Georgetown University Round Table on Languages and Linguistics 1981

Analyzing Discourse:
Text and Talk

Deborah Tannen

Editor

Georgetown University Press, Washington, D.C. 20057

Bibliographic Notice

Since this series has been variously and confusingly cited as: *Georgetown University Monographic Series on Languages and Linguistics, Monograph Series on Languages and Linguistics, Reports of the Annual Round Table Meetings on Linguistics and Language Study*, etc., beginning with the 1973 volume, the title of the series was changed.

The new title of the series includes the year of a Round Table and omits both the monograph number and the meeting number, thus: *Georgetown University Round Table on Languages and Linguistics 1981*, with the regular abbreviation *GURT 1981*. Full bibliographical references should show the form:

Becker, Alton L. 1981. On Emerson on language. In: *Georgetown University Round Table on Languages and Linguistics 1981*. Edited by Deborah Tannen. Washington, D.C.: Georgetown University Press. 1-11.

Library of Congress Catalog Number: 58-31607
ISBN 0-87840-116-4
ISSN 0196-7207

CONTENTS

iv / Contents

WELCOMING REMARKS

James E. Alatis
Dean, School of Languages and Linguistics
Georgetown University

Good evening. Welcome to Georgetown University, the School of Languages and Linguistics, and to the 32nd Annual Georgetown University Round Table on Languages and Linguistics.

In previous years, when I chaired the Round Table, I was never at liberty to say just how great a program had been put together. This year, however, since the Round Table is the work of Deborah Tannen and her able assistant, Susan Dodge, I may say, with all modesty, that the program is impressive indeed.

In looking over the program this year I was amazed to note that the pre-conference sessions present as wide and interesting a range of topics as the conference itself. This is a tribute to Dr. Tannen's energy and enthusiasm, as well as a mark of the widespread interest that the Georgetown University Round Table program generates. I was particularly pleased to note today's pre-conference session on oral proficiency testing (1) because it marks the continuation of our joint efforts with the inter-agency round table and further cooperation between government and university, and (2) because oral proficiency testing is a field of language activity which is of common interest to professionals in the fields of foreign language, EFL, ESL, and bilingual education.

The topic of the Georgetown University Round Table on Languages and Linguistics 1981--Discourse Analysis--is a very exciting one, and appropriate to a coming of age in linguistics. Now that the tide has turned, it is safe for me to say in public that, when I was introduced to linguistics, it was billed as the key to the ultimate understanding of literature and discourse. I am, therefore, very pleased to welcome you to a conference that will indeed further understanding in this area.

I was going to make a few more rousing remarks, but I understand that I have been upstaged by one of the world's last medicine and side show pitchmen, Mr. Fred Bloodgood. That's a tough act to follow, so I will simply turn over the microphone to Deborah Tannen, with my thanks and appreciation for a job well done.

INTRODUCTION

The topic of the Georgetown University Round Table on Languages and Linguistics 1981 is 'Analyzing Discourse: Text and Talk.' Perhaps a word is in order concerning the meaning and use of the terms 'discourse', 'text', and 'talk'.

The subtitle, 'Text and Talk', can be understood to refer to two separate modes of discourse: text as written prose, and talk as spoken conversation. This is a common use of these terms (for example, Cicourel 1975). But 'text' is often used interchangeably with 'discourse'. Indeed, the term 'discourse' is used in varied ways, to refer to anything 'beyond the sentence'. The term appears in reference to studies of the structure of arguments underlying written prose (for example, van Dijk in the present collection), and to analysis of pairs of hypothetical sentences (for example, Bolinger 1979). However, 'discourse' is also used to refer to conversational interaction. In fact, a book entitled *An Introduction to Discourse Analysis*, written by a participant in this meeting (Coulthard 1977), is concerned only with conversational interaction. Schegloff (this volume) argues that rather than conversation being a subvariety of discourse, all forms of discourse are subvarieties of conversation.

Discourse, as the term appears in the title, and as it is used in the papers collected here, encompasses all these. It refers to both text and talk, and these not as two separate genres to be compared and contrasted, but rather as overlapping aspects of a single entity. As the object of study, spoken discourse is 'text', much as words spoken in a speech are commonly referred to as the text of the speech. In this sense, 'discourse' and 'text' are synonymous.

In a nonlinguistic discussion of what linguists know as the Sapir-Whorf Hypothesis, Laing (1959) suggests that speakers of English cannot conceive of mind and body as one, because their language does not provide a word to express them so. The best that English speakers can do is attempt to conceptualize *mindandbody*, squishing them together but never really perceiving them as a single entity. It is fortunate, therefore, that there exists in English a word that refers to language in context across all forms and modes. That word is discourse, and that is the sense in which it is intended here.

Given this unified approach to discourse, it would be infelicitous to think of written and spoken language as separate, that is, of text as anything written and talk as spontaneous conversation. The inadequacy of such a division is a recurrent theme in recent research (see papers collected in Tannen 1982a and 1982b). Features that have been associated exclusively with spoken or written language are often found in discourse of the other mode. For example, Bright (this volume) shows spoken discourse to exhibit verse markers previously considered poetic; Chafe (1981) finds spoken ritual Seneca to share many features with written language; and written fiction exhibits many features expected in spontaneous conversation (Tannen 1982c).

In their study of all forms of discourse, linguists are concerned with central questions: of structure, of meaning, and of how these function to create coherence. How do people put words together? How do particular combinations of words yield particular meanings? In short, what makes individual words into discourse?

Discourse analysis raises another issue which is dramatized in the following personal experience. Recently, my parents visited me, and my father asked about my work: How do I really know when I have made a discovery? How can I prove my findings? How scientific is the study of language? I began to comment on interpretive vs. statistical methods; that statistics may lie; that sometimes it is necessary to look beyond what will fit into a test tube, to understand what is in the world. My voice must have taken on an intoning quality, because my father (who is a lawyer) hesitated, looked at me, smiled slightly, and said, 'It sounds as if you've had this discussion before, but I'm having it for the first time, and that gives you an advantage'.

It is likely that many analysts of discourse have had this discussion before, from one or more of these perspectives. How and to what extent can linguistics claim to be--and does it aspire to be?--a science? The expansion (or, more accurately, the return) of our sphere of study to discourse, to language in context, raises more and more troubling questions of accountability, reliability, and verifiability; the role and nature of interpretation, or hermeneutics; and, again and again, the question of whether linguistics is one of the sciences, or of the humanities, or of the arts.[1]

Perhaps the choice is not really a choice at all. In a well-reasoned argument identifying science as an art, Judson (1980) quotes Nobel laureate physicist Paul Dirac: 'It is more important to have beauty in one's equations than to have them fit experiment' (p. 11). 'It seems that if one is working from the point of view of getting beauty into one's equations, and if one has really a sound insight, one is on a sure line of progress' (p. 199).

How can science be seen as an endeavor seeking beauty? For one thing, in searching for explanations, science, like art, discovers patterns and relationships. It seeks to understand the exhilarating tension of creativity within constraints. Just so, linguists seek to discover patterns that create and reflect coherence. Just so, the linguists whose work is collected here have discovered the principles and processes underlying coherence in a wide variety of texts. Thus linguistics, at the same time that it is scientific, is also concerned with aesthetics, for aesthetics is (in the terms of Becker 1979, citing Bateson), 'the emergent sense of coherence'. An aesthetic response is made possible by the discovery of the coherence principles underlying a text.

In Christopher Hampton's play, *The Philanthropist*, a linguist is introduced to a novelist, who asks him how he can bear to do such narrow work. The linguist replies that he is interested in the same thing as the novelist--words. The novelist, unimpressed, scoffs, 'But one at a time--not in a sequence'.

The study of discourse means that linguists are indeed interested in words in a sequence, and in that mysterious moving force that creeps in between the words and between the lines, sparking ideas, images, and emotions that are not contained in any of the words one at a time--the force that makes words into discourse.

Those who came to linguistics from the study of literature, and those who came from mathematics, or anthropology, join together in the study of discourse, seeking to discover patterns in language--a pursuit that is humanistic as well as reasoned, that is relevant at the same time that it is elegant, that is theoretical and empirical, and even beautiful.

The diversity of work in discourse analysis is reflected in the papers collected here, and in the range of pre-conference sessions that were organized in conjunction with the Georgetown University Round Table on Languages and Linguistics, as can be seen in the following list of session titles (organizers are shown in parentheses).

1. Oral proficiency assessment (James Frith, Foreign Service Institute)
2. Applications of discourse analysis to teaching: Spanish and international affairs (William Cressey, Georgetown University)
3. Toward adequate formal models of natural discourse (Jerry R. Hobbs, SRI International)
4. Functions of silence (Muriel Saville-Troike, University of Illinois)
5. Pragmatics (Nancy Yanofsky, Georgetown University)

Proceedings of many of these sessions will be published in collections edited by their organizers. Papers from Hobbs' session will appear in a special issue of the journal *Text*, and papers from Tannen's session are included in Tannen (1982a) and (1982b).

I want to thank the organizers of and participants in the pre-conference sessions, and the participants in the plenary sessions whose papers appear in this volume. Indeed, there are many people--far more than I can name--who deserve heart-felt thanks. First, I am grateful to Dean James E. Alatis for giving me the opportunity to organize this year's Georgetown University Round Table. I want to thank my colleagues, especially Roger Shuy, for their generous support, and the many Georgetown students who selflessly volunteered time and enthusiasm. Finally, my deep thanks go to Susan Dodge, who was at my side from start to finish, and without whose able and cheerful assistance I cannot imagine this year's Round Table having materialized at all.

Deborah Tannen

NOTES

These remarks have gone through a number of transformations, from typed notes to oral face-to-face discourse (a blend of reading and extemporaneous talk) to typed transcription (for which I thank Marta Dmytrenko) to revision for print. In the last stage, I was helped by comments from Alton Becker, Wallace Chafe, Robin Lakoff, Fr. Richard O'Brien, and Roger Shuy.

1. Becker suggests, following Burke (1961), that linguistics may be none of these, but something else entirely: a unique epistemological realm.

REFERENCES

Becker, Alton L. 1979. Text-building, epistemology and aesthetics in Javanese shadow theatre. In: The imagination of reality. Edited by A. L. Becker and Aram A. Yengoyan. Norwood, N.J.: Ablex. 211-243.

Bolinger, Dwight. 1979. Pronouns in discourse. In: Discourse and syntax. Edited by Talmy Givon. New York: Academic Press. 289-309.

Burke, Kenneth. 1961. The rhetoric of religion. Boston: Beacon Press.

Cicourel, Aaron V. 1975. Discourse and text: Cognitive and linguistic processes in studies of social structure. Versus 12.33-84.

Coulthard, Malcolm. 1977. An introduction to discourse analysis. London: Longmans.

Judson, Horace Freeland. 1980. The search for solutions. New York: Holt Rinehart Winston.

Laing, R. D. 1959. The divided self. Middlesex and Baltimore: Penguin.

Tannen, Deborah, ed. 1982a. Spoken and written language: Exploring orality and literacy. Norwood, N.J.: Ablex.

Tannen, Deborah, ed. 1982b. Coherence in spoken and written language. Norwood, N.J.: Ablex.

Tannen, Deborah. 1982c. Oral and literate strategies in spoken and written narratives. Lg. 58:1.

ON EMERSON ON LANGUAGE

Alton L. Becker
University of Michigan

'Emerson wrote by sentences or phrases rather than
by logical sequence...The unity of one sentence in-
spires the unity of the whole--though its physique is
as ragged as the Dolomites.'

Charles Ives, *Emerson*, p. 23.

'The maker of a sentence...launches out into the infinite and builds a road into Chaos and old Night, and is
followed by those who hear him with something of wild,
creative delight.'

R. W. Emerson, *Journals*,
October 18, 1834.

1. **Comparative noetics.** For a philologist, the task is to
build a road across time to an old text, or across space to a
distant one, and to try to understand it. It is a utopian task,
but nonetheless essential, at least to the extent that such
understanding of distant texts is crucial in an age of rapidly
growing, increasingly powerful systems of communication, and
diminishing resources. What does it mean that Balinese watch
Star Trek on television, followed by a propaganda film on the
American space program, and mix the two? There are few
more difficult questions right now. Is there something like
noetic pollution, a spoiling of the noosphere by some cancer-
ous overgrowth? And where might we be--American linguists--
in the sweep of the noetic history we are just beginning to
write?

The term *noetic* is an old word in English; its turbulent
history is traced in the Oxford English Dictionary. Coleridge
used it to designate a science of the intellect, drawing on the
Kantian philosophers of Germany. Emerson knew Coleridge's

1

work well, and visited him on his first visit to England in 1833. In Emerson's early work, the mental realm--the noetic sphere, or, as Pierre Teilhard de Chardin called it, the noosphere--is called Spirit or Thought. Walter Ong has given currency to the old word *noetic*. (In Javanese, the term for reviving old words is *jarwa dhosok*, forcing--literally 'pushing'--old language into the present.) In his essay on the drum languages of Africa, Ong (1977) defines noetics as the study of the shaping, storing, retrieving, and communicating of knowledge. He has also laid the groundwork for a new kind of study: comparative and historical noetics, or looking out in space to other cultures and back in time, even within our own, at others' ways of shaping, storing, retrieving, and communicating knowledge. Surely the whole process is language-ful, which is what Benjamin Lee Whorf has had such a hard time trying to tell us: that language is involved in the whole process of shaping, storing, retrieving, and communicating knowledge.

In the histories of particular noetic traditions, there appear to be a very few powerful laws, among them a one-way sequence of changes from orality to writing to printing to secondary orality (this latter is Ong's term for the print-based, electronic orality of our American present). Each stage in this continuum seems to recontextualize the prior stage, so that certain kinds of knowledge remain in the medium of the past: most prayers are still spoken (or thought), many personal letters are still appropriately handwritten, and most books are still printed, though photocopy would allow mass circulation of manuscripts. As Ong and others have shown us, each of these media entails its own noetic economy, its own power and authority: the power of the voice, of the signed document, of print, and of television. Furthermore, major changes in noetic systems seem to happen initially in a few places and then spread to other places, across language boundaries. That is to say, noetic changes for most people in the world have involved language contact, within which a noetically more powerful language exports the secret of its power to the weaker. What increases over time appears to be the scope of central control, as a language adds media. In making these statements, one is forced to hedge, with terms like *appear* and *seem*, in acknowledgment that a new myth of history is being shaped, and like most myths it is to some extent self-serving. As Sartre (1964) wrote: 'Progress, that long, steep path which leads to me'.

Yet the myth has its power in helping one interpret changes one sees going on. For instance, imagine a village, small, in the hills, where knowledge is stored in the cultivated memories of a few old people, often blind, often women. They sit in special places in trials and other village meetings and tell who is related to whom, and who did what, and who owns what bit of land, and what the last ruler said. And now imagine what happens to them when a young person who can read and write the new national language returns, after a few years of schooling, to the village. The old blind people enter their own new dark ages. This is a dramatic, but oft repeated, instance of noetic change.

Or imagine what happens when a foreign colonial language, always more powerful noetically, replaces--as a source of knowledge--important functions of the local language. Sometimes a voice across time and space lets us share a feeling of noetic change. A Javanese poet writes, in a world in which understanding of the present was shaped by Dutch, in the late nineteenth century:

Anglakoni zaman edan
Ewuh aya ing pambudi
'(We) walk in an unstable world
Not at home, struggling against our own imagination'

I have written elsewhere (Becker in press) about this remarkable poem, and the difficulties we have in reading it and understanding it; the English meanings at the deepest levels we must abandon, even as we encounter meanings of tense and person as background cohesion, and the presence of elaborate focus and deixis--to mention only a few of the more obvious grammatical differences one encounters.

The paradox of philology (to paraphrase Ortega y Gassett 1959) is that distant texts are always both exuberant and deficient at the same time. I read too much in, and I am unperceptive of what is there, and so I understand only through successive approximation, by giving up--unexpectedly--various etic aspects of English and slowly getting attuned to new emic possibilities of language. Noetic exploration into terra incognita is, of necessity, a very slow and very difficult process of abduction.

2. **Pontification.** But one can go back into one's own language, too, as Michel Foucault has done in French, to another episteme, another noetic era. Many years ago I began a lingual biography of Emerson. He left us an abundant record of letters, journals, lectures, and essays from throughout his life--plenty of data, and the primary philology has been done very well. It is all laid out chronologically, well annotated. Furthermore, Emerson was self-conscious about language itself and was keenly interested in the ideas and books the New England ships brought back from India. His European correspondents kept him in touch with the exploration of Sanskrit. For many generations of academics his 'The American Scholar' has provided our own version of the Hippocratic oath. However, the task of understanding Emerson on language is not unlike other philological excursions: it is slow and difficult.

Emerson's own language changes noticeably when he leaves
America on Christmas day, 1832. He was very sick, his 19-
year-old wife had died, and he had resigned his prestigious
Unitarian pulpit in Boston, agitated with religious doubt. He
was sailing to Italy in search of health. Up until then, his
writing was quite conventional. When he arrived in Italy, well
and energetic, the voice we recognize as Emerson's has
emerged, and one begins to read him as the words quoted
earlier suggest, 'with something of wild, creative delight'.
Just one sample: he writes his brother William from Messina:

> The fault of travellers is like that of American farmers,
> both lay out too much ground & so slur, one the insight
> the other the cultivation of every part. Aetna I have
> not ascended. (Rusk 1939:364)

Writers in different times and places innovate at various
levels of language, some at the levels of sentences, like Emerson. (The reader is invited to parse the sentence just quoted,
in whatever methodology seems comportable.) Some writers
innovate at the level of words, like James Joyce. Some innovate in drawing on new sources of prior text, like the Irish
mythology which Yeats both shaped and drew from. Some
innovate in the language act they perform, like the opening
of the inner newsreel in Virginia Woolf or, again, Joyce. It
is very Emersonian to ask: what are the ways people can innovate in language? In what different ways can we deviate from
the norms we inherit? Emerson, like his literary descendent,
Gertrude Stein, is an innovator in sentences.
His sources vary, and he sometimes uses odd words, but the
language act he performs is constant. Kenneth Burke (1966:5)
has called it pontification:

> pontificate; that is, to "make a bridge." Viewed as a
> sheerly terministic, or symbolic, function, that's what
> transcendence is: the building of a *terministic bridge*
> whereby one realm is *transcended* by being viewed in
> terms of a realm "beyond" it.

As a writer of sentences, Emerson slows us way down. We
academics have come to expect innovation at higher levels and
a certain 'stereotypicity' at the level of the figure of a sentence. We can read rapidly only if the lower figures are regular. Some see our field of linguistics as one big text we are
all engaged in writing, and of necessity we must agree,
therefore, to certain conventions, and still our individual
voices. In what language acts do personal constraints matter?
If there is one idea popularly associated with Emerson, it is
his celebration, like Gertrude Stein's, of the individual voice
shaping sentences. 'The maker of a sentence...launches out
into the infinite and builds a road into Chaos and old Night,

and is followed by those who hear him with something of wild, creative delight'.

3. **Norm and deviation: The individual voice.** The most difficult task of the philologist is to hear the individual voice. In reading an Old Javanese text, I have very little sense of what is stereotypic and what is innovative, what is norm and what is deviation. That means that an essential feature of aesthetic response, deviation (however so slight it may be in a traditional genre), is inaccessible. More often than not, in a new language one sees everything as unfamiliar innovation. A few years ago, when I wrote about constraints on the creation of a Javanese shadow play (Becker 1979), where etymologizing is an opportunity for innovation, where stories have no climax, where several languages are used simultaneously-- the repeated response of my Javanese friends was, 'What's so new about that?' Their stereotypes were innovations for me, and therein lies the odd aesthetic excitement of philology.

Emerson saw the American scholar as a deviation from the European norm. A new context brought new meanings, a new relationship with the world. But before he presented his well-known lecture, 'The American Scholar', he published a small book called *Nature*, in which there is a section called 'Language'. If we read it as one must an Old Javanese text, not as something to agree or disagree with but rather first as something to understand, it makes an interesting noetic journey for a linguist, back to our own chirographic age, as it is preserved in print. In his own day, as many people heard Emerson as read him, even as far off as Kalamazoo or Ann Arbor. Though the book *Nature* was prepared for printing, Emerson's sentences were hand-shaped, first, in his letters and journals. The journals became sources for lectures, the lectures sources for essays. The essays are talks to be read, meant to be heard, with the voice in them, shaped by hand-writing. The best way to enjoy Emerson is to read him aloud, slowly. I suspect it may be impossible to read him fast.

4. **Nature as a source of constraints.** Nature, Emerson writes, is 'all that is separate from us, all which philosophy distinguishes as the *not me*'. The aim of science, he says, is 'to find a theory of nature'.[1] He lists those aspects of nature not only unexplained but previously thought inexplicable: sleep, madness, dreams, beasts, sex, and language. Central to the essay, then, is the image of I and Other, a particular ego and its context. How does an 'I' relate to its context? Emerson lists four ways:

I use nature as a commodity
I use nature as a source of beauty
I use nature as a source of language
I use nature as a source of discipline

Note the order in the list. I relate to the world as first subject to my will and finally as subjecting me to its discipline, with aesthetics and language in between.

The section on language explores the nonarbitrariness (or iconicity) of the relations between language, nature, and thought. For Emerson, language consists of signs for Nature (as he defined it, the 'not me'), while Nature in turn is symbolic for what he calls Spirit, but which we might call, after Bateson (1979: 89-128), *mind*, what phenomenologists call *noema*. [2]

5. Iconicity and double metaphors. One sentence from the section on language of Emerson's *Nature* first struck me a few years ago when I was trying to understand the root metaphors behind the Burmese system of classifiers (Becker 1975): 'Parts of speech are metaphors because the whole of nature is a metaphor of the human mind' (p. 18).

This is a puzzling statement. It seems to require some adjustment in our thinking in order to make it appear true. It is not self-evidently true.

There is some prior text. In a lecture entitled 'The Uses of Natural History', given in 1833, Emerson expressed a similar idea (Whicher, Spiller, and Williams 1959: 24):

The strongest distinction of which we have an idea is
that between thought and matter. The very existence
of thought and speech supposes and is a new nature
totally distinct from the material world; yet we find it
impossible to speak of it and its laws in any other language than that borrowed from our experience in the
material world. We not only speak in continual metaphors
of the *morn*, the *noon* and the *evening* of life, of dark
and bright thought, of sweet and bitter moments, of the
healthy mind and the fading memory, but all our most
literal and direct modes of speech--as right and wrong,
form and substance, honest and dishonest...are, when
hunted up to their original signification, found to be
metaphors also. And this, because the whole of Nature
is a metaphor or image of the human mind.

The deeply metaphoric nature of one's own language is most clearly seen across cultures, in that 'passage to India' that motivates the philologist-linguist. Emerson had a mistaken opinion about the language of 'savages': he thought it was like the language of children (Sealts and Ferguson 1969: 15). It remained for his student, Henry Thoreau, to begin to understand the language of 'savages' by living close to them and listening. Yet Emerson's notion that parts of speech are metaphors is strongly confirmed in the work of the comparative philologist, for whom even nouns and verbs lose their iconicity, as does the notion of grammar itself. Languages seem to select from nature one or another pattern--a set of regularities to build coherence around: temporal sequences, perspectives from the speaker or from the hearer, the basic dramatis personae of case, the distinctions of the sexes, or the division between changing actions and stable things--all the etic icons that cohesion may be built around. These regularities perceived in nature are all, in a sense, available in nature--in the relation of person and context--to build language around. The deepest regularities are the most backgrounded features of language--the most iconic. (By *iconic* I mean felt by the observer--culturally defined--to be the most natural--as ordinary speakers of English feel tense to be a natural fact, not a lingual metaphor, or as Burmese speakers feel their classifiers to be in nature, mirrored in language.) To learn a new distant language is, in Emerson's terms, to develop a new relationship with nature, a new set of iconicities, at least in part. 'Parts of speech are metaphors because the whole of nature is a metaphor of the human mind'. Or, as Gregory Bateson (1979:17) put it, 'contextual shaping is only another term for grammar'.

6. A figure for defamiliarization. 'Parts of speech are metaphors because the whole of nature is a metaphor of the human mind'. This is a favorite Emersonian figure, the strategy of the double metaphor. It dominates this section of his essay, where about 75 percent of the sentences are equative strategies, simple and complex. A figure is a sentence or larger unit conceived of as a substitution frame, in which certain points are more open to substitution than others, for example, the figure of a recent riddle, 'How many ___ does it take to change a lightbulb?', in which one substitutes a name of a human category, such as a nationality, a profession, a religion, etc. The answers evoke the stereotypes of each category. (A new point of substitution, and a new impact, came later, when someone substituted 'government' for 'lightbulb'.) All language can be conceived of as sets of partially remembered figures. [3]

The general shape of Emerson's figure might be rendered as: 'X is Y because the A of B is a Y of C'. It is a complex equative or identificational strategy, the figure of definition and of metaphor, of overlays. For Emerson and others in the Kantian tradition, metaphor is a strategy of reason, which, as readers of philosophy know, meant just the opposite then of its normal present meaning: it meant intuition--direct apprehension, 'first thought'. Part of the difficulty in moving into another episteme (in time or space) is learning not only new words but new meanings for old ones, a variety of what has been called *ostranenije* 'defamiliarization' or even 'alienization', making things strange, [4] or what Burke (1964) calls

'perspective by incongruity'. Defamiliarization is essentially a
metaphoric process: seeing the familiar in a new way. Javanese makes one see English in a new way: it defamiliarizes it.
Javanese is a metaphor of English, and vice versa.

Within the metaphoric figure that recurs in the text, Emerson
plays with three classes of terms: terms for language, terms
for nature, and terms for what he calls spirit or mind. What
are the relations of language, nature, and thought? The central proportion, expressed in the sentence we are considering,
is that 'Language is to Nature as Nature is to Thought'.
'Parts of speech are metaphors because the whole of nature is
a metaphor of the human mind'.

7. **Linguistics of particularity.** There have been hundreds
of books and articles written about this one essay by Emerson,
but only Kenneth Burke penetrates below the macrostructure
to the kinds of microstrategies Emerson uses in order to make
possible higher level meanings. Is there not artistic and
philosophical creation at the level of sentences, a play of
figures and lexical classes at a level below that usually noticed
by the literary scholars, and a bit above that usually studied
by linguists, a level where, as Isidore of Seville wrote, 'grammar is joined to the art of rhetoric' (quoted in Murphy 1974)?
It is here that we encounter what Kenneth Pike has called the
linguistics of particularity, and Paul Ricoeur calls discourse.
For Ricoeur (1971:529-562), discourse differs from language
(i.e. Saussurian 'langue') in that discourse has a particular
writer or speaker, a particular reader or hearer, a particular
time, and a particular world. I would add, any discourse
also evokes a particular set of prior texts for the participants.
A discourse can be understood only in its particularity.

For the study of particular discourse, we need techniques of
textual parsing which include all the kinds of discourse variables which constrain its particularity--which help shape it.
Such techniques will have to allow us to move across levels of
discourse and discern the different kinds of constraints operating at various levels: word, phrase, clause, sentence,
paragraph, monologue, exchange.

One of the reasons why I never found local grammars of
Southeast Asian languages, although I looked hard for them,
was that Southeast Asians do not customarily view language,
I recently realized, at the level of the clause and the sentence. In Java, for instance, people have a rich vocabulary
(much richer than ours) for what they call *unda usuk*, i.e.
the choices of words or phrases in given positions within
figures. (*Unda usuk* means literally the parallel wooden strips
on a pitched roof on which one hangs ceramic tiles.) This set
of terms represents a conventional understanding of paradigmatic choices. One might imagine a traditional Javanese
student of language beginning his or her study of English
with a description of the difference between 'Close the door'

and 'Shut the door'. That is, the Javanese would begin with paradigmatics rather than with syntagmatics, with constraints on substitution rather than immediate constituents.

Returning to Emerson's figure--X is Y because the A of B is a Y of C--one notices that it includes two equative clauses, although rhetorically they might better be called identificational clauses. In general, identificational strategies operate at noun phrase level, and--as is well known--many languages have no equivalent of an identificational copula; in those languages, equational clauses are structurally identical with noun phrases. Without a copula, the copula strategies are awkward to express. In the West, copula strategies characterize some of our most important figures: definitions, syllogisms, generics, even passives--all our most evaluative figures. In pontification (i.e. writing the moral essay) copula strategies dominate. (It is interesting to think of the essay as the reverse of narration, to some extent: in narration, narrative strategies dominate, and are evaluated by, among other figures, generic copula strategies; while in the moral essay, copula strategies dominate and are evaluated by short bits of exemplary narrative.)

Within copula strategies, Emerson relates three sets of terms to one another over and over again, offering evaluative instances: terms for language, terms for nature, terms for spirit or mind. A double metaphor is established, in which language is metaphoric of nature, and nature--now considered as text--is metaphoric of mind. The essay establishes terministic depth, via a sequence of overlays. Each time a term for nature, mind, or language reappears, it has acquired more context. 'Parts of speech are metaphors because the whole of nature is a metaphor of the human mind.'

This sentence, like the fragment of a hologram, projects an image of the whole essay, *Nature*.[5] This double metaphor is at the heart of transcendentalism, where grammar, rhetoric, and epistemology meet, in a figure 'as ragged as the Dolomites' (Ives 1970:23). To understand it means to be reshaped by it, to let it defamiliarize one's world. It means to think and write for a moment like Emerson, who concludes his section on language with these words:

'Every scripture is to be interpreted in the same spirit which gave it forth,' is the fundamental law of criticism. A life in harmony with Nature, the love of truth and virtue, will purge the eye to understand her text. By degrees we may come to know the primitive sense of the permanent objects of nature, so that the world shall be to us an open book and every form significant of its hidden life and final cause.

A new interest surprises us whilst, under the view now suggested, we contemplate the fearful extent and multitude

of objects, since 'every object rightly seen unlocks a new
faculty of the soul.' That which was unconscious truth
becomes, when interpreted and defined in an object, a
part of the domain of knowledge,--a new amount in the
magazine of power. (pp. 18-19)

The goal of this short excursion into a few lines of Emerson's
'Language' has been to think about another episteme, another
conceptual world, another noema, another mind. Our difficulty
on so many levels--including the grammatical--in reading Emerson's words as currently relevant knowledge, tells us much
about ourselves and the distance--even within our own culture,
within our own language, and within our own field of study--
of the conceptual world of 1836. The task requires, I think,
that we change ourselves as readers, moving from an etic to an
emic understanding, by imagining a world in which those words
could be true: 'Every scripture is to be interpreted in the
same spirit which gave it forth'--words Emerson quotes from
George Fox--might also be the fundamental law of modern
philology, and hence a discipline for one important approach
to the study of text.

NOTES

Dedicated to Marvin Felheim, 1914-1979. Thanks for critical
readings of a prior draft to J. Becker, A. Yengoyan, and D.
Tannen.
1. Quotations from Emerson's *Nature* are from Sealts and
Ferguson (1969). These passages are from page 5. Page
references for later quotations will be cited in the text.
2. For an overall view of phenomenological methodology, see
Ihde (1977). 'Noesis' and 'noema' are discussed on pages 43-
54.
3. Most medieval rhetorics and grammars included discussion
of figures, or common deviations from ordinary language. The
number of figures varied, but it was common to distinguish 45
figures of diction and 19 figures of thought. Ten of the
figures of diction were called tropes. Later writers described
up to 200 figures. For details, see Murphy (1974). I use the
term *figure* here to designate a minimal text strategy.
4. This term is fully explicated in Stacy (1977). The term
was first used by the Russian critic, Viktor Shklovsky.
5. The hologram has given rise to a new sense of whole-
ness. See Bortoft (1971:43-73).

REFERENCES

Bateson, Gregory. 1979. Criteria of mental process. In:
Mind and nature. New York: E. P. Dutton. 89-128.

Becker, Alton L. 1975. A linguistic image of nature: The
Burmese numerative classifier system. International Journal
of the Sociology of Language 5.109-121.
Becker, Alton L. 1979. Text-building, epistemology, and
aesthetics in Javanese shadow theatre. In: The imagination
of reality: Essays in Southeast Asian coherence systems.
Edited by A. L. Becker and Aram Yengoyan. Norwood,
N.J.: Ablex.
Becker, Alton L. (in press) The poetics and noetics of a
Javanese poem. In: Spoken and written language: Explor-
ing orality and literacy. Edited by Deborah Tannen.
Norwood, N.J.: Ablex.
Bortoft, Henri. 1971. The whole: Counterfeit and authentic.
Systematics 9.2:43-73.
Burke, Kenneth. 1964. Perspectives by incongruity. Bloom-
ington: Indiana University Press.
Burke, Kenneth. 1966. I, eye, ay--Emerson's early essay
"Nature": Thoughts on the machinery of transcendence.
In: Transcendentalism and its legacy. Edited by Myron
Simon and Thornton H. Parsons. Ann Arbor: University
of Michigan Press.
Ihde, Don. 1977. Experimental phenomenology: An intro-
duction. New York: Capricorn Books.
Ives, Charles. 1970. Emerson. In: Essays before a sonata.
Edited by Howard Boatwright. New York: Norton.
Murphy, James J. 1974. Rhetoric in the Middle Ages.
Berkeley: University of California Press.
Ong, Walter J. 1977. African talking drums and oral noetics.
In: Interfaces of the word: Studies in the evolution of
consciousness and culture. Ithaca: Cornell University
Press.
Ortega y Gassett, José. 1959. The difficulty of reading.
Diogenes 28.1-17.
Ricoeur, Paul. 1971. The model of the text: Meaningful
action considered as text. Social Research 38.529-562.
Rusk, Ralph L., ed. 1939. The letters of Ralph Waldo
Emerson. Vol. 1. New York: Columbia University Press.
Sartre, Jean-Paul. 1964. The words. Greenwich, Conn.:
Fawcett.
Sealts, Merton M. Jr., and Alfred R. Ferguson, eds. 1969.
Emerson's Nature: Origin, growth, meaning. Carbondale,
Ill.: Southern Illinois University Press.
Stacy, R. H. 1977. Defamiliarization in language and litera-
ture. Syracuse: Syracuse University Press.
Whicher, Stephen E., Robert E. Spiller, and Wallace E.
Williams, eds. 1959. The early lectures of Ralph Waldo
Emerson. Vol. I. Cambridge, Mass.: Harvard University
Press.

ORAL REMEMBERING AND
NARRATIVE STRUCTURES

Walter J. Ong, S.J.
Saint Louis University

1. Of all verbal genres, narrative has the most evident and straightforward relationship to memory. Narrative is fundamentally retrospective. Even a live radio broadcast of a football game tells you what is just over with. A science fiction story cast in the future is normally written in the past tense.

The creative imagination as such has curious alliances with memory. Wordsworth insisted that poetry 'takes its origin from emotion recollected in tranquility'. I have heard a fiction writer from the Midwest explain passionately to an audience how in creating a story his entire imaginative activity is one of memory. What he is making up--his plot and his characters--present themselves to him as remembrances of what has been. Creative activity is nostalgic. This is why the artist who deals with the future, as perhaps artists now must, is under particularly heavy strain.

All narrative, moreover, is artificial, and the time it creates out of memory is artificial, variously related to existential time. Reality never occurs in narrative form. The totality of what has happened to and in and around me since I got up this morning is not organized as narrative and as a totality cannot be expressed as narrative. To make a narrative, I have to isolate certain elements out of the unbroken and seamless web of history with a view to fitting them into a particular construct which I have more or less consciously or unconsciously in mind. Not everything in the web will fit a given design. There may be, for example, no way to fit in the total series of indescribable moods that I lived through in the few moments after I was shaving. It is hard even to distinguish these clearly from everything else that was going on in and around me. So, with almost everything else, such matters are dropped in favor of more standard topoi. Writers such as

James Joyce or William Faulkner enlarge the number of topoi--
to the dismay of complacent readers--but the number remains
always limited. The totality of existence-saturated time is
simply too much to manage. 'There are still many other things
that Jesus did, yet if they were written about in detail, I
doubt there would be room enough in the entire world to hold
the books to record them' (John 21:25).

Something other than the events themselves must determine
which events the narrator cuts out of the incessant and dark
flow of life through the density of time and frames in words.
He or she must have a conscious or unconscious rationale for
the selection and shaping. But what the rationale is in any
given case it is difficult and often impossible to state fully or
even adequately. 'Jesus performed many other signs as well--
signs not recorded here--in the presence of his disciples. But
these have been recorded to help you believe that Jesus is the
Messiah, the Son of God, so that through this faith you may
have life in his name' (John 20:30-31). Here a rationale is
stated. It is what we call 'salvation history': the author
picks from Jesus' life what is particularly relevant to human
beings' salvation. But such statement is exceptional. Few
historians can put down so straightforwardly as the author of
the Fourth Gospel the rationale they have settled on for their
selection and structure of events. Even fewer fiction writers
could adequately state their own rationale when they bring
into being the artificial construct that we call narrative.
There is no reason why they should have to. But neither is
there any reason why we should not ask what the rationale is.

The ways of articulating memory, of bringing to mind and
representing the past, are various. They differ from culture
to culture and from age to age. In particular, as we have
become increasingly aware, bringing to mind and representing
the past is quite different in oral cultures from what it is in
cultures such as our own where writing and print, and now
electronic processes, have been interiorized so deeply that
without great learning, skill, and labor we cannot identify
what in our thought processes depends on our appropriation
of writing and the other technologies into our psyche, and
what does not. Often oral narrative processes strike us as
divergent from what we consider 'normal', whereas in fact
many mental processes which seem 'normal' to us have only
recently been feasible at all.

Here I propose a few reflections concerning oral noetic processes centering on the way memory and narrative plot are
related in some primary oral cultures as contrasted with the
ways they are related in chirographic and typographic cultures
and electronic cultures, the ones to which we ourselves are
closer. I understand plot in the ordinary sense of the temporal and causal sequence in which events are presented in a
narrative.

2. Memory, in its initial role and in its transformations, is in one way or another a clue to nearly everything that went on as discourse moved out of the pristine oral world to literacy and beyond. Memory is still with us, but it is no longer with us in the way it used to be.

The retention and recall of knowledge in primary oral culture calls for noetic structures and procedures, largely formulaic, of a sort quite unfamiliar to us and often enough scorned by us. One of the places where oral noetic structures and procedures manifest themselves most spectacularly is in their effect on narrative plot, which in an oral culture is not quite what we take plot typically to be. Persons from today's literate and typographic cultures are likely to think of consciously contrived narrative as typically designed in a climactic linear plot often diagrammed as the well-known 'Freytag's Pyramid': an ascending action builds tension, rising to a climactic point, which consists often of a recognition or other incident bringing about a *peripeteia* or reversal of action, and which is followed by a dénouement or untying--for this standard climactic linear plot has been likened to the tying and untying of a knot. This is the kind of plot Aristotle finds in the drama (*Poetics* 1451b-1452b)--a significant locale, for Greek drama, though orally performed, was composed as a written text and was the first verbal genre, and for centuries was the only verbal genre, to be controlled completely by writing in the West.

Ancient Greek oral narrative, the epic, was not plotted this way. In his *Ars Poetica*, Horace writes that the epic poet 'hastens into the action and precipitates the hearer into the middle of things' (lines 148-149). Horace has chiefly in mind the epic poet's disregard for temporal sequence: the poet reports a situation and only much later explains, often in detail, how it came to be. He probably has also in mind Homer's conciseness and vigor (Brink 1971:221-222): he wants to get immediately to 'where the action is'. But whatever these further implications, literate poets eventually interpreted Horace's *in medias res* as making hysteron proteron obligatory in the epic. Thus John Milton explains in the 'Argument' to Book I of *Paradise Lost* that, after proposing 'in brief the whole Subject' of the poem and touching upon 'the prime cause' of Adam's fall, 'the Poem hasts into the midst of things'.

Milton's words here show that he had from the start a control of his subject and of the causes powering its action that no oral poet could command. Milton had in mind a plot, with a beginning, middle, and end (Aristotle, *Poetics* 1450b) in a sequence corresponding temporally to that of the events he was reporting. This plot he deliberately dismembered in order to reassemble its parts in a consciously contrived anachronistic pattern.

Exegesis of oral epic has commonly seen oral epic poets as doing this same thing, imputing to them conscious deviation from an organization which was in fact unavailable without writing. Such exegesis smacks of the same chirographic bias evident in the term 'oral literature'--which is to say, 'oral writing'. Radically unfamiliar with the psychodynamics of a given phenomenon, you take a later or secondary phenomenon and describe the earlier or primary phenomenon as the later or secondary phenomenon reorganized. Oral performance is thought of as a variant of writing, and the oral epic plot as a variant of the plot worked out in writing for drama. Aristotle was already doing this sort of thing in his *Poetics* (1447-1448a, 1451a, and elsewhere), which for obvious reasons shows a better understanding of the drama, written and acted in his own chirographic culture, than of the epic, the product of an oral culture long vanished.

In fact, an oral culture has no experience of a lengthy, epic-size, or novel-size climactic linear plot, nor can it imagine such organization of lengthy material. In fact, it cannot organize even shorter narrative in the highly climactic way that readers of literature for the past 200 years have learned more and more to expect. It hardly does justice to oral composition to describe it as varying from an organization it does not know, and cannot conceive of. The 'things' that the action is supposed to start in the middle of have never, except for brief passages, in anyone's experience been ranged in a chronological order to establish a 'plot'. There is no *res*, in the sense of linear plot to start in the middle of. The *res* is a construct of literacy. It has to be made, fictionalized, and it cannot be made before writing. You do not find climactic linear plots ready formed in people's lives, although real lives may provide material out of which such a plot may be constructed. Any real Othello would have had thousands more incidents in his life than can be put into a play. Introducing them all would destroy the plot. The full story of Othello's whole life would be a bore.

Oral poets characteristically experience difficulty in getting a song under way: Hesiod's *Theogony*, on the borderline between oral performance and written composition, makes three tries at the same material to get going (Peabody 1975:432-433). Oral poets commonly plunged the reader *in medias res* not because of any grand design, but perforce. They had no choice, no alternative. Having heard perhaps scores of singers singing hundreds of songs of variable lengths about the Trojan War, Homer had a huge repertoire of episodes to string together but, without writing, absolutely no way to organize them in strict chronological order. There was no list of the episodes nor, in the absence of writing, was there any possibility even of conceiving of such a list. If he were to try to proceed in strict chronological order, the oral poet would on any given occasion be sure to leave out one or another episode at the point where it should fit chronologically and would have to put it in later on. If, on the next occasion, hypothetically smarting under the earlier disgrace, he remembered to put the episode in at the right time, he would be sure to leave out other episodes or get them in the wrong order. Neither he nor any other poet ever had the poem by heart at all. Oral narrative poets do not memorize a poem word-for-word, but only a potentially infinite number of recitations or rhapsodies of formulas and themes in various configurations, depending on the particular situation. (The Greek *rhapsoidein* means to stitch together song.)

Moreover, the material in an epic is not the sort of thing that would of itself yield a climactic linear plot in any event. If the episodes in the *Iliad* or the *Odyssey* are rearranged in strict chronological order, the whole has a progression but it does not have the tight climactic structure of the typical drama. It might be given that sort of structure, as might the real life of a real person, by careful selection of certain incidents and bypassing of others. But then most of the episodes would vanish. An epic put in straight chronological order remains a loose concatenation of individual episodes, with only very weak climactic progression. There is really no *res*, in the sense of linear plot, in the epic, waiting to be revealed.

What made a good epic poet was not mastery of a climactic linear plot which he manipulated by dint of a sophisticated trick called plunging his hearer *in medias res*. What made a good epic poet was--among other things, of course--tacit acceptance of the fact that episodic structure was the only way and the totally natural way of handling lengthy narrative, and possession of supreme skill in managing flashbacks and other episodic techniques. Starting in 'the middle of things' is the original, natural way to proceed for lengthy narrative (very short accounts are perhaps another thing). Lengthy climactic linear plot, with a beginning, a middle, and an end is essentially artificial. Historically, the classic dramatic plot is a literate transmutation of episodic procedure, not vice versa. If we take the climactic linear plot as the paradigm of plot, the epic has no plot. Strict plot comes with writing.

Why is it that climactic linear plot comes into being only with writing, comes into being first in the drama, where there is no narrator, and does not make its way into lengthy narrative until more than two thousand years later with the novels of the age of Jane Austen? Earlier so-called 'novels' were all more or less episodic, although Mme de La Fayette's *La Princesse de Clèves* (1678) and a few others are less so than most. The climactic linear plot reaches a kind of plenary form in the detective story--relentlessly rising tension, exquisitely tidy discovery and reversal, perfectly resolved denouement. The detective story is generally considered to have begun in 1841 with Edgar Allen Poe's *The Murders in the Rue Morgue*. Why was all lengthy narrative before the early 1800s more or less episodic, so far as we know, all over the world (even Lady Murasaki Shikibu's otherwise precocious *The Tale of*

Genji)? Why had no one written a detective story before 1841?

The answers to these questions must be sought in a deeper understanding of the history of narrative than we have thus far had, an understanding beginning from the fact that in lengthy oral narrative climactic plot is not really central to what the narrative is 'about', to the aims of the narrator, or to the audience's participation and enjoyment. Structuralist analysis by Claude Lévi-Strauss (1970 and elsewhere) and others has revealed some of the organizing principles of oral narrative as these can be described in terms of binary themes and parts. But structuralism leaves out a lot of what is going on. It is unfamiliar with much relevant scholarship, largely American.

3. Some new insights into the relationship of memory and plot have been opened in a recent lengthy work by Peabody (1975). Peabody builds on the work of American scholars now famous for their pioneering work on oral epic, notably Milman Parry and Albert Lord and (less obviously) Eric Havelock, as well as upon work of earlier Europeans such as Antoine Meillet, Theodor Bergk, Hermann Usener, and Ulrich von Wilamowitz-Moellendorff, and upon some cybernetic and structuralist literature. He situates the psychodynamics of Greek epos in the Indo-European tradition, showing the intimate connection between Greek metrics and Avestan and Indian Vedic and other Sanskrit metrics, and the connections between the evolution of the hexameter line and noetic processes. This larger ambience in which Peabody situates his conclusions suggests still wider horizons beyond: very likely, what he has to say about the place of plot and about related matters in ancient Greek narrative song will be found to apply in various ways to oral narrative in cultures around the entire world. And indeed Peabody, in his abundant notes, makes reference from time to time to Native American Indian and other non-Indo-European traditions and practices.

Partly explicitly and partly by implication, Peabody brings out the negative correlation of linear plot (Freytag's Pyramid) and memory, as earlier works were unable to do. He makes it clear that the true 'thought' or content of ancient Greek oral epos dwells in the remembered traditional formulaic and stanzaic patterns rather than in the conscious intentions of the singer to organize or 'plot' the narrative a certain way (1975:172-179). 'A singer effects, not a transfer of his own intentions, but a conventional realization of traditional thought for his listeners, including himself' (1975:176). The singer is not conveying 'information' in our ordinary sense of 'a pipeline transfer' of data from singer to listener. Basically, the singer is remembering in a curiously public way--remembering not a memorized text, for there is no such thing, nor any verbatim succession of words, but the themes and formulas that he has heard other singers sing. He remembers these always differently, as rhapsodized or stitched together in his own way on this particular occasion for this particular audience. 'Song is the remembrance of songs sung' (1975:216).

Creative imagination, in the modern sense of this term, has nothing to do with the oral epic (or, by hypothetical extension, with other forms of oral narrative in other cultures). 'Our own pleasure in deliberately forming new concepts, abstractions, and patterns of fancy must not be attributed to the traditional singer' (1975:216). The bard is always caught in a situation not entirely under his control: these people on this occasion want him to sing (1975:174). The song is the result of interaction between him, his audience, and his memories of songs sung. Since no one has ever sung the songs, for example, of the Trojan Wars in any chronological sequence, neither he nor any other bard can even think of singing them that way. His objective is not framed in terms of an overall plot. In modern Zaire (then the Democratic Republic of the Congo), Candi Rureke, when asked to narrate all the stories of the Nyanga hero Mwindo, was astonished (Biebuyck and Mateene 1969:14): never, he protested, had anyone performed all the Mwindo episodes in sequence. We know how this performance was elicited from Rureke: as he narrated, now in prose, now in verse, with occasional choral accompaniment, before a (somewhat fluid) audience for 12 days, three scribes--two Nyanga and one Belgian--took down his words. For print, the text, of course, had to be massively edited. How the entire *Iliad* and *Odyssey* were elicited from a singer and doubtless edited to give us our texts in the complete--though still episodic--forms in which we have them, we do not quite know, but it was very likely in some similar fashion.

What the singer remembered in ancient Greece--and seemingly also in modern Zaire--were themes and formulas, although the formulas are apparently more obtrusive in the Greek than in the Nyanga story because the Greek is all in verse, while the Nyanga is a mixture of verse and prose narrative. For the simple reason that the singer has never heard a linear plot in chronological sequence from beginning to end of a lengthy narration, he does not remember such a chronological sequence-- though he may keep pretty close to temporal sequence in shorter narrative of a few lines generated out of a theme. He cannot create a linear plot out of his ordinary resources, since he is a rememberer, not a creator--in the sense of a creative narrator, though he is a creator in the sense that he creates an interaction between this specific audience, himself at this particular period in his development, and the memories he has. In this sense, a full linear plot of the *Iliad* and the *Odyssey* in chronological sequence never existed in anyone's imagination or plans, which is the only place it could have existed before writing. These and other comparable oral performances came

into existence episodically, and in no other way. Episodes is
what they are, however masterfully strung together.

By contrast, the situation was utterly different with Milton
when he sat down to compose *Paradise Lost* aloud, for, even
though he was now blind and composing by dictating, he was
doing essentially the same sort of thing he did when he
learned to compose in writing. His epic was designed primarily as a whole. Milton could have his dictated lines read
back to him and revise them, as an oral narrator can never
revise a line spoken or sung: Milton was creating, not
remembering. Though he of course used some memory in his
creating, it was not the communal memory of themes and
formulas that Homer had dwelt in. *Paradise Lost* is not the
'remembrance of songs sung' as the *Iliad* and the *Odyssey* and
The Mwindo Epic are.

Peabody's profound treatment of memory throws bright new
light on many of the characteristics of orally based thought
and expression, notably on its additive, aggregative character,
its conservatism, its redundancy or copia (which helps produce the constant feedback that characterizes oral thought
development and gives it its often bombastic quality), and its
participatory economy.

Of course, narrative has to do with the temporal sequence
of events, and thus in all narrative there is some kind of
story line. As the result of a sequence of events, the situation at the end is subsequent to what it was at the beginning.
Nevertheless, memory, as it guides the oral poet, often has
little to do with strict linear presentation of events in temporal
sequence. The poet will get caught up with the description
of the hero's shield and lose completely the narrative track.
We find ourselves today, in our typographic and electronic
culture, delighted by exact correspondence between the linear
order of elements in discourse and the referential order, the
world to which the discourse refers. We like the sequence in
verbal reports to parallel exactly what we experience or can
arrange to experience. When narrative abandons or distorts
this parallelism, as in Robbe-Grillet's *Marienbad* or Julio
Cortazar's *Rayuela*, the effect is utterly self-conscious: one
is aware of the absence of the normally expected parallelism.

Oral narrative is not much concerned with exact sequential
parallelism, which becomes an objective of the mind possessed
by literacy. Parallelism between the sequence of events in a
narrative and its real-life referent was precociously exploited,
Peabody points out, by Sappho and gives her poems their curious modernity as reports on temporally lived personal experience (1975:221). By Sappho's time (fl. c. 600 B.C.) writing
was already structuring the Greek psyche. But there is little
of this parallelism at all in epos--or, for that matter, in other
discourse in oral cultures (Ong 1967:50-53, 258-259). Similarly,
'narrative description in the epos is seldom the description of
an Aristotelian causal chain' (Peabody 1975:214). Philosophical

and scientific analysis are entirely dependent on the interiorization effected by writing.

Thought in oral cultures develops, but it develops with
glacial slowness, for individuals cannot move far from the tradition in which oral culture stores its knowledge without losing
both their auditors and themselves (Ong 1967:231-234). 'The
amount of effort, inventive imagination, and technical skill'
needed for an oral performer to work up in recitation (his
only resource for working out thought) a store of new information discovered and organized by himself is simply pro-
hibitive, as Peabody points out. For an individual to work out
with conscious intent truly original thought on any appreciable
scale, 'some time-obviating mechanism like writing is necessary
to organize, formulate, and realize' the thought. Instead of
being analytically linear, oral thought is highly redundant and
echoic: this is the only way it can proceed, by feedback
loops out of and into itself (1975:173-176).

Further details of Peabody's creative extension and deepening
of recent scholarship on orality are too complex and at times
involuted for full treatment here, especially since his most
fecund and wide-ranging discussions emerge from his primary
concern with the sources of the pentameter line as such--
sources which are treated not just metrically, however, but
psychodynamically in full social contexts. One can question
or qualify certain features of his argument, as Havelock has
done in a lengthy article-review (1979), but one must at the
same time affirm, as Havelock forthrightly does, the incontro-
vertible value of a work 'so close to the realities of the oral
situation' (1979:189) and to the mentality that uses the oral
medium in what I have called a primary oral culture. Peabody's work shows how profoundly and suggestively our
understanding of the shift from orality can be expanded and
deepened.

4. With writing, and even more intensively with print and
the computer, the operation of human memory is drastically
altered and the noetic processes that mark oral cultures are
transformed. Writing, and later print and computer, enable
knowledge to be stored outside the mind--though of course
only after a manner of speaking, because there is no knowledge outside the mind. Unless a human mind knows the code
for interpreting writing, letters on a page are no more knowledge than random scratchings would be. It is what is in the
mind that makes the letters signify. Writing and its sequels
do not, strictly speaking, store 'knowledge' outside the mind
but rather set up structures outside the mind which enable
the mind to engage in intellectual activity otherwise unavailable
to it. This is why writing and its sequels become more effective as the human mind 'interiorizes' them more and more, incorporates them into itself by adjusting itself to using them
without having to reflect on them, so that operations

supported by the technology of writing, and later of print and electronics, seem to it as normal as its unsupported natural operations. Today, as we have seen, most literates are totally unaware that their most characteristic kinds of thinking--those that organize a school textbook or even a newspaper article, for example--are unavailable to oral peoples, are not 'natural' at all in the sense that they cannot be carried on by a mind unaffected, directly or indirectly, by writing. Chirographically conditioned or implemented thought is technologically powered, although at the same time it is, of course, 'natural' in the sense that it is totally natural to man to devise artificial technologies to improve his own native prowess.

A helpful analog for the use of writing is performance on a musical instrument. Musical instruments are tools, the products of technology, totally outside the human being who plays them, as a written or printed text is outside the reader. When Beethoven composed, he was imagining sounds made with tools ('instruments' is the more commendatory word, but it says the same thing), and he was writing down exquisitely specific directions on how to manipulate the tools. *Fortissimo*: hit the keys very hard. *Legato*: do not take your finger off one key until you have hit the next. An orchestral performance is a demonstration of what human beings can do with tools. Some music-making devices, such as a pipe organ, are not just tools but huge, complex machines, with sources of power separate from the player. Electric guitars and other electrified instruments are machines, too. Modern instrumental music, whether that of an electronic orchestra, a classical orchestra, or a piano or a flute, is a technological triumph. Try to make a musical instrument and see.

And yet, the violinist has interiorized his tool, the violin cradled in his arm, so deeply that its sound seems to come from the very depths of his soul. He has humanized the tool, interiorized it, so that to him and his audience it seems a part of himself. The organist similarly humanizes, interiorizes a huge machine whose mechanism he by no means fully understands. This is what human beings have also done with the technologies of writing, print, and computers. Writing can be compared to a violin or flute or trumpet, print to a piano (far more mechanical and dismayingly complex), the computer to the pipe organ or electronic organ.

Human memory does not naturally work like a written or printed text or like a computer. Natural, orally sustained verbal memory is redundant, essentially and not by default, echoic, nonlinear, and, unless supplemented by special intensive training, it is never verbatim for any very lengthy passage. Rather, it is thematic and formulaic, and it proceeds by 'rhapsodizing', stitching together formulas and themes in various orders triggered by the specific occasion in which the rememberer is remembering. It works out of and with the unconscious as much as within consciousness. Peabody has

made the point that the performance of the oral narrator or
singer is very little determined by conscious intent: the
formulas and themes--the tradition--control him more than he
controls them.   This is the ultimate difference between human
memory and language on the one hand and, on the other, the
retrieval and communication systems set up by writing and
print and electronics.   Human memory and language grow out
of the unconscious into consciousness.   Writing and print
and electronic devices are produced by conscious planning--
though of course their use, like all human activities, involves
the unconscious as well as consciousness.

We have interiorized tools and machines so deeply that we
are likely--unconsciously--to use them as models for human
activity.   We think of retrieval of material from the written or
printed text or from the computer as the model of native human
memory.   It is not an adequate model.   Human memory never
recalls simply words.   It recalls also their associations.   Literate scholars of an earlier age, predisposed to take as the model
of mnemonic activity the literate's verbatim memorization of
texts, commonly supposed that since oral peoples clearly had
prodigious memories, they had prodigiously accurate verbatim
memories.   This supposition is untrue.   Literates can normally
reproduce a lengthy narrative in metrically regular verse only
when they have memorized a preexisting text.   Oral performers
can reproduce a lengthy narrative in metrically regular verse,
as Lord has shown (1960), by quite different techniques--not
by learning verbatim a string of words but by expressing
themselves with vast stores of metrically tailored formulas,
accommodated to the narrative themes and forms they know.
Out of these formulas they construct metrical lines ad libitum
which tell the same story in perfect metrics but not at all
word for word.   Memory here works not out of an actively
conscious attempt to reconstitute perfectly a string of words,
but rather out of a passion for what Peabody styles the 'flight
of song'.

This is not to say that oral cultures never ambition or
achieve verbatim repetition, particularly in ritualized recitation
learned by intensive drill (Sherzer 1980: 2-3 of typescript,
and n. 3; 1981, n. 3).   But even ritual is not typically altogether verbatim, either in oral cultures or in chirographic
cultures retaining a heavy oral residue.   'Do this in memory
of me' (Luke 22:19), Jesus said at the Last Supper.   Christians celebrate the Eucharist because of Jesus' command.   But
the words of institution which he spoke before he gave this
command and to which the command refers, the words that
Christians repeat in their liturgy as Jesus' words ('This is
my body...; this is the cup of my blood...'), are not set
down in exactly the same way in any two passages of the
New Testament that report them.   The command to remember
does not call for verbatim memory.   Even in a text here, the
still highly oral Christian Church remembered in the original,

resonant, pretextual way, rich in content and meaning--a way that can frighten unreflective literate and computer people disposed to associate recall with verbatim retrieval, which is to say with itemization rather that with truth.

With the new and radically analytic ways of thought that are set up by writing and print and electronics, and that revamp the field in which memory had moved, human intellectual and verbal activity enters radically new phases, which actively develop over the generations as writing and its sequels are more and more interiorized. For interiorization is a lengthy and complex process. We are only now beginning to learn what it has really meant.

NOTE

This paper is an adaptation of a section of a forthcoming book, *Orality and Literacy*, by Walter J. Ong, to be published by Methuen (London and New York) in their New Accents series. Copyright 1981, Walter J. Ong.

REFERENCES

Abrahams, Roger D. 1968. Introductory remarks to a rhetorical theory of folklore. Journal of American Folklore 81.143-158.

Abrahams, Roger D. 1972. The training of the man of words in talking sweet. Language in Society 1.15-29.

Biebuyck, Daniel, and Kahombo C. Mateene, eds. 1969. The Mwindo epic from the Banyanga. Berkeley: University of California Press.

Brink, C[harles] O[scar]. 1971. Horace on poetry: The 'Ars Poetica.' Cambridge, England: Cambridge University Press.

Havelock, Eric A. 1963. Preface to Plato. Cambridge, Mass.: Belknap Press of Harvard University Press.

Havelock, Eric A. 1979. The ancient art of oral poetry. Philosophy and Rhetoric 12.187-202. [A review article treating Peabody (1975).]

Kelber, Werner H. 1979. Markus und die Mündliche Tradition. Linguistica Biblica 45.5-58.

Kelber, Werner H. 1980. Mark and oral tradition. Semeia 16.7-55.

Lord, Albert B. 1960. The singer of tales. Harvard Studies in Comparative Literature 24. Cambridge, Mass.: Harvard University Press.

Ong, Walter J. 1967. The presence of the word. New Haven and London: Yale University Press.

Ong, Walter J. 1971. Rhetoric, romance, and technology. Ithaca and London: Cornell University Press.

Ong, Walter J. 1977. Interfaces of the word. Ithaca and London: Cornell University Press.

Ong, Walter J. 1978. Literacy and orality in our times. ADE Bulletin No. 58, September, 1-7.

Peabody, Berkley. 1975. The winged word: A study in the technique of Ancient Greek oral composition as seen principally through Hesiod's works and days. Albany: State University of New York Press.

Sherzer, Joel. 1980. Tellings, retellings, and tellings within tellings: The structuring and organization of narrative in Cuna Indian discourse. Paper presented at the Centro Internazionale de Semiotica e Linguistica, Urbino, Italy, July [to be published in the Proceedings].

Sherzer, Joel. 1981. The interplay of structure and function in Kuna narrative, or, How to grab a snake in the Darien. [This volume, 307-323.]

PERSUASIVE DISCOURSE
AND ORDINARY CONVERSATION,
WITH EXAMPLES FROM ADVERTISING

Robin Tolmach Lakoff
University of California, Berkeley

The very work that engaged him [in an advertising
agency] ... wafted him into a sphere of dim platonic arche-
types, bearing a scarcely recognizable relationship to anything in the living world. Here those strange entities, the
Thrifty Housewife, the Man of Discrimination, the Keen
Buyer and the Good Judge, for ever young, for ever hand-
some, for ever virtuous, economical and inquisitive, moved
to and fro upon their complicated orbits, comparing prices
and values, making tests of purity, asking indiscreet questions about each other's ailments, household expenses, bed-
springs, shaving cream, diet, laundry, work and boots,
perpetually spending to save and saving to spend, cutting
out coupons and collecting cartons, surprising husbands
with margarine and wives with patent washers and vacuum
cleaners, occupied from morning to night in washing, cooking, dusting, filing, saving their children from germs, their
complexions from wind and weather, their teeth from decay
and their stomachs from indigestion, and yet adding so
many hours to the day by labour-saving appliances that
they had always leisure for visiting the talkies, sprawling
on the beach to picnic upon Potted Meats and Tinned Fruit,
and (when adorned by So-and-so's Silks, Blank's Gloves,
Dash's Footwear, Whatnot's Weatherproof Complexion Cream
and Thingummy's Beautifying Shampoos), even attending
Ranelagh, Cowes, and Grand Stand at Ascot, Monte Carlo
and the Queen's Drawing-Rooms.
    --Dorothy L. Sayers, *Murder Must Advertise*

In the field of discourse analysis, much attention has been focused on certain forms of discourse, much less on others. In particular, scholars have been concerned with ordinary conversation, on the one hand, and written expository text, on the other. While the treatment of these types as separate entities has certainly taught us a great deal about the characteristics of each of them individually, and something about the nature of discourse in general, it leaves a great many questions unexplored. For one thing, how do they relate to other types of discourse--which may superficially or even more deeply resemble one or the other? What are the universal characteristics of all types of discourse, and what characteristics are specific to just one or two? Can we devise a taxonomy of discourse types, a means of unambiguously differentiating among them?

Classifying the basic forms of discourse in terms of their differing and similar characteristics seems rather less glamorous than writing a grammar, a system of rules, for one or all discourse types. But in fact, it is impossible to write a grammar without knowing the basic units involved: grammar consists of instructions for the combinations of these basic elements.

It would also be profitable to look at discourse not from its surface form (as conversation, say, or literary text) but more deeply, with interest in its deeper purpose. When we look at a range of discourse types, we notice that they appear quite different from one another. Clearly, this disparity is due to differences in what each is intended to accomplish, so that a successful performance of a type of discourse is one that accomplishes what the speaker, or the participants as a whole, had set out to do, rather than merely one that conforms to some particular surface configuration.

This paper is somewhat experimental in nature, as I want to address some of these questions, and see how far we can get toward at least preliminary answers. As a start, I want to consider one possible distinction among discourse types in terms of function or purpose: ordinary conversation, on the one hand, and something we can call 'persuasive discourse' (PD), on the other. I will come to the problem of the definition of the latter shortly. I am not suggesting that this is the only distinction one can make among discourse types, nor that it is necessarily the major one. Certainly, we can divide up the spectrum in many ways, all intersecting: oral/written, formal/informal, spontaneous/nonspontaneous--just to list some possibilities. I am phrasing the question as if we are to inspect and perhaps justify a dichotomy, but we should keep in mind the possibility that no dichotomy will emerge--that we cannot divide discourse neatly into persuasive/nonpersuasive realms, that some types may cut across this distinction and it may prove irrelevant for others.

With all these caveats in mind, however, it still seems useful to begin as I proposed, since persuasion is a function attributable to at least some discourse types. I would suggest at the start that ordinary conversation is not persuasive in the sense of having persuasion as its major goal. That is not to say that in ordinary conversation (OC) we do not persuade, or try to persuade, other participants. But persuasion is not what we enter into the conversational experience for. We do not come away from an informal chat saying, 'Wow, that was a great talk! I persuaded Harry that bats eat cats!' Rather, an experience of OC is good if we come away feeling that a good interaction has been had by all, that we all like each other and wouldn't mind talking to each other again. Granted that getting these ideas across is in a sense persuasive, it is not so in the sense that getting someone to worry about ring-around-the-collar is persuasive.

One important determinant of technically persuasive discourse is nonreciprocity: discourse is defined as reciprocal only in case both, or all, participants in it are able to do the same things, and if similar contributions are always understood similarly. A classroom lecture obviously is nonreciprocal: one participant selects the topics, does most of the speaking, and determines the start and finish of the discourse. The power in such discourse is held by the person holding the floor, at least to the extent that that person makes most of the explicit decisions as to the direction the discourse takes, its start and finish. On the other hand, it can be argued that the audience holds power in such a situation, for it can go or stay, be attentive or not--and by these decisions negate the effect and purpose of the other's speaking. I return later to the question of what constitutes power in a discourse, but here it can be noted that it is meaningful to raise this question only for nonreciprocal discourse.

Discourse that is truly reciprocal is, at the same time, necessarily egalitarian, at least ostensibly. Ordinary conversation, for example, is normally fully reciprocal: any participant has the same conversational options as any others, and if one can ask a question and expect an answer, so can the others; if one can ask a particular type of question, or make a certain sort of statement (say, a question as to the other's financial affairs; a statement about the other's personal appearance), the other has the same privilege in turn, and if one can refuse to answer, so can the other. Violations of this principle do, of course, occur in OC, but when they do, participants feel a rule has been violated, that the conversation is making them uncomfortable, while nonreciprocity in a lecture is expected and reasonably comfortable.

An example of an intermediate, hence problematic, case is psychotherapeutic discourse. In many of its forms, there is the appearance of an egalitarian, reciprocal conversation, but in terms of deeper intention, the reciprocity turns out to be only superficial. The therapist can ask questions which the client soon learns not to ask; and if the latter should attempt to ask such a question, the therapist, rather than give an answer, will usually treat the question as a tacit invitation to ask another question, or make an interpretation: 'I notice you're curious about my personal life'. Further, many of the marks of power that belong to the lecturer in the classroom also belong to the therapist: the decision when to begin and end, and--while the client ostensibly picks the topics of discourse-- the determination of what the client's contributions actually mean. The client, however, typically holds the floor for the major part of the discourse--an anomaly in terms of the relation between floor-holding and power-holding in typical conversational settings, which makes it especially difficult to acquire proficiency in therapeutic dialog.

With these assumptions in mind, one can attempt a definition of persuasive discourse as a type of discourse that nonreciprocally attempts to effect persuasion. Discourse, then, is to be considered persuasive only in case it is nonreciprocal, and the intent to persuade is recognized explicitly as such by at least one party to the discourse. By 'persuasion' I mean the attempt or intention of one participant to change the behavior, feelings, intentions or viewpoint of another by communicative means. The last is important. Communicative means may be linguistic or nonlinguistic (say, gestures), but they are abstract and symbolic. A gun held to the head may indeed induce a change in someone's behavior, but it is not communicative in this sense. Hence I do not consider a direct physical threat a type of persuasive discourse. Types such as advertising, propaganda, political rhetoric and religious sermons clearly do fall into this category. While lectures, psychotherapy, and literature might belong here under some interpretations, they are problematic and are dealt with later: they seem intermediate between PD and OC. On the other side, while direct physical intervention is clearly outside of our definition of PD, brainwashing is more difficult to assign to either category. It is true that very often there is no direct physical force involved. But in brainwashing, as the term is ordinarily used, there almost necessarily are physical interventions--whether isolation from other people and familiar surroundings, privations of numerous kinds, physical discomfort and torture--so that, perhaps, on the grounds that brainwashing is rooted, however indirectly, in nonsymbolic physical means of motivation, we ought not to consider brainwashing among the types of persuasive discourse, although it is a demonstrably effective means of persuasion.

As we attempt to make more precise our definition of what is persuasive and what is not, we are confronted with a problem that has, itself, propagandistic overtones. Perhaps because we live in a society in which egalitarianism is upheld as a paramount virtue, we extol anything that has the appearance of equality, distrust anything that does not. We are not apt to ask whether there are certain kinds of activities and situations in which equality is unnecessary or even impossible, and find it hard to imagine using phrases like 'power imbalance', 'inequality', or 'nonreciprocity' without negative connotations. Hence, to talk about discourse as 'reciprocal' implies that it is somehow good, or beneficent; to call something 'nonegalitarian' is to imply that those who customarily utilize it are manipulative and hungry for control. (This may, of course, be true, and certainly there are situations where a position of power is misused or abused. It is further true that using the surface appearance of egalitarian and reciprocal discourse for deeper nonreciprocal and power-seeking purposes is illegitimate and deserves censure, unless justification can be given for this deceptiveness. But discourse that is overtly and explicitly nonegalitarian seems not to present any danger, nor to deserve the opprobrium heaped upon it so often.)

Additionally, for numerous reasons, there are certain cultural preferences in discourse types. Some we are prone to admire and respect; others are illegitimate, 'dirty', debauched. We would prefer to keep our likes and dislikes in neat, overlapping piles: what we like for one reason should be admirable on all grounds, and vice versa. Hence, if we have been trained to despise one type of discourse--say, commercials or political propaganda--we would like to believe that it is 'persuasive' because we consider persuasive discourse, since it is nonreciprocal, malign; and if a type of discourse is, at least to its practitioners, beneficent and pure--for example, psychotherapeutic discourse--there is tremendous pressure to deny that it is 'persuasive', that there is anything nonreciprocal about it, or that there is any sort of power imbalance involved, for believing these claims would seem, to its proponents, to vitiate the claims for benignness for the discourse type in question.

Uncertainty and conflict arise, of course, when we simultaneously judge a type of behavior good or bad, depending on which aspects of it we focus on; but we have to dispense with the idea that the attribution of power imbalance and nonreciprocity is name-calling. It is not; it is mere definition and should be considered value-free, with the added assumption that some discourse types must, to be effective, be nonreciprocal and power-imbalanced, the only issue in this kind of word being whether it is effective, not the value of the method by which that effect is achieved. We must try not to heap obloquy on the commercial, and praise on the therapeutic discourse, because of their purposes, at least not while we are trying to discover their properties and their positions within a taxonomy, and eventually a grammar, of discourse.

With this problem out of the way, let us turn to the question of definition. Some of the factors have already been alluded to at greater or lesser length in this paper, but I summarize here all the relevant points as they appear to me, in classifying discourse types, determining how they differ and what aspects are universal, and differentiating between persuasive and nonpersuasive discourse.

First, and perhaps most important, is reciprocity, about which
much has been said earlier in this paper. Connected with reciprocity is bilaterality. A discourse may be reciprocal and bilateral, like OC; nonreciprocal and unilateral, in that true participation occurs on only one side, like a classroom lecture
(though I make amendments even to this statement shortly); or,
most complex, nonreciprocal but bilateral, like psychotherapeutic discourse, where both parties most typically can make true
contributions to the conversations, but the contributions may be
of different surface forms, and certainly are open to different
interpretations. Turn-taking is a natural concomitant of reciprocity, though (as in psychotherapeutic discourse which involves turn-taking) the two can be separated; but a non-turn-
taking, or unilateral, discourse can never be reciprocal.[1]

Discourse may be spontaneous or not, or rather, can be conventionally spontaneous or not. Thus, OC is at least conventionally spontaneous: we distrust apparent OC if we have
reason to suspect any of the participants is working from a
script, or has planned significantly in advance. But a work of
art, or a lecture, is not supposed to be spontaneous, and the
lecturer feels no embarrassment about referring to notes.
Hence, we find differences in the use of hesitation devices,
pragmatic particles, cohesion, and so forth. A spate of
y'knows distresses us far less in OC than in a lecture--and
an ordinary conversation style without hesitations and other
devices reflective of spontaneity would make most of us very
uncomfortable. Spontaneity is, of course, related to reciprocity
and bilaterality: it is almost impossible to plan the flow of your
conversation when another participant has as much right as you
to determine its direction.

Another characteristic of persuasive discourse is novelty.
Ordinary conversation thrives on ritual and custom: while the
topics of our conversation, and the precise way we talk about
them, differ from time to time, our overall style does not shift,
nor in general does the way in which a given society holds an
informal conversation change over time. The general mode of
conversation today is not, at least judging from novels and
other contemporary evidence, significantly different from the
way it was done 200 years ago. Openings and closings--the
most ritualized elements--have changed very little over time:
while colloquially we introduce new forms of these occasionally--
Hiya, ciao, and so on--we eventually return to the old standbys,
hello and goodbye. The rest of the conversation follows a style
that can best be described as unstylized: it has no set pattern,
and hence no new patterns can be substituted for the old. Persuasive discourse, in all forms, is different: a defining feature
of persuasive discourse is its quest for novelty. This is manifested on the lexical level, in the form of slogans and neologisms; syntactically; semantically, in that new concepts are
continually being introduced and talked about; and pragmatically,
in the way in which PD addresses hearers, its register, its

directness or indirectness, and many other factors. What is
crucial here is that PD wears out; OC does not.

A feature common to most forms of PD is that there is an
audience, rather than an addressee. Actually, audiencehood
goes along with unilaterality: an audience is a hearer or group
of hearers who play only that role, and do not take the active
role of speaker. The role of an audience is much more passive
than that of an addressee. In some forms of discourse, we
find both, at least ostensibly: in dramatic performances in
any medium, we often find conversations--involving speaker
and addressee in ordinary conversation--taking place in the
hearing of an audience, which does not participate. But much
of the dialogue uttered by the participants in the drama itself
differs in striking ways from true ordinary spontaneous conversation. Some of the difference, of course, has to do with the
fact that the dialogue is constructed rather than spontaneous,
so that many of the uses of spontaneity are absent. [2] But
other differences are directly due to the fact that the dialogue
is occurring, in such situations, for the benefit not of the immediate participants, but of the audience, and therefore many
of the contributions found in OC designed to make the other
feel good, or inform the other about necessary facts, are absent, and other things are present which would ordinarily not
be found in OC because all participants are already aware of
them and the contribution is therefore redundant. But the
audience is not aware, and needs to be apprised of the information, and so it is. An audience has a different role than
does an eavesdropper in true OC.

In addition to the major distinction of audience/addressee,
there are distinct types of audience, based on the role the
latter is to play in the discourse. The role of audience ranges
from totally nonparticipatory to a conscious and active involvement. Indeed, an audience can exist even in case the speaker
is not aware of its presence--an eavesdropper, that is, whose
role is precisely to remain undiscovered and therefore to give
no clues whatsoever as to its presence. In ceremonial functions
--at a wedding, for instance--the audience is known to be present, and indeed its presence as witness to the ritual is necessary if the ritual is to be transacted successfully, but there its
role ends. It does not participate, it is not expected to understand, or signal its understanding. Typically, the audience at
a wedding does not indicate by any means, verbal or otherwise,
its agreement or complicity. In fact, it does not matter to the
members of such an audience if the ceremony is conducted in a
language they do not understand (say, Hebrew at an Orthodox
Jewish wedding). Their role is simply to be present, not to
derive anything themselves from what they hear. On the other
hand, an audience at a classroom lecture has as part of its
function to understand and, perhaps, give approbation--in the
form of evaluations later, yes, but more importantly, immediately
in the form of nodding and other nonverbal backchannels. A

good lecturer, however large the audience, devises ways of discovering and utilizing this nonverbal response, and without it--say, speaking to a television audience--someone accustomed to lecturing in the presence of an audience is lost. Hence, we often find television discourse being taped in the presence of a live audience, to provide speakers with this all-important, though nonverbal and unconscious, feedback.

A third level of audience response is seen in certain forms of religious and political gatherings: the audience is expected to participate with audible and explicit backchannels: 'amen/right on!' or applause and cheers. The audience here is very important to the speaker: it signals by its response whether persuasion is occurring in these maximally persuasive forms of discourse.

Related to the foregoing, but perceptible at a more abstract level of analysis, is the use of the Gricean conversational maxims. The maxims themselves are problematic for conversational analysis in that they were formulated by Grice (1975) for quite different purposes than providing an understanding of how discourse functions. Actually, in OC Grice's maxims are seldom encountered directly. Rather, they are understood via rules of implicature, and any ordinary conversations that adhered for any length of time to the maxims themselves would certainly strike participants as strange, oddly impersonal, often literally unintelligible. By contrast, a lecture is expected to adhere pretty closely to the maxims, and when implicature is utilized it is for special purposes--irony, for instance--which the audience is expected to appreciate as special. Indeed, Grice's Conversational Logic, as he set it out, is optimally applicable to the lecture, not the ordinary conversation. When we attempt to extend the notion to other forms of discourse, we find still more complicated difficulties, as I show in greater detail later.

The presence of a power relationship among participants was noted earlier. Important in this regard is the question of how power is determined. It has been suggested that conversational power belongs to the one who controls topic and floor, but there is an alternative view that power is in the hands of whoever has the choice of whether to continue to participate, whether to be persuaded. The hearers at a lecture may listen attentively or may whisper and shuffle; or they might even leave, individually or en masse, and then the lecture truly ceases to exist. Psychotherapeutic clients may or may not continue to appear for their sessions. The audience for the commercials may buy the sponsor's product or not. Still, while this may in some general sense be power, we can distinguish from it power within the discourse: the power to motivate the discourse in a certain direction, to begin or terminate it explicitly. And this power rests with the floor-holder (or with the therapist in the case of psychotherapeutic discourse). As with the issue of persuasion generally, we tend to consider power an evil, and its appearance in discourse a sign of the corruptness of the discourse. But in fact, as long as it is explicitly acknowledged that the imbalance exists, there is no problem.

Finally, as a distinguishing feature among discourse types, we can think about the means of persuasion. Again, this is an area heavily laden with value judgment, which is not helpful for our present purposes. We can make distinctions among the means of persuasion, in those types of discourse that fall into the range that we have called truly 'persuasive': propaganda, advertising, and political rhetoric, and those that have strong persuasive elements: lectures, psychotherapeutic discourse, and literature. In fact, it can be argued that what distinguishes the first category from the second is precisely the means--ostensible in any case--of persuasion. The first operates by appeal to the emotions, the second--largely, or at least theoretically--by appeal to the intellect. We tend to assign a desirable connotation to intellectual persuasion, since it appears to treat us with respect, take our most crucial human values into account, give us a real chance to weigh and judge, and so on; while emotional appeals seem to circumvent our reason and to appeal to our base nature, giving us no chance to make a real decision. In particular, within the last several decades, 'subliminal' advertising designed to present a tachistoscopic image to the mind so that conscious perception is circumvented, leaving only the appeal to the unconscious, by definition motivated only by appeals to emotion and instinct, has aroused particular outrage and inspired a good deal of preventive legislation, despite more recent evidence that it is less effective than its proponents hope and others fear.

I discuss further on the use of Gricean maxims in persuasion. It is important here to note that the Rules of Conversation are perhaps deceptively applied, or nonapplied; but they are certainly invoked, because they constitute, for the audience, evidence that we are being persuaded by reason, intellectual argumentation. Hence the appearance of conformity to the Gricean maxims is critical if we as newly sophisticated consumers are to be subliminally seduced. The appearance of reason conceals the appeal to emotions and justifies it for the buyer.

Indeed, all forms of persuasive discourse have gone through changes over time--partly necessitated by the requirement of novelty, but also in part by the increasing sophistication of the consumer and the need to present products as reasonable ones to purchase. The change in the realm of advertising is especially interesting. In older advertising (say, up till the 1930s, roughly speaking), there was a heavy preponderance of print, of words, and far fewer and less striking pictures. This was in part due to the state of reproductive techniques: photography was rather primitive, color reproduction ruinously expensive, and graphic techniques relatively unsophisticated so that, for the money, words were the most economical means of

persuasion. But the words, if we examine them, were far more
directly an appeal to the emotions than is wording--or, perhaps,
even illustrations--in advertising today. Part of the change is
due, of course, to increasingly vigilant regulation by federal
agencies concerned with truth in advertising. But ironically--
and not surprisingly, given our bias toward seeing ourselves
as logical and rational--regulations have almost invariably been
framed in terms of the wording used in advertising, at most
encompassing explicit illustration: marbles in the soup, for instance. You cannot, in an ad, say in words, 'Glotz Detergent
will make your marriage happy': the Fair Trade Commission
(FTC) will come down hard on you. But you can say in words,
'Glotz gets your husband's shirts their whitest', alongside a
picture of a young, vital couple glowing at each other, surrounded by cheerful children, a dog, a white picket fence.
The irony is that, in fact, the second approach is far more effective than the first, since it circumvents intellectual judgment
('How can using a detergent make Harry more responsive to
me?') and goes directly to the realm of the unconscious, capable
only of desires, fears, and needs.

If much of this discussion has the ring of a psychology textbook, many modern advertising techniques trace their genealogy
directly to the far-famed couch in Vienna. Indeed, much of
modern motivational psychology, the basis of advertising, derives from Freud, directly or indirectly. For it was Freud
(1900/1953) who pointed out the basic distinction between the
processes of the conscious and the unconscious mind. The unconscious works by the laws of the primary process; the conscious, by the secondary process. Primary process thought is
preverbal--symbolic, nonsequential, and visual--while secondary
process thought, more directly 'rational', is auditory and
verbal. Hence, if one wants to persuade by circumventing the
processes of rational thought, it makes good sense to emphasize
abstract images--music and pictures, for instance, rather than
words in logical sequence. And if the FTC is concerned with
deception in advertising, it would do better to pay attention to
the nonverbal means of persuasion which can be much more de-
ceptive. But the problem is, of course, that it is difficult for
the investigator to prove what the picture of the happy family,
or the vital adolescents guzzling Coke, is communicating, since
we think of communication in terms of logical symbols--words.

Edward L. Bernays (perhaps not coincidentally Freud's
nephew), the inventor of modern public relations and hence of
many of the modern forms of persuasion, spoke of 'the engineering of consent' (1952). It is this that upsets us as consumers
and intrigues us as investigators. If we are so suspicious of
persuasion and its techniques, how are we 'engineered' to give
consent? Bernays referred not only to the relatively harmless
influence of advertising, but also to the more baneful effects of
political rhetoric, including propaganda. The latter term itself
can be given some scrutiny.

Originating in a religious context, with positive connotations (the 'propagating' of the faith), the term 'propaganda' eventually came to mean, viewed from the perspective of another religion, a form of improper influence or pressure. Hence 'propaganda' today is exclusively a pejorative term (though Bernays makes a plea for its rehabilitation).[3] One question is whether the term really has true denotative meaning, as a special kind of persuasion identifiable even when the argument is one with which we are in sympathy; or whether 'propaganda' simply means emotional persuasion, when the argument is not one we approve of. We would agree that 'propaganda' is mainly applicable to forms of persuasiveness that utilize emotion, usually of a high intensity, often invoking fear and irrational desires. But advertising typically does this, yet is not considered 'propaganda'. So we might want to add the proviso that propaganda concerns changes in beliefs, rather than concrete buying habits alone. Yet we might argue that much advertising is propagandistic--not only the 'public service' advertising and institutional advertising by power companies, but even advertisements for soft drinks that suggest indirectly that youth and a svelte body are minimal conditions for being allowed to exist, or that create and reinforce all sorts of traditional sexual and other stereotypes. This then suggests another facet of propaganda: it is normally indirect. It is not present in the explicit message, but somewhere in the presuppositions. When we are serenaded to the effect that 'Coke adds life', the propaganda is not in the admonition to buy Coke, but in the inference that youth is desirable (and young people drink Coke).

This brings us back a bit roundaboutly to the relation between the Gricean maxims and discourse types. I have argued that the Cooperative Principle (CP) is more directly applicable to the classroom lecture than to any other type of discourse--certainly more than to ordinary conversation. But even OC makes reference to the maxims, if only via implicature. And in OC, we understand that flouting of the maxims is due to our desire to adhere to more socially (as opposed to intellectually) relevant rules, rules of Rapport: when we have a choice between being offensive and being unclear, we invariably choose the latter, and a majority of cases of OC implicature can be seen to stem from this assumption.

But in persuasive discourse, the situation is rather different. Whereas in OC and the lecture, our aim is to inform--at least, it is so, other things being equal--in PD our aim is, of course, to persuade. The politician does not especially want a knowledgeable electorate: he wants votes. The advertiser is not interested in educating people about hygiene: he wants to sell deodorant. It is not that the maxims are violated only in case a more peremptory need intervenes, as in OC--they are regularly infringed without explanation, cue, or apology.

Indeed, it might be argued that the PD need for novelty alone is responsible for many instances of violations of the maxims,

especially in advertising. For in OC, we have seen, novelty
is not especially valued. Part of the reason for this is that
familiarity aids intelligibility--that is, aids in the keeping of
the Cooperative Principle. What is new and requires interpretation is in violation of the maxim of Manner (be clear). But
in PD it is this very violation that is striking, memorable--
efficacious.

If we understand this preference for novelty as an intrinsic
aim of PD, we can perhaps understand better why advertisers
cling to certain formulas despite--or rather, because of--the
contempt to which they are subjected by critics. For example,
many of us remember a slogan from the fifties: 'Winston tastes
good like a cigarette should'. The criticism heaped on the hap-
less preposition was staggering, yet the commercial continued to
appear in that form. (Lip service was later paid to linguistic
chastity by the addition, after the infamous slogan, of the re-
joinder, 'What do you want, good grammar or good taste?' which
was cold comfort for traditional grammarians.) We can understand the company's clinging to the solecism if we understand it
as a Manner violation: focusing the hearer's (or reader's)
attention on style tended to obscure content, and thus to flout
Manner, if a bit indirectly. Indeed, anything neologistic will
have much the same effect, and will serve as good persuasion
for two reasons: first, because it violates Manner as just explained, and thus attracts the audience's attention; and second,
in the case of obvious neologism--as opposed to the simple un-
grammaticality of *like* for *as*--it forces the audience to interpret
--as any violation of the Cooperative Principle does.

It is axiomatic among proponents of all forms of persuasive or
semipersuasive discourse (e.g. psychotherapeutic discourse and
the classroom lecture) that if the audience can be made to participate at some level--that is, to function as addressee, not
wholly as audience--learning, or persuasion, will be much more
successful. Hence, if the audience is forced to interpret neologism, or relate 'ungrammatical' forms to their textbook version,
they will probably remember better. And memory is the name
of the game in PD.

We find violation of the Cooperative Principle not only in Manner, but in other maxims as well. In terms of neologisms and
other sorts of linguistic novelty--most easily considered as
Manner violations--we find:

(1) Lexical novelty (neologism):
    stroft, a portmanteau of *strong* and *soft*; *devilicious*.

(2) Morphological/Syntactic novelty (in terms of category
    shifts: *like* for *as* may belong here):
    Gentles the smoke and makes it mild
    Travels the smoke further

The soup that eats like a meal
Peanuttiest

(3) Syntactic innovation:
(Some of these can also be viewed as Quantity violations, in that either not enough or too much information is given for ordinary conversation understanding. These include such odd usages as the following.)

(3a) Absence of subjects and often the absence of verbal auxiliaries as well:[4]
Tastes good! And nutritious too!

(3b) Odd uses of the definite article, which is sometimes unexpectedly inserted and is sometimes unaccountably absent:
Next time, I'll buy the Tylenol!
Baby stays dry! Diaper keeps moisture away from baby's skin!

(4) Semantic anomaly (other than lexical anomaly):
(These include quantity violations, among other things.)
Cleans better than another leading oven cleaner.
Works better than a leading detergent.

In instance (4) we expect, because of Quantity (or perhaps Relevance), a definite article in the item being compared with the product being touted. Otherwise, the information is non-informative, or useless: after all, what we need to know is which is best. Here is a good example of persuasive discourse adopting the surface trappings of informative (i.e. Cooperative Principle obeying) discourse and thereby leading us to conclude that it is informative (if it looks like a duck, and walks like a duck ...). Hence we understand it as informative, that is, in keeping with the CP. Notice that when a maxim is infringed in OC via implicature, we do not interpret the utterance as being in keeping with the maxim by virtue of its surface appearance. Rather, in these cases we are given signals by the infringing speaker that the contribution is in violation of the CP, and we are thus implicitly directed to put our interpretive skills to work. In PD, on the other hand, the flouting of the maxim is covert, and we are tricked into assuming that an act of information is taking place in cases like this, where in fact it is not.

(5) Pragmatic novelty.
This includes anything aberrant about the discourse form itself. In particular, since many commercials are framed as mini-dramas, we see many unusual bits of dialogue within these 30-second segments. One such type much in vogue lately is the following.

--You still use Good Seasons Italian?
--Not any more!
--No?
--I use new improved Good Seasons Italian!

Now in terms of ordinary conversation, the second speaker's contribution violates Quantity, and would probably be treated not as the joke it functions as in the commercial, but as a rather stupid bit of obfuscation, if it were to occur in real OC. This is generally true of the 'jokes' highly favored in recent commercial genres, especially coffee commercials:

--Fill it to the rim!
--With Brim! [laughter]

Wife [with camera]: Give me a smile!
Husband [at breakfast table]: Only if *you* give *me* another cup of your coffee. [5]

Humor, in ordinary conversation, can often be viewed as a permissible Manner violation. But the humor here is of a rather different order, especially as it seems both strained and puerile. This may in part even be purposeful: reassuring the audience that the folks in the commercial are no different from them, they make awkward jokes too, and this just shows they are good, spontaneous people. That this seems especially characteristic of coffee commercials, I think, is because the ambiance of these commercials is intended to suggest a sort of easy-going informality where joking of this kind is in place. But beyond this, these jokes fulfill another communicative purpose: if we assume that, unlike OC, the major purpose in commercials is to ensure that the sponsor's name is remembered, rather than creating an easy and natural atmosphere of warmth (but, in many types of commercials, the summum bonum is getting the sponsor's name memorably associated with an easy and natural atmosphere of warmth--that is, superficial rapport), these 'jokes' see to it that the sponsor's name gets mentioned in a prominent position, usually at the very end of the commercial, and in a loud voice with stress--as we stress the punchline of a joke more than the end of a normal sentence.
Another pragmatic anomaly is seen in unusual patterns of intonation. For example (a commercial for Sunrise coffee):
I like it I'll drink it,
with no pause between the clauses. In fact, the stress of this utterance is what we would expect if we had a syntactic dependent clause at the left (e.g. Since I like it so much ...). The intonation here is steady rather than falling, as would be normal for two syntactically independent sentences. I think the only way we can make sense of this is as an attention-getting novelty.

It seems that in the past, most advertisers focused their attention on lexical and syntactic novelty, while more recently, pragmatic novelty seems to be favored. What we may be seeing here is metanovelty: the audience is jaded with the older forms of newness, and advertisers must press ever onward into the more mysterious reaches of language to get a response from us at all.

Some of the novelties I have been talking about can be justi- fied on additional grounds, beyond their usefulness as floutings of some part of the Cooperative Principle. For example, many of these work for brevity, a real desideratum when the point must be made in 30 seconds. But I think that brevity alone seldom justifies any special usage. Rather, all the special fea- tures of PD are overdetermined.

I have illustrated the flouting of the Cooperative Principle with regard to advertising, in which it is particularly glaring and has, indeed, been exalted to an aesthetic feature of the medium. But it can be found just as easily in other forms of PD. Its function in psychotherapeutic discourse is special, and is not dealt with here. But certainly we are accustomed to it in political rhetoric--especially in the form of hyperbolic viola- tions of Quantity, and metaphorical floutings of Manner. It is noteworthy that, of all the forms of violations of CP that are found and tolerated in PD, Quality alone is missing. Quality violations are what bring the FTC down on the sponsor, im- peachment threats down on the politician. The others seem be- yond reproach. We may want to examine again the assumption that Quality is on the same level as the other maxims, when in fact we feel that abrogation of this maxim has very different psychological and social implications. Indeed, violation of the other maxims can always be justified for either aesthetic or social reasons, without further ado; but we have only a sub- category of Quality violations that are tolerable--and only dubiously so: the 'fib' or 'white lie'. In fact, Quality viola- tions are the only ones ordinary language has a separate word for--and a word with bad connotations at that. [6]

I have referred to the importance of Rapport rules and strate- gies in OC, and their superseding of the Cooperative Principle when they conflict with it. Since PD is nonreciprocal and has an audience, rather than participating addressees, it is not surprising that Rapport as such plays no role. We do find, in some types of commercials, attempts to establish a one-to-one relationship with the audience on television: eye contact and twinkling, casual register, and the like. But in fact, most of the conventions of OC that exist for Rapport purposes are ab- sent from commercials, and from most forms of PD as well-- openings and closings, for example, are either totally missing or heavily truncated (as in psychotherapeutic discourse).

All this discussion raises a very troubling issue in discourse analysis of the kind I am attempting here: what is the role of the CP in persuasive discourse, and especially in advertising?

I have spoken as if the CP were involved in our understanding of commercials as it is in OC or the lecture--and yet we saw it was utilized very differently in even these two types of discourse. Certainly the CP gives us a much needed and illuminating handle on the workings of commercials and our understanding of them. But at the same time, invoking the CP as the basis of our understanding of a discourse type makes an implicit claim: since the CP enjoins us to be as informative as possible, to say that our discourse is understood in relation to it is to imply that the true underlying purpose of that discourse is to inform; and that, if information is not exchanged in some utterance in an optimal way, there is a special reason for it--politeness, for instance, in OC. This assumption works splendidly for discourse that is explicitly intended above all to inform--that is, of course, the lecture. But even with OC, it gets us into trouble. For the main purpose of OC is not to inform, or even to exchange information. This can occur, and conversations frequently are loaded with useful information, but most often the information serves only as a sort of carrier, enabling the real business of the interaction to get done--interacting. Hence Rapport supersedes the Cooperative Principle, since Rapport is the point in OC. Then we might argue that OC is not really CP-based, but Rules of Rapport-based, with the CP a mere auxiliary. This is unsatisfactory, though, in that we invoke the mechanisms of the CP to account for our understanding of the utterance--implicature is, logically if not psychologically speaking, secondary to the operations of the Cooperative Principle.

The problem with persuasive discourse, however, is more complex still. We are not intended to understand PD through the use of implicature; there is no apparent reason that might justify infractions, yet infractions are common and, as we have seen, quite different from the sort we get with OC. Yet in PD there is an appeal to our knowledge of the workings of the Cooperative Principle. It is our very awareness of its being violated, in such unexpected and inexplicable ways, that creates the memorability and effectiveness of all forms of PD, especially advertising. It is not clear, then, whether we should say that PD, like OC, is predicated on a base of the CP, but merely is expected to be in violation of it (it is not really clear what this would mean), or whether a completely different basis must be proposed. But if the latter, how do we account for our recognition of the CP through its flagrant violation in PD? Or our insistence on interpreting PD as if it were in accord with the CP, although it is not (which, as we have seen, makes it persuasive)? I am not sure how to resolve this issue, and present it here as something that will have to be determined by future research, if we are to devise a taxonomy of discourse that accounts not only for surface form, but for deeper intentions and the relations between the two.

In any event, we have made a beginning, I think, and some interesting facts as well as problems have emerged. We have seen that there are valid bases on which to distinguish between ordinary conversation and other types of discourse, and between truly persuasive discourse and intermediate types. I have discussed the meaning of 'the engineering of consent', and argued that it has to do with the manipulation of our expectations about the form and function of OC, translated into PD: both surface form and deeper intention, in terms of the Cooperative Principle, can be turned to persuasive effect. I have argued that we must take a number of factors into account in making these determinations: reciprocity and bilaterality; spontaneity and novelty; power; the function of the audience/ addressee; the means of persuasion; and finally, the use of the Cooperative Principle and the Maxims of Conversation.

In short, many discourse types which superficially look similar, at a deeper level of analysis function quite differently; and many types which look different turn out to have deeper similarities. We cannot understand discourse until our classification includes, and compares, form and function together, and we can hope to have a satisfactory grammar of discourse only when we have arrived at a valid taxonomy. This brief discussion of one parameter--persuasive and nonpersuasive discourse--is presented as a beginning.

NOTES

The quotation from Dorothy L. Sayers which appears at the beginning of this paper is from her book *Murder Must Advertise* (New York: Harper and Row, Publishers, Inc.).

The ideas in this paper owe much to discussion with many others. In particular, Linda Coleman's (in press) work on advertising, as well as other forms of persuasive discourse, has been stimulating. Students in Linguistics 153, Pragmatics (Spring 1981), have been invaluable in refining my thoughts, and their forbearance in serving as sounding-boards is gratefully acknowledged. Deborah Tannen's suggestions and inspiration are similarly much appreciated.

1. An odd apparent counterexample occurred at the end of the Phil Donahue show, June 16, 1981. At this point Donahue turned to the camera (not the studio audience) and said: 'We're glad you were with us. You were terrific!' It is hard to imagine how the TV audience could have demonstrated its terrificness.

2. More discussion of these points can be found in Lakoff (in press).

3. Curiously, the Oxford English Dictionary has a definition of *propaganda* that is wholly without negative connotations-- quite different, I think, from its normal use: 'Any association, systematic scheme, or concerned movement for the propagation of a particular doctrine or practice'.

4. An added benefit of this form of utterance is that it
mimics a casual register and thus suggest folksy informality.
Comparison of these segments with true OC casual register
makes it clear, however, that the truncations found in commercials do not occur in OC. One more advantage, of course:
a micro-millisecond saved is a tidy sum of money earned, given
current rates on prime time television.

5. The use of *your* here is typical of many kinds of commercials (preceding the name of the sponsor's product, or its
generic category, as here) and is characteristic of the genre,
and not OC. Normal here is 'another cup of coffee', perhaps
'that coffee'. *Your* in this environment (a quantity violation in
that it provides unnecessary information) perhaps is intended
to suggest the addressee's responsibility for the adequacy of
the product.

6. And only with Quality do we find it necessary to differentiate between purposeful ('lying') and accidental or neutral ('mis-
information', etc.) violations. For more discussion of the linguistic and communicative problems about lying, see Coleman and
Kay (1981).

REFERENCES

Bernays, Edward L. 1952. Public relations. Norman, Okla.:
University of Oklahoma Press.
Coleman, Linda. (in press) Semantic and prosodic manipulation
in advertising. In: Information processing research in ad-
versiting. Edited by Richard J. Harris. Hillsdale, N.J.:
Erlbaum.
Coleman, Linda, and Paul Kay. 1981. Prototype semantics.
Lg. 57.1:26-44.
Freud, Sigmund. 1900/1953. The interpretation of dreams.
Vols. 4 and 5 of the Standard Edition of the Complete Psycho-
logical Works of Sigmund Freud. London: Hogarth Press.
Grice, H. Paul. 1975. Logic and conversation. In: Syntax
and semantics 3: Speech acts. Edited by Peter Cole and
Jerry L. Morgan. New York: Academic Press.
Lakoff, Robin Tolmach. (in press) Some of my favorite
writers are literate: The mingling of oral and literate
strategies in written communication. In: Spoken and written
language: Exploring orality and literacy. Edited by Deborah
Tannen. Norwood, N.J.: Ablex.

MONEY TREE, LASAGNA BUSH, SALT AND PEPPER: SOCIAL CONSTRUCTION OF TOPICAL COHESION IN A CONVERSATION AMONG ITALIAN-AMERICANS

Frederick Erickson
Michigan State University

Introduction. This is an analysis of a dinner table conversation in an Italian-American family. Two issues are of special interest: (1) how topics and topical items are cohesively tied together in strips of discourse across turns at speaking and (2) how this cohesion is maintained within and across multiple conversational floors, as individuals talk simultaneously without apparent interference, interruption, or other damage to intelligibility or appropriateness.

Both topical cohesion and floor management are seen as practical problems of social organization in conversation. They are work which must get done by the collective action of individuals who are partners in listening and speaking relationships that are enacted in real time.

The paper begins by reviewing a few key notions: 'conversational work', 'social construction and production resources', 'floor', and 'topic'. This is followed by an introduction to the transcript, describing the nature of the conversation as a social occasion. An interpretive analysis follows the transcript itself. The analysis attempts to identify some of the social interactional grounds of topical cohesion and floor maintenance, to shed light on the organization of a conversation in which such apparently disparate topical items as a money tree, lasagna bush, and salt and pepper could cohere and make sense.

The notion of 'conversational work' can be thought of both as effort exerted toward a set of ends, and as the ends to which the effort is exerted. The activity of conversation--speaking and listening behavior--is thus seen as effort exerted for purposes beyond itself. The organization of conversation is constituted not simply by its own activity, but by the larger purposes to which the activity of conversation contributes.

The portion of the dinner conversation to be considered here involved talk that occurred near the end of the main course of the meal, just before dessert was to be served. The dinner partners were finishing up the instrumental work of eating. Their talk can be seen as an expressive accompaniment to that work. The talk did not accomplish discrete instrumental functions, as in the promises, requests, and other 'speech acts' that have been considered by speech act theorists and by linguistic pragmaticists. Nor did talk in this conversation accomplish discrete expressive purposes as ends in themselves, as in highly stylized displays of verbal art, e.g. toasts, ritual insults, jokes. Unlike the 'speech events' that have been studied in much of the literature of ethnography of speaking (see the discussion in Sherzer 1977), speech itself did not constitute the activity being undertaken.

The overall functions of talk before dessert seem to have involved what Malinowski termed 'phatic communion'--the conduct of sociability for its own sake (Malinowski 1923:315). Even this communicative purpose was not an end entirely accomplished in the talk itself, since the food and its shared consumption was another communication channel by which phatic communion was being accomplished. But one can't talk fluently with one's mouth full, as had been the case in the phase of the dinner in which the primary focus was on food consumption. At the point at which the transcript begins, there was a shift in channel dominance from the gustatory work of eating and passing dishes to the conversational work of talking and allocating turns at speaking. Despite the shift in channel dominance, the overall event remained 'having dinner'. As we will see more closely, the contents of the dinner table before the dishes were cleared for dessert--the residue of unconsumed food, the condiments, and the utensils for eating--provided an important resource for topical content.

Conversation as social construction. The work done in conversation is socially accomplished construction. The term 'social' is meant here in a particular way: that of Weber's definition of 'social action' as action that is taken in account of the actions of others (Weber 1922:30):

> A social relationship may be said to exist when several people reciprocally adjust their behavior to each other with respect to the meaning which they give to it, and when this reciprocal adjustment determines the form which it takes.

'Construction' involves making use of constraints provided by the actions of others as structure points around which one's own activity can be shaped. The constraints can thus be seen as 'production resources' rather than as limitations or as deterministic pressures.

There are at least three types of production resources that conversationalists can make use of: 'immediately local' resources, 'local resources once removed' from the immediate scene, and 'nonlocal' resources. Since the latter two types are defined here in relation to the first, it is appropriate to consider the notion of local production resources before considering the others.

Local production resources are those available within the immediate physical setting and within the immediate action of conversation as it occurs in real time. The term 'local production' was developed by conversational analysts in sociology to identify the socially adaptive character of talk as it naturally occurs. Speakers are not seen as simply producing strings of syntax, but as responding at one moment to what the self or others did in the moment before, or prefiguring what will come in the moment next. The adjacency relationships of 'next' (e.g. answer slot as a reply to the adjacently prior question slot) and the character of speech as addressed to a hearer (termed 'recipient design') have been elegantly described by conversational analysts (see Sacks, Schegloff, and Jefferson 1974). Their emphasis on sequential adjacency highlights the reciprocal dimension of social organization in conversation; individual actions are seen as taking account of the actions of others back and forth across strategic moments of real time.

Another aspect of local production has been emphasized more by researchers in the tradition of context analysis, in which nonverbal and verbal aspects of interaction are studied together (see Birdwhistell 1970; Scheflen 1973; Kendon 1977). Here it is the complementary dimension of social organization that has received the most attention, e.g. looking at the ways in which the listening behavior of the listeners and the speaking behavior of the speakers, cooccurring synchronously, complete each other's actions and thus mutually influence each other.

While conversational analysts have emphasized more the reciprocal and sequential aspects of interaction, and context analysts have emphasized more the complementary and simultaneous aspects of interaction, both see the social organization of interaction as radically local. (Indeed, the reciprocity and complementarity I have been describing can be thought of as horizontal and vertical relationships of adjacency in real time). Conversation is seen as a highly coordinated partnership, as in the relations of immediate influence and regulation between partners in a ballroom dance. Conversational partners are seen as enabling and completing one another's actions in real time performance through speaking and listening activity that is both reciprocal and complementary.

From this perspective, an essential aspect of local production is the continual activity of the partners in telling each other what is going on in real time--what time it is, what activity it is now. This telling is done explicitly and implicitly, verbally and nonverbally, by a host of surface structural means that

Gumperz (1977) calls contextualization cues. These cues are a
subset of the devices that Bateson (1972) called 'metacommunicative'.

This is to take a special view of the relations between text
and context, one that is not usual among linguists. In conversation, text and context can be seen as mutually constitutive rather than as dichotomous. To paraphrase McDermott
(1976:33), 'people in interaction form environments for each
other.'

Necessary as these local resources are, they are not the only
ones drawn on by conversationalists. As Goffman (1976) has
pointed out, conversation is organized not only in terms of
locally adjacent next relationships, but in terms of connections
across larger chunks of discourse, connections across the whole
history of the conversation.

These connections can extend across even longer strips of
time and across space, beyond the conversation itself. Influences on the immediate conversation can come from outside it,
across days, weeks, even years, as in the recurring meetings
of a committee, in long-standing family disputes ('Oh God,
you're not going to bring *that* up again!'), or in a military
attack, in which various subgroups begin an assault simultaneously, the officers having synchronized their watches. In
responding to what others have done outside the immediate encounter, conversationalists take action that is social by Weber's
definition, even though there is only an indirect connection between their actions inside the encounter and the actions of
other persons outside the encounter.

There is no current term for these indirect sources of influences on conversation which are still specific to the immediate
situation at hand (in that the influences have to do with the
particular biographies and shared history of the conversational
partners). Since the relationships of immediate adjacency in
conversational action have been called 'local' production resources, we can call the influences that are not fully local--
but still group-member specific--'local production resources
once removed'.

This resource type can in turn be distinguished from a third
type: those nonlocal production resources that derive from the
wider social structure. Among these nonlocal resources are
knowledge of cultural traditions shared within a given speech
community that define appropriateness in ways of speaking,
knowledge that at the individual level Hymes and others have
called 'communicative competence' (Hymes 1974). Another nonlocal resource is 'linguistic competence', knowledge of the grammar and sound system of a language. While these nonlocal resources are not specific to the members of the interacting group,
they influence the shape of collective action in the group through
the medium of the individual members' particular knowledge and
performance skills.

In summary, three sources of social influence on the conduct of conversation can be distinguished: the nonlocal, the local once removed, and the immediately local. These can be thought of as production resources. All three types of production resources are employed in naturally occurring conversation. All three are often employed simultaneously and need to be considered together in a holistic analysis of conversation.

Conversational floors and topical cohesion. Topics and the speakers who produce them must have a floor to be in. Conversational floors are thus a local production resource for the construction of topical cohesion. The 'floor' is a sustained focus of cognitive, verbal, and nonverbal attention and response between speaker and audience.

In maintaining a floor, audience and speaker interact socially in the reciprocal and complementary ways discussed earlier. Talk is addressed by recipient design to the audience, and the audience responds to the talk. Without the ratification of audience response, a speaker has nowhere to go with a topic once it has been introduced. In consequence, as Keenan and Schieffelin (1976) have pointed out, the notion of topic in conversation entails a relationship between speaker and audience.

It is possible for conversations to be socially organized with more than one floor being sustained simultaneously by multiple speakers and multiple audiences. The conversation studied in this analysis is a case in point. For members of the Italian-American speech community from which the conversational partners came, multiple floored conversations are appropriate and frequent occurrences.

In this type of conversational arrangement, a fundamental organizational task for conversationalists involves determining where the floors are, how many of them there are now (see the discussion in Shultz, Florio, and Erickson in press). That task is even more fundamental than the task of allocating access to the floor through a turn exchange economy, an issue that has been discussed by the conversational analysts (Sacks, Schegloff, and Jefferson 1974).

'Topics' themselves involve social construction within the conversational floor. Once allocated, a turn at speaking must have some topical content and some duration in real time. The real-time nature of performance places practical constraints on appropriateness of topic. These can be thought of as constraints on intelligibility and of fluency, which can also be considered as production resources.

Since the topic occurs in a floor, and floors are jointly maintained by speaker and audience participation, a topic must be intelligible to the audience if the audience is to be able to do its part in collaboration with the speaker. Because the topic is spoken in real time, topical content must be immediately intelligible in the moment, since the flow of action cannot be suspended to give the audience time out for extensive reflection.

Moreover, since floor time is occupied by topical content, it is strategically necessary for speakers to produce topical content fluently--continuously across real time--in order to be able to maintain their position of participation in the floor.

The etymology of the term 'topic' points to the issue of fluency as well as to the issue of intelligibility. As Ong (1977: 147ff., 166) points out, the Classical Greek term for topic is a spatial metaphor (*topos* 'place'). The notion of topic was that of a location in semantic space. Knowledge of certain of these 'places' was widely shared conventionally within a speech community. Among Classical and Renaissance rhetoricians, the term for these widely recognized topics was 'commonplaces' (see the discussion in Lechner 1962). The orator memorized many of these commonplaces: an assertion, together with constituent topical items such as metaphors, anecdotes, citations of evidence, quotes from literature, or previous oratory. As a cognitive resource, the commonplace functioned as a memory storage device, since retrieval of the general topical category ('place') entailed a connected set of specific items of information. As a social interactional resource, the commonplace functioned as a device enabling fluent production and comprehension. The easily remembered topical items could be continuously spoken in real time by the orator and were readily understandable in real time by members of the audience.

While ordinary conversation differs from oratory in a number of ways (ordinary conversation being characterized by short turns at speaking and a relative lack of preplanning in discourse), people in ordinary conversation face the same fundamental practical problems faced by orator and audience--the problems of achieving and maintaining fluently reciprocal and complementary coordination of speech production and comprehension in real time. It is not surprising, then, that people in ordinary conversation draw on some of the same production resources as those found in formal rhetoric. In fact, the improvisatory character of ordinary conversation requires the ready availability of commonplace topics as formulaic themes around which conversational partners can improvise situational variations.

As resources, the sources of commonplace topics in ordinary conversation can be thought of as immediately local, local once removed, and nonlocal. Immediately local topical resources are those experiences currently being shared among the conversational partners, for example, the fact that it is raining now, the food is on the table now. Local resources once removed are topics derived from experiences previously shared among the conversational partners, for example, what we did on our summer vacation, what happened in last week's meeting. Nonlocal topical resources involve knowledge of semantic domains that is widely shared within the speech community, for example, talk about sports, current national events, cars, the arts, religion. Topics and their constituent topical items are used as commonplaces at each of these levels. Conversational partners have experience in how to organize informal conversation around the topics; for example, they already know how to talk about the immediately local topic of what the weather is now, or the nonlocal topic of what kind of car one might or might not want to buy.

The conversation. The dinner conversation discussed here occurred in an Italian-American family living in a working class neighborhood in a suburb of Boston. The conversation was videotaped as part of a study of the communicative competence of Bobby, the youngest boy in the family. His communication was also studied at school in the first grade classroom he attended (for discussions of the larger study, see Bremme 1977; Florio 1978, Shultz and Florio 1979; and Shultz, Florio, and Erickson in press).

Bobby's interaction with other family members was videotaped on two days, one week apart, in early September, from the time he came home from school through the end of dinner. Other family members besides Bobby included his mother and father, three older brothers, and a sister. Bobby was the youngest. The portion of the dinner conversation presented here comes from the second of the two dinners that were videotaped. The night of the second dinner, Bobby's father was not home; he had gone out of town on an overnight trip. The guest, an Italian-American woman research assistant, sat in the father's usual place at one end of the table (see diagram at the top of the transcript). The mother sat in her usual place, at the opposite end of the table from the guest. Some of the other children in the family had left the table at the point in the meal at which the transcript begins. The two remaining children, 7-year-old Bobby and his next older sibling, an 8-1/2-year-old sister, sat facing one another on the opposite axis of the dinner table from that along which the mother and guest were seated.

As the conversation progressed, the arrangement of social participation changed. At first, the conversation was organized around a single conversational floor, with all four partners orienting to it as a quartet of speakers. Later, the conversational duet or team--mother-guest along one axis of the table, and brother-sister along the other axis. Then after a few minutes, the conversational arrangement returned to a single conversational floor. Thus the spatial arrangement of the partners around the table was made use of as an immediately local resource in the social construction of discourse in the conversation.

Local resources once removed and nonlocal resources were also used in the conversation. Since a major source of local resources once removed were topics from the dinner that was videotaped the week before, some description of what happened in that dinner is necessary here by way of introduction.

During the first videotaped dinner, the father and mother
had functioned together as a conversational team. In the
second videotaped dinner, the guest occupied the role of the
other adult in the scene, a position usually occupied by the
father. In the previously recorded dinner, the father had a
significant role of leadership in the conversation; many of the
new topics that came up were either introduced by the father,
or were ratified by him through his giving attention to the
speaker who introduced the topic.

The previously videotaped dinner conversation had included
considerable discussion of the home-grown vegetables that were
part of the meal and that had come from the family's large garden in the back yard. Another major topic had been how expensive things were becoming nowadays. This was linked to
the other major topic, since gardening and canning was a way
the family saved money on food. Discussion of the topics
'food from the garden' and 'things that are expensive nowadays' involved the use of listing as a prominent resource for
discourse organization. In the listing sequences, various family
members would alternate in contributing a single item in the list.
This seemed to be a conversational arrangement that was especially easy for the youngest children in the family to participate
in. All they had to do was come up with a list item every now
and then, and say that item at the point in real time in which
it was appropriate for the next item slot in the list sequence to
be performed. Fun was had with this; sometimes the list item
matched the overall topic by a kind of ironic connection rather
like punning. Talk was used in other kinds of playful ways;
for example, the father said that things are so expensive nowadays, they need a money tree in the back yard as well as a
vegetable garden.

During the second videotaped dinner, speakers drew upon
topical resources from the previous videotaped dinner. In its
content, the topic 'things to eat that come from the garden'
harked back to last week's conversation. In terms of process,
the listing routines and playful uses of talk recalled the previous week's topics and the roles of family members as humor-
ists in the previous conversation.

Before turning to the transcript, a few notes about transcription conventions are in order. Generally, the transcription follows the conventions of the conversational analysts.
Special emphasis is placed on rhythmic and intonational features of speech prosody. Dramatic shifts in pitch are occasionally indicated by placing letters above or below the ordinary
line of text. Volume stress is occasionally indicated by an
underline. It is usually indicated by placement of the stressed
syllable at the left margin (without underline). A single line
of text usually represents a single breath group or tone group
of speech. Thus, the first syllable of each new line of text
is usually a stressed syllable, and syllables at the right margin

of the line are enclitic to the syllable at the left margin of the
next line, as in pickup notes in music:

  (6) G: I
        love your s<u>al</u>ad

Periods (dots) indicate silence, with two periods indicating
approximately one-half second of silence (a sentence-terminal
pause), four dots indicating approximately one second of silence, and a single dot indicating one-fourth second of silence
(roughly equivalent to a comma).
    Sustained loud volume is indicated by capitalized letters.
This is used for Bobby's speech. In this conversation, he uses
two distinct pitch and volume registers: one very loud and
high pitched, with steeply rising and falling intonation contours, and another at more normal volume and pitch level.
    Elongation of syllables is indicated by successive colons
(SPOO::N). Simultaneously overlapping talk by two or more
speakers is indicated by a bracket:

  (12) S: did
      all this come ⌈outta our ga:den?
           M: ⌊<u>Don</u>'t put your fingers in there.

Alternation of speech between which there is no overlap but
also no gap ('latching') is indicated by a bracket whose flaps
point in opposite directions, as in the following latched laugh-
ing between the mother and the guest:

  (15) M: mhmhmh⌉
  (16) G: ⌊Mhmhmh/
        didn't you grow that in your yard?

The latching symbol is also used occasionally in the speech of
a single individual to indicate the absence of a gap between
the word or syllable at the end of one line and the beginning
of the next. This is more usually indicated by the slant mark
at the right margin of a line of text, as in (15). When a
slanted line is not followed by further speech by an individual,
the line indicates an interruption in speech which leaves a
word or phrase incomplete, e.g. 'n the di/ for 'n the dishes.
The numbers in the text do not indicate a constant unit (a
'turn' at speaking) because, given the frequent overlap of
speech and the interpenetration of one another's sentence and
clause units between multiple speakers, the notion of turn as
a discrete sequential unit often does not apply at various
points in this conversation. Consequently, the numbers in the
text are to be thought of as reference points for the reader
rather than as turn units. When the conversation splits into
two simultaneously occurring duets, this is indicated by the
subscript letters *a* and *b*.

   The postural positions and interpersonal distance of the conversationalists are indicated in the transcript by diagrams accompanying the text. The rectangle represents the dinner
table, the brackets indicate the lines of the shoulders and
upper torso of an individual, and the arrow indicates the direction of gaze of that individual. If there is no arrow for a
given individual, that means the individual was apparently
looking down at his/her plate. Bobby, the son (indicated by
S in the transcript) shifts back and forth from one chair to
another during the conversation (see the diagram at the head
of the transcript), and this is shown in the postural diagrams
that appear throughout the transcript.
   As the transcript begins, the people remaining at the dinner
table were finishing eating the main course of the meal, which
was lasagna and a salad. After a pause in talk during which
people were chewing their food, the mother addressed the
guest with an invitation to another helping of food (see Figure
1, pages 54-58).

Discussion. Let us consider four sets of production resources
and their use in social construction of topical cohesion within
and across multiple conversational floors: (1) posture and gaze,
(2) listing routines, (3) commonplace sources of topical content,
and (4) rhythmic organization of speech prosody.

Posture and gaze. As sources of contextualization cues, posture and gaze are nonverbal communication media that play an
important role at the immediately local level of production in the
establishment and maintenance of conversational floors. Speakers in this conversation oriented to one another in three ways;
on the nonverbal channel by postural position and by gaze direction, and on the verbal channel by the addressing of speech
to particular individuals as audience. These three dimensions
of orientation shifted together throughout the conversation, i.e.
a change in floor management (speaker-audience relationship)
cooccurred with changes in postural and gaze orientation. This
can be seen in the transcript by noting the configurations of
posture and gaze that were sustained from points (1) through
(19), across points (20a,b) through (28a,b), and across points
(29) through (43). The second of these three chunks of discourse is the one in which the conversational participation
structure shifted from a single floor, in which all four partners
interacted as a conversational quartet, to a double floor, participated in by two pairs of partners: mother-guest, son-
daughter. Notice in the postural and gaze diagrams that in
the whole section before (20a), gaze and postural orientation
was shared across the two pairs of partners; for example, at
points (4) and (5), the guest and son faced one another and
looked directly at one another. From (20a,b) through (28b),
however, this pattern changed. Across that whole strip of
activity, mutual gaze and postural focus were not shared across

the pairs of conversational partners. While the double floor
arrangement of talk lasted, the mother and guest focused posture and gaze orientation only on each other. This was also
true for the son and daughter, with what seems to be a momen-
tary exception at (24a), where the son gazed in the direction
of the mother. But what the son was actually doing at (24a)
was to gaze at the salad bowl, which was placed on the table
to his immediate left. Moreover, the mother did not direct gaze
or postural focus to the son, but continued at that point to
focus on the guest. So the pattern of across-team avoidance
of gaze and posture sharing continued to be maintained through
point (28b).

Looking now at point (29), it is apparent that the pattern of
postural and gaze configuration changed as the conversational
arrangement changed back to a single conversational floor. The
mother and son oriented to one another at point (29). From
then on, mutual orientation was again exchanged across the
pairs of the partners who from (20a,b) through (28b) had never
exchanged mutual gaze or postural focus. In sum, throughout
the whole conversation configurations of mutually sustained posture and gaze orientation seem to have been functioning as contextualization cues; by these means as well as by the content
of their talk, the conversational partners were telling each other
where the floor is now, and who is in it.

Topical content and process: Commonplaces and lists. There
are three main sources of topical resources in the conversation:
things in the garden, things on the dinner table, and topical
items said just previously. The first topical resource draws
upon the shared past history of the conversational partners by
invoking topics from last week's videotaped dinner conversation.
This is a matter of local production once removed from the immediate scene. The second topical resource is derived from the
geography of the dinner table. Since the table and its contents
are there to be seen in the here and now by all the participants,
the use of the table by the son as a resource in the generation
of list items is a matter of immediately local production. Retrospective semantic tying back to the topical item said just previously is also a matter of immediately local production. All
three sources of topical content (especially the first two sources)
can be thought of as commonplaces, in that (1) all three sources
draw on understanding and experience shared in common by the
participants in the conversation, and (2) as places in semantic
space they are readily identifiable. Moreover, the first two
sources of topical content are semantic domains whose constituent parts--subtopics and list items--are connected by semantic
ties that are extremely obvious. All three sources of topical
content function well as resources for the fluency of speaker
production and listener comprehension in real time.

The overall sequence of topics and topical items in the transcript is shown in Figure 2, which also identifies the individual

Figure 1.

PL = plate

tinfoil pan of lasagna

salad bowl

Mother (M)

chair

Son (S)

G's salad plate

Guest (G)

grated cheese

S's glass

salt

pepper

milk

Drinks

Daughter (D)

Main course of meal is almost finished. At this point G puts fork down on plate, and wipes mouth with napkin

(1) G looks at M

(1) M: Can I get you S'more?

(2) G: Oh no thanks . . .

        This is great
(3) S: M::::::::::::: (very loud)

(4) G: More, yeah?

(5) S: (single nod)

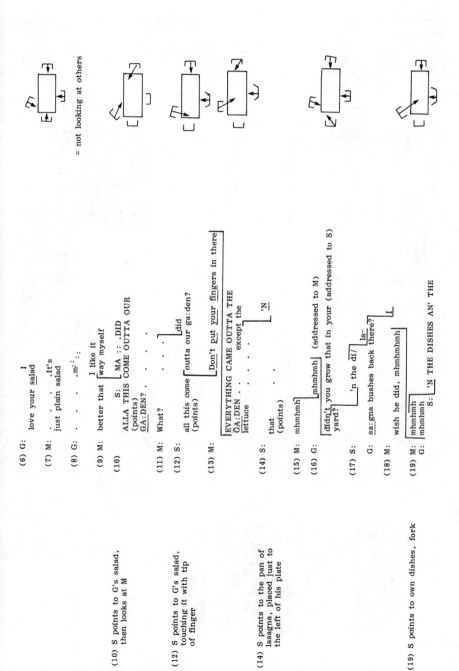

= not looking at others

(6) G: I love your salad

(7) M: . . . .It's just plain salad

(8) G: . . . .m·::

(9) M: better that [I like it way myself

(10) S: [MA::.DID ALLA THIS COME OUTTA OUR GA:DEN? (points)

(11) M: What?

(12) S: all this come [outta our ga:den? (points) [did

(13) M: Don't put your fingers in there
EVERYTHING CAME OUTTA THE GA:DEN . . . except the lettuce 'N

(14) S: that (points)

(15) M: mhmhmh

(16) G: [mhmhmh] (addressed to M) [didn't you grow that in your (addressed to S) yard?

(17) S: 'n the di/ [la-
G: sa:gna bushes back there?

(18) M: wish he did, mhmhmhmh

(19) M: mhmhmh
G: mhmhmh
S: 'N THE DISHES AN' THE

(10) S points to G's salad, then looks at M

(12) S points to G's salad, touching it with tip of finger

(14) S points to the pan of lasagna, placed just to the left of his plate

(19) S points to own dishes, fork

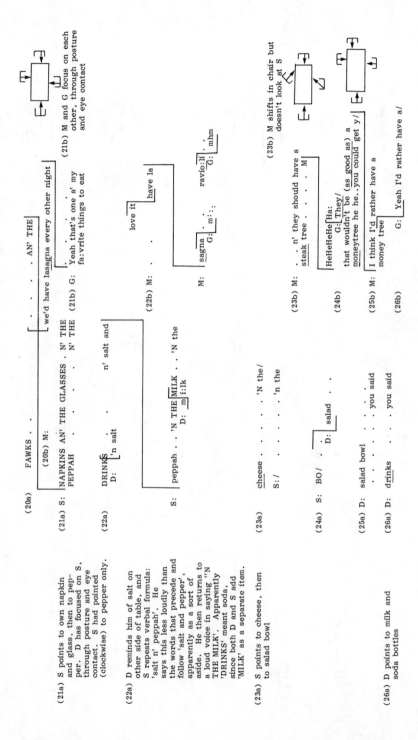

(20a) FAWKS . . [. . . . AN' THE]

(20b) M: [we'd have lasagna every other night]

(21a) S: NAPKINS AN' THE GLASSES . N' THE N' THE
PEPPAH . . .

(21b) G: Yeah that's one a' my fa:vrite things to eat

(21b) M and G focus on each other, through posture and eye contact

(21a) S points to own napkin and glass, then to pepper. D has focused on S, through posture and eye contact. S had pointed (clockwise) to pepper only.

(22a) DRINKS [n' salt and]
D: [n salt]

(22b) M: . . . love it [have la]

S: peppah . . 'N THE MILK . . 'N the
D: m i:lk

M: sagna ravio:li . .
G: m:::. G: mhm

(22a) D reminds him of salt on other side of table, and S repeats verbal formula: 'salt n' peppah'. He says this less loudly than the words that precede and follow 'salt and pepper', apparently as a sort of aside. He then returns to a loud voice in saying "N THE MILK'. Apparently 'DRINKS' meant soda, since both D and S add 'MILK' as a separate item.

(23a) cheese . . . . 'N the/
S:/ . . . . . 'n the

(23b) M: . . n' they should have a steak tree . . M

(23b) M shifts in chair but doesn't look at S

(23a) S points to cheese, then to salad bowl

(24a) S: BO/ . . salad . .
D: salad

(24b) HeHeHeHe[Ha:
G: They/
that wouldn't be (as good as) a
moneytree he he..you could get y/

(25a) D: salad bowl . . you said

(25b) M: [I think I'd rather have a money tree]

(26a) D: drinks . . . you said

(26b) G: [Yeah I'd rather have a/]

(26a) D points to milk and soda bottles

(27a) D: dri:nks, and milk . .

(27b) M: /I'd rather have a big (27b) M looks at salad bowl and tree. HA HA . . . shifts in posture but does not look at S

(28a) S: I sat here and got drink . . . . .

(28b) stea:ks. . I mean y 'know I'll cook CHA:COAL BROI:L or somethin'

(28a) S looks to and points to drink spilled on table around his plate

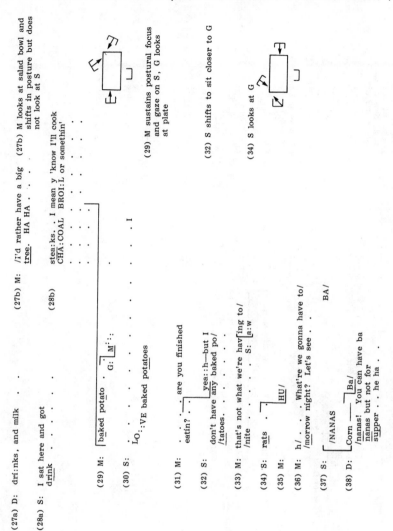

(29) M sustains postural focus and gaze on S, G looks at plate

(32) S shifts to sit closer to G

(34) S looks at G

(29) M: baked potato . G: M::

(30) S: LO::VE baked potatoes I

(31) M: . . are you finished eatin? . .

(32) S: yea::h—but I don't have any baked po/ /tatoes . .

(33) M: that's not what we're hav[ing to/ /nite . . . . . S: [a:w

(34) S: rats . . [HU/

(35) M: [HU/

(36) M: h/ . . . What're we gonna have to/ /morrow night? Let's see . . BA/

(37) S: /NANAS

(38) D: [Corn——[Ba/ /nanas! You can have ba nanas but not for supper . . he ha . .

(39) M does not move, speak, or
look at S--D is drinking
milk. At 'cuz I' D puts
down glass on table. It
hits with a rap. D looks at
S

(40) D looks at S but S looks
at M

(41) As D says 'yea::h' S turns
to face D

(39) S: N, N, N, N, N, I WANNA MAKE/
          LET'S MAKE SOME CAKE

          . . . . I get the
          bowl . . . . .   Cuz I
          never get the
          bo:w⌐
                ⌊Neither do
(40) D: I:::   . . . .

(41) S: YEA : : : ⌈: H? WHEN I MADE A⌉
                     ⌊Yea::h?   ⌋

(42) S: ⌈CAKE YOU GOT THE
          ⌊SPOO::N: . . 'N . . 'N/

(43)   /EVERYTHING

Figure 2. Flow chart of topical items.

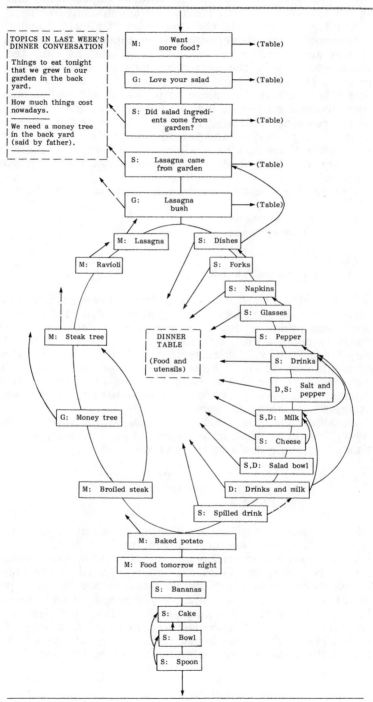

who introduced the topic or constituent topical item, and illustrates the shift between single and double conversational floors.

Keeping in mind both the flow chart in Figure 2 and the transcript of the conversation, it is apparent that topical content is drawn from what has just been said (as indicated by arrows pointing to the next previous topical item), from the objects on the dinner table (also indicated by arrows), and by direct and indirect reference to topics of last week's conversation (indirect reference indicated by arrows with dotted lines, direct reference indicated by arrows with straight lines).

At the beginning of the transcribed portion of the conversation, after there had been a long silence while people at the table chewed their food the mother offered the guest more food.

The guest responded with compliments about the food:

(2) G: Oh no thanks ..
         this is <u>great</u>

(6) G: I
         <u>love</u> your <u>salad</u>

This marks a transition in the dinner between a food consumption-dominated period of chewing work and a talk production-dominated period of conversational work. Reciprocally, the guest responded with 'talk items' to the mother's offer of 'food items' (on what was characterized earlier as the 'food channel' of phatic communion). From that point on in the meal, talk became the foregrounded activity (and the talk channel became the primary medium of phatic communion), with food consumption relegated to the background.

At point (10), the son harked back indirectly to last week's topic, 'things to eat that came out of our garden', as he pointed to the guest's salad bowl and said:

(10) S: MA::, DID
         ALLA THIS COME OUTTA OUR
         GA:DEN?

After the mother replied 'Everything came out of the garden', the son introduced another feature from the previous week's conversation, the overall character of playfulness in dinner table talk. At point (14), the son responded to the mother by playfully reading her previous *everything* literally, pointing to the aluminum pan of (commercially prepared and frozen) lasagna, and asking counterfactually if that, too, had come from the garden. The mother acknowledged this sally of wit with a laugh which was joined in by the guest, who then continued the counterfactual play by saying to the son:

(16) G: didn't you grow that in your
          yard?
      S: 'n the di/
                        la
      G: sagna bushes back there?

While the guest introduced the imaginary plant into the conversation, she also was interrupting the son, who had begun
to generate another item in a counterfactual list: 'things on
the table that grew in the garden'. His next item was *dishes*.
As he started to say this ('di/'), he was pointing to the plate
in front of him, which was right next to the pan of lasagna on
the table (refer again to the diagram of the table at the head
of the transcript). The next list items, *napkins* and *glasses*,
were said while pointing to his own napkin and glass, located
next to his plate. Next to his glass was the pepper shaker
(see table diagram). His pointing to the pepper began what
from his point of view was a counterclockwise movement of
pointing around the table. Next in the counterclockwise arc
came the drinks (soda) and milk, followed by the grated cheese.
Past the cheese was the guest's plate and her individual salad
bowl, but plates and the guest's salad had already been mentioned earlier, as had the items at the son's own place setting.
Continuing on the counterclockwise arc, the next item found on
the table was the lasagna pan, but that, too, had already been
mentioned. The only item yet unmentioned was the salad bowl,
which was the last item the son mentioned in his list.
  It seems clear that the son was using the geographic location
of objects on the dinner table as a means of generating a list.
Further evidence for this inference is found in the comment of
the sister at (22a) and in her brother's reaction to that comment. Apparently, the brother's idiosyncratic list formula was
not yet understood fully by his sister--it did not yet perform
a commonplace role for both speaker and audience, as evidenced
by the sister's apparent mistake in comprehension at this point.

(21a) S: AN THE
         NAPKINS AN' THE GLASSES . 'N THE
         PEPPAH . . . .   . 'N THE
(22a)   DRINKS   .   .   'n salt and| (said more
                                              softly)
      D: 'n salt
      S: peppah .   . 'N THE MILK

At (21a) the son had begun his counterclockwise pointing routine, going from his glass to the pepper shaker to the drinks
(see the table diagram). As he got past the pepper to the
drinks (which were in next position according to his geographic
listing formula), his sister corrected him by reminding him that
salt goes with the pepper. But this was an apparent mistake

on her part. *Salt and pepper* go together as a pair (with pepper in second position) on the basis of a commonplace verbal formula in American English. The two do not go together according to the commonplace table geography formula the son appears to have been using. (According to the table geography, salt would have come next after the cheese). The sister here seems to have been trying to cooperate in her brother's list item-generating, but not to have understood the generative principle he was using. The less loud way in which the brother said "n salt and peppah' seems to have acknowledged only as an aside the sister's irrelevant correction. After the aside, the brother returned to his own list formula, speaking again in his loud voice register.

The use of the dinner table as an immediately local production resource for item-generation was accompanied by use of an entirely nonlocal production resource. This was the syntactic structure of the listing formula itself, knowledge of which is shared not only beyond this family with the Boston area Italian-American speech community, but beyond that speech community with the linguistic community of English speakers generally. Syntactically, the son's listing formula is of the very simplest sort: noun slot plus conjunction plus definite article, reiterated: 'the X and the Y and the Z'. This syntactic string is produced with the simplest possible speech rhythm, a recurring anapaest: (♫ ♩ ♫ ♩). This speech rhythm, too, is a nonlocal resource. Taken together, the simple syntax, simple speech rhythm, and obvious table geography are sets of resources that make for an almost foolproof system for fluent production of topical items in real time. The listing rhythm continues like an air hammer, continuously cutting through the conversation that is being carried on by the mother and guest on the cooccurring second conversational floor. Let us turn now to consider the organization of conversation between the mother and guest, from (20b) through (28b).

The sources of topical items are two: the immediately local resource of the content of prior turns (especially the son's mention of lasagna), and the local once-removed resource of the money tree topic from last week's conversation (see Figure 2).

In the mother-guest conversation, there is a listing connection as a cohesion device, but it is of a slightly more complex sort than the list found in the son-daughter conversation. The list items are three counterfactual plants: lasagna bush, steak tree, and money tree. The lasagna bush topic was initiated by the guest at (17) and responded to by the mother at (18) and (20a). The steak tree was introduced, after a brief pause, by the mother at (23b). This was a play upon both *lasagna bush* (from the conversation) and *money tree* (from the father's funny line in last week's conversation). Reference by the guest to the money tree immediately followed at (24b):

```
(23b) M:    .   .     an' they should have a
            steak tree    .    .    .    .     M
            hehehehe┌ha:
(24b) G:            └They/
            that wouldn't be (as good as)     a
            moneytree hehe . . you could get y/
(25b) M:    I think I'd rather have a
            money tree
```

Interspersed between the mentions of the three imaginary plants are other comments. From (20b) through (22b), there was a brief, elliptical discussion of lasagna and its pasta 'cousin', ravioli, in which the guest collaborated by saying that she liked those foods, too:

```
(20b) M:    If we actually had a lasagna bush in the back yard
            we'd have lasagna every other night
(21b) G:    Yeah that's one a' my
            fa:vrite things to eat .
                 .     .    love it
(22b)                          M:   have    la┐
      M:    ┌sagna   .    . ravio:li┐.    .
            G:   m·:.           └ mhm
(23b) M:    .        . an' they should have a
            steak tree
```

The *steak tree* appeared in (23b) as the next item in the list consisting of *lasagna, ravioli, steak*. *Steak tree* also tied back semantically to the prior *lasagna bush*, and to the previous week's *money tree*. From (23b) on, the interspersed comments had to do with what one would prefer, a steak tree or a money tree.

The whole strip involves counterfactual conditions. It was tied together across turns by manipulation of syntactic and lexical choices through the use of conditional tense, by the modals *would, should,* and *could,* and later by the conditional *would rather.* These syntactic construction patterns offer alternative opportunities--full form, contraction, and deletion-- altering the length and rhythm of utterances. The full form is found only three times:

```
(23b) M:    an' they should have a steak tree
(24b) G:    that wouldn't be as good as a money tree
            you could get y/
```

More common is the contracted form, as in (20b) and (24b), where *we'd* substitutes for *we would,* and *I'd* substitutes for *I would.*

```
(20b) M:    We'd have lasagna every other night.
(24b) M:    I'd rather have a money tree.
```

Deletion of the modal also occurs, as in (22b), where the deleted item seems to be *we would*:

```
      G:      (I)| love it
 (22b) M:   . .    (we would)| have la
      M:    sagna         .        ravio:li
```

Notice here that the pronouns can also be deleted, as in the guest's substitution at (22b) of *love it* for *I love it*.

The ultimate deletion seems to have occurred right at the end of the strip, at (27b) and (28b).

```
 (27b) M:   /I'd rather have a big
            tree. HA HA .   .   .
 (28b)      stea:ks.  . I mean y'know I'll cook
            CHA:COAL    BROI:L  or   somethin'
```

By contrastive stress on *stea:ks* and by contrastive sustained loudness on *CHA:COAL BROIL* the mother seems to have been saying something like 'I wouldn't want steak all the time. But I'd like it sometimes, and if we had a money tree we could have steak whenever we want it. And then we'd have it the best way --charcoal broiled'.

It may be that after a pause she said *stea:ks* so elliptically (deleting both noun and verb) because of the increased dead air time in the other conversation (see full transcript). At that point the son-daughter conversation had begun to run down. The topic resources of the table had been exhausted, and the syntactic listing formula had also been abandoned. What was left were stressed one-syllable words--drinks, milk-- separated by pause (see (26a)-(28b)). Perhaps the mother's utterance, *stea:ks* was echoing the food items in the other conversation.

There is considerable evidence that some attention was being paid across the pairs of conversational partners. At the end of the double conversational floor, as the mother said *CHA:COAL BROIL* after just having said *stea:ks*, the son looked across at the mother (in the pause at (28b)). Talk between the son and the daughter had stopped. Then the mother turned to the son, looked directly at him, and at (29) said "ba̲ked pota̲to'. This is both a food item tie (*baked potato* is the second part of the conventional verbal pair *steak and baked potato*) and a social inclusion tie (the mother knows the son likes baked potato). At this point the single conversational floor resumed.

Even better evidence for attention across pairs of conversational partners comes from close investigation of speech rhythm, and it is to this final issue that we now turn.

Roles of rhythm in maintaining cohesion in topics and in floors. The regular periodicity of speech and nonverbal behavior rhythm appears to enable conversational partners to coordinate their action together within an overall ensemble. Through rhythm, strategic next moments in real time can be anticipated. This seems to be a necessary condition for inter- action that is fully 'social', in the sense in which I have used that term here (see also the discussions in Erickson 1981, Erick- son and Shultz 1981, Scollon this volume, and Sudnow 1980).

In this conversation, the role of the reiterated anapaest rhythm pattern in maintaining fluency in list-item production has already been discussed. In that pattern the stressed sylla- bles, which occur at a regularly periodic interval in relation to each other, contain the next piece of new information--the next noun in the list.

The tendency for a piece of new information to be found at the point of the stressed tonal nucleus in a breath group occurs not only in the relatively simple anapaest in the son's listing formula. It occurs as well in the more complex patterns of the speech of the mother and guest. In the doubly floored phase of the transcribed text (20a,b)-(28a,b) in the adults' speech, the stressed tonal nucleus often not only is a point of new informa- tional content, but occurs at the end of a syntactic clause. In real time performance, the stressed tonal nuclei occur at a regu- lar rhythmic interval. In performance, these chunks of speech are almost identical in length:

(20b) we'd have lasagna every other night
(21b) yeah that's one a'my fa:vrite things to eat
(23b) an' they should have a steak tree

When these clause units in the mother-guest conversation are juxtaposed with anapaest units in the simultaneously occurring son-daughter conversation, the two sets of conversational rhythm pattern articulate together in an overall rhythmic shape, or ensemble. Moreover, the two conversations are articulated so that the stressed tonal nuclei in each conversation occur either at a point of silence in the other conversation, or occur simultaneously. In either case, this rhythmic integration across the two pairs of conversational partners enables both conversa- tions to proceed with neither one upsetting either the rhythmic cohesion of the other or the points in the other conversation at which important new information is being communicated.

In short, it seems that rhythmic fine tuning enables this multiply floored conversation to proceed without having the overlapping talk constitute an interruption. I am arguing that this rhythmic integration is social in nature. Conversational partners appear to be rhythmically field-sensitive. They appear to be taking action on account of the rhythmic action of others, not only within conversational pairs, but across pairs as well. More generally, rhythm seems to be the fundamental social glue by which cohesive discourse is maintained in conversation,

within and across turns and sets of turns, and within and between the speech of speakers in conversational floors.

These points can be illustrated by displaying the rhythmic
patterns of speech in musical notation. The passage in Figure
3 comes from points (18) through (23b) in the transcript.

Notice that in measure 2, as the son had gotten his list going, ''n the dishes n' the forks', he completed that unit in time
for the mother's 'we'd have lasagna every other night' not to
interfere with his speech or be interfered with by his speech.
In that instance, the two avoided interference by avoiding
overlap. In measure 3, even though the mother's and son's
speech overlapped, interference was avoided by the exact matching of stressed syllables (*night* and *napkin*) and by the mother's
doubling of speed relative to that of the son right before the
next stressed syllable (see *every other* in relation to *'n the*).

Another way of avoiding interference while preserving overall
rhythmic ensemble is rapid-fire alternation between speakers, of
onsets and offsets of speech. The Western musical term for this
alternation, found in medieval European vocal duets, is 'hocket'.
Hocketing can be seen in measures 6 and 7, where the most
finely tuned coordination across the two conversations is appar-
ent--from the son's *drinks* to the daughter's *'n salt*, to the
guest's *love it* to the mother's *lasagna* which was accompanied by
the son's *'n salt 'n* and was followed by the guest's *mm*. This
is a dramatic example of individuals interacting closely in real
time and yet staying out of one another's way in time. Viewed
in the total rhythmic context at this point, the mother's deletion
of the modal *we would* before *have lasagna* can be seen as a
syntactic accommodation to the rhythmic organization of what the
other speakers were doing reciprocally and complementarily in
immediately adjacent and simultaneous moments of real time.
People do, indeed, seem here to have been functioning as environments for one another.

Conclusion. In the musical notation we can see local production resources being used in a radically local way to maintain
cohesion at the level of utterance and topical item. But in the
same time we are also seeing nonlocal production resources being used, for what is being produced locally in the conversation
is an instance of a culturally patterned way of speaking that is
widely and nonlocally shared within the ethnic speech community:
the Italian-American way of conducting multiply floored conversation in which simultaneously occurring and rapidly alternating
speech does not constitute interruption. The overall pattern of
multiple flooring is not specific to Italian-Americans. It has
been found among Americans of East European Jewish descent
(Tannen 1981) and Americans of Cape Verdean descent (Gomes
1979). However, the specific organizational features by which
multiply floored conversations are managed by speakers do appear to be speech community-specific.

Figure 3.

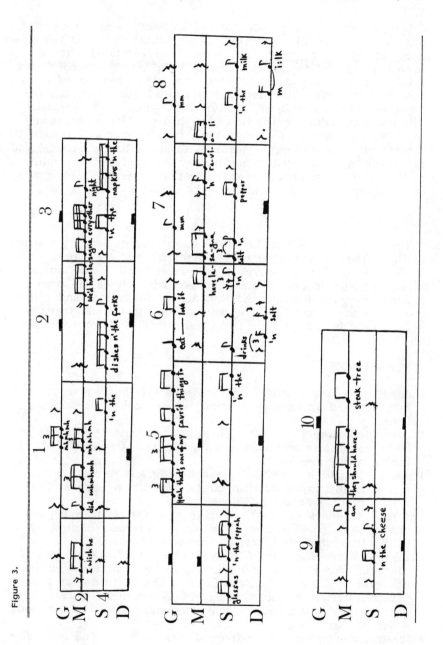

In addition, we have seen both immediately local resources for topical content being used (the dinner table) and local resources once removed being used (last week's conversation). It has been argued that topical cohesion and the conversational floors within which topics are manifested, are both products of social construction. The resources for this production are seen as being simultaneously local, local once removed, and nonlocal. The analysis points to the need for theory which comprehends these various levels of organization, from syntax and moment-to-moment rhythm, through discourse, to social life in general and to broadly shared cultural patterns. The analysis also points to the need for empirical procedures that unite the ethnography of speaking with sociolinguistic and linguistic microanalysis.

NOTE

The research reported here was supported in part by a grant to the author from the Spencer Foundation and by a post-doctoral fellowship to Jeffrey Shultz from NIMH. The author is indebted to Deborah Tannen for editorial advice, to Doro Franck, Brigitte Jordan, and Ron Simons for advice and criticism, and to Susan Florio for collaboration in the original research (she is the 'guest' in the transcript) and for comments on this analysis.

REFERENCES

Bateson, Gregory. 1972. The message this is play. In: Steps toward an ecology of mind. New York. Ballantine Books.

Birdwhistell, Ray L. 1970. Kinesics and context: Essays on body motion communication. Philadelphia: University of Pennsylvania Press.

Bremme, Donald W. 1977. Accomplishing a classroom event: A microethnography of first circle. Qualifying paper, Harvard Graduate School of Education.

Erickson, Frederick. 1981. Timing and context in everyday discourse. In: Children's oral communication. Edited by O. W. Dickson. New York: Academic Press.

Erickson, Frederick, and Jeffrey Shultz. 1977. When is a context? Some issues and methods in the analysis of social competence. Quarterly Newsletter of the Institute for Comparative Human Development 1(2).5-10. Reprinted 1981 in: Ethnography and language in educational settings. Norwood, N.J.: Ablex Press.

Erickson, Frederick, and Jeffrey Shultz. 1981. The counselor as gatekeeper: Social interaction in interviews. New York: Academic Press.

Florio, Susan. 1978. Learning how to go to school: An ethnography of interaction in a kindergarten/first grade classroom. Doctoral dissertation. Harvard Graduate School of Education.

Goffman, Erving. 1976. Replies and responses. Language in Society 5.257-313.

Gomes, Louis Antone, Jr. 1979. Social interaction and social identity: A study of two kindergarten children. Ph.D. dissertation. Harvard Graduate School of Education.

Gumperz, John J. 1977. Sociocultural knowledge in conversational inference. In: Georgetown University Round Table on Languages and Linguistics 1977. Edited by Muriel Saville-Troike. Washington, D.C.: Georgetown University Press. 191-212.

Hymes, Dell. 1974. Foundations in sociolinguistics: An ethnographic approach. Philadelphia: University of Pennsylvania Press.

Keenan, Elinor, and Bambi Schieffelin. 1976. Topic as a discourse notion. In: Subject and topic. Edited by C. Li. New York: Academic Press.

Kendon, Adam. 1977. Studies in the behavior of social interaction. Bloomington: University of Indiana Press.

Lechner, Joan Marie, O.S.U. 1962. Renaissance concepts of the commonplaces. New York: Pageant Press.

Malinowski, Bronislaw. 1923. The problem of meaning in primitive languages. In: The meaning of meaning. By C. K. Ogden and I. A. Richards. New York: Harcourt, Brace and World. Supplement 1, 296-336.

McDermott, Ray P. 1976. Kids make sense: An ethnographic account of the interactional management of success and failure in one first grade classroom. Unpublished dissertation. Stanford University.

Ong, Walter, S.J. 1977. Typographic rhapsody. In: Interfaces of the word: Studies in the evolution of consciousness and culture. Ithaca and London: Cornell University Press.

Sacks, Harvey, Emmanuel Schegloff, and Gail Jefferson. 1974. A simplest systematics for the organization of turn-taking for conversation. Lg. 50.696-735.

Scheflen, Albert E. 1973. Communicational structure: Analysis of a psychotherapy transaction. Bloomington: University of Indiana Press.

Sherzer, Joel. 1977. The ethnography of speaking: A critical appraisal. In: Georgetown University Round Table on Languages and Linguistics 1977. Edited by Muriel Saville-Troike. Washington, D.C.: Georgetown University Press. 43-58.

Shultz, Jeffrey, and Susan Florio. 1979. Stop and freeze: The negotiation of social and physical space in a kindergarten/first grade classroom. Anthropology and Education Quarterly 10.3:166-181.

Shultz, Jeffrey, Susan Florio, and Frederick Erickson. (in press) Where's the floor? Aspects of the cultural organization of social relationships in communication at home and at school. In: Ethnography and education: Children in and

out of school. Edited by Perry Gilmore and Alan Glatthorn.
Washington, D.C.: Center for Applied Linguistics.
Sudnow, David. 1980. Talk's body: A meditation between two
keyboards. Harmondsworth, Middlesex, England: Penguin.
Tannen, Deborah. 1981. New York Jewish conversational style.
International Journal of the Sociology of Language 30.133-149.
Weber, Max. 1922 (1978). Wirtschaft und Gesellschaft. Vol. 1,
pp. 1-14 (Tübingen, 1911). Translated as: The nature of
social activity. In: Weber: Selections in translation. Edited
by W. G. Runciman. Cambridge: Cambridge University Press.
7-32.

DISCOURSE AS AN INTERACTIONAL ACHIEVEMENT: SOME USES OF 'UH HUH' AND OTHER THINGS THAT COME BETWEEN SENTENCES

Emanuel A. Schegloff
University of California, Los Angeles

1. From the standpoint of students of 'discourse', conversation and other forms of talk in interaction are subvarieties of discourse. What comes to be minimally criterial for discourse is the presence, in some sort of coherent relationship, of a spate of language use composed of more than one sentence (or whatever other unit is treated as grammatically fundamental). It is then common to be concerned (1) with the basis for the apparent coherence between the several components of the discourse, (2) with the cognitive structure of the unit, and (3) with the mechanisms by which it is analyzed or decoded on reception. There may be an effort to discern quasi-syntactic relationships between successive parts of the discourse--between successive sentences, for example. And discourse units, such as paragraphs, may be found to be constituted by such quasi-syntactic relationships. The actual enactment of the discourse--for example, its telling--often seems to be treated as the behavioral realization of a preplanned cognitive unit. The prototype discourse for such an approach is the narrative or lecture, which readily lends itself to treatment as the product of a single speaker, whose cognitive apparatus underlies and shapes it.

For the student of talk in interaction, discourse (still minimally defined as a spate of talk composed of more than one sentence or other fundamental unit) is more usefully treated as one type of production in conversation (or other speech-exchange situation). Note that, although some sorts of objects for analysis, such as written stories, memoranda, and legal documents, may appear suitable for analysis under the former conception but not the latter, in many cases the same objects of inquiry are seen differently from the two points of view. The common discourse-analytic standpoint treats the lecture, or sermon, or story told in an elicitation interview, campfire setting, or around the table, as the product of a single speaker and a single mind; the conversation-analytic angle of inquiry does not let go of the fact that speech-exchange systems are involved, in which more than one participant is present and relevant to the talk, even when only one does any talking.

Let me recount an old experience. Once I had trouble understanding certain monologues in Shakespeare. I was watching a series of rehearsals of *The Winter's Tale* by the Canadian Shakespeare Company on public television, and had gotten down my *Complete Shakespeare* and was following the text. In the monologue in question, I could see how line 2 followed 1, 3 followed 2, and line 4 followed 3; but I just could not figure out how line 5 followed line 4. And then I saw in a series of rehearsals that, the authoritative text in front of me to the contrary notwithstanding, line 5 did not follow line 4; some action followed line 4, and line 5 followed that action. And what was at issue in the rehearsals was what that action should be and who should do it, for the sense of line 5, and ensuing lines, would be affected in a major way by it.

Anyone who has lectured to a class knows that the (often silent) reactions of the audience--the wrinkling of brows at some point in its course, a few smiles or chuckles or nods, or their absence--can have marked consequences for the talk which follows: whether, for example, the just preceding point is reviewed, elaborated, put more simply, etc., or whether the talk moves quickly on to the next point, and perhaps to a more subtle point than was previously planned.[1] If this is the case in such a situation of talk-in-interaction as the lecture, then its relevance should be entertained as well for experiments, elicitation interviews, and ordinary conversation.

Clearly, different speech-exchange systems are involved in lectures and ordinary conversation, with different turn-taking practices providing quite differently structured opportunities to talk or participate in other ways. That is one reason why the reference to lecture situations describes wrinkled brows and smiles and nods, rather than utterances or even 'uh huh's. Clearly, as well, in several different types of speech-exchange situations, there can be occasions in which participation is constructed by a speaker in continuing response to interactional contingencies and opportunities from moment to moment, and occasions in which a participant has a preformed notion, and sometimes a prespecified text, of what is to be said, and plows ahead with it in substantial (though rarely total) disregard for what is transpiring in the course of this talking. But these two extremes are not equally likely to occur in the various types of speech-exchange situations; the prespecified text, adhered to 'no matter what', is much less common (and for good structural reasons) in ordinary conversation than in sermons or lectures. Even the wholly prespecified talk, which most approximates the enactment of a cognitive object, must be adapted in its delivery to its occasion, and will certainly have been designed with attention to its recipients and the situation of its delivery in the first place--both aspects of interactional sensitivity. However, it should be clear at the outset that in what follows I am most centrally concerned with what I take to be both the primordial and the most common setting and organization for the use of language--ordinary conversation. Although much of what I have to say is relevant to other settings, the way in which orientation to co-participants and interactional structure matter to discourse and its formation, will vary in different speech exchange systems with different turn-taking systems.

Important analytic leverage can be gained if the examination of any discourse is conducted in a manner guided by the following.[2] (1) The discourse should be treated as an achievement; that involves treating the discourse as something 'produced' over time, incrementally accomplished, rather than born naturally whole out of the speaker's forehead, the delivery of a cognitive plan. (2) The accomplishment or achievement is an interactional one. Quite aside from whatever individual cognitive or processing achievements might be involved (which are not to be treated only as anterior to the interactional), the production of a spate of talk by one speaker is something which involves collaboration with the other parties present, and that collaboration is interactive in character, and interlaced throughout the discourse, that is, it is an ongoing accomplishment, rather than a pact signed at the beginning, after which the discourse is produced entirely as a matter of individual effort. (3) The character of this interactional accomplishment is at least in part shaped by the sociosequential organization of participation in conversation, for example by its turn-taking organization, which is not organized to be indifferent to the size of the turns parties take, but whose underlying (though supercessable) organization is designed to minimize turn size. It is this feature which requires us to see 'discourse' and 'discourse units' which have overcome this bias as achievements and accomplishments. (4) Because the actual outcome will have been achieved by the parties in real time and as, at each point, a contingent accomplishment, the mechanisms of the achievement and its effort are displayed, or are analyzably hidden in or absent from, various bits of behavior composing and accompanying that discourse, and analyzable with it.

One class of such behavior which is implicated in the achievement of discourses in conversation is the concern of this paper. Instances of the class take the form of vocalizations such as 'uh huh', 'mm hmm', 'yeah', and others as well

as head-gestures such as nods.[3] These, as well as other,
bits of talk and behavior produced by other than the 'main
speaker' are regularly discarded when discourses--the stories,
the arguments, etc.--are extracted from the tangle of detail
which composed their actual occurrence. 'The story' is puri-
fied of them in the course of its extraction, both by lay re-
counters and by professional analysts. It is this separation
of bits of talk, otherwise intercalated with each other and contingent on one another, into two distinct classes, of which one
is the 'real talk' (the story, the 'what-was-being-said') and the
other conversational 'detritus' (apparently lacking semantic
content, and seemingly not contributing to the substance of
what the discourse ends up having said), which makes possible the notion of 'discourse' as a single speaker's, and a single
mind's, product. It is a consequence as well that the interactional animus and dynamic of the spate of talk can disappear
into the cognitive structure and quasi-syntactic composition of
the discourse. What has been discarded may itself be picked
up by investigators--typically other investigators, even other
sorts of investigators--for separate treatment under such
rubrics as 'accompaniment signals' (Kendon 1967) or 'back-
channel' actions (Yngve 1970; cf. Duncan and Fiske 1977).

But, as I urge later, the fact that both parts of the occa-
sion--the teller's telling and the behavior of the recipients--
may be subjected to study does not restore the interactivity
lost when the former is extracted from the latter. For the
parts of the telling appear to follow one another, rather than
each following some responsive behavior by a recipient (or the
lack thereof); and what recipients produced after this or that
part of the telling has been removed from the environment of
that to which it was responsive. From 'discourse' and 'listener
behavior' so conceived and studied, it is unlikely that one will
be able to reassemble the actual structure of 'talking at length
in conversation'.

In what follows, I first elaborate a bit on the meaning of,
and the reasons for, treating the occurrence of discourse in
conversation as 'an achievement'. One mechanism for that
achievement has its focus at points at which recipients or
hearers could begin talking but content themselves with 'uh
huh' and the like instead, after which prior speakers continue.
I briefly discuss recent treatments of vocalizations such as 'uh
huh' and 'yeah', and then offer some alternatives.

2. Why should the existence of a 'discourse' (a multi-
sentence unit) in ordinary conversation be treated as an
achievement? Elsewhere (Sacks, Schegloff, and Jefferson
1974) it has been argued that speakers construct utterances
in turns at talk out of describable structured units, with
recognizable possible completions. In English, some lexical
items (e.g. 'hello', 'yes', 'who'), some phrasal units, some
clausal units, and sentences constitute such 'turn-constructional

units'. The end of any such unit is a possible completion of
a turn, and possible completions of turns are places at which
potential next speakers appropriately start next turns. If
this is the case, then an underlying structure of turn distribution is in operation which organizes interactive enforcement,
or potential enforcement, of a minimization of turn size.

If such a system is in operation, then a constraint for
single-unit turns has at least two sources. First, there is an
organizational basis for current nonspeakers to monitor for the
possible completion of first units in a current turn as a place
to start next turns. And second, there is an orientation by
speakers starting a turn to the organizationally motivated orientation of others to so start up, which can engender a designing of the talk in a turn to be so organized as to get what
needs to be said said before the end of the first unit's completion. The second of these can contribute to making the
smooth operation of the first viable and routine. A great many
turns at talk in conversation thus end up being one unit long.

With all of this, it is obvious that some turns at talk end up
having more than one unit in them. Nor is this an anomaly,
or counterevidence. It does invite exploration of the possible
existence (and features) of methodical ways in which such
multi-unit turns are achieved. If there are such ways, then
their use may serve as additional evidence of the underlying
organization which these methods are used to supersede, at
the same time as they explicate the work of achieving the
supersession--the discourse. Although this is not the place
to undertake an extensive, let alone exhaustive, account of
such methodical devices, several may be mentioned to supply
a sense of the sorts of phenomena that are involved.

One class of methods by which multi-unit turns may be
achieved is that composed of devices initiated by the potential
speaker of the multi-unit turn.

(a) The potential discourse-speaker may indicate from the
beginning of the turn an interest in producing a more-than-
one-unit turn. For example, the speaker may begin with a
list-initiating marker, such as 'first of all',[4] projecting thereby
that after the turn-unit in which the 'first' is done, more will
follow. Note that there may otherwise be no particular need
to pre-mark an item as first in a list (i.e. besides leaving it
to be so discovered over the course of extended talk, by virtue of eventual subsequent items) other than the problem of
getting to produce subsequent items. Beginning a turn this
way recognizes the turn-taking contingency, and, by projecting a multi-unit turn, invites recipients to hold off talking
where they might otherwise start, so that the 'post-first-units'
may have room to be produced.

(b) Indeed, the turn-position, or turn-opportunity, in which
the beginning of a projected multi-unit turn could be produced, may instead be entirely devoted to a whole turn which
is focused on doing the projecting (as the list-initiating marker

does within a turn). Some years ago, Sacks (1974) described one such operation under the rubric 'story prefaces', and more recently, I have described under the term 'pre-pre' a similar logic of use underlying one class of occurrences of utterances of the form 'Can I ask you a question' (Schegloff 1980). In both cases, a course of talk is projected which involves more than one turn-constructional unit, and the talk begins with a display of that projection. Note that it remains for recipients to honor this projection, and to withhold talk at the points at which it would otherwise be appropriate. Although initiated by the intending extended-turn speaker, if an extended turn results, it will have involved interactive accomplishment by both speaker and recipients, the latter being recipients only by abjuring their possible status as speakers. The list-initiating marker, or story preface, or 'pre-pre' (i.e. 'Can I ask you a question') are the overt markers of orientation to the constraints making achievement of discourse problematic, and of the effort directed to superseding them.

(c) Speakers may also employ methodical devices for achieving a multi-unit turn at positions other than the beginning of the turn in question. There is, for example, what can be called the 'rush through'--a practice in which a speaker, approaching a possible completion of a turn-constructional unit, speeds up the pace of the talk, withholds a dropping pitch or the intake of breath, and phrases the talk to bridge what would otherwise be the juncture at the end of a unit. Instead, the speaker 'rushes through' the juncture without in-breath, reaches a point well into a next unit (e.g. next sentence), and there stops for a bit, for an inbreath, etc. (Schegloff 1973). Here the turn-extension device is initiated near the otherwise-possible-end of the turn, rather than at its beginning. Once again, interaction and collaboration are involved, for recipients could start up despite the displayed intention of current speaker to continue, and produce thereby at least a 'floor fight'. Once again, the turn-extension device exhibits, on the speaker's part, an orientation to the imminent possibility of another starting up as s/he approaches the end of the turn-unit. Once again, if successful at getting to produce a multi-unit turn or discourse, the talk displays the special effort involved in achieving it.

Of course, not all multi-unit turns are the result of speaker-initiated methods designed to achieve them. Some multi-unit turns are the outcome of a different methodical production. A speaker produces a one-unit turn, at whose possible completion no co-participant starts a next turn. Then one way the talk may continue is by the prior speaker talking again, sometimes by starting a new turn unit.[5] On possible completion of the now added second unit, a multi-unit turn has been produced; of course, the same cycle may occur on the next possible completion as well.[6] In cases of this sort, the course of action which issues in a multi-unit turn is 'initiated' by a recipient, and not by an (intending) speaker of (what ends up as) the multi-unit turn, or discourse unit. Once again, interactional achievement is involved, each participant orienting to the other(s), and all oriented to the underlying turn-taking organization, which is itself an interactionally driven and constrained organization. Once again, signs of the collaborative work are marbled through the talk--in this case, in the form of a frequent slight gap of silence at the possible turn completion which can issue in prior speaker resuming and extending the turn into a multi-unit one.

In the preceding, I have tried to point to several methodical routes by which multi-unit turns or discourses can come to be. Each concerns how a second turn-constructional unit can come to be produced at the point at which the underlying turn-taking organization otherwise provides for turn-transition. But sometimes quite extended spates of talk are involved-- stories, chains of argument, long descriptions, etc. The point about the joint, interactive achievement of discourse is not limited to the beginning of spates of discourse--the initial possible transition point at which the turn stays with the same speaker. Recurrently through an extended spate of talk, places where others could start up appear, and when others do not start up full utterances, there are commonly small behavioral tokens by which interactive management of the possible transition occasion is effected--bits of assessment or the absence of them where they are relevant, tokens of interest, nods, smiles, 'uh huh's, and withholding of these, gaze direction with or without mutual gaze, and the like. It is on one class of these that I concentrate in what follows.

3.   The modern literature in which bits of talk, vocalization or related behavior are extracted from what becomes ongoing talk by another, and are subjected to treatment in the aggregate, begins with the linguist Fries (1952). Fries treated together the following sorts of forms (1952:49): 'yes', 'unh hunh', 'yeah', 'I see', 'good', 'oh', and others of lesser frequency. Others have dealt with body-behavioral versions of this behavior, and have discussed the vocalized forms in the course of doing so (Kendon 1967; Dittman and Llewellyn 1967, 1968). The most common term now in use for such items, 'back-channel communication', was introduced by Yngve (1970), and includes a much broader range of utterance types, including much longer stretches of talk. The term 'back-channel' has been adopted by Duncan and his associates (for example, Duncan and Fiske 1977), together with the broadened definition of the class. Duncan and Fiske (201-202) include not only expressions such as 'uh huh', 'yeah', and the like, but also completions by a recipient of sentences begun by another, requests for clarification, 'brief restatement' of something just said by another, and 'head nods and shakes'.[7]

Throughout this literature, two related characterizations have been offered to deal with these bits of behavior. According to one, these bits of behavior are evidence of attention, interest, and/or understanding on the listener's part. (Thus Fries 1952:49, '...signals of this continued attention...', or Kendon 1967:44, '...appears to do no more than signal... that he is attending and following what is being said...').[8] A second use of such behavior proposed in this literature is that it '...keeps the conversation going smoothly' (Dittman and Llewellyn 1967:342), or '...appears to provide the auditor with a means for participating actively in the conversation, thus facilitating the general coordination of action by both participants...' (Duncan and Fiske 1977:202-203).

I do not intend to comment extensively on this second characterization beyond noting that once an organization of conversation is established in which nonspeaker interpositions are a recurrent part, their presence will be part of 'going smoothly' or of active participation; but this does not tell us why active participation is taken to involve this sort of behavior, or why the absence of such interpolations undercuts the 'smoothness' of the conversation, if indeed it does (cf. Schegloff 1968:1092-1093). However, it is the capacity of 'uh huh' and cognate bits of behavior to betoken attention and understanding which is the most common proposal about these events taken in the aggregate, with each removed from its context of occurrence; and it is to this sort of characterization that the following points are addressed.

(1) The term often used in the literature to describe 'uh huh' and similar productions is 'signal', and it is unclear what the implications of this term are for the strength of what is believed to be done by these bits of behavior. It is worth noting, however, that 'uh huh', 'mm hmm', 'yeah', head nods, and the like at best *claim* attention and/or understanding, rather than *showing* it or *evidencing* it. The references to 'signals of continued attention' or 'signal...that he is attending and following' treat these as more than claims, but as correct claims, and this need not be the case; it is, at any rate, a contingent outcome, and not an intrinsic characteristic of the behavior being described.

(2) It is unclear why any particular behavior--such as 'uh huh' or a head nod--should be needed to address the issue of attention, whether to claim it or to show it. Regularly, these bits of behavior are produced when there are otherwise present on a continuous basis sorts of behavior which are understood as manifestations or exhibits of attention, such as continuing gaze direction at speaker.[9] Aside, then, from the issue of whether 'uh huh' etc. evidence attention or claim it, there is the issue of why attention is taken to be problematic in the first place, in need of showing *or* claiming.

(3) If, for the moment, we treat the issue of attention as having its relevance established, then it may be noted that any instance of an indefinitely extendable set of utterances

would either claim or show attention to, or understanding of, an immediately preceding utterance by another. That is, a vast array of types of talk following an utterance by another exhibit an orientation to it; accordingly, the claim that 'uh huh' exhibits an orientation to, or attention to, preceding talk does not help discriminate 'uh huh' from any other talk, or tell us what 'uh huh' in particular does or can do, and therefore why a participant might choose to produce it rather than something else.

(d) If, however, we aim to understand how bits of behavior such as 'uh huh' and the like may be taken as bearing on the attention, interest, or understanding of their producers with respect to the talk being produced by another, then we should also note that 'uh huh', 'yeah', and the like are regularly taken as betokening agreement as well. A search for the mechanism by which interest, attention, or understanding are exhibited by this behavior, should also deal with the apparent exhibiting of agreement.

When 'uh huh's etc. are considered in the aggregate, then, the characterization of the class as signaling attention, interest, or understanding appears equivocal. Although it can be argued that attention and understanding are generically relevant in conversation, no ready account is at hand (when the aggregate of cases is considered) for why these issues need specially to be addressed, why they are addressed with these tokens, why addressed at these particular points (if, indeed, it is at particular points, on this account, that these tokens are placed).

However, examination of particular occurrences of the sort of behavior under discussion--of particular 'uh huh's, 'yeah's, etc.--might yield answers to some of these questions. In particular instances, for example, analysis may show that attention was indeed problematic for the parties, and that an 'uh huh' or a nod was produced 'in response to' an extended gaze by the speaker which appeared to solicit a sign of attention/interest/understanding. Or, analysis may show that certain usages by speakers regularly involve addressing the issue of understanding in their immediate aftermath. Thus, as described elsewhere (Sacks and Schegloff 1979), speakers may use 'recognitional reference forms' (such as proper names) to refer to persons they think recipients know; but if speakers are not certain that recipients know the intended referent, they may mark the reference form with an upward intonation, soliciting some signal of recognition (a special kind of understanding); if no such display is forthcoming, further tries, involving further clues to the identification of the referent, are provided, with display of recognition again solicited. Recipients may betoken such a recognition with 'uh huh' or may add to this token (especially if recognition was delayed) some demonstration of recognition, as in (1) and (2).

(1) A: Ya still in the real estate business, Lawrence
     B: → Wah e' uh no my dear heart uh, ya know Max
           Rickler h
        → (0.5)
     B: with whom I've been 'ssociated since I've been out
           here in Brentwood has had a series of um (0.?)=
     A: →   [yeah
     B: =bad experiences uhh hhh I guess he calls it a
           nervous breakdown.
     A: Yeah
           (Sacks and Schegloff 1979:19)

(2) L: ...well I was the only one other than than the uhm
        → tch Fords? Uh Missiz Holmes Ford? You know uh
           the the cellist?
           [
     W: →   Oh yes. She's she's the cellist.
     L: Yes
           (Sacks and Schegloff 1979:19)

With this background, one can note that even in the absence
of overt solicitation by upward intonation of some display of
recognition, after recognitional reference one commonly finds
'uh huh' and the like,[10] as in (3).

(3) Bee: hh This feller I have- (iv-) "felluh"; this ma:n.
           (0.2) t! ⁻·hhh He ha::(s)- uff-eh-who-who I have
           fer Linguistics is real   ly too much, ·hh h=
     Ava: →   [Mm hm?]   [Mm hm,
           (TG, 198-201)

It is not that some substantial proportion of 'uh huh's etc. are
thus accounted for, but that an analytically coherent set of
cases can be assembled in this way from a series of analyses
of individual cases, the basis for the coherence of the class
being derived from the sequential environment in which those
particular tokens are produced. Although appeals to signalling
attention, interest, and/or understanding appear equivocal when
invoked on behalf of the aggregated occurrence of tokens such
as 'uh huh', 'yeah', and the like removed from their particular
environments, such accounts may be viable and strong when
introduced for delimited and described cases in which the relevance of these issues *for the parties to the conversation at
that point in the talk* can be shown. Appropriate sets of such
analyzed single cases may then be assembled to display recurrent practices, themes, structures, etc.

4. Is there nothing more general, then, that can be said
about such utterances as 'uh huh' and the like, when they
compose all of their producer's vocalization on that occasion

of talking? Two observations seem to me to have sufficiently
general relevance to bear mention in this connection.

Perhaps the most common usage of 'uh huh', etc. (in environments other than after yes/no questions) is to exhibit on
the part of its producer an understanding that an extended
unit of talk is underway by another, and that it is not yet,
or may not yet be (even ought not yet be), complete. It
takes the stance that the speaker of that extended unit should
continue talking, and in that continued talking should continue that extended unit. 'Uh huh', etc. exhibit this understanding, and take this stance, precisely by passing an opportunity to produce a full turn at talk. When so used, utterances such as 'uh huh' may properly be termed 'continuers'.

Note that the sorts of issues mentioned earlier as arising
with respect to the 'signalling attention and understanding'
accounts bear differently here.

(a) For talk-in-interaction whose turn-taking organization
makes possible-completion-of-one-speaker's-talk a place where
another can start up a next turn, it is structurally relevant
at such places for parties to display their understanding of
the current state of the talk. For example, as Sacks pointed
out years ago, participants sometimes begin a turn by producing an 'uhm' just after the possible completion of a prior turn,
then pausing, and then producing a turn, rather than just
delaying the start of their turn until they are 'ready'. They
may be understood to proceed in this fashion precisely in
order first to show their understanding of the current state
of the talk and their stance toward it (i.e. 'a prior turn is
over, it is an appropriate occasion for a next turn, I will
produce one'), in some independence of the actual production
of the turn they eventually produce. So also is it relevant
for parties to display their understanding, when appropriate,
that an extended turn is underway, and to show their intention to pass the opportunity to take a turn at talk that they
might otherwise initiate at that point.

(b) 'Uh huh's, etc. as continuers do not merely claim an
understanding without displaying anything of the understanding they claim. The production of talk in a possible turn
position which is nothing other than 'uh huh' claims not only
'I understand the state of the talk', but embodies the understanding that extended talk by another is going on by declin-
ing to produce a fuller turn in that position. It does not
claim understanding in general, but displays a particular
understanding through production of an action fitted to that
understanding.[11]

(c) Except for the limited set of behavioral productions that
are used to do 'continuers', it is not the case that any instance of an indefinitely extendable set of utterances would
achieve this outcome or do this job. Most other forms of talk
would be full turns in their own right, rather than ways of
passing the opportunity to produce such a turn, and would

fail precisely thereby to display understanding of, or respect for, an extended unit still in progress.

The 'continuer' usage is most readily illustrated by data in which clear marking of the end of the extended unit, or discourse, is provided, and until the occurrence of which the 'in-progress' character of the talk is clearly visible. Among the ways in which such marking may be done are the several ways of announcing, at the beginning of the unit, the sort of thing that will be its possible end. For example, there are story prefaces (cf. Sacks 1974) which may characterize the sort of event the forthcoming story is about (for example, 'a funny thing happened...'), such that the unit will not be possibly complete until such an event has been mentioned, and may be over at the end of its mention. Or there are 'preliminaries to preliminaries' (Schegloff 1980) in which an 'action-type' is projected (like 'question' in 'Can I ask you a question?') as that to which preliminaries are leading; the preliminaries may then be developed as an extended discourse (e.g. a description, a story, etc.) until such an action is done (e.g. such a question is asked) as these preliminaries could be leading up to. Several instances are given in (4) and (5).

```
(4)  1  B°:    I've listen' to all the things that chu've said,
                an' I agree with
     2          you so much.
     3  B°:    Now,
     4  B°: →  I wanna ask you something,
     5  B°:    I wrote a letter.
     6          (pause)
     7  A:     Mh hm,
     8  B°:    T'the governor.
     9  A:     Mh hm::,
    10  B°:    -telling 'im what I thought about i(hh)m!
    11 (A):    (Sh:::!)
    12  B°: →  Will I get an answer d'you think,
    13  A:     Ye:s,
                (BC, Red:190)
```

```
(5)  1  B:  →  Now listen, Mister Crandall, Let me ask you
                this.
     2          A cab. You're standing onna corner. I
                heardjuh
     3          talking to a cab driver.
     4  A:     Uh::uh
     5  B:     Uh was it- uh was a cab driver, wasn' i'?
     6  A:     Yup,
     7  B:     Now, yer standing onna corner,
     8  A:     Mm hm,
     9  B:     I live up here in Queens.
    10  A:     Mm hm,
    11  B:     Near Queens Boulevard,
```

```
12  A:    Mm hm,
13  B:    I'm standing on the corner of Queens
              Boulevard a::nd
14        uh::m (     ) Street.
15  A:    Right?
16  B:    Uh, I- a cab comes along.  An' I wave my
              arm, "Okay,
17        I wancha I wancha."  You know,
18  A:    Mm hm,
19  B:    Uh::m, I'm waving my arm now.  Here in
              my living room.
20        hhhh!
               [
21  A:    heh heh!
22  B:    A:nd uh, he just goes right on by me.
23  A:    Mm hm,
24  B:    A::nd uh-two::, three:, (.) about three
              blocks,
25        beyond me, where- in the direction I'm going,
              there
26        is a cab stand.
27  A:    Mm hm,
28  B:    Uh-there is a hospital, (0.?) uh, a block
              (0.?) up,
29        and there is a subway station, right there.
30  A:    Mm hm.
31  B:    Uh now I could 've walked, the three or
              four blocks,
32        to that cab stand,
33  A:    Mm hm,
               [
34  B:        Bud I, had come out-of where I was,
              right there
35        on the corner.
36  A:    Right?
37  B:  → Now is he not suppose' tuh stop fuh me?
38  A:    If he is on duty,
              (BC, Red:191-193)
```

Note that after the projection of a question upcoming, the recipient of the extended talk confines himself almost entirely
(the alternatives are touched on below) to continuers--'uh huh',
'mm hmm', 'right', and the like, until a question is asked (of
the sort analyzably projected; not just any subsequent question; not, therefore, the one at line 5 in (5). The extended
unit then being completed, and a determinate action being
called for by the question, the recipient of the discourse
addresses himself to the question. The same form of utterance may be produced (for example, the 'yes' at line 13 in
(4)), but in this sequential environment it is a full turn,
rather than passing one.

What will constitute the end of an extended spate of talk is
not always named or characterized as it is in the aforemen-
tioned forms; still it is regularly readily recognized by the
participants. Sometimes, however, misunderstandings occur,
and a continuer produced to display an understanding that an
extended unit is in progress and is not yet completed thereby
displays a misunderstanding, as in (6) (taken from the same
corpus of telephone calls to a radio talk show, as was the
source of (4) and (5).

```
(6)   1  B:    This is in reference to a call, that was made
                  about a
      2         month ago.
      3  A:    Yessir?
      4  B:    A woman called, uh sayin she uh signed a
                  contract for
      5         huh son who is- who was a minuh.
      6  A:    Mm hm,
      7  B:    And she claims inna contract, there were
                  things given,
      8         and then taken away, in small writing.
      9         ((pause))
     10  A:    Mm hm
     11  B:    Uh, now meanwhile, about a month ehh no
                  about two weeks
     12         before she made the call I read in, I read or
                  either
     13         heard-uh I either read or hoid onna television,
                  where
     14         the judge, hadda case like this.
     15  A:    Mhhm,
     16  B:    And he got disgusted an' he says 'I'- he's
                  sick of these
     17         cases where they give things in big writing,
                  an' take
     18         'em, an' take 'em away in small writing.
     19  A:    Mhhm,
     20  B:    An' 'e claimed the contract void.
     21  A:    Mhhm,
     22  B:    Uh what I mean is it c'd help this woman
                  that called.
     23         You know uh, that's the reason I called.
               (BC, Gray, 74-75)
```

At line 21, A produces another in the series of continuers
that have helped propel B's telling; this one, it turns out, is
'mistaken', for the caller had apparently intended 'An' 'e
claimed the contract void' to be the end--perhaps hearable as
'a solution' for the woman to whose earlier call he refers.[12]
It is worth noting that 'trouble' around the end boundary of
discourse units need not be understood as 'cognitive' or

processing error; it can be the vehicle for thoroughly designed interactional effects (cf. the discussion of reengage-
ment of turn-by-turn talk at emergence from a story in
Jefferson 1978).

These instances allow me to remark on several additional
points which may provide some sense of the interactional texture involved here.

1. Note that after a continuer, the speaker of the extended
unit may 'do the continuing' in various ways (and it should
be underscored that this locus of talk should be investigated
precisely for the work of 'doing continuing'). In (4), the
first continuers are followed by increments to the turn-unit
(sentence) already in progress; in (5), some continuers are
followed by increments to the prior sentence (for example,
lines 10-11); others are followed by starts of new sentences,
(for example, lines 12-13); still others are followed by what
could be counted as new sentences by virtue of their grammatical independence, or as increments to the prior by virtue
of their linkage by conjunction--by just such a token as marks
'continuation' (for example, lines 22-26). In this respect,
then, there is no major differentiation between sentences and
multi-sentence units or discourses; the same mechanism can
engender an elaborated version of the former or the latter.

2. Note that the bits of behavior produced by the recipient
of the extended talk vary. Two points may be advanced here.
First, even when little other than continuer usage is involved,
the tokens employed for it vary. I have referred to 'uh huh',
'yeah', etc. throughout this paper, and have not addressed
myself to the differences between these tokens. I note here
only that the availability of a range of tokens may matter less
for the difference of meaning or usage between them (if any)
than for the possibility thereby allowed of varying the composition of a series of them. Use in four or five consecutive
slots of the same token may then be used to hint incipient
disinterest, while varying the tokens across the series, whatever tokens are employed, may mark a baseline of interest.

Second, in some of the positions at which some sort of continuer is relevant (as may be shown, for example, by the
speaker withholding further talk until one is produced, as in
(4), lines 5-7, or (6), lines 8-11), the immediately preceding
talk may be such as to invite some sort of 'reaction' aside
from, instead of, or in addition to the continuer. And one
does find throughout extended units--especially stories--
markers of surprise ('Really?'), assessments ('oh my', 'wow',
'you're kidding', 'isn't that weird', 'wonderful', etc.), and
the like. In the fragments I have cited, we may note the
laugh in (5) at line 21, and in (4) the laugh/assessment/
expletive at line 11. Note in the case of the latter that it
follows a selection of idiomatic phrasing that indicates 'scold-
ing' (and this has already been reported as directed to a high
political official), and its last word is delivered with a laugh

token as well.[13] In the case of (5), note that at lines 16-17,
the teller 'packages' the telling in a very dramatic format with
exaggerated self-quotation, which could have been designed
to engender a more forthcoming appreciation than this 'mm hmm'
provides.[14] Note, then, that although B does continue talking
after the continuer, here she does not continue with the extended unit that was 'in progress', but shifts from a description of the events being told about to a description of the current scene of the telling, using the recurrence of 'waving the
arm' as the bridge. The description appears designed to
underscore 'incongruity' and to elicit a response to it, but
even the first effort at this fails to get a response ('I'm waving my arm now.'); she then adds another (she could have
resumed the story) to underscore the incongruity even further
('Here in my living room'), to which she appends a laugh token
as well. This time she does get a response of the sort she
has apparently been after. (Note: one is tempted to write
'of a sort fitted to the character of her talk', but, of course,
it is precisely the assessment of the character of her talk
which is at issue in the sort of response A makes or withholds.
It may be suggested that the mechanism by which a series of
same continuer tokens displays incipient disinterest involves
the availability of tokens of surprise, special interest, assessment etc., the nonproduction of which shows the recipient not
to be finding in the talk anything newsworthy, interesting, or
assessable. Varying the continuer tokens may mask the absence of other types of response token; using the same one
continuously may underscore it.)

The general point I want to make here is that the operation
of continuers and of the other bits of behavior produced by
recipients in the course of, or rather in the enabling of, extended talk or discourse by another, is designed in a detailed
way to fit to the ongoing talk by the teller, and 'to fit' may
involve either 'cooperating' with what that talk seems designed
to get, or withholding; both of these are fitted to the details
of the locally preceding talk, and cannot be properly understood or appreciated when disengaged from it. When disengaged, there is no way of telling that the 'mm hmm' at line 18
in (5) is not only a continuer, but is possibly withholding a
laugh; and without that, one may not be in a position to understand why the teller next abandons the story for a description
of her telling posture. In brief, disengaging the listener behavior from its local sequential context not only undercuts the
possibility of understanding what it is doing; it can remove an
important basis for understanding what is going on *in the discourse itself*.

The preceding discussion having ended with an account of
some of the interactional texture in particular data fragments,
it is in point to recall that the concern of this section is to
see what more general assertions can defensibly be put forth

to characterize what tokens like 'uh huh' may be doing. One
I have suggested is the usage as 'continuer'.

The continuer usage rests on the observation that 'uh huh',
etc. passes the opportunity to do any sort of fuller turn at
all, on the grounds that an extended unit is already in progress. Note, however, that, were a fuller turn done, it
would be some particular type--it would be of some particular
form, and would be doing some particular action or actions.
In passing the opportunity to do a fuller turn, a participant
therefore is also passing the opportunity to *do something in
particular*--the opportunity to do whatever might have relevantly been done at that point. We just discussed a case in
which an 'mmhm' was alternative to a laugh; but we clearly
cannot say that 'uh huh', etc. is generally a way of withholding laughter, because there is no way of showing that
doing laughter is generally relevant, and if something cannot
be shown to be relevantly present, then it cannot be relevantly absent, or withheld. Of course, laughter is not generally relevant; it was relevant in the case I have discussed because the other party did something to make it relevant, and
that is why one needs the local sequential environment--to see
what the other parties have done that makes some sorts of
next actions relevant, which 'uh huh' may be displaying the
withholding of. The question is: are there any kinds of
actions which have some kind of 'general relevance' in conversation, by which is meant that they are not made relevant by
the particulars of someone's immediately preceding talk or behavior? There is at least one candidate.

One kind of talk that appears to have quite a general potential provenance is what has elsewhere (Schegloff, Jefferson,
and Sacks 1977) been termed 'other-initiated repair' or 'next-
turn repair initiation'. A variety of constructional formats are
used to do the job of initiating the remedying of some problem
of hearing or understanding the just prior talk of another--
several of the WH-question terms, such as 'who', 'what', etc.,
as well as 'huh', partial (and sometimes full) repeats of prior
turn, partial repeats plus one of the question words, and
others (pp. 367-369). It appears that there are no systematic
exclusion rules on the possible relevance of next-turn repair
initiation in any possible turn position. Although next-turn
repair initiation is generally withheld until after completion of
the turn in which the trouble-source occurred, it appears correct to say that such repair initiation is regularly potentially
relevant after completion of any unit of talk by another.[15]
Its use exploits its positioning--next after the unit in which
the trouble-source occurred. If it is the case (Schegloff,
Jefferson, and Sacks 1977:363) that any talk can be a trouble-
source, then 'after any talk' can be a place for repair to be
initiated on it. Speakers can look to the moments after some
unit of talk to find whether repair on that talk is being initiated; indeed, speakers who will be continuing can leave a

moment of nontalk for such repair to be initiated if the talk
just produced is to be treated by others as a trouble-source.
Then 'uh huh', nods, and the like, in passing the opportunity
to do a full turn at talk, can be seen to be passing an opportunity to initiate repair on the immediately preceding talk.[16]

Note that, if tokens such as 'uh huh' operate to pass an
opportunity to initiate repair, the basis seems clear for the
ordinary inference that the talk into which they are interpo-
lated is being understood, and for the treatment in the literature that they signal understanding. It is not that there is
a direct semantic convention in which 'uh huh' equals a claim
or signal of understanding. It is rather that devices are
available for the repair of problems of understanding the prior
talk, and the passing up of those opportunities, which 'uh
huh' can do, is taken as betokening the absence of such
problems.

Further, the use of other-initiated repair as one way of
pre-indicating the imminent occurrence of disagreement
(Schegloff, Jefferson, and Sacks 1977:380) suggests why 'uh
huh's and the like can be taken as indications of agreement
with the speaker of an ongoing extended unit. For if disagreement were brewing, then opportunities to initiate repair
would supply a ready vehicle for the display and potential de-
flection of that disagreement. Passing the opportunity to raise
problems of understanding may be taken as indicating the absence of such problems. It may also be taken as indicating
the absence of that which such problems might have por-
tended--disagreement--and thus be taken as indications of
agreement.

It must be noted, however, that there is a difference between this usage and the continuer usage. It was noted
earlier that with regard to the 'current state of the talk',
'uh huh' does more than claim an understanding, but embodies
it in particulars and acts on it. With respect to the understanding of, and agreement with, what a prior speaker has
said and done, 'uh huh' is merely a claim of understanding.
Such a claim may turn out to be incorrect; and passing one
opportunity to initiate repair is compatible with initiating repair later. The status of 'uh huh' as an indication of understanding or agreement is equivocal in a way in which its status
as a continuer is not, as participants who have relied on it will
have discovered and regretted.

In this section, I have tried to formulate what appear to me
to be the only two general characterizations that can be sustained when applied to singular, particular, situated instances
of vocalizations such as 'uh huh': a usage as continuer and a
usage to pass an opportunity to initiate repair. For the rest,
the treatment of them in the aggregate, separated from the
talk immediately preceding them, loses what they are doing.
Perhaps more germane to the official topic of this Georgetown
University Round Table, along with that is lost the character

of the ongoing talk during which they have been produced. Thereby our understanding of discourse is weakened. I close with several observations on this theme.

5. Among the themes I have stressed most strongly is that, at least in conversation, discourse must be treated as an achievement. There is a real, recurrent contingency concerning 'who should talk now'; the fact that someone continues is an outcome coordinatedly achieved out of that contingency. There is a real, recurrent contingency concerning what who-ever-gets-to-talk should talk on; the fact that the same speaker who talked before talks again *and talks more of the same thing* is an outcome achieved out of this contingency (they could have gone on to repair what preceded; they could have paren-thesized into a comment about their talking; they could have 'touched-off' into something entirely different, etc.).

Once it has happened that 'a speaker continues' (for exam-ple, 'a teller continues his story'), that appears entirely 'natural'; we lose sight of what were contingent alternatives; they do not become 'ex-alternatives' or 'alternatives-not-taken'; they simply disappear, and leave the achieved outcome in the splendid isolation of seeming inescapability. For ana-lysts, this is a great loss. Good analysis retains a sense of the actual as an achievement from among possibilities; it re-tains a lively sense of the contingency of real things. It is worth an alert, therefore, that too easy a notion of 'discourse' can lose us that.

If certain stable forms appear to emerge or recur in talk, they should be understood as an orderliness wrested by the participants from interactional contingency, rather than as automatic products of standardized plans. Form, one might say, is also the distillate of action and/in interaction, not only its blueprint. If that is so, then the description of forms of behavior, forms of discourse (such as stories) included, has to include interaction among their constitutive domains, and not just as the stage on which scripts written in the mind are played out.

NOTES

My appreciation to the Netherlands Institute for Advanced Study in the Social Sciences and Humanities (NIAS) for time to reflect on some of the matters discussed here, while I was a Fellow during 1978-1979, and to Anita Pomerantz and Michael Lynch for useful discussion.
1. The behavioral vehicles for interaction between 'per-former' and 'audience' may vary among various 'single speaker' settings, but the fact of interaction is certainly not limited to the academic lecture. Max Atkinson (private communication) has been exploring it in political speeches in Great Britain.

2. See, for example, the paper by Marjorie Goodwin (1980). These themes are relevant not only for discourse units, but for 'sentences' as well. Cf. Charles Goodwin (1979).

3. Of course, not every occurrence of one of these vocalizations is an instance of the usage I am concerned with; not, for example, occurrences which follow so-called 'yes/no questions'.

4. Once again, not all utterances of 'first' or 'first of all' are list-initiating, although they do commonly project some form of extended talk, if only by indicating that before an already relevant action, something else is to be done, as in the following segment:

```
Vic:     I know who didit.
James:   You know who didit,
         [
Vic:     Yeeah,
Vic:     Ye:s.
James:   Who wuzzit.
         (0.7)
Vic:  →  First of a:::ll, un Michael came by:,...
         (US, 33)
```

5. The alternative is adding to the turn unit already produced, which can then be recompleted, as in the following:

```
Anne:    Apparently Marcia went shopping fer all these things.
         (1.0)
Anne:    Becuz uh: (0.5) Leah didn't seem t'kno:w, which
         kid//d-
         (Post-Party, I, 5)
```

6. On the possibilities discussed in this paragraph, cf. Sacks et al. (1974:704, 709, 715).

7. Cf. note 16.

8. Kendon does describe another use of such interpolations --a 'point granting' use.

9. In Fries' materials from telephone conversation, and in Dittman and Llewellyn's experimental format (1967:348), the parties are not visually mutually accessible, and this remark is not in point.

10. As it happens, a number of Yngve's instances are of this sort; cf. Yngve 1970:574.

11. Cf. Fragment 6, lines 20-23, and the discussion in note 12.

12. Note that B's 'what I mean...' shows an orientation to 'having been misunderstood'. He does not *go on* to say he means to help the woman and this was the reason for his call; he uses a repair format to indicate that this is what he meant before, which was not understood by A, as displayed by the 'mh hm' which indicates waiting for more to come. This bears

on the remark earlier in the text that continuer tokens display an understanding of the current state of the talk, and do not merely claim an understanding. It is the displaying of what understanding their producer has which makes it possible for recipient of the continuer to find that understanding flawed.

13. On the ways in which a laugh token can solicit a response from a coparticipant, cf. Jefferson (1979).

14. If so, then the 'mm hm' may be used in lieu of, or to display the withholding of, such a more forthcoming response, a possibility further examined later. Note too that 'uh huh', etc. can be delivered in an indefinitely extendable range of ways; some 'uh huh's can mark surprise, appreciation, assessment, etc.

15. Indeed, it can be relevant after a suspected talk unit by another, as exchanges such as the following show:

        (Silence)
    A: Huh?
    B: I didn't say anything.
        (EAS: FN)

16. In this respect, 'uh huh', 'mm hmm', nods, and the like are specifically alternatives to utterances such as 'huh?', 'what?', 'who?', and the like, rather than being comembers of a category such as 'back-channel communications', as in Yngve (1970) and Duncan and Fiske (1977). On the other hand, 'uh huh', etc., in being alternatives to repair initiation, are in a sense part of the organizational domain of repair.

In writing in the text of 'passing the opportunity to do a full turn at talk', I appear to be joining the consensus reported on, and joined by, Duncan and Fiske (1977:203) that 'back-channel actions, in themselves, do not constitute speaking turns'. However, I do not believe that (a) this question should be settled on conceptual or definitional grounds; (b) the various components included in the term 'back-channel' fare identically on this question; or (c) positions on the turn-status of 'uh huh' are invariant to the occasion for the issue being posed. I can here only suggest the basis for this stance. Consider the fragments in (i) through (iii).

    (i)   D: But listen tuh how long-
                  [   ]
          R: →   In other words, you gotta string up the-
                    you gotta string up the colors, is that it?
                    (KC-4, 37)

    (ii) R: Hey::, the place looks different.
          F: Yea::hh.

```
        K:          Ya have to see all ou r new-
                                  [          ]
        D:    →                         It does?
        R:          Oh yeah.
                    (KC-4,2; cf. Sacks et al.; p. 720)

(iii)   1 B:        hhh And he's going to make his own paint-
                    ings,
        2 A:        mm hmm.
        3 B:        And- or I mean his own frames.
        4 A:        yeah.
                    (SBL: 1, 1, 12-11)
```

Note first that in both (i) and (ii), talk which requests clarification (in (ii)) or repeats and solicits confirmation (in (i)),
which are two types of back-channel for Duncan and Fiske,
win out in floor fights, though, according to Duncan and Fiske,
it is a consequence of back-channels not being turns that instances like these are not even counted by them as simultaneous turns. In my view, the issue of the turn-status of
some utterance should be approached empirically, i.e. do the
parties treat it as a turn; in (i) and (ii), clarification talk is
so treated. I believe much talk of this sort is treated by
participants as having full turn status. However, other sorts
of vocalization, such as 'uh huh', are not so treated, as Duncan and Fiske note, at least with respect to simultaneous talk
and its resolution.

When the issue is a different one, however, a different position may be warranted. In (iii), for example, 'paintings' in
line 1 is an error, which is corrected at line 3 by its speaker.
This correction is undertaken after the recipient has had an
opportunity to do so, and has passed. With respect to the
organization of repair and its interactional import, it can
matter that B's self-correction follows a passed opportunity
for A to initiate repair. A silence by A in that position may
well have called attention to the presence of a repairable;
the 'mm hm', in specifically not doing so, is doing something.
'Mm hm' is more than 'not a turn'; with respect to the repair
issue, it is very much like one.

Accordingly, it seems appropriate to me that the turn-status
of 'uh huh' etc. be assessed on a case-by-case basis, by
reference to the local sequential environment, and by reference to the sequential and interactional issues which animate
that environment.

REFERENCES

Dittman, Allen T., and Lynn G. Llewellyn. 1967. The pho-
    nemic clause as a unit of speech decoding. Journal of Per-
    sonality and Social Psychology 6.341-349.

Dittman, Allen T., and Lynn G. Llewellyn. 1968. Relationship between vocalizations and head nods as listener responses. Journal of Personality and Social Psychology 9.79-84.
Duncan, Starkey, and Donald W. Fiske. 1977. Face-to-face interaction: Research, methods, and theory. Hillsdale, N.J.: Lawrence Erlbaum Associates.
Fries, Charles C. 1952. The structure of English. New York: Harcourt, Brace.
Goodwin, Charles. 1979. The interactive construction of a sentence in natural conversation. In: Everyday language: Studies in ethnomethodology. Edited by George Psathas. New York: Irvington Publishers.
Goodwin, Marjorie. 1980. Processes of mutual monitoring implicated in the production of description sequences. Sociological Inquiry 50.303-317.
Jefferson, Gail. 1978. Sequential aspects of storytelling in conversation. In: Studies in the organization of conversational interaction. Edited by Jim Schenkein. New York: Academic Press.
Jefferson, Gail. 1979. A technique for inviting laughter and its subsequent acceptance/declination. In: Everyday language: Studies in ethnomethodology. Edited by George Psathas. New York: Irvington Publishers.
Kendon, Adam. 1967. Some functions of gaze direction in social interaction. Acta Psychologica 26.22-63.
Sacks, Harvey. 1974. An analysis of the course of a joke's telling in conversation. In: Explorations in the ethnography of speaking. Edited by R. Baumann and J. Sherzer. Cambridge: Cambridge University Press.
Sacks, Harvey, and Emanuel A. Schegloff. 1979. Two preferences in the organization of reference to persons in conversation and their interaction. In: Everyday language: Studies in ethnomethodology. Edited by George Psathas. New York: Irvington Publishers.
Sacks, Harvey, Emanuel A. Schegloff, and Gail Jefferson. 1974. A simplest systematics for the organization of turn-taking for conversation. Lg. 50.696-735.
Schegloff, Emanuel A. 1968. Sequencing in conversational openings. American Anthropologist 70.1075-1095.
Schegloff, Emanuel A. 1973. Recycled turn beginnings. Public lecture at Linguistic Institute, University of Michigan, Ann Arbor. Mimeo.
Schegloff, Emanuel A. 1980. Preliminaries to preliminaries: 'Can I ask you a question'. Sociological Inquiry 50.104-152.
Schegloff, Emanuel A., Gail Jefferson, and Harvey Sacks. 1977. The preference for self-correction in the organization of repair in conversation. Lg. 53.361-382.
Yngve, Victor. 1970. On getting a word in edgewise. In: Papers from the Sixth Regional Meeting, Chicago Linguistic Society. Chicago: Chicago Linguistic Society. 567-577.

THE PLACE OF INTONATION
IN THE DESCRIPTION OF INTERACTION

Malcolm Coulthard and David Brazil
University of Birmingham, U.K.

Paralinguistic phenomena in general and intonation in particular are areas of language patterning which have received comparatively little attention from linguists, who, for differing reasons, have chosen to concentrate on segmental phonology, morphology, syntax, and lexis. Although detailed descriptions of intonation do exist and there is a fair measure of agreement about the phonetic and phonological facts, at least of British English, little work has been done on interactive significance of intonation, though the recent work of Gumperz (1977 and this volume) is an obvious and notable exception. Crystal (1969) contents himself with a very detailed description of all the phonological options without attempting to assign significance to them. Halliday (1967) asserts that all 'English intonation contrasts are grammatical' and thus restricts their significance to the language system, while Crystal (1975) argues that 'the vast majority of tones in connected speech carry no meaning', although a few do carry attitudinal options like 'absence of emotional involvement'.

Only O'Connor and Arnold set out to describe all intonation choices as interactively meaningful, asserting that a major function of intonation is to express 'the speaker's attitude to the situation in which he is placed' (1973:2). However, until there is some set of agreed and mutually exclusive attitudinal labels to match against the intonation choices, an attitudinal description must be impossible: the experiment reported by Crystal (1969:297ff.) shows the difficulties native speakers have in matching attitudinal labels with intonation contours, while the examples O'Connor and Arnold choose to present undermine their claim to have managed to do so. For example, they describe the significance of the rise-fall in relation to a number of exemplificatory sentences. In (1), B is said to be

'quietly impressed, perhaps awed', whereas in (2), B is
thought to be expressing a 'challenging' or 'censorious' attitude.

(1) A: Have you heard about Pat? B: ^Yes!
(2) A: Why don't you like it? B: I^do.

In other examples, this same tone choice is said to convey that
the speaker is 'impressed, favourably or unfavourably--by
something not entirely expected', 'complacent, self-satisfied or
smug', or 'disclaiming responsibility, shrugging aside any involvement or refusing to be embroiled'. It soon becomes evident that some, if not much, of the claimed attitudinal meaning
of the intonation contour is, in fact, being derived from the
lexico-grammatical and contextual features of the examples
themselves.

Thus, although there is no dispute that speakers can vary
independently tempo, loudness, pitch, and voice quality, and
thereby alter aspects of the meaning of their utterances, any
systematic relationship between physical changes and semantic
ones has so far remained undiscovered. Indeed, Labov and
Fanshel imply that a search for systematic relationships may
be misguided when they suggest that the lack of clarity or
discreteness in the intonational signals is not 'an unfortunate
limitation of this channel, but an essential and important aspect of it' (1977:46). The result is that, in the absence of
any satisfying theory to account systematically for the interactional meaning of intonation, those involved in the analysis
of interaction have, of necessity, taken only intermittent notice
of intonation choices, at those points where they felt they
could attach significance to them.

Perhaps the paradigm example of this approach to intonation
is the way in which Sinclair and Coulthard (1975) used the co-
occurrence of the prosodic features 'high falling intonation'
and a 'following silent stress' with now, well, OK, right, good,
to isolate those occasions when these lexical items were functioning as 'frames', markers of boundary points in the ongoing
lesson.

More generally, most analysts have felt able as native speakers to recognise, though not necessarily to describe, the intonational features that mark certain declarative clauses as questioning in function and certain words as 'stressed', while
Jefferson's (1978) transcription system, which sets out to be
'one that will look to the eye how it sounds to the ear' (p. xi),
marks also a 'continuing intonation', a 'stopping fall', and
three degrees of stress. Nevertheless, as none of the published transcriptions have an accompanying tape and only
Labov and Fanshel provide fundamental frequency traces, it
is impossible to be sure what phonological features analysts
are focusing on, how consistently they are recognising and
marking them, how much agreement there is between analysts

on what constitutes a question-marking intonation or a particular degree of stress, and how far it is only the phonological features they are responding to.

Thus, although no one else has explicitly stated it, it is evident from the use made of intonational information that all those involved in the analysis of verbal interaction would agree with Labov and Fanshel (1977:46) that it is at the moment impossible 'to provide a context-free set of interpretations of prosodic cues'.

Towards an interactionally motivated description of intonation. For the past eight years, we have been developing a description which has as its final goal an account of the interactional significance of paralinguistic cues. We do not claim, by any means, to be able to handle the way in which all paralinguistic features carry meaning (not, indeed, that they all have interactional meaning), but we do feel we have a workable description of many pitch phenomena and sound principles for setting up a description of other paralinguistic phenomena.

The first principle is that features which are acoustically on a continuum must be analysed as realisations of a small number of discrete units that 'form a closed set, defined by their mutual oppositions' (Labov and Fanshel 1977:42). The second principle is that there is no constant relationship between particular acoustic phenomena and particular analytic categories; it is contrasts and not absolute values which are important. These two principles are not, of course, novel and create no problems theoretically or practically, as analysts of tone languages discovered long ago:

...tone languages have a major characteristic in common: it is the relative height of their tonemes, not their actual pitch which is pertinent to their linguistic analysis...the important feature is the relative height of a syllable in relation to preceding and following syllables. A toneme is 'high' only if it is higher than its neighbours in the sentence, not if its frequency of vibrations is high. (Pike 1948:4)

A third principle is that there is no necessary one-to-one relationship between paralinguistic cues and interactional significances: on the one hand, as Bolinger's (1964) 'wave' and 'swell' metaphor suggests, a given pitch choice can at the very least be simultaneously carrying both general information about emotional state and a specific local meaning of the kind described in detail further on in this paper; on the other hand, certain interactionally significant signals--for instance, a request for back-channel support--may be carried by the co-occurrence of a particular pitch choice and a particular kinesic one, each of which singly has a different significance (Gosling forthcoming).

Our final principle is to see intonation as primarily concerned with adding specific interactional significance to lexico-grammatical items. Indeed, one of its major functions is to enable the speaker to refine and at times redefine the meanings and oppositions given by the language system. Thus we argue that the intonational divisions speakers make in their utterances are not grammatically motivated (though for explainable reasons intonation unit boundaries frequently coincide with major grammatical boundaries); rather they are motivated by a need to add moment-by-moment situationally specific, intonationally conveyed meanings to particular words or groups of words.

The description we are going to propose here is expressed in terms of pitch choices, though this is almost certainly a simplification. Intensity and durational features regularly co-occur with the pitch choices, and it may well turn out that the choices we describe as being realised by pitch phenomena are being identified by hearers through associated intensity and durational phenomena--we are only too aware of Lieberman's (1960) experiments on stress.

Our description sets out to account for the paradigmatic options available at any point to a speaker and for the syntagmatic structures he can build up. We have so far isolated four systems of options--tone, prominence, key, and termination--all realised by pitch phenomena and all potentially realisable in a single syllable; and we have four units of structure--syllable, segment, tone unit, and pitch sequence--of which the most important is the tone unit. The four intonation systems we have isolated all work within and attach meaning to the tone unit; divisions in utterances are, as we argued earlier in this paper, intonationally and not grammatically motivated, and we agree with Laver (1970) that the tone unit rather than the clause is 'the most likely unit of neuro-linguistic pre-assembly'.

We see the tone unit as having the following structure:

(Proclitic segment) Tonic segment (Enclitic segment)

As this structure implies, tone units may consist simply of a tonic segment, and many do; indeed, a considerable number consist of no more than a tonic syllable, i.e. the syllable on which there is a major pitch movement, as in (3).

(3) // GOOD //, // YES //, // ME //, // JOHN //

Most tone units, of course, do consist of more than the minimal tonic segment, and then the question of segmentation arises. With the syllables following the tonic there is, in fact, no analytic problem: even though the pitch movement of the tone may be continued over succeeding syllables, for

reasons which we explain later, the tonic segment is considered
to end with the tonic syllable,[1] as shown in (4).

(4) Tonic segment: Enclitic segment:
    // GOOD   ness knows //
    // YES   sir //
    // WE   did //
    // JOHN   ny's coming //

However, while the final boundary of the tonic segment is
obviously unproblematic, recognising where the tonic segment
begins is a more difficult matter and depends on an understanding of the concept of prominent syllable.

It is not always easy, in the literature of phonology, to be
sure what significance is attached to such terms as 'stress',
'accent', 'salience', and 'prominence'. We hope we are not
gratuitously adding to the confusion by redefining two of these
terms, accent and prominence, to fit the conceptual framework
of our own description. By 'accent' we mean the attribute
which invariably distinguishes the marked from the unmarked
syllables in words like *'curtain, con'tain, re 'la tion*, and distinguishes the lexical items from the others in a sentence like
'Tom is the 'best 'boy in the 'class. The expression 'word
accent', although tautologous from our point of view, may
serve usefully as a reminder that accent is an inherent
property of the word, which, being inherent, has no possible
contrastive significance. When we say *Tom is the best boy in
the class* we are not 'accenting' *is*; we are making it pitch
'prominent'.[2] 'Prominence' is thus a property associated with
a word by virtue of its function as a constituent of a tone-
unit.

We are now in a position to define the scope of the tonic
segment. The presentation is simplified if we begin with some
examples in which prominence and word accent do cooccur.
(Prominent syllables are capitalised; the tonic ones are also
underlined.)

(5) // he was GOing to GO //
    // that's a VERy TALL STORy //
    // it was a WEDnesday //

The tonic segment begins with the first prominent syllable,
henceforth called the 'onset', and ends with the last prominent
syllable, the 'tonic'; in fact, these can be and often are one
and the same syllable. There are thus, by definition, no
prominent syllables in the proclitic and enclitic segments, as
shown in (6). If we expand the first example in (6) to (6a),
we can see that we now have four classes of syllable: unaccented, *he, was, -ing, to, a-*; accented, *-gain*; prominent,
GO; and tonic, *GO*; it is interesting to speculate how far these

are, in fact, the four degrees of stress which Trager and Smith (1951) proposed.

(6)
Proclitic segment	Tonic segment	Enclitic segment
he was	GOing to GO	
that's a	VERy TALL STOR	y
it was a	WED	nesday

(6a) // he was GOing to GO again //

Prominence, then, is a linguistic choice available to the speaker independent of the grammatical structure of his utterance and the accents of the constituent words' citation forms; what then // IS its significance //? Consider the question/ response pair in (7).

(7) Q: What card did you play?
    R: // the QUEEN of HEARTS //

It is easy to see that in the response the word *of* is the only word that could occupy the place between *queen* and *hearts*. If we think of each word as representing a selection from a set of words available at successive places, then at the place filled by *of* there is a set of one. In this respect it can be compared with the places filled by *queen* and *hearts*. If we leave aside for the moment the slightly less straightforward case of *the*, we can show the total range of possibilities as in (8).

(8)
	ace		
	two		hearts
(the)	.	of	clubs
	.		diamonds
	queen		spades
	king		

The speaker has a limited choice of 13 possibilities at the first place and of four at the second, but this time the limitation has nothing to do with the working of the language system: there is no linguistic reason why the response should not have been *the prince of forks* or the *17 of rubies*, or any of an enormous number of combinations. What imposes the limitation is an extralinguistic factor, the conventional composition of the pack of playing cards.

We use the term 'existential paradigm' for that set of possibilities that a speaker can regard as actually available in a given situation. This enables us to distinguish it from the 'general paradigm' which is inherent in the language system. It is clear that at the place occupied by *of*, the two paradigms coincide: there can be no possibility of selection in the existential paradigm because there is none in the general paradigm. We now want to argue that items are marked as prominent to indicate that the speaker is selecting from a range of oppositions in the existential paradigm. Thus we can invent a context in which *of* can be situationally selective --a correction of a foreigner's *the queen in hearts* would certainly be as shown in (9), and also a context in which *queen* and *hearts* would not be selective and therefore nonprominent, as in (10) and (11).

(9) // the queen OF hearts //

(10) Q: What heart did you play?
     R: // the QUEEN of hearts //

(11) Q: Which queen did you play?
     R: // the queen of HEARTS //

In each of these examples the questioner sets up a context which effectively removes the possibility of choice for one of the items by indicating that he knows either the suit or the denomination of the card. Thus the answerer's use of *hearts* in (10) and *queen* in (11) is not the outcome of his making any kind of selection, a fact which would probably result, in many circumstances, in their being omitted altogether.

(12) Q: What heart did you play?
     R: // the QUEEN //

(13) Q: What queen did you play?
     R: // HEARTS //

Here again the existential paradigm is reduced to a set of one by something additional to the language system. It is because shared understanding with respect to one of the variables has already been acknowledged in the conversation that no selection is involved. One may think, in this particular case, of the wide range of options that comprise the general paradigm at each of the two places being reduced by shared card-playing conventions and then further reduced by shared experience of the immediate conversational environment of the response.

The examples we have used so far suggest that the non-prominent/prominent distinction is very similar to the textually given/textually new distinction, but this is misleading; rather we are concerned with the interactionally given. All interaction proceeds, and can only proceed, on the basis of the existence of a great deal of common ground between the participants: that is, what knowledge speakers (think they) share about the world, about each other's experience, attitudes, and emotions. Common ground is not restricted to shared experience of a particular linguistic interaction up to the moment of utterance; rather it is a product of the interpenetrating biographies of the participants, of which common involvement in a particular ongoing interaction constitutes only a part.

Thus one can create a situation in which items are contextually given, as in a game of cards when one person has, without saying anything, put down the jack of hearts and a next player verbalises, as in (14).

(14) // QUEEN of hearts //

Or one can create a situation in which items are available from past experience, as in (15), when the addressee is known to only drink coffee and the question is 'cup or mug'.

(15) // CUP of coffee //

It is perhaps more useful to see the situation not as one in which a certain configuration of contextual features results in the speaker choosing a particular prominence treatment for his utterance, but rather as one in which his intonation choices project a certain context of interaction. Thus in (15) it is assumed and marked as assumed that *coffee* is not in doubt.

Key. In addition to making choices in the prominence system, a speaker must also, for each tone unit, select relative pitch or 'key' from a three-term system: high, mid, and low. However, unlike Sweet (1906), we do not see mid key as the norm for the speaker; rather we see key choices as made and recognised with reference to the key of the immediately preceding tone unit. In other words, there are no absolute values for high, mid, and low key, even for a particular speaker; in fact, a given high key tone unit may well be lower than an earlier mid key one. As we noted earlier, the continually varying reference point is already well attested in analyses of tone languages.

The key choice is realised on the first prominent syllable of the tonic segment and adds a meaning that can be glossed at the most general level as:

High key   contrastive
Mid key   additive
Low key   equative

The way in which these intonational meanings combine with lexico-grammatical ones is discussed in detail in Brazil et al. (1980) but can be simply illustrated in the invented examples in (16), where only key[3] is varied. In example (16), we see key being used to indicate particular relationships between successive tone units in a single utterance, but the same relationships can occur between successive utterances. If we begin with the polar options 'yes' and 'no', we quickly realise that

only when they cooccur with high key are they in opposition.
In other words, when wishing to convey 'yes not no' or 'no
not yes', a speaker must select high key.

(16) he GAMbled // and $\overline{\underline{LOST}}$

Contrastive (contrary to expectations; i.e. there is an
interaction-bound opposition between the two)

he GAMbled // and LOST

Additive (he did both)

he GAMbled // and $_{LOST}$

Equative (as you would expect; i.e. there is an
interaction-bound equivalence between them)

(17a) well you $^{WON'T\ be}$ HOME // $\Big\{$ (i) $\overline{YES}$ // I $\underline{WILL}$ //

before SEVen (ii) $\overline{NO}$ // I WON'T //

In (i),[4] the speaker chooses contrastive high key to mark the
choice of opposite polarity in his response; in (ii), the speaker
chooses to highlight an agreed polarity, and this apparently
unnecessary action is usually interpreted as emphatic, and
then in a particular context as 'surprised', 'delighted', 'an-
noyed', and so on. Much more usual than (ii) is (iii) in (17b).

(17b) well you $^{WON'T\ be}$ HOME //$\Big\{$ (iii) NO //p I WON'T //

before SEVEN *(iv) YES // p I WILL//

Item (iv) in (17b) sounds odd because the speaker is heard as
simultaneously agreeing and contradicting, or perhaps rather
agreeing with something that has not been said; the normal
interpretation would be that he had misheard. The contradiction is, in fact, only made evident by the repeated auxiliary,
which carries the polarity, because interestingly, 'yes' is the
unmarked term of the pair and as a result, if the speaker does
not repeat the auxiliary he can choose either 'yes' or 'no', an
option which at times causes confusion even for native speakers, as in (17c).

(17c) well you $^{WON'T\ be}$ HOME // $\Big\{$ (v) NO// (I agree I
                                                      won't)
before SEVen// (vi) YES// (I agree with
                                             your assess-
                                             ment)

When the polarity is positive, however, there is only one choice, as in (17d).

(17d) well you'll be $\underline{HOME}$ //

     before $\underline{SEV}$en //

     (vii) $\underline{YES}$// (I agree I will/I agree with your assessment)

     *(viii) $\underline{NO}$// (I agree I won't)

Instead of the mid key 'yes' and 'no' items in (17b,c,d), a mid key 'right' could equally well have been chosen to express agreement; with high key, however, the speaker is using the item to assert 'right not wrong', and this is the use we see in the example from Labov and Fanshel (1977:147).

(18) Rhoda: then nobody else knows an' everybody
                thinks everything is fine, and good
     Therapist: mhm
     Rhoda: and I end up--hurting myself
     Therapist: // $\underline{RIGHT}$ //

In (18) and Figure 1, the therapist is seen using high key to mark 'right' as evaluative, and thus to let Rhoda know that she is 'restating one of the most important lessons she had learned in treatment' (p. 148).

Figure 1. (Labov and Fanshel 1977.)

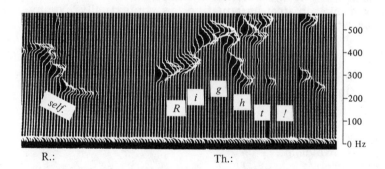

R.:   Th.:

Garfinkel (1967) emphasized that it is impossible for speakers to 'say in so many words' what they actually mean. Use of high key is one major way in which speakers make appeal to and use of information which they assume their listener(s) to have. The following 'misreading' from a BBC newscast is amusing because of the contrast which listeners were forced to derive from the utterance to make sense of it.

(19) and tomorrow Mrs. Thatcher will make
     // a con$\underline{SID}$ered statement // on immi$\underline{GRA}$tion //

The previous day, Mrs. Thatcher had made a speech including comments on immigration and the newscast was supposed to be saying that in addition to other things she was going to do, Mrs. Thatcher would make a statement on immigration that would be 'considered', i.e. reasonable and well presented.

(19a) // a conSIDered STATEment on immiGRAtion //

The high key choice in (19) for 'considered' marked this statement as contrastive and the obvious contrast was with the previous day's statement, which must therefore be seen as not 'considered' or even as 'ill-considered'.

Our examples of high key contrastivity have so far implied that the contrast is a binary one between polar opposites, but this is not necessarily so. In example (20), 'wife' could in some contexts be heard as in contrast with the only other possibility, 'daughter', and therefore as a flattering introduction (i.e. doesn't she look young?).

(20) //^{MEET} el_{IZabeth} // johns <u>WIFE</u> //

But given the right context, 'wife' could be heard as in contrast to a whole series of other relations one might, in the context, have assumed Elizabeth to be: his secretary, sister, sister-in-law, friend, mistress... Thus high key marks for the listener that an item is to be heard as in contrast but leaves him to fill out the existential paradigm.

Low key marks an item as equative, as contextually synonymous; thus when the option is co-selected with 'yes' or a repetition, the utterance does little more than acknowledge receipt of the information, as in (21) and (22).

(21) D: Whereabouts in your chest?
    P: On the heart side.
    D: // <u>YES</u> //

(22) A: What's the time?
    B: Ten o'clock.
    A: //Ten o'<u>CLOCK</u> //

If a speaker reformulates in low key, he is indicating that he does not feel he is adding any new information, but is simply verbalising an agreement that the two versions are situationally equivalent in meaning.

(23) A: What's the time?
    B: Ten o'clock.
    A: //<u>BEDtime</u> //

(24) HE'S <u>DEAD</u> // and _{BURied} //

The choice of mid key marks the matter of the tone unit as additionally informing, and thus (24a) is slightly odd.

(24a) //HE'S <u>DEAD</u> // and <u>BUR</u>ied //

So is (25), from a newscast reporting how a Palestinian terrorist organisation had tried to invade Israel by balloon, but had met disaster when the balloon

(25) //<u>CRASHED</u> // and <u>BURNED</u> //.

This listener, at least, expected a low key for 'burned', indicating 'as you would have expected'.

Pitch concord. It has long been accepted that some polar questions seem to expect or even predict a particular answer like (26i), while others like (26ii) appear to allow for either.

(26i) You'll come, won't you?
(26ii) Will you come?

We want to suggest that, in fact, all utterances set up expectations at a very general level about what will follow. In order to demonstrate this, we need to discuss 'termination', a second three-term pitch choice made this time at the tonic syllable. When we look at transcribed texts, we discover a remarkable tendency for concord between the 'termination' choice of the final tone unit of one utterance and the 'initial key' choice of the next; in other words, it appears that with his termination choice a speaker predicts or asks for a particular key choice and therefore, by implication, a particular meaning from the next speaker. This is easiest to exemplify with questions. In example (26i), the speaker is looking for agreement, i.e. a mid key 'yes', and his utterance is likely, therefore, to end with mid termination, as in (26a), to constrain the required response (remember that key and termination can be realised in the same syllable).

(26a) A: // you'll <u>COME</u> // <u>WON'T</u> you //
    B: <u>YES</u> // (I agree I <u>will</u>)

Choice of high termination for 'won't you' needs some ingenuity to contextualize; the conflict between the lexico-grammatical markers of a search for agreement and the intonational indication that there is a 'yes/no' choice makes it sound like either a threat or a plea.

(26b) // you'll COME // $\overline{\underline{\text{WON'T}}}$ you //

Example (26ii), by contrast, naturally takes a high termination, looking for a 'yes/no' contrastive answer, as in (26c), although the persuasiveness of (26d) can be explained simply as the intonation choice converting an apparently open request into one looking for agreement.

(26c) A: // Will you $\underline{\text{COME}}$ // B: $\dfrac{\text{YES}}{\text{NO}}$ // //

(26d) A: //$^{\text{WILL you}}$ COME // B: YES //

We can see this pitch concord working in examples (27) and (28), both from the same doctor/patient interview.

(27) D: // its $\underline{\text{DRY}}$ skin // $\underline{\text{IS}}$n't it// P: $\underline{\text{MM}}$//

(28) D: VERy $\underline{\text{IR}}$ritating you say // P: $\underline{\text{VER}}$y irritating//

The initial key choices in the answers have the meanings we have already discussed, and in both we can see the first speaker asking for or constraining a response of a particular kind by his final termination choice. Thus, in (27), the doctor ends with mid termination because he wants the patient to agree with his observation, while in (28), he wants the patient to exploit the contrastive 'yes not no' meaning of high key to confirm what he has said. Had the doctor stopped at 'skin', in example (27), his question would have had a very different force, and he would again have been heard as asking for confirmation of a fact in doubt; but both the key and the lexical realisation of the rest of the utterance show that what is required is agreement with a presumed shared opinion.

The pressure towards pitch concord can, of course, be disregarded; the patient could have responded to the doctor's mid key 'isn't it' with a high key 'yes' or 'mm', but telling the doctor he was right would, in these circumstances, sound like noncompliant behaviour, suggesting perhaps annoyance at an unnecessary question. In example (29), the patient solves his dilemma by selecting the predicted agreeing mid key but lexicalising the correctness just to be sure.

(29) D: // $\underline{\text{FIVE tiller}}$ ROAD// $\underline{\text{IS}}$n't it//
P: // THAT'S cor$\underline{\text{RECT}}$// $\overline{\text{YES}}$ //

All the examples we have discussed so far have been of pitch concord between questions and answers, but this phenomenon of pitch concord now enables us to explain a paradox in classroom discourse. On the one hand, the third, follow-up item in an exchange is, as defined by Sinclair and Coulthard (1975), optional; on the other, it is so important that 'if it does not occur we feel confident in saying that the teacher has deliberately withheld it for some strategic purpose' (1975:51). One explanation of the paradox lies in the peculiar nature of much classroom questioning--the teacher is not seeking infor- mation in the accepted sense, as he already knows the answer, whereas it is essential for the pupils to know whether their answer is the one the teacher was looking for; hence there is a situational necessity for the follow-up. There is, however, a more satisfactory explanation. When we look at examples like (30), we discover that very often the pupils are in a very real sense requesting a high key, evaluative follow-up by end- ing their response with high termination. Only when they are confident do they end with mid termination requesting the teacher's agreement with what they have said.

(30) T: //^{WHY} would you want to be STRONG//

    P: // to MAKE MUSCLES//

    T: // to MAKE MUSCLES// YES //

While high and mid termination place concord constraints on what follows, low termination does not; it marks, in fact, the point at which prospective constraints stop and thus occurs frequently at the boundaries of exchanges, as in (31a,b).

(31a) D: Where abouts in your chest?
     P: On the heart side
     D: // YES//

(31b) D: And how long have you had those for?
     P: Well I had them a--week last Wednesday.
     D: // a WEEK last WEDnesday//

It is not unusual in certain types of interaction for an answer to end with low termination. Example (32) is unremarkable.

(32) A: // have you GOT the TIME//
    B: // its THREE o' CLOCK//

In choosing low termination, the second speaker does not pre- clude the first from making a follow-up move but he certainly does not constrain him to do so as he could have done by choice of high termination. If the first speaker chooses to continue in the same exchange and produce a follow-up, one option is a low key 'thanks', which one might expect if the ex- change occurred between strangers in the street in Britain, in which case the item would serve simultaneously to acknowledge

receipt of the information and to terminate the encounter.
(In the United States, one would expect a mid or even high
termination 'thanks', allowing for or constraining, respectively,
the 'you're welcome', 'sure', 'OK' which invariably follows.)
If the exchange had occurred during a longish interaction,
the acknowledging function could equally well have been realised by an 'mm', a repetition, or an equative reformulation.

(32a) // $_{mm}$ //
     // THREE o'CLOCK //
     // TIME to GO //

Form and function. We can now use these observations on
the significance of pitch concord to explain one of the major
problems in discourse analysis: why some items which are
declarative or moodless in form are taken to be questioning in
function. Following example (32), we discussed the possibilities for the follow-up; options we did not discuss were those
in which the speaker ends in mid or high termination, rather
than low. The exchange could have ended as in (32b), and
the message would have been 'I take "three o'clock" as equivalent in meaning in this context to "time to go" (indicated by
choice of low key), and I assume you will agree' (mid termination predicting mid key 'yes I agree').

(32b) A: Have you got the time?
     B: It's three o'clock.
     A: // TIME to GO //

Another alternative would be (32c), and this time the speaker
is heard as both adding the information that he considers
'three o'clock' to be 'time to go' and asking for positive confirmation in the form of a 'yes/no' response.

(32c) // TIME to GO //

We can see the difference that termination choice makes in
these two extracts from a doctor/patient interview: in (33),
the repetition with low termination is heard as exchange final;
in (34), the repeated item with high termination is heard as
eliciting.

(33) D: How long have you had these for?
     P: Well I had them a week last Wednesday
     D: // a WEEK last WEDnesday // /
     D: // HOW many atTACKS have you HAD //

(34) D: What were you doing at the time?
P: Coming home in the car. I felt a tight pain in
the middle of the chest.
D: //$\overline{\text{TIGHT}}$ pain//
P: //^{YOU} $\underline{\text{KNOW}}$ // like a - // DULL $_{\underline{\text{ACHE}}}$ //

There are two significant points about these observations:
first, although the items with mid or high termination are
initiating and in some sense questioning, the pitch movement
on the tonic is falling--not rising, as is often claimed in the
intonation manuals; in other words, it is definitely termination
and not tone choice which carries the eliciting function;
second, we are now able to identify the function of these items
through the phonological criteria which realise them and do not
need to draw on assumptions about speaker's and hearer's
knowledge or A-events and B-events, as suggested by Labov
(1972).

As philosophers have frequently pointed out, the two major
assumptions underlying orders are that the speaker has the
right to tell the listener to do X and that the listener is, in
the most general sense, willing or agreeable to doing X. From
what has been said here about termination choices, key concord, and the meanings of choices in the key system, one
would expect orders to end with a mid termination choice,
looking for a mid key agreeing //YES//, //$\underline{\text{SUREly}}$//, //$\underline{\text{CER}}$-
tainly//. It is thus quite fascinating to discover that most
classroom instructions, even those in a series and to the
whole class, when no acknowledgment is possible or expected,
also end with mid termination, symbolically predicting the absent agreement.

(35) FOLD your $_{\underline{\text{ARMS}}}$ // LOOK at the $_{\text{WINdow}}$ // LOOK
at the $_{\text{CEILing}}$ //

LOOK at the $_{\underline{\text{FLOOR}}}$ // LOOK at the $_{\underline{\text{DOOR}}}$//

It is also instructive, if not worrying, to realise that when
parents and teachers get cross because their instructions are
being ignored, they typically switch to high termination which
paradoxically allows for the high key contrastive refusal.

(36) P: // PUT it $\underline{\text{DOWN}}$ // C: // $\underline{\text{NO}}$ //

The pitch sequence. There have been several unsuccessful
attempts to isolate a phonological unit above the tone unit and
defined as a sequence of particular tones; it is possible, however, to see tone units linked together by pitch phenomena.

We noted earlier that the particular significance of low termination is that it does not place any constraints on a succeeding utterance, and we find it useful to regard all the tone
units occurring between two successive low terminations as a
phonological unit which we have called the 'pitch sequence'.
Pitch sequences are often closely associated with topic--
speakers appear to use a drop to low termination to signal
their apprehension that a particular mini-topic is ended. The
next pitch sequence may begin in mid key, in which case the
key choice indicates that what follows is additively related, or
topically linked, with what has just ended. In (37), the
doctor ends one part of the examination and begins another
linked one.

(37) D: //It's <u>DRY</u> skin// <u>IS</u>n't it //
      P: // MM //
      D: // <u>SCAL</u>y // LET'S have a _{<u>LOOK</u>} /// OPen your
           mouth <u>WIDE</u> //

On other occasions, the next pitch sequence begins in high
key and the contrastive meaning serves to mark the beginning
of a completely new topic. In fact, if we now generalise, we
discover that the frames which Sinclair and Coulthard isolated
on item-specific intonation criteria are actually high key, pitch
sequence initial items following low termination, pitch sequence
final ones.

(38) T: So we get energy from petrol and we get--energy
           from food
           // TWO kinds of _{<u>ENergy</u>} /// <u>NOW</u> then // ...

Indeed, once one recognises them, the pitch phenomena appear
to be much more important than the lexical items in marking
boundaries; a reexamination of some of the classroom data
shows that at certain points, where on topical grounds one
felt a need for a boundary but had accepted that as no frame
occurred the teacher had not marked and probably had not intended one, there are pitch marked boundaries.

(39) T: Good girl, energy, yes, you can have a team
           point; that's a very good word
           // we <u>USE</u> // we're <u>USing</u>// <u>ENergy</u> // we're
           <u>USing</u>// //_{<u>ENergy</u>} /// when a <u>CAR</u>// GOES
           into the _{<u>GARage</u>} //...

In other words, the low termination/high key, pitch sequence
boundary, here occurring between 'energy', and 'when a car',
appears to carry the transaction boundary signal.

In these few pages we have tried to present principles for describing paralinguistic phenomena, and an analysis of how certain pitch phenomena mean. We hope to have convinced you of the validity of both.

// but <u>NOW</u> // for <u>US</u> // the REST is _{SIlence} /// <u>THANK</u> you //

NOTES

1. Apart from its function in determining tonic segment boundaries, the significance of tonic pitch movement is not discussed further in this paper as there are marked differences here between British and American English.
2. A full discussion of the fundamental frequency characteristics of prominent syllables can be found in Brazil (1978), and a briefer but more accessible discussion in Brazil, Coulthard, and Johns (1980).
3. In all subsequent examples, // marks the mid line; items that are high or low key are printed above or below this notational line.
4. All examples are assumed to have a falling tone.

REFERENCES

Bolinger, D. 1964. Around the edge of language: Intonation. Harvard Educational Review 34.282-293.

Brazil, D. C. 1978. An investigation of discourse intonation. Final report to SSRC on research project HR 3316/1.

Brazil, D. C., R. M. Coulthard, and C. M. Johns. 1980. Discourse intonation and language teaching. London: Longman.

Crystal, D. 1969. Prosodic systems and intonation in English. London: Cambridge University Press.

Crystal, D. 1975. The English tone of voice. London: Edward Arnold.

Garfinkel, H. 1967. Studies in ethnomethodology. Englewood Cliffs, N.J.: Prentice-Hall.

Gosling, J. (forthcoming) Kinesics in discourse. University of Birmingham: English Language Research.

Gumperz, J. 1977. Sociocultural knowledge in conversational inference. In: Georgetown University Round Table on Languages and Linguistics 1977. Edited by Muriel Saville-Troike. Washington, D.C.: Georgetown University Press.

Halliday, M. A. K. 1967. Intonation and grammar in British English. The Hague: Mouton.

Jefferson, G. 1978. Transcript notation. In: Studies in the organisation of conversational interaction. Edited by J. Schenkein. New York: Academic Press. xi-xvi.

Labov, W. 1972. Rules for ritual insults. In: Studies in
social interaction. Edited by D. Sudnow. New York: Free
Press. 120-169.
Labov, W., and D. Fanshel. 1977. Therapeutic discourse.
New York: Academic Press.
Laver, J. 1970. The production of speech. In: New hori-
zons in linguistics. Edited by J. Lyons. Harmondsworth,
England: Penguin.
Lieberman, P. 1960. Some acoustic correlates of word stress
in American English. Journal of the Acoustical Society of
America 32. 451-454.
O'Connor, J. D., and G. F. Arnold. 1973. Intonation of
colloquial English. 2nd edition. London: Longman.
Pike, K. L. 1948. Tone languages. Ann Arbor: University
of Michigan Press.
Sinclair, J. McH., and R. M. Coulthard. 1975. Towards an
analysis of discourse. London: Oxford University Press.
Sweet, H. 1906. A primer of phonetics. Oxford: Clarendon
Press.

TOPIC AS THE UNIT OF ANALYSIS
IN A CRIMINAL LAW CASE

Roger W. Shuy
Georgetown University and
Center for Applied Linguistics

Whenever a research project involves a large amount of data, an obvious problem develops: 'How can we get a handle on the data in order to find its salient aspects?' Vygotsky (1962) warned that the most critical aspect of data analysis is finding the appropriate unit of measurement. For years, language research has suffered from the existence of its analytical routines. Because of the development of mean length of utterance, T-units, word frequency, and other commonly used measures of language, such routines were applied to masses of data, whether they needed it or not. We also often misused the more traditional analytical approaches of our field. But, if the body of data under investigation consists of a half-hour of tape-recorded conversation between suspected criminals, and if the purpose of the analysis is to help determine whether or not criminal activity has taken place, even a traditional phonological analysis may not be the best approach to take. If we follow Vygotsky's advice to find the appropriate unit of analysis, we need to begin with the reason for the analysis rather than the inventory of known analytical routines. We ask ourselves, under such circumstances, 'What is the best unit of analysis I can find in order to address the problem I am attempting to solve?'

In this paper I describe how topic analysis was selected as a crucial unit of analysis for the evidence presented by the defense in the case of the State vs. Arthur Jones in the Fall of 1979.[1] But first it is necessary to describe this case briefly.

The State vs. Jones case. Arthur Jones is a wealthy businessman whose life has been plagued with court litigation.

Jones married a woman named Gwendolyn, with whom he lived for several years before they began to have marital difficulties. During the ensuing divorce proceedings, which were bitter and extended, a man who had worked for the Jones-owned business went to the FBI with the story that Jones had asked him to find someone to murder Gwendolyn along with the judge in their divorce trial. This employee, Roy Foster, a salesman, was told that he should engage in some linguistic fieldwork. The FBI attached a Nagra tape recorder to his body and told him to surreptitiously record Jones on tape actually soliciting these murders. The resulting tape, of course, could then be used as evidence against Jones.

Roy Foster then arranged a meeting with Arthur Jones in the city parking lot. Foster attempted his linguistic fieldwork with the goal of eliciting from Jones the agreement to solicit these murders. The conversation lasted about 20 minutes. Two days later, a second meeting between Foster and Jones was also arranged. This 10-minute conversation was also recorded with the surreptitious body tape recorder, but with a new twist. The FBI also video taped this event from a camera hidden in a van in the same parking lot.

The District Attorney was satisfied, from these tape recordings, that Jones had actually solicited the murder of his wife and the judge. An indictment was made and Jones stood trial in a local state court in the following autumn. The trial ended in a hung jury (8 against and 4 in favor) and a re-trial was scheduled for the following winter.

Topic analysis. Elsewhere (Shuy 1981) I have described the agonies one goes through when confronted with an opportunity to participate in a court case. After listening to the tapes and reading the state's transcripts, I finally hit on a way to address the language issues involved. The basic linguistic questions were clear: exactly what did Jones agree to do? What were his intentions? What were Foster's intentions? In order to address these questions it was clearly necessary to see them in relationship to the specific conversational topics in which they occurred.

In such analysis of topic, I followed the general outlines of topic-comment analysis as described by Chafe (1972) and Kates (1980). That is, the structure is not defined by the grammatical relations of the terms, nor by the semantic structure. Kates observes (1980):

> In general, something is treated as a topic, whether it is linguistically expressed or not, when it is taken as an intentional object or structure (invariant) of some type. A comment refers to some way in which that object can or should or will or does, etc., appear or manifest itself.

By mapping the topics of an interaction, therefore, one can obtain a macro picture of one aspect of the structure of the conversation which highlights the cognitive thrust of its direction.

Such a mapping is particularly important for the purposes of a court case such as State vs. Jones for two reasons. For analysis purposes, it divides the conversation into meaningful units of analysis in which propositions can be seen in direct relationship to their responses, as we shall see. For the presentation to the jury, topic analysis provides a clear guide to the conversation at a macro level, to enable the untrained laymen of the jury to see holistically and not be bogged down with memory lapses or details. Furthermore, as Greenfield (1980) has observed, '...if we can establish directedness and termination in the presence of the goal, we have established a particular intention'. The very existence of the topics establishes this kind of directness, and clear evidence of resolution establishes termination. A criminal court case is little more than the establishment of intentions and the evidence of having carried them out. The issue in the Jones case, it became clear, was one of determining what was intended and what was accomplished. Intentionality is a slippery thing, verifiable perhaps only in the mind of the person who intends. Traditional court procedure is to ask defendants to tell what their intentions were, but this is, at best, self-report data in which it is not reasonable to expect anything but bias. When the actual conversation is recorded, however, there is more to work with. My question became, 'How can the structure of taped conversation help the jury infer the intentions of the speakers?'

Although my topic analysis of the Jones tapes was begun initially to serve my own needs in determining the content of the conversation, it soon became apparent that this same topic mapping, if displayed properly, could prove equally beneficial to the jury's understanding of what was actually going on.

Identifying topics. One question remained to be solved: how could I know for sure when one topic ended and another began? Several methods suggested themselves. First, there is the clear and uncontestable change of subject focus. The two separate conversations presented as evidence in this case included talk about many things, including:

Doing Gwendolyn and the judge
Fred
Arrangements for future meetings
Some unidentified objects in their possession
The trunk of the car
Jones' sunglasses
A local activist group
The original plan

    Favors of friends
    Their health
    Jones' divorce
    A car part that was broken

These topics were clearly separable from each other on the
basis of logic and content. The responses of the other
speaker, the one who did not introduce these topics, however,
were not as easy to categorize. I chose to use the term,
topic 'response', to characterize the speech (or absence of
speech) once one of the foregoing topics was introduced. The
more commonly used term, 'comment' (Kates 1980; Keenan and
Schieffelin 1976) was not as descriptive for two reasons.
First, 'comment' did not effectively differentiate 'response'
from 'resolution', a distinction which has tremendous significance in this case. That is, not every response was a resolution, and it is in the matter of resolution of topic that a court
case rests. Second, the term 'comment' is not as forceful,
familiar, or clear to a jury as is 'response'.
    In addition to a content definition of topic, there are also
structural evidences for topic introduction or change. These
include intonation changes (Sacks, Schegloff, and Jefferson
1974), pauses, and either individualized or general topic-
marking devices at the onset of a speaker change (Keenan
and Schieffelin 1976), such as:

    Hey, I got something here. + new topic.
    Uh... + new topic.
    Hold it. Wait a second. + new topic.
    Now. + new topic.
    Just one problem. + new topic.
    Well, + new topic.
    Uh, What else? + new topic.

This combination of internal cohesion of the subject matter
and prosodic and topic-marker phrases enabled me to be
reasonably certain of the topic units of these conversations.

    Topics in the State vs. Jones case. At this point it would
be well to show what the topics of the conversations looked
like when displayed to the jury in the form of a chart. In
the first 20-minute tape there were 22 topics, as Figure 1
indicates.
    By displaying these topics by speaker, we can gain insights
into which speaker was dominant in topic introduction and
which speaker recycled which topics. Color was used on the
chart presented to the jury (through expert witness testimony)
to enable them to visualize the differences between the topic
types (transitions, proposals, Fred, and details) and to mark
the topic recycling. In addition, key words from the actual
transcript were also written underneath the topic boxes to

Figure 1. Topic introduction and recycling, Jones case, first tape.

	1	2	3	4	5	6	7	8	9	10	11	12	13	14	15	16	17	18	19	20	21	22
Jones									P							Tr			D	Tr	D	P
Foster	Tr	P		Tr		Tr	F	Tr	P	F	P	Tr	P	Tr	F		P	Tr		Tr	D	

Tr = Transitions (in brown)
P = Proposal (in red)
F = Fred (in green)
D = Details (in blue)

Figure 2. Topic introduction and recycling, Jones case, first tape, topics 8-12.

Topics	8	9	10	11	12
Jones		Prop			
Foster	Prop		Fred	Prop	Tr

Original plan

Price on Gwendolyn / Talk to shooter (8)   Alibi (10)   Do her first? (11)   Divorce (12)

118 / Roger W. Shuy

remind the jurors of that portion of the conversations which they had actually heard on the tape. Figure 2 provides a close-up picture of a portion of that chart (topics 8-12) for illustrative purposes.

In the 10-minute April 20 tape, there were 13 topics, as Figure 3 indicates.

The second conversation. These charts, as I have indicated, were actually used as part of my expert witness testimony in this case. The defense attorney asked me questions about the significance of the charts. Perhaps the best way to illustrate this procedure is to quote directly from the proceedings of my direct examination by the defense attorney during the trial.

> Attorney: Let me ask you this, Dr. Shuy: What--
> generally, what is the purpose of a linguist in the
> analysis of breaking down the tape recording of a con-
> versation and the topics?
> Shuy: One major purpose is to show the balance of
> the introduction to topics, or the imbalance in this case,
> of the introduction of topics. In normal conversation you
> have a balance of topics introduced. Speakers are obliged
> in conversation to introduce approximately equal numbers
> of topics. One way to determine the nature of conver-
> sation, the structure of conversation, is to determine not
> only who introduced what topics, but what the equilibrium
> is--what is the balance of topics introduced by each
> speaker.
> Attorney: And is there a balance of introduction of
> topics in this tape?
> Shuy: No, it's not balanced.

Then after questioning me about what topic recycling meant, the attorney asked:

> Attorney: Is there any observation you can make as
> an expert in linguistics to the imbalance of the number
> of topics that were introduced by Mr. Foster (18) as
> opposed to the four that were introduced by Mr. Jones?
> Shuy: Yes. One of the characteristics of a conver-
> sation is that once a topic is introduced in a conversa-
> tion, it does not tend to be reintroduced or recycled
> over and over again if it is resolved...one doesn't keep
> bringing up the same topic over and over again if the
> listener does not respond to it.

This line of questioning went on for about one court day, during which time I branched out from the macro picture which was set by the topic introduction charts to the various segments of each topic which were germane to the case. I

Figure 3. Topic introduction and recycling, Jones case, second tape.

	1	2	3	4	5	6	7	8	9	10	11	12	13
Jones	[Tr] Greeting			[Obj.] What do with these?			[Tr] Forgot sunglasses			[Det.] Money		[Det.] Wait three days	[Tr] Leave-taking
Foster		[Obj.] Walk around car	[Now What] Couldn't change plans		[Now What] Got to go	[Trunk] Going to trunk?		[Trunk] Walk around car	[Now What] Operate tonight		[Fred] Tell Fred		

[Tr] = Transitions (in brown)
[Obj.] = Objects (in orange)
[Now What] = Now what? (in red)

[Trunk] = Trunk (in purple)
[Det.] = Details (in blue)
[Fred] = Fred (in green)

pointed out that a pattern could be seen by noting who introduced which topics, as in Figure 4.

Figure 4.   Summary of topic types by speaker,
             Jones case, first tape.

	Foster	Jones
Transition	8	1
Proposal	6	2
Fred	3	0
Details	1	1
	18	4

This simple breakdown for the jury made it clear that Jones
was not in control of this conversation and that Foster was
dominant. The defense position, of course, was that if Jones
was the instigator of a plot to kill his wife and judge, isn't it
odd that he never brought up the subject?

Transition topics. From the transition topic control of Foster
it also is clear that he, not Jones, took responsibility for providing the conversational glue, the transitional, less substantive topics which provided spacing for his recycling the proposal topics which were his conversational agenda. One initiates conversational transition to facilitate progress on a larger
agenda by offering small breaks from it or to uphold the social
obligations of conversation. The first way is more cognitive
and planned; the second is more social and spontaneous. The
single transition topic which Jones introduced in the first conversation came in the last third of the conversation, likely out
of a realization that he had not been holding up his end of the
conversation. Foster's transition topics, however, were more
planfully timed to move his agenda along. Jones had responded
to his substantive proposal topics in one of four ways: with
total silence; with token noises such as *uh, well,* or coughs;
by changing the subject entirely; or by responding to the
least significant part of a proposal topic. Foster reacts to
Jones' minimal responsiveness by moving the topic to less
threatening ones, trying to make Jones feel more comfortable
and perhaps even utter a few words. His theory of transition topic introduction seems to parallel that of a salesman who
is trying to get a customer to respond to his pitch. If the
customer does not bite on one product, the salesman tries
another line to elicit a response. When I called this phenomenon to the attention of the attorney, he reacted enthusi-
astically, for Roy Foster's occupation was, in reality, that of
a salesman.

Details topic. In the same conversation, Jones introduced
one details topic (19), interestingly enough bounded on each

side by Foster transition topics (18 and 20). This details topic, harmlessly enough, involved whether or not it was all right for his secretary to take the message if Foster should call him back.

Fred topic. The topic of a person named Fred, Foster's boss at the company which Jones owns, was introduced only by Foster. It appears that Foster had to miss work occasionally in order to do personal work for Jones, and Foster introduced this topic as a means of asking Jones to supply an alibi for him to Fred. The topic is introduced three times (4, 10, and 15). On the surface, this topic did not appear to be favorable to Jones' innocence but, from my position, it had to be noted for what it was. As it turns out, however, unknown to me until after my testimony, Jones had testified that he had hired Foster earlier to keep an eye on his wife's activities before and during their divorce hearings. Jones claimed that this topic referred to that set of events.

Proposal topics. Jones did introduce proposal topics twice. Rather than convicting him, however, these instances actually argued for his defense. The proposal which he introduced first as topic 9 and recycled as topic 22 was actually an alternative to Foster's proposal topic of 'doing the judge and doing Gwendolyn'. The substance of Jones' alternative proposal was that they should 'go back to the original plan'. To this day I do not know what the original plan was. As an expert witness who could not know the facts external to the data presented as evidence, this information was not available to me. If the prosecution were to discover what the original plan was, they would have to get it from Jones himself, not from my analysis.

The second tape. The second tape yielded a similar pattern. Jones introduced 5 of the 13 topics, all nonsubstantive. He introduced the greetings, mentioned the objects they held in their hands, one transition topic, and two details topics. Foster, on the other hand, introduced three substantive topics about the presumed killer he had hired, two topics about their activity at the trunk of their car, one reference to the objects in their hands, one fleeting reference to Fred, and their leave-taking.

Responses to topics. Once the topics have been clearly identified and presented, it becomes possible to examine the really crucial aspects of a court case of this type, the responses. One should keep in mind that the jury had no experience in listening to a mass of conversation largely about killing people, and separating who said what to whom about what topics. It is not accidental that over 99 percent of all court cases involving tape recorded evidence result in convictions (Fishman 1973). There is said to be predisposition on the part of jurors that if persons are taped they are most likely to be guilty. There is also the contamination factor to be dealt with. That is, if two people are talking and one of them talks about murder, it is likely to be overgeneralized that both of them are talking about murder.

After a topic is introduced, it is expected of the conversational partner to respond. There are several alternative possibilities of response available to such a partner: to add something to the topic during his/her turn; to deny the premise or facts of the topic; to ignore the topic with silence or irrelevance; to respond to some, but not all, aspects of the topic; to defer or change the topic to something else; or to request clarification or amplification of the topic.

Participant responsiveness in a conversation can be an indication of intentionality at a level much deeper than the semantic meaning of the words themselves. A participant tends to be responsive when interested in or knowledgeable about the topic being discussed. Once the conversation has been segmented into topics, one can observe an interesting pattern in Jones' responsiveness. If we discount transition topics on the grounds that they call out only social responsiveness, not cognitive responsiveness, we are left, in the first tape, with only Fred's topics: proposals and details. The details topics are all resolved when introduced. They are recycled only for additional details. Jones' responses to the topic of Fred are more animated and fuller than are his responses to the proposal topics. Jones appears to be interested in Foster's absence from work more than in any other topic introduced by Foster. This may be from relief that he is finally on a topic about which the stakes are lower, or it may be because he understands the topic better than the proposal topic.

Figure 5 is a representation of the topic resolutions of the first conversation which I prepared for the jury during my testimony in this case. Notice that the point of this chart is to isolate for the jury the responses to the more substantive topics of this tape: proposals and Fred. Although the Fred topic turns out to be not terribly substantive, it still serves a very useful purpose: that of contrasting with Foster's proposals by showing what a clear resolution can look like. Jones finally commits himself to helping Foster with his alibi to Fred in topic 15, the third time it is introduced. In sharp contrast to this resolution is the lack of commitment by Jones to Foster's repeated recycling of his proposals about killing people. Jones avoids resolution by using the strategies of incomplete responses (false starts and incomplete utterances); unclear responses (well..., uh..., etc.); requests for clarification; off-topic comments; presumed hearing failure; and responses to a minor aspect of the topic not germane to its substance. In short, there was no commitment, no resolution. In topic 17,

Figure 5. Topic resolution, Jones case, first tape.

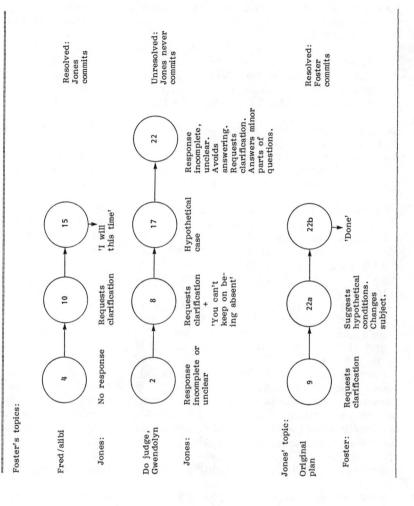

however, there are some anxious moments. Following the
state's transcript, in reference to the supposed hired killer,
Jones responds:

> Jones: Well, he's not going to go wandering in there
> if there's anybody else there. He's gonna--He'll know
> what he's doing better than that. Do the judge, and
> then his wife, and that would be it.

On the surface these words appear to negate my assertion that
in topic 17 Jones does not resolve the topic. The reason it
does not negate my assertion is that the state's transcript of
the tape, provided by the FBI, is in error. Foster's statement preceding those Jones remarks is as follows:

> Foster: I mean I'll go along with whatever you say but
> uh, what...are you gonna do *if* the son-of-a-bitch wants
> to do...You know, They...They're awful close together.
> Uh *if* he grabs that judge up and puts him in his car...
> There's gonna be a hell of a stink but not near as much
> as *if* he left that son-of-a-bitch bloody and bleeding in
> his driveway...
> Jones: Well, he's not going to go wandering in there
> if there's anybody there. He's gonna--*He'd* know what
> he's going to do better than that. *He'd* do the judge,
> and then his wife and that *would* be it.

Careful listening to this tape revealed one deleted *He'd* in
Jones' speech transcript, converting a conditional into an imperative. The media cited the incorrect transcript for weeks
before and during the trial. The context of Foster's question
is clearly hypothetical. Jones' answer is equally hypothetical.
He goes on immediately after this, in fact, saying:

> Jones: Or *if* he...or he *might* catch the judge coming in.

Since Jones' response is to a hypothetical case, not a specific one, it cannot be considered a resolution to Foster's proposal to hire someone to kill Gwendolyn and the judge. For
this reason it is possible to say that there was no resolution
to this topic on this tape.

In contrast, Jones' proposal topic, 'go back to the original
plan', is resolved by Foster in topic 22 of the first conversation. After responding by requesting clarification, com-
plaining, suggesting hypothetical conditions, and changing
the subject in topics 9, 17, and earlier in 22, Foster finally
commits to Jones' proposal with the word 'Done' at the end of
the conversation.

What this leaves us with, then, is topic resolution for
Foster's topic of Fred and for Jones' topic of the original plan.

What remains unresolved is Foster's topic of doing the judge and Gwendolyn.

  Other aspects of topic analysis. It is almost always the case that an analysis which attempts to segment one aspect of the data out of convenience or necessity runs risks of artificiality. Here it is clear that the separation of topic from response is difficult if not impossible. The process is more cyclical than linear, and the reductionist fallacy is as present here as it is in the current vogues in educational practice. The part does not isolate from the whole; it only explains it. Nevertheless, as a procedure, the isolation of topic served a very useful end both for the analysis and for the presentation to (actually the teaching of) the jury. Other aspects of the analysis used in the defense of Arthur Jones could be presented separately, but they really can be seen more clearly as part of the topic-response patterns found in these conversations. Pauses, for example, were shown to be significant aspects of Jones' responses to Foster's topic initiations. Interruptions played a crucial role in the jury's understanding of both topics and responses. Lax tokens were seen to be useful indications of uncertain responses, and the analysis of uh-huh, all right, and OK as place holders also proved to be very important indications to linguistic laymen that not every response which seemed to be positive actually was.

  Conclusions. Several points of interest can be deduced from this experience of utilizing topic as a unit of analysis in a criminal law case. Perhaps the most crucial is that the problem being addressed dictated the selection of the unit of analysis. The problem was to determine what the structure of the conversations could tell us about the meaning of the event. It was up to the jury, of course, to decide for themselves exactly what had taken place from what was said on the tapes. It was not appropriate for me to tell them what the intentions of the speakers were or what their words actually meant. The court agreed that this was the sole province of the jury to determine. My role, quite differently, was to help the jury understand the structure of the conversation as a clue to the possible intentions of the speakers and to help them distinguish exactly what was said by whom. This is partly linguistic analysis and partly teaching, which was largely accomplished through visual displays in the form of charts of the sort noted here.
  Topic analysis helped the jury understand who controlled the conversation and who produced minimal and often evasive responses to those topics. It helped them understand the separate agendas of Foster and Jones by noting their topic recycling patterns. It helped them obtain a holistic or macro picture of the entire conversation to use as a reference point into which micro elements of the conversation could be

appropriately placed. It helped them separate the substantive aspects of the conversation from the less substantive ones.

Response analysis helped the jury determine exactly what was avoided, deferred, or rejected. It was necessary for the jury to understand the difference between the social requirements of conversation which require some sort of response, even if evasive, and the cognitive requirements which require positive or negative resolution. Conversational partners are pressured by both types of requirements, but the social requirements offer constraints based on context and intentions which are not easily recognized by the linguistic layman. Response analysis sorted out for the jury the topics Jones was willing to elaborate on or resolve from those which he was unwilling to advance or commit to.

Topic and response were not the only linguistic analyses used in the Jones case, but they turned out to be extremely useful in helping to meet the major goals of my expert witness testimony: to determine the structure of the conversations.

NOTE

1. For obvious reasons, the names of all participants in this case have been changed.

REFERENCES

Chafe, Wallace. 1972. Discourse structure and human knowledge. In: Language comprehension and the acquisition of knowledge. Edited by Roy O. Freedle and John B. Carroll. Washington, D.C.: V. H. Winston.

Fishman, Clifford. 1973. Wiretapping and eavesdropping.

Greenfield, Patricia Marks. 1980. Towards an operational and logical analysis of intentionality. In: The social foundations of language and cognition: Essays in honor of J. S. Bruner. Edited by David Olson. New York: W. W. Norton.

Kates, Carol A. 1980. Pragmatics and semantics: An empiricist theory. Ithaca, N.Y.: Cornell University Press.

Keenan, Elinor Ochs, and Bambi Schieffelin. 1976. Topic as a discourse notion: A study of topic in the conversations of children and adults. In: Subject and topic. Edited by Charles Li. New York: Academic Press.

Sacks, Harvey, Emanuel Schegloff, and Gail Jefferson. 1974. A simplest systematics for the organization of turn taking for conversation. Lg. 50.

Shuy, Roger W. 1981. Linguistics in the courtroom. Paper presented at Conference on Linguistics and the Humanities, Arlington, Texas. Mimeo.

Vygotsky, Lev S. 1962. Thought and language. Cambridge, Mass.: MIT Press.

BUILDING STORIES:
THE EMERGENCE OF INFORMATION STRUCTURES
FROM CONVERSATION

Catherine E. Snow and Beverly A. Goldfield
Harvard University

One way of thinking about the nature of the development in children's language ability between the ages of 2 and 3-1/2 years is as a reorganization of the relationship between syntactic and discourse skills in the service of transmitting information. From this point of view, the following significant developments are characteristic of the growth in language between 2 and 3-1/2 years of age.

1. Semantic relationships that had been encoded by simple intraspeaker apposition come to be encoded syntactically. Thus, the young 2-year-old typically says things like (1) and (2), or engages in conversations like (3), in which the semantic relationships are derivable from context and world knowledge, not made explicit in the utterances.

(1) sweater
    chair

(2) mommy
    cookie
    eat

(3) Mother: Do you want a banana?
    Child: Lunch.

The 3-1/2-year-old, on the other hand, typically says things like (4), (5), and (6), encoding the semantic relationships syntactically within one utterance.

(4) sweater on the chair

(5) Mommy's eating a cookie.
(6) I want a banana for lunch.

2. Information structures that at 2 years are expressed in a sketchy, incomplete way, are by 4 years of age more complete, more decontextualized, and less egocentric presentations of the information.
3. Information structures that had been largely idiosyncratic, dependent upon the child's own experience related to the topic, become conventional. By 4 years, children can encode information in structures conventional enough to be understood even if the information is new to the listener.

In this paper, we hope to demonstrate that the three indices of language development we have sketched are related, and that they emerge in a very concrete way from the child's history of talking about specific things, again and again, with a knowledgeable adult; the data base analyzed to support these claims is a series of conversations between a mother and her child about the pictures in one book. The conversations occurred on 13 separate occasions, in the course of 11 months, starting when the child was 2;5.18 (that is, 2 years, five months, 18 days). We presume that the types of conversation and the effects of recurrent discussion of a single topic on children's language growth presented here are possible in a wide variety of contexts, certainly not limited to book-reading; nonetheless, for the purposes of clarity, analysis and discussion in this paper are limited to situations of talking about events in pictures.

The knowledgeable adult can be hypothesized to fulfill a number of functions during the conversations with the child that produce the developments sketched earlier. These functions can be identified as the product of two dichotomies (see Table 1), the first relevant to the information structure and the second relevant to the time at which the adult's effect is felt. The first dichotomy is the distinction between (a) the categories of information that need to be included for an adequate representation of some set of similar events and (b) the specific informative content relevant to each specific event. The second dichotomy is the distinction between (a) synchronic and (b) diachronic effects of the adult partner in the conversations. These two sets of distinctions are discussed in greater detail in the next two sections. Table 1 presents the ways in which they interact to provide four categories of functions which the knowledgeable adult can fulfill in conversations with children.

The structure of information. A good description, a good story, or a good argument has a certain structure--a skeleton of categories or slots around which the details of any particular description, narrative, or argument are built. The notion of an abstract structure which underlies the organization of any narrative is the basis for proposals such as story grammars (see, for example, Mandler and Johnson 1977, Rumelhart 1975) and, without committing ourselves to any particular claim about the nature of such a structure, an assumption of its existence is crucial to our understanding of the developments in children's language skills sketched earlier.

Table 1. Hypothesized functions of the knowledgeable adult in the child's presentation of information structures.

	Synchronic	Diachronic
Categories of information:	Adult uses questions to elicit informative content, so that an adequate information structure is presented. Child has content, but does not know the relevant categories.	Adult models the categories that are relevant for understanding a particular picture. Child acquires these for later use.
Informative content:	Adult answers the child's questions, providing the informative content relevant to a particular picture. Child knows the categories, not the content.	Adult models the informative content relevant to a particular picture, and in subsequent discussions, the child provides that informative content.

This skeleton of the information structure is referred to in this paper as 'categories of information'. The assumption is that categories of information are quite general, relatively abstract, and that some small set of them is adequate for dealing with a wide variety of specific pictures or events.

The categories of information contrast with the 'informative content', which is specific to a particular picture or event. The informative content is the flesh hung on the skeleton--the concrete understanding, meanings, lexical items, perhaps even syntactic structures needed to talk about a particular picture or event.

With reference to Table 1, it is proposed that a knowledgeable adult can elicit and model the categories of information and the informative content independently of one another, and in separate utterances. Questions, for example, provide evidence about the categories of information appropriate to the picture under discussion, not about informative content, whereas responses to questions normally provide informative content after the category of information has been established. (Responses to questions may also provide evidence that a chosen category of information is inappropriate, e.g. 'Why is he doing that?' 'Just because. No reason.')

Synchronic and diachronic effects. In the course of talking to a child about a picture in a book--especially if the picture is complex, action filled, and intrinsically narrative, as was the case for the pictures analyzed here--the knowledgeable adult can provide structure and add informative content in such a way that a good, complete, and conventional information structure emerges from the conversation. The skillful adult elicits from the child all the relevant informative content, but weaves that (typically incomplete or unstructured) content into a conversation whose sum total constitutes a good information structure. This process is referred to here as the synchronic function of the adult. It was abundantly in evidence in the conversations analyzed, but is not discussed in detail here. The synchronic function has been described, for a variety of situations, in other studies. Most closely related to this one, for instance, McNamee (1979) documented the way in which a kindergarten teacher elicited knowledge about a story from a child, knowledge which the child possessed but could not display without the interactive support of the knowledgeable adult.

Wertsch (1979) has described a similar adult role in supporting children's problem-solving in a puzzle task; the adult analyzed and structured the task so that the child's knowledge and skills could be deployed to solve it. With younger children, Scollon (1979), Snow (1977, 1978), Shugar (1978), and others have described how adults structure conversations so that children are effective conversational partners as well as good providers of information. Michaels (1981) has described how a match between child and adult in the way they organize their information facilitates the interactive construction of good information structuring. The synchronic function of the knowledgeable adult is very important, both for parent-child and for teacher-student interaction, but this paper concentrates on the as yet unreported and unanalyzed diachronic function.

By diachronic function, we mean the effect of the adult's elicitation and modelling on the child's performance at a later time; in other words, that the child's presentation of the information structure looks like the adult's presentation of a few weeks or months earlier. The diachronic function can be differentiated in terms of whether the child is learning the adult's presentation of categories of information, or of informative content, or both (see Table 1). It is for the diachronic function of the knowledgeable adult that we present evidence in this paper.

Growth of knowledge as a basis for language development. In the foregoing discussion, we have repeatedly introduced the notions of 'knowledge' and 'knowledgeable adult'. This emphasis is intentional. We would like to argue that the development in the child's ability to present complete, complex, conventionalized information structures with reference to any particular picture (or object, event, situation, or relationship) is the product of accretion of knowledge about that picture (object, event, situation, or relationship).

This is, clearly, an extreme statement, which probably has to be moderated. Some development in cognitive capacity independent of specific knowledge is surely occurring during the period studied, and the growth in complexity, completeness, and elaboration of information structures achieved at later discussions is no doubt partly attributable to that development. Nonetheless, we feel a strong case can be made that the more important process is the simple accretion of knowledge concerning: (a) what questions need to be answered about a given picture, (b) what the central items and events in the picture are, and (c) how one talks about the central items and events. It is useful at least to try to push as far as it will go our explanation that this development is the result of the accretion of knowledge, before reverting to more general, vaguer, and less testable explanations in terms of the child's developing cognitive capacity.

The data base. The findings to be analyzed here are based on 13 tapes of conversation between a mother and her firstborn child, Nathaniel. The tapes are a subset of recordings made at regular intervals during Nathaniel's third and fourth years. Those selected for analysis here include all occasions on which Nathaniel and his mother were reading Richard Scarry's *Storybook Dictionary* (London: Hamlyn 1967). Table 2 gives more information on the data base.

Table 2. Nathaniel's age and information about the pictures discussed at each of the three series of book-reading sessions.

Series	1	2	3
Nathaniel's age	2;5.18-2;6.2	2;6.19-2;6.22	3;4.8-3;4.21
Number of different pictures of which discussions are included in the analysis	41	27	45
Number of picture discussions analyzed	96	59	102

For ease of presentation, we analyze the 13 occasions as three series: Series 1 includes the first four recordings, all of which occurred on separate days within a period of two weeks; Series 2 includes the next four, which occurred within a period of four days starting about two weeks about Series 1; and Series 3 includes five recordings within two weeks,

starting nine months after Series 2. Within each series, only
those pictures have been analyzed which were discussed at
least twice within that series; this selection was made because
we felt that the pictures which were discussed several times
within a period of a few days best reflected Nathaniel's development of integrated and complete information structures.
Pictures which were discussed only once or only at six-month
intervals were talked about in much less sophisticated ways
than those discussed intensively over a shorter period of time;
often the discussions of the more rarely talked about pictures
focused only on the vocabulary items needed to identify the
major characters or objects in the picture.

During the period of time under consideration, all of Nathaniel's readings of this book with his mother (or, occasionally,
father) were recorded, so the conversations analyzed here
represent his total exposure to discussions with a knowledgeable adult about this book for these 11 months. He had read
the book with his parents on several occasions before taping
started.

Because we are interested in those pictures for which some
elaborated knowledge structure is built up, we have analyzed
only those conversations about pictures discussed more than
once within a session. In fact, there was considerable rou-
tinization in Nathaniel's structuring of the book-reading
activity, at several levels (see Snow in press, Snow and Goldfield 1980, for other analyses revealing the levels of routini-
zation), including the level of picture selection. Of the more
than 800 pictures available for discussion in the book, more
than 500 were never discussed in any of the 13 readings, and
352 were discussed more than once.

The character of the pictures is crucial both to the nature
of the conversations held and to the kind of analysis done (and
probably to the popularity of the Richard Scarry books with
Nathaniel and other children as well). The pictures, each
meant to illustrate one of the entries in the dictionary, are
highly narrative, presenting both actual and impending action.
The text is in most cases only supplementary to the narrative
presented in the picture (as well as being without notable
literary merit). In fact, only at Session 3 was the text read
aloud during the conversations between Nathaniel and his
mother, and then often the conversation proceeded without
reference to the information that had been read.

Analysis of the recurrent conversations. As we have outlined, the conversations were analyzed to reveal two functions:
laying out the relevant categories of information, and laying
out the relevant informative content. The following coding
scheme emerged from our attempts to make sense of the data
(note that, though some of these categories may be reminiscent
of story grammar categories, our categories were all generated

by the data themselves, not imposed by us in accordance with any theoretical presuppositions).

1. Item labels. The item label category was indicated by questions like 'What's that?' and 'Who's that?' The informative content within this category included labels for unique referents, e.g. 'That's Dingo', or 'That's Dingo's car', as well as class labels, e.g. 'That's a truck' or 'Those are all trees'.

2. Item elaborations. This category was introduced by questions like 'What kind of an airplane?', 'What's that part of a car called?' 'How many pigs?', or 'What color is it?' The informative content scored under this category included labels for superordinates or subclasses, for parts, and for specifications of type, number, and color.

3. Event. The category was typically introduced by 'What's happening?' Content consisted of simple event descriptions, including the main arguments of the relevant verb, e.g. 'Dingo hit the apple cart' or 'The apples got knocked all over.'

4. Event elaborations. Content within this category included provision of event labels (e.g. 'There was an accident'), or of elaboration of an already introduced event by providing information on location, position, consequence, or by explaining it.

5. Motive/cause. This category was introduced by 'Why' or 'How come', and content consisted of explanations for events in terms of physical causality or psychological motives.

6. Evaluation/reaction. Content in this category consisted of responses to the characters or the events by the readers, e.g. 'Dingo's sure a bad driver' or 'That was silly, Dingo.'

7. Relation to the real world. The content in this category consisted of explicating a relationship between a pictured item or event and a real world item or event known to the child, e.g. 'That's just like your fire engine' or 'The pigs are taking a bath. You did that this morning!'

With reference to any of these seven categories, two tasks had to be accomplished if the category were to be successfully incorporated in the conversation: (a) the category of information had to be introduced and (b) the informative content had to be introduced. Two basic questions we asked of the data were: (a) who undertook these tasks for the various pictures discussed? and (b) did the responsibility for these tasks shift from the adult in the earlier discussions to the child in later discussions of particular pictures?

Results and discussion

Development of information structures. The first question of importance in assessing the development of Nathaniel's knowledge structures for these pictures is: how do the categories of information discussed change from the first to the last sessions? Is there any evidence that the information structure built up around particular pictures grows more complex, complete, or sophisticated?

Frequencies with which the various categories of information were introduced at each series of sessions are presented in Table 3. It is clear that there is enormous change over time, with most of the discussion concentrated on items, item elaborations, events, and event elaborations during Series 1 and 2, and a striking increase in motive/cause at Series 3.

Table 3. Frequencies of the various categories of information at each of the three series.

	1	2	3
Item label	133	74	72
Item elaboration	51	27	0
Event	71	38	136/78*
Event elaboration	67	6	37
Motive/cause	6	5	77
Evaluation/reaction	2	3	19
Real world	21	8	14

*At the third session, the event was presented 58 times in the text which was read at the beginning of the discussion, whereas the event was presented 78 times by Nathaniel or his mother in spontaneous speech. Thus, the category event was presented 136 times, though only 78 of those were equivalent to the mode of presentation of Series 1 and 2.

Of course, the introduction of new categories for discussion does not cause reduction in discussion of the old categories-- one must mention the characters and objects involved in order to talk about the event, and one must mention the event in order to discuss its cause or consequences. The more sophisticated categories are introduced to elaborate on the information structure created in and remembered from the earlier discussions, not to replace the earlier categories.

Shifting of responsibility. Given the development in the information structures achieved by Nathaniel and his mother, the question arises: which of them is responsible? Is the introduction of the information category 'event' during the early series and the category motive/cause during the third series due to Nathaniel's mother asking the relevant questions and providing answers? Or do those changes reflect Nathaniel's changing behavior? Evidence to answer this question comes from calculating the proportion of introductions of a particular category or of provisions of informative content within a category that were due to Nathaniel (see Tables 4 and 5).

In the first series of conversations, Nathaniel took primary responsibility for introducing the category item label (see Table 4) and shared about equally with his mother the tasks of introducing the categories item elaboration and event.

Table 4. Percentages of use of a given information category introduced by Nathaniel or his mother.

	1 M	N	2 M	N	3 M	N
Item label	16.5	83.5	6.8	93.2	65.3	34.7
Item elaboration	52.9	47.1	29.6	70.4	0.0	0.0
Event	50.7	49.3	28.9	71.0	58.9	41.0
Event elaboration	61.2	38.8	66.7	33.3	33.3	66.7
Motive/cause	83.3	16.7	80.0	20.0	18.2	81.8
Evaluation/ reaction	100.0	0.0	66.7	33.3	84.2	15.8
Real world	57.1	42.8	37.5	62.5	100.0	0.0

His mother was responsible for all or most of the introductions of evaluation/reaction, motive/cause, event elaboration, and real world references. In the course of the 11 months, Nathaniel gradually assumed more responsibility for introducing all these categories; especially striking is the high frequency of his introducing event at Series 2 and motive/cause at Series 3.

The responsibilities for providing informative content were assigned somewhat differently (see Table 5). During the first series, Nathaniel provided more than half the content only for item labels, and close to half only for event and real world reference.

Table 5. Percentages of provision of informative content in a given category by Nathaniel or his mother.

	1 M	N	2 M	N	3 M	N
Item label	42.8	57.1	27.0	73.0	27.1	72.9
Item elaboration	68.6	31.4	44.7	55.3	--	--
Event	53.5	46.5	55.3	44.7	32.1	67.9
Event elaboration	67.2	32.8	83.3	16.7	21.2	78.8
Motive/cause	83.3	16.7	100.0	30.0	86.8	13.2
Evaluation/ reaction	100.0	0.0	33.3	66.7	84.2	15.8
Real world	55.0	45.0	37.5	62.5	71.4	28.6

By the third series, Nathaniel was providing most of the information about items and events, and his mother supplied most of the information with reference to motive/cause. These highly event-related categories, unlike the more peripheral evaluation/ reaction and real world references, show a pattern of complementarity between category and content during the third series, reflecting the by now well developed and smooth question and answer organization of the dialogue.

In summary, then, at the earliest sessions Nathaniel most often asked 'What's that?', often provided item labels himself, and collaborated with his mother in describing and elaborating events. He rarely asked or answered questions about motive/ cause. During the second series, he both introduced events and provided informative content about events more than previously. By the third series, he shared the responsibility for asking questions about items and events, and provided most of the informative content about items and events. He did almost all the asking, but very little answering, about motive/cause.

Those results reflect a real shift in responsibility from mother to child, and the child's growing understanding of how to talk about the pictures discussed. The nature of this shift may be clearer if we take some examples of the dialogue. Consider, for instance, the first recorded discussion of the picture of an accident, held when Nathaniel was 2;5.18.

Nathaniel:	Mother:
car	
car	
	that's a car
car de de go up a apples	
	Yeah, Dingo crashed into the apples.
apples, crash	
	crash
going backwards	
	Is Dingo going backwards?

Here, Nathaniel identified two items (*apples* and *car*) and two events (*go* and *going backwards*), while his mother initiated neither category nor content. The second discussion, at 2;6.0, was shorter.

Nathaniel:	Mother:
dat	
	What's that?
a bable	
	Spilled the apples, didn't he?
	Dingo ran into the apples.
	Had an accident.

Here, Nathaniel introduced category and content for item label (*dat* and *a bable*), while his mother supplied content for event and various event elaborations. Two days later, the following discussion took place.

Nathaniel:	Mother:
dis is dis	
	Who's that?
Who's dat?	
	Who's that?
Who's dat?	
	That's Dingo.
Dingo	
	Dingo Dingo is a terrible driver.
er de de de crashing...	
er de	
	Dingo's always having crashes, yeah.

Here, Nathaniel introduces the category item label, eliciting the content *Dingo* from his mother, then provides a miminal description of the central event *crashing*, while his mother gives a fuller description of the event and a reaction to it.

Ten months later, the conversations begin almost ritually with the new form 'read dis one'. As mentioned earlier, Nathaniel's mother sometimes did read the text upon request, although she often (as in the first conversation below, at 3;4.9) avoided doing so.

Nathaniel:	Mother:
Read dis one	
	What's happening there?
Dingo crashed in	
	What did he crash?
De apples in in dis apple cart	
	Dingo had an...
accident	
	My goodness!
accident	

Here, Nathaniel's mother introduced the event and two event elaborations, but Nathaniel provided all the informative content. The next day, the same sequence occurs, but then Nathaniel's mother provided a motive for the event.

Nathaniel:	Mother:
Read dis one	
	accident. Dingo had an accident. My goodness. What'd Dingo do?
Bump the apple underneath the apple cart. turnin'	

Nathaniel: Mother:

                                    yep

slow
                                    _?_ think 'cause he likes to
                                    bump into apple carts. He
                                    turned so he could bump into
                                    the apple carts. Oh Dingo!

On the final recorded reading, at 3; 4.21, Nathaniel described
the event, asked why, then provided a cause after his mother
had provided a motive.

Nathaniel: Mother:

Read dis one

                                    accident. Dingo had an acci-
                                    dent. My goodness. What
                                    happened?

What happened? It gonna
  get into the whole apple
  cart. His car turned all
  by itself.

                                    yep because...Dingo wasn't
                                    being very careful I guess.

Why?
                                    Well, you know Dingo, don't
                                    you?

He he wasn't watch he was
  going?
                                    Wasn't watching was going

What de what mm what
  Dingo Dingo waved?
                                    Did he wave?

yeah
                                    Maybe.

waved Dingo

   Another example of the degree to which Nathaniel's interests
had shifted in the later sessions to the category motive/cause
comes from the following dialogue, about the picture labelled
'Back'. The picture shows Mr. Fixit's truck, the back of
which has just been smashed by Dingo. Mr. Fixit is emerging
from a shop with a stove on his back. He is presumably intending to put the stove in the back of his truck, which is
now, however, squashed beyond utility. The conversation
(held at 3; 4.8) proceeded as follows:

Nathaniel:	Mother:
What he doin?	
	What's he carrying on his back?
Has a oven	
Why nowhere to where to put the oven?	
Why?	
Why?	
	What did Dingo do to Mr. Fixit's lorry?
Smash	
	Right.
He's gonna fix it with the oven?	

This discussion builds on several previous ones, as shown by Nathaniel's ability to presuppose a joint understanding of the problem in his third utterance, 'Why is there nowhere to put the oven?' (Nathaniel referred to stoves as ovens during this period.) The most interesting aspect of this discussion is what it reveals about Nathaniel's strategy at this age for understanding these pictures: take two salient events in the picture, and try to integrate them into a cause and effect structure. In this particular case, that strategy yields a proposition which is somewhat implausible by adult standards. Just as morphological overgeneralizations reveal a child's knowledge of morphological rules, this violation of reasonable real world relationships reveals Nathaniel's control of the obligatory information structure for these narrative pictures.

Similar overgeneralizations of the notion that the pictures should be understood as events occurred during the second series. The first example shows Nathaniel imposing the category 'event' on a picture which presented no event, but only an object to label (2;6.19).

Nathaniel:	Mother:
Who's this	
	cake
da bake da cake	
	There's the cake, in the bakery window.

The second example shows Nathaniel interpreting what is actually a pictured motive structure as an event. The picture being discussed shows three beggars gazing wistfully at a cake (2;6.22).

Nathaniel:	Mother:
Who's the cake	
	That's the cake.
eh they're pushing the cake	
	They're pushing it?
pushing it	
	They're wishing they could eat it.

These attempts to impose event structures on pictures to which they are not appropriate reveal Nathaniel's implicit rules for understanding and for talking about these pictures at 2-1/2, just as the later search for motives and causes reveals that he considered a causal structure to be crucial to a complete understanding of the pictures at 3; 4.

Conclusion. It has been the purpose of this paper to demonstrate that what children say when describing pictured events is a function of (a) their general knowledge about the categories of information necessary for structuring such discussions and (b) the picture-specific knowledge of the necessary informative content. Furthermore, we have shown how both these levels of knowledge emerge diachronically as well as synchronically from interactions with knowledgeable adults. Children learn from adults first, what questions to ask and second, how to answer those questions. The learning is facilitated by the kind of interactive situation analyzed here, in which precisely identical contexts for discussion recur over time (see Snow and Goldfield 1980, for further discussion of context specificity in language acquisition).

We conclude from the data presented here that Nathaniel was learning from the conversations with his mother how to talk about the pictures in the Richard Scarry Storybook Dictionary. Presumably, that rather restricted learning had more general effects in three areas: (1) the language forms that Nathaniel acquired in the context of these discussions were eventually available to him for talking about a wide variety of things; (2) the notions of item, event, motive, and cause as organizing structures for talking about these pictures were also seen to be relevant for discussing other kinds of phenomena, for example, real-world events; and (3) Nathaniel was learning how to think about both pictured and nonpictured events, internalizing the interactively produced information structures in such a way that they organized knowledge for him without any further dependence on interaction.

REFEFENCES

Mandler, Jean, and Nancy Johnson. 1977. Remembrance of things parsed: Story structure and recall. Cognitive Psychology 9.111-115.
McNamee, Gillian D. 1979. The social interaction origins of narrative skills. The Quarterly Newsletter of the Laboratory of Comparative Human Cognition 1.4:63-68.
Michaels, Sarah. 1981. Sharing time revisited. Paper presented at the Ethnography in Education Research Forum, University of Pennsylvania, March.
Rumelhart, David. 1975. Notes on a schema for stories. In: Representation and understanding: Studies in cognitive science. Edited by D. G. Bobrow and A. Collins. New York: Academic Press.
Scollon, Ron. 1979. A real early stage: An unzippered condensation of a dissertation on child language. In: Developmental pragmatics. Edited by E. Ochs and B. Schieffelin. New York: Academic Press.
Shugar, Grace. 1978. Text analysis as an approach to the study of early linguistic operations. In: The development of communication. Edited by N. Waterson and C. Snow. Chichester: Wiley.
Snow, Catherine E. 1977. The development of conversation between mothers and babies. Journal of Child Language 4.1-22.
Snow, Catherine E. 1978. The conversational context of language learning. In: Recent advances in the psychology of language: Language development and mother-child interaction. Edited by R. N. Campbell and P. Smith. London: Plenum Press.
Snow, Catherine E. (in press) Saying it again: The role of expanded and deferred imitations in language acquisitions. In: Children's language, Vol. 4. Edited by K. E. Nelson. New York: Gardner Press.
Snow, Catherine E., and B. A. Goldfield. 1980. Turn the page please: Situation-specific language learning. Unpublished MS.
Wertsch, James. 1979. From social interaction to higher psychological processes: A clarification and application of Vygotsky's theory. Human Development 22.1-22.

COMPETENCE FOR IMPLICIT TEXT ANALYSIS:
LITERARY STYLE DISCRIMINATION
IN FIVE-YEAR-OLDS

Georgia M. Green
University of Illinois

Why on earth would anyone imagine that 5-year-olds could tell one literary style from another? I certainly would not have if someone had not asked me if they could.

A couple of years ago, I remarked to someone that when my daughter Robin was $2\frac{1}{2}$, she claimed to recognize illustrations she had never seen before, saying that we already had books we had just gotten. In fact, what we already had were books illustrated by the same artist, but the illustrations were of course not identical: what she recognized was the illustrator's artistic style. My interlocutor, who was a well-known expert in language acquisition, asked if Robin also thought she recognized stories she had never heard before when they were by the same author as ones she had heard, if she recognized verbal style as easily as artistic style. My response was that not only did I not know if she had been able to do that at $2\frac{1}{2}$; I had no idea if she could do it at the time, when she was $4\frac{1}{2}$.

By the time I had figured out how to find out, I realized that it would be about as easy to investigate the abilities of a more representative population of children as it would be to explore the abilities of one child, and there would be a lot to be gained, for the question is of more than passing interest, and my interest in it was more than idle curiosity: if children at the age when reading instruction typically begins are sensitive to stylistic properties of texts, then this has far-ranging implications for their text-processing abilities, and these in turn have implications for diverse aspects of the practice of reading instruction. I am going to return to these eventually.

So, the question was: given that one child, and I presumed many others, interpreted the similarities in the illustrations of

142

artists like Lionel Kalish, as shown in (1) and (2), as 'identities' of a sort at age $2\frac{1}{2}$, could children recognize similarities in verbal (or literary) style as indicating identity of authorship?

I arranged to carry out a small-scale experiment, with the aid of a research assistant, Margaret Laff, in the kindergarten class of a day-care center in a midwestern university community of 95,000. The participants were five girls and eight boys, ranging in age from 5;0 to 6;1 years. These children had not begun formal reading instruction, although two of them could read unfamiliar texts with some facility.

At our request, the regular classroom teacher read 10 books to the class at times normal for such an activity and in the way she normally would read to the children, showing the illustrations and answering questions. It took 14 days for the books, 2 by each of 5 authors, to be read once. The 10 books, read in the order in which they are listed, are indicated in (3).

(3) Exposure books:

1. Dr. Seuss. *The Lorax*. New York: Random House, 1971.
2. Margaret Wise Brown. *Wait Till the Moon is Full*. New York: Harper and Row, 1948.
3. Bill Peet. *The Ant and the Elephant*. Boston: Houghton Mifflin, 1972.
4. Virginia Kahl. *The Habits of Rabbits*. New York: Charles Scribner's Sons, 1957.
5. Beatrix Potter. *The Tale of Mr. Jeremy Fisher*. New York: Warne, 1906.
6. Dr. Seuss. *Happy Birthday to You*. New York: Random House, 1959.
7. Margaret Wise Brown. *The Runaway Bunny*. New York: Harper and Row, 1942.
8. Bill Peet. *Big Bad Bruce*. Boston: Houghton Mifflin, 1977.
9. Virginia Kahl. *The Baron's Booty*. New York: Charles Scribner's Sons, 1963.
10. Beatrix Potter. *The Tale of Peter Rabbit*. New York: Warne, 1902.

Shortly after the last book was read to the group, we prepared the group for the task of indicating their identification of new stories with an activity where they noted whether they recognized which book an illustration was from. Five-page booklets were distributed to the children. On each page of the booklets five pictures had been photocopied in black and white. Each picture represented a major character from a book by a different one of the five authors mentioned in (3). In every case the character came from one of the books read to the children in class, and with only one exception, the character's name occurred in the title of the book. The same five pictures

(2)

(1)

appeared on each page but they were arranged in different orders. For each page, the children were asked to put a crayon mark on 'the picture that looks like it was drawn by the person who drew the pictures in (title) and (title)'; the two titles by each author were cited in turn. This was an unusual task for the children and a few seemed puzzled by it. Though most seemed to know the correct answers, some may have been distracted by wondering why we would ask something so obvious. We also observed in at least one case that a child would point to the correct answer, but for some reason could not be persuaded to mark it. The children got from 2-5 correct, as indicated in (4); 9 got 3 or more correct.

(4) Illustrations task results:

Number correct	2	3	4	5	Total
Number of children	4	5	1	3	13

Then, five tape recordings of other stories by the same authors were played individually to each child. The stories on the tapes are indicated in (5).

(5) Test books:

1. Dr. Seuss. *I Had Trouble in Getting to Solla Sollew*. New York: Random House, 1965.
2. Beatrix Potter. *The Tale of Two Bad Mice*. New York: Warne, 1904.
3. Bill Peet. *Eli*. Boston: Houghton Mifflin, 1978.
4. Margaret Wise Brown. *Fox Eyes*. New York: Pantheon Books, 1951.
5. Margaret Wise Brown. *The Little Fur Family*. New York: Harper and Row, 1946.

Each child heard the tapes in a different order. Some children heard one story by each author; some heard 2 stories by one author and one by each of 3 others. Thus, not all the children heard all the authors. This was intended to serve as a check on guessing strategies. Unfortunately, one-third of the children in the second condition did not complete the task, so we did not draw any conclusions about guessing strategies.

Before each story, the children were told that at the end of the story they would be asked to think about which of the books read by the teacher the new story most reminded them of. The children were also told that when the story was over, they would be asked to make a mark on a picture in a booklet similar or identical to one used in the illustration identification task.[1] Not all booklets were identical: the children who heard two stories by the same author had five 4-item pages, while those who heard one story by each author had five 5-item pages.

When each story was over, the interviewer read these instructions to the child:

If you think this story was written by Beatrix Potter, who
wrote the stories about Peter Rabbit and Jeremy Fisher, put
a mark on the picture of Peter Rabbit.

If you think the story you just heard was written by
Virginia Kahl, who wrote the stories about Gunhilde and the
rabbits, put a mark on the picture of Gunhilde.

If you think that the story was written by Margaret Wise
Brown, who wrote the stories about the runaway bunny and
the raccoon who wanted to go out at night, put a mark on
the little raccoon's picture.

If you think the story was written by Dr. Seuss, who wrote
the stories about the Lorax and the Birthday Bird, put a
mark on the picture of the Lorax.

(5-item group only) If you think the story was written by
Bill Peet, who wrote the stories about Big Bad Bruce and
the ant and the elephant, put a mark on the picture of the
bear.

After the child had marked a choice, the interviewer asked the
child three questions: (1) Have you ever heard this story before? (2) How did you know it was that one? (3) Tell me
something about the story that made you know who wrote it.
    We did not expect to get much in the way of revealing or
even true answers to such questions (5-year-olds have been
observed to have no qualms about making up answers to such
questions out of whole cloth), but we were prepared to consider anything indicating awareness of any stylistic property
to be significant.
    Responses fell into one of three categories. Many were either
'off the wall' or simply uninformative. For example, in response to the second question, 'How did you know it was that
one?', we got such responses as:

Well my dad told me.
I just knew. I was just thinking in my head. I remembered
    in my mind who it was always written by.

Some of these children had correctly matched the author. Some
had matched it incorrectly. A good number of responses, however, seemed to indicate at least a vague awareness of style.
For instance, in response to the same question, 'How did you
know it was that one?', children who had correctly identified
the authorship of the story said things like:

Because ... uh ... because they were talking the same.

Um, because of how they were talking.

Well, it sounds like she's the one (pause) that was talking. It really sounds like the Lorax girl. See, in little parts of it it sounded like she was talking. And she was talking in the Lorax, I think, because she sounds the same as the Lorax girl.

And a few comments showed that at least one child was conscious of certain determinants of style. For example, responding to the same question, this child said:

Because I heard the story of Big Bad Bruce and they said something about the s ... nort, and they said it too.

Most of the children, predictably, did not have the concentration to perform the entire task at a single sitting (about 55 minutes), and did one or two stories at a time. Three or four children did have the concentration to do this, however (two of these were readers), and several were so intrigued with the task of guessing the authorship that they interrupted the tape to tell us the author (usually correctly) and preferred, contrary to our expectations, to go on to the next tape, rather than hear the end of the story.

This part of the experiment was not conducted under the best of circumstances. The tapes were unfortunately excessively 'noisy', and the listening accommodations were not particularly comfortable--usually the floor of a small room that was not in use.

Children were allowed to discontinue the experiment at any time if they did not wish to go on. Three children did not complete the task. One listened to 4 out of 5 stories, one to 3 out of 5, one to 2 out of 5.

Thus the experiment was performed under a number of conditions that could be expected to bias the results against the hypothesis that children can identify stylistic traits of texts well enough to match the authorship of novel texts to texts they have already heard. (1) Children were exposed to only two exemplars by each author prior to the testing. (2) Children were exposed to each exemplar only once. (3) Exposure stretched over 14 days. The two books by each author were read for the most part 7 days apart. (4) The testing task was lengthy. (5) The testing was conducted under uncomfortable and distracting conditions. Nonetheless, when they listened to tapes of a third work by each of the 5 authors, 6 of the 13 children who participated in the interviews were able to identify correctly the authorship of 3 or more of the 5 stories, as indicated in (6).

(6) Style test results

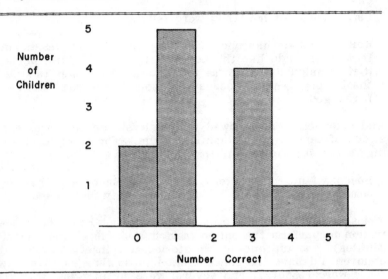

The probability of randomly choosing the correct item out of 5 is 0.2. The probability of doing this 3 or more times in 5 trials is around 0.06. This means that 6 children performed at a level of accuracy highly unlikely to be attributable to chance. The other 4 who completed the interviews performed with far below chance accuracy. In other words, a large percentage of the children performed in such a fashion as to imply that their comprehension of stories was not limited to vague outlines of plot and characterization, but extended to appreciation of the subtler rhetorical and linguistic aspects of style. Apparently, the other part of the group either (a) misunderstood the task, (b) did not attend to the discriminants of style, or (c) fixed upon arbitrary guessing strategies.

Correlations. There was no apparent correlation of the percentage correct with the participants' age or sex, as shown in (7).

Furthermore, there was no direct correlation between the children's ability to do well on the illustration pretest and their ability to perform the style recognition task. This indicates that performance on the style recognition task is not a simple function of intelligence or ability to follow directions. Specifically, of the 10 children who completed the style recognition task, the 3 children who did best on the illustration recognition task (matched all 5 pictures correctly) got 0 or 1 correct on the style recognition task. The children who did poorest (2 correct) on the illustration task, with one exception, got 0 or 1 correct on the style recognition task. But the children who did moderately well on the illustration task (3-4 correct) got 3-5 correct on the style recognition task.

(7) Comparison of number of correct responses with age and with sex.

Average age of:
Total group	64.3 months
3-5 Correct group	64.8 months
0-1 Correct group	63.8 months

Percentage of girls in:
Total group	.38 (5/13)
3-5 Correct group	.33 (2/6)
0-1 Correct group	.43 (3/7)

A possible explanation for this is that the group that got 100 percent correct on the illustration task were accustomed to attending much more to the illustrations in listening to stories than to rhetorical and linguistic properties of the text, and that most of the children in the group that did poorest on the illustration task simply were not accustomed to attending to either style or illustrations in listening to stories. But the reason why the children who did best on the style recognition task did only moderately well in recognizing illustrations may be that their concentration on the aspects of literary style that allowed them to recognize authorship precluded their paying more attention to the illustrations.

In the absence, however, of confirmatory observations of the individual children, it seems just as justifiable to attribute the gap between the 0-1 correct group and the 3-5 correct group to individual differences (e.g. sensitivity to language) or linguistic maturity. Another possibility is that the children in the 0-1 correct group simply had less prior experience with the authors whose style we chose to investigate. Logically, this would seem to be a significant variable only if, in being read to before the experiment, these children were made aware of the names of the authors of the relevant books. I have no idea whether this was true in the case of the children tested. I would guess that the practice of reading the title page is not widespread, but I know of no definitive investigations. Personally, I never used to read aloud even the titles of the books I read to my children, and as a consequence, they developed their own designations for books. Thus, my daughter's name for *The Cat Who Stamped His Feet*, by Betty Ren Wright (Golden Press, 1974) was 'the cat-in-the-attic book', and her name for *The Sheep of the Lal Bagh*, (2) by David Mark (Parents Magazine Press, 1967) was 'the Ramesh book'.

On the other hand, Cazden suggests (personal communication) that prior exposure to other books by the same authors, even when the author's name is not mentioned, might provide a child with a frame in which to assimilate and categorize stylistic properties of texts.

Before I go on to describe with more specificity the linguistic and rhetorical aspects of text that these children must have been attending to in order to make the correct judgments that they made, I am going to describe how we selected the materials for this task, because we took great pains to avoid using materials that would allow a participant to make correct answers based on text properties that we considered not particularly linguistic, such as similarities of subject matter, or familiarly named protagonists.

Selection of materials was not a matter to be taken lightly. We knew that children might use subject matter or characters' names to decide authorship. For example, in a similar forced-choice task, one child correctly chose 'the author of the Babar books' as the author of an unfamiliar paragraph referring to an individual named Arthur, and 'the author of *Hi, Cat* and *Whistle for Willie*' as the author of an unfamiliar paragraph referring to a dog named Willie. When questioned, she replied that she had made her judgments on the basis of the name Arthur and the name Willie, respectively. Thus, our materials had to meet all of the following criteria:

1. The author had to have a distinct style. If we were not able, intuitively, to identify an author's works as stylistically unique, we did not consider her or his works as candidates for inclusion in the study. This eliminated a number of celebrated children's authors, including Ezra Jack Keats and Robert McCloskey.

2. The author had to have written at least three books which were not all about the same unique subject matter. This ruled out, for example, Jay Williams, among whose books we could find only one that was not about princesses or kings.

3. The author had to have written at least two books with nonoverlapping sets of characters. This, regrettably, ruled out many authors with strongly individual styles--for example, the de Brunhoffs, authors of the Babar books. We considered including such authors, and changing the characters' names so as not to 'give away' the authorship. We rejected this strategy however, on the grounds that (a) the kinds of names an author chooses are an aspect of style, and we did not want to compromise the integrity of the experiment by meddling with even one aspect of an author's style; and (b) if a child did know such an author's works well, it might be unfairly confusing to ask for judgment on a work that both is and is not that author's.

4. We had to have access to at least three books by the author that shared a distinct style. This eliminated such stylistically interesting authors as Maurice Sendak and Rosemary Wells,

since we could not find three books (on the shelf at the local library) that met our other criteria and shared the same style.

5. At least one of the books, and preferably all three, had to have a text which could present the story independently of the illustrations, so that (a) the familiarization stories could be equally well assimilated by children sitting farther from the teacher and by children clustered closely around her, and (b) the taped story would not be incomprehensible.

The testing had to be done with tapes of the books rather than exemplars, even exemplars that obliterated the author's name, in order to eliminate the possibility that the children might identify the authorship by identifying the illustrations, which in most cases here were done by the author. Also, we wanted to eliminate the graphics (type face, layout) as a possible source of identification, since we had observed that at least some 2-year-olds can recognize these things and 'read' the Crest, K-Mart, Sears, and Special K logos. (One 2-year-old insisted for months that a certain supermarket was an ice cream store, despite regular correction. Eventually, his mother noticed that the lettering on the store's sign was very similar to that used by the Baskin-Robbins chain, and made some headway in clearing up the confusion.) We figured that 5-year-olds might also use such cues, and we wanted to eliminate them.

What we finally ended up with was the following: two authors who wrote in rhymed couplets and used many long words: Dr. Seuss and Virginia Kahl; and three authors who wrote about anthropomorphized animals: Beatrix Potter, Margaret Wise Brown, and Bill Peet.

Finding five authors who met all of our criteria was very difficult. In the initial planning of the study, we feared that including Dr. Seuss might bias the experiment in favor of the hypothesis. However, the discovery of Virginia Kahl allowed us to include both authors in the study, as both write verse fantasy in similar meter. Samples are reproduced in (8) and (9).

(8a) "Oh, help!" cried the Duchess. "Our children are gone!
They're not in the castle--they're not on the lawn--
They're not in the gardens. Are they down in the moat?"
"If they are," said the Duke, "let us hope they can
float."
"They have vanished, they've all disappeared from our
sight.
Our dear little daughters give one such a fright."

(Virginia Kahl: *The Baron's Booty*)

(8b) The message told what the men had seen:
An enormous beast of yellowy-green,
With a sinuous neck and a small fierce head
That had no hair but had horns instead.

(*How Do You Hide a Monster?*)

(8c) And everyone cried, "There's been an error.
That beast is never a cause for terror.
He'd never harm us; he's kind and true.
We must protect him; what shall we do?"
At last they announced, after due reflection,
"We'll send the men off in the wrong direction."

(*How Do You Hide a Monster?*)

(8d) They all ate their pancakes--the very last crumb;
But when they had finished, they all remained dumb.
Then said the Good Wife, "Now, why don't you praise
    me?
Your manners are dreadful--you really amaze me.
You know that my pancakes are fluffy and flavory,
Tender and toothsome, incredibly savory--
Served with a syrup so pure and delightful,
That you've often swooned when you've bitten a
    biteful."

(*The Perfect Pancake*)

(9a) Down slupps the Whisper-ma-Phone to your ear
and the old Once-ler's whispers are not very clear,
since they have to come down through a snergelly hose,
and it sounds as if he had smallish bees up his nose.

(Dr. Seuss, *The Lorax*)

(9b) But I'm also in charge of the brown Bar-ba-Loots
Who played in the shade in their Bar-ba-loot suits
and happily lived, eating Truffula fruits.
NOW ... Thanks to your hacking my trees to the ground,
there's not enough Truffula fruit to go 'round.
And my poor Bar-ba-Loots are all getting the crummies
because they have gas, and no food in their tummies.

(*The Lorax*)

(9c) I was real happy and carefree and young
and I lived in a place called the Valley of Vung
And nothing, not anything, ever went wrong
Until ... well, one day I was walking along
And I guess I got careless, I guess I got gawking
At daisies and not looking where I was walking.

(*I Had Trouble in Getting to Solla Sollew*)

(9d) I dreamed I was sleeping in Solla Sollew
On the banks of the beautiful River Wah-Hoo
Where they never have troubles. At least very few.
Then I woke up. And it just wasn't true.
I was crashing downhill in a flubbulous flood
With suds in my eyes and my mouth full of mud.

(*Solla Sollew*)

(9e) Our camel, he said, had a bad case of gleeks
and should be flat in bed for at least twenty weeks.

(*Solla Sollew*)

(9f) I listened all night to the growls and the yowls
And the chattering teeth of those mice and those owls.
While the Midwinter Jicker howled horrible howls.
I tossed and I flipped and I flopped and I flepped.
It was quarter past five when I finally slept.

(*Solla Sollew*)

(9g) We're marching to battle. We need you, my boy.
We're about to attack. We're about to destroy
The Perilous Poozer of Pamplemousse Pass!
So, get into line! You're a Private, First Class.

(*Solla Sollew*)

(9h) They smell like licorice! And cheese!
Send forty Who-Bubs up the trees
To snip with snippers! Nip with nippers!
Clip and clop with clapping clippers!
Nip and snip with clipping cloppers!
Snip and snop with snipping snoppers!

(*Happy Birthday to You!*)

Similarly, by choosing three animal story authors, we hoped to eliminate topic as a cue to authorship, and force the judgments to depend on subtler cues. Indicative samples of the three authors' texts are reproduced in (10)-(12).

(10a) "If you are a gardener and find me," said the little
    bunny,
    "I will be a bird and fly away from you."
    "If you become a bird and fly away from me," said his
    mother,
    "I will be a tree that you come home to."

    (Margaret Wise Brown: *The Runaway Bunny*)

(10b) Once upon a time in the dark of the moon there was a
    little raccoon.

    (*Wait Till the Moon Is Full*)

(10c) "Does everyone sleep at night?" asked the little
    raccoon.
    "No," said his mother, "not everyone."
    "Who doesn't?" asked the little raccoon.
    "All things that love the night," said his mother.
      "Wait till the moon is full."
    "Is the moon a rabbit?" asked the little raccoon.
    "No," said his mother. "The moon is a moon. A big
    round golden moon."
    "Will I see it soon?"
    "Wait," said the mother. "Wait till the moon is full."

    (*Wait Till the Moon Is Full*)

(10d) There was a little fur family
    warm as toast
    smaller than most
    in little fur coats
    and they lived in a warm wooden tree.

    (*Little Fur Family*)

(10e) Then the little fox climbed an apple tree. Along the
    bark of the tree the eye of a tree toad closed suddenly.
    The fox coughed, "Whiskerchew!" And the tree toad
    knew that someone had seen him hiding there in plain
    sight against the bark of the tree. Some children who
    were supposed to be taking a nap in the afternoon
    weren't sleeping at all. "Whiskerchew!" the fox
    coughed. And the children knew that the fox knew
    that they were not sleeping. All this the fox noted,
    and he went on his way.

    (*Fox Eyes*)

(11a) Peter gave himself up for lost, and shed big tears; but his sobs were overheard by some friendly sparrows, who flew to him in great excitement, and implored him to exert himself.

(Beatrix Potter: *The Tale of Peter Rabbit*)

(11b) I am sorry to say that Peter was not very well during the evening.

(*Peter Rabbit*)

(11c) So that is the story of the two Bad Mice,--but they were not so very very naughty after all, because Tom Thumb paid for everything he broke.

(*The Tale of Two Bad Mice*)

(11d) "What a mercy that was not a pike!" said Mr. Jeremy Fisher. "I have lost my rod and basket; but it does not much matter for I am sure I should never have dared to go fishing again!"

(*The Tale of Mr. Jeremy Fisher*)

(11e) And instead of a nice dish of minnows--they had a roasted grasshopper with lady-bird sauce; which frogs consider a beautiful treat; but I think it must have been nasty!

(*Jeremy Fisher*)

(12a) "Where in blazes did you come from?!!" she shrieked, giving the boulder a vicious kick.

(Bill Peet: *Big Bad Bruce*)

(12b) Once upon a time there was a lion named Eli who lived in the faraway land of Kumbumbazango. He was a decrepit old cat with a scruffy mop of mane, and most of the thunder had gone out of his roar. Now, after many long years as a proud king of beasts, the old lion had finally become as meek as a mouse.

(*Eli*)

(12c) In one frantic leap, and with a wild swing of a paw, Eli caught the jackal with a clout to the snout that sent the little rascal yelping away with his tail between his legs.

(*Eli*)

(12d) Raising his voice to a rumble to make sure all the birds could hear, the lion let them have it. "You good-for-nothing grubby old bone-pickers! You flea-bitten beggars! You ugly old coots! You give me the creeps! Skedaddle! Take off! Get a tree of your own! Leave me be!"

(*Eli*)

(12e) "Wade out into that soup and scrunch down in the gunkazunk grass. The Zoobangas will never look for you there."

(*Eli*)

What might the children have been picking up on to make the correct identifications that they made? Let us begin with the verse selections. At first, the similarities between Kahl and Seuss may seem more striking than the differences. Both write obvious fantasy with a strong four-foot meter, mostly anapests. And both do not hesitate to use words likely to be unfamiliar to young children. But here the similarity ends. Seuss' unfamiliar words tend to be unfamiliar because they are invented (*slupps, snergelly, gleeks, flubbulous, snop*), whereas Kahl's are likely to be unfamiliar because they are drawn from the formal, academic register of language, to which few young children have been exposed, and hardly any have attended. Sometimes she uses basically academic or literary words in her verses (*error, toothsome, swooned*), but much of the unfamiliar word usage is just academic senses of words in common usage in children's books (for example, *reflection* in the sense 'thought', *due* in the sense 'sufficient', *true* in the sense 'loyal', *dumb* in the sense 'mute'). Although the plots are comparatively simple and predictable, the whole tone of Kahl's stories is old-fashioned and/or mock academic, and this is reflected in the syntax as well, in such phrases as *cause for terror*, and *after due reflection*, and in the nonanaphoric use of the pronoun *one* to mean 'a person', and the Germanic verb-second syntax of *Then said the Good Wife*.

In contrast, the tone of the Dr. Seuss stories is very intimate and conversational. This is reflected in the vocabulary, where one finds such colloquial items as *smallish, tummies, the crummies, real* used to intensify an adjective, and the contraction *go 'round*. The conversational tone shows up just as strikingly in the syntax, in such locutions as the introductory *well*, the hedge *I guess*, and the *get* + present participle construction (*got walking*).

Then there are the Seuss trademarks—the made-up species (*Bar-ba-Loots, Truffula, Who-Bubs*), and the coined place names (*Valley of Vung, River Wah-Hoo*), and the novel compound nouns (*Bar-ba-loot suits, Super-Axe-Hacker,*

Key-Slapping Slippard). Finally, alliteration, assonance, and consonance, as in selections (9g-i), are much more character-istic of Seuss' verse than of Kahl's.

There are differences in length (the Seuss stories are longer) and in plot construction: the Seuss stories involve more epi-sodes, are less predictable, and generally involve a human protagonist in interaction with nonhuman species (or only non-human characters), whereas Kahl's stories involve almost ex-clusively human protagonists (the sole exception is a Loch Ness-type monster). However, I suspect that these global properties of the texts were less salient to the children than the more lin-guistic differences, and this feeling is supported by the fact that several children made judgments (usually correct) before they had heard one-tenth of a story. Without hearing a longer selection, they could not easily have formed correct judgments about such global properties as length and plot construction.

Furthermore, when the children mentioned reasons for their choices, they were usually framed in terms like 'it sounded like ...', although one child, justifying an incorrect choice, mentioned particular actions:

I think it's (by the author of) Peter Rabbit because they were planting things and stuff. They were planting carrots.

As it turned out, the Dr. Seuss story was identified correctly 7 out of 12 times; one Kahl story was identified correctly 4 out of 11 times, the other once in 2 trials. Among the 6 children who identified the authorship of 3 or more stories correctly, the Dr. Seuss story was misidentified only once (as being written by Kahl), and the Kahl story was misidentified twice.

What cues allowed the children to recognize stories as being written by Brown, Potter, and Peet? First of all, although all three begin their stories traditionally enough with *Once upon a time* or *Once there was* or *There once was*, there are striking differences in the register used to tell the stories. Peet's stories have a colloquial (*scrunch, clout, snout*), even earthy tone. He minces no words; his characters are *scruffy, de-crepit, crafty*. They do not just say or cry or even shout things, they *shriek* and *let them have it*. And his characters, who tend to be rather bad-tempered, do not mince words either. Roxy comes as close to cursing in (12a) as you can in a picture book, and Eli sounds almost like a Marine drill in-structor when he calls the vultures all those colorfully rude names in (12d).

On the other hand, Potter's stories, written in Edwardian England, sound like it. When Mr. Jeremy Fisher curses, it's *'What a mercy that was not a pike!'* Some of the vocabulary is very formal and literary (*implored, exert*). Many of the phrases strike the modern ear as old-fashioned or maiden-auntish, for example, *shed big tears, so very very naughty, it does not much matter, I should never have dared to.*

The register of Brown's stories is that of bedtime storytelling. As in the Bank Street College's 'Here and Now' stories, for which Brown was a principal writer, these stories are almost exclusively dialog, with a little bit of narration and description, and the description is exclusively literal. In this way, her comparatively plain prose contrasts with Peet's, which makes copious use of figurative language: Eli has a *mop* of mane, and the *thunder* had gone out of his roar. When the vultures urge Eli to wade into the swamp (12e), they call it *soup*. It also contrasts with Potter's, in that Potter almost always interrupts her narrative at the end and makes her presence felt with comments like those in (11b), (11d), and (11e).

I do not mean, by saying that Brown's prose is plain, to imply that it is either colorless and boring, or lacking in style. It has a lyrical rhythmicity, clear in the refrain *'Wait,' said his mother. 'Wait till the moon is full'*, as well as in the selections in (10b), (10d), and (10e). And there is so much internal rhyme and half-rhyme, as in (10b), (10d), and (10e), that some of the passages almost seem to be in verse. Furthermore, Brown's prose has a cyclical structure that also marks it as unique, at least among this group of authors. This structural cyclicity shows up plainly in the conditional-counterconditional repartee (exemplified in (10a)) that constitutes almost the whole of *The Runaway Bunny*, and it is no less clear in the repeated requests in *Wait Till the Moon Is Full* that are answered, every page or so, with the refrain *'Wait,' said his mother. 'Wait till the moon is full'*, as in (10c).

All of the Brown stories used in the experiment are quiet, calm stories, with no violence and a comparatively low level of suspense--what is going to happen is never a matter of life and death.[2] In contrast to Brown's simple, almost plotless stories, Peet's and Potter's stories involve unpredictable chains of episodes, and in Peet's these involve embedded and conflicting plans. All of the stories by these three authors that the children heard have animals as the main protagonists, but Brown's are almost always presented as juvenile and 'pedomorphized', while many of Potter's and all of Peet's are full-grown, though not grown-up--they act and react like children. At least one of the stories by each author also involves human beings, though always as minor characters.

The Potter book in the test (*The Tale of Two Bad Mice*) was correctly identified 4 times out of 11; the Brown books (*Fox Eyes* and *Little Fur Family*) 7 times out of 13, and 1 time out of 4, respectively; and the Peet book (*Eli*), 2 times out of 6. Among the 6 children who correctly identified the authorship of 3 or more books, *Fox Eyes* was correctly identified 5 out of 6 times, and *Little Fur Family* 1 time out of 2; *The Tale of Two Bad Mice* was correctly identified 4 times out of 6, and *Eli*, 2 times out of 4.

Let us turn for a moment to address the question of accounting for the errors that were made. What might have caused some of the confusions? We can identify a number of cross-author similarities that might account for some of the errors. Both Peet and Seuss use very colloquial vocabulary and syntax. And Peet, like Seuss, refers to obviously invented species and places (*gunkazunk grass, Zoobangas, Kumbumbazango*), though Seuss' are more often compounded of familiar morphemes than Peet's. Both Potter and Kahl use a fairly formal and literary vocabulary and syntax. Seuss as well as Potter intrudes into the narrative and makes the author's presence felt. *Happy Birthday to You* and *The Lorax* are specifically addressed to the reader, the former as an extended wish, the latter as a sort of reverie. *I Had Trouble in Getting to Solla Sollew* unsurprisingly is a first-person narrative. Both Kahl and Brown tell simple stories, with relatively predictable plots, though Kahl's are more complex, and some of Brown's have hardly any plot at all. Finally, while Potter's stories are not as lullaby-like as Brown's, the suspense is muted, the action damped, by the calm, matter-of-fact tone of the telling.

How well do these similarities account for the errors that were actually made? If the errors had been random and evenly distributed, half of them would have been in cells predicted by these similarities. In fact, 56 percent of the errors were in these cells (56.5 percent of the errors by the 0-2 correct group, and 55 percent of the errors by the 3-5 correct group). And 4 children made symmetrical errors--for example, identifying the Potter story as by Kahl and vice versa, suggesting that the errors were not random, but were based on some perception of similarity.

Implications. This study appears to show that at least some 5-year-olds have the ability to appreciate and discriminate among the literary styles available in books intended for young children. Indeed, several children found the challenge of testing this ability exhilarating.

I cannot show that what the children were attending to when they correctly identified the authorship of stories they had not heard before was, in fact, the linguistic and rhetorical aspects of literary style that I have indicated (I could not prove that, even if the experiment had been conducted with well-read and highly articulate adults), but it seems a good bet. In any case, it means that the children understood a whole lot more than the bare outlines (or even dressed-out outlines) of plot. Making the correct judgments almost certainly entailed not only noticing and abstracting from very fine details of wordcraft, but also attending to and abstracting from global structural matters of form and content.

If it is true that 5-year-olds generally, and by extension, 6- and 7-year-olds, have the ability to make such fine discriminations, then it seems likely that they would be able to tell the difference between the prose in ordinary children's books of the sort I have been discussing, and the prose in their readers, a sample of which is given in (13).

(13) Rabbit said, "I can run. I can run fast. You can't run fast."

Turtle said, "Look Rabbit, See the park. You and I will run. We'll run to the park."

Rabbit said, "I want to stop. I'll stop here. I can run, but Turtle can't. I can get to the park fast."

Turtle said, "I can't run fast. But I will not stop. Rabbit can't see me. I'll get to the park."

Such prose is edited to conform to readability formulae which impose strict limits on sentence length and vocabulary. Owing to the strict constraints imposed by the publishers of basal readers [3] on sentence length, vocabulary, and story length, these works end up being designed in such a way that they are devoid of most characteristics of individual style. If it is generally true that at the age when reading instruction begins, children attend to and appreciate stylistic differences, then it would seem to follow that expecting them to read such basal readers is, to say the least, inconsiderate. At best, it is pointless; at worst, it is counterproductive. It wastes valuable time that could be spent in more profitable ways and risks boring the children and conveying to them that there is nothing interesting to be learned in books, or even in school. Is it possible that Johnny does not learn to read because there is no thrill in being able to read texts like (13), which is from what is supposed to be a version of Aesop's fable about the hare and the tortoise?

The objection is likely to be raised that the fact that 5-year-olds can appreciate the differences between works by Beatrix Potter and Margaret Wise Brown does not mean that 7-year-olds could read the works of either author independently, that 7-year-olds have enough trouble reading the admittedly anemic prose in the basals. It is certainly true that there is no direct entailment from what 5-year-olds can comprehend orally to what 7-year-olds can independently read, but I think this study suggests that 7-year-olds might be able to read Margaret Wise Brown and Beatrix Potter; the fact that some have trouble with second-grade basals might be due to stylistic properties of the basals that are introduced in the process of writing a graded reader. Work at the Center for the Study of Reading (Davison, Kantor, et al. 1980) has shown that many of the devices used in adapting a text to meet sentence-length, vocabulary, and passage-length requirements contribute to a marked decrease in the coherence and interest of the text. In addition, it is a basic principle of attention theory that perceptual activities which demand more mental processing tend to be favored over less demanding activities (Hardiman and Zernich 1978). Successfully meeting a challenge is itself a source of pleasure and satisfaction. If some 7-year-olds have trouble with grade-level basal readers, it may be a problem of motivation; it may be that they would do better on more complex, more difficult, more challenging, more rewarding material.

If the ability to discriminate literary styles is general among primary-grade children, then it may be that by editing their readers to meet someone's preconceived notions of what is easy, we are depriving children of the satisfaction of meeting a challenge, and contributing to making learning to read an unpleasant experience.

NOTES

Permission for use of illustrations and quotations in this paper is gratefully acknowledged, as follows:

Illustrations:
Examples (1) and (2): By Lionel Kalish, from *The Cat and the Fiddler*, by Jacky Jeter (copyright © 1968 by Parents Magazine Press), and *The Sheep of the Lal Bagh*, by David Mark (copyright © 1967 by Lionel Kalish), respectively. Englewood Cliffs, N.J.: Four Winds Press. Used with permission.
Quotations:
Example (8a): From Virginia Kahl, *The Baron's Booty*. Copyright © 1963 by Virginia Kahl. (New York: Charles Scribner's Sons, 1963) Reprinted with the permission of Charles Scribner's Sons.

Examples (8b), (8c): From Virginia Kahl, *How Do You Hide a Monster?* Copyright © 1971 by Virginia Kahl. (New York: Charles Scribner's Sons, 1971) Reprinted with the permission of Charles Scribner's Sons.

Example (8d): From Virginia Kahl, *The Perfect Pancake*. Copyright © 1960 by Virginia Kahl. (New York: Charles Scribner's Sons, 1960) Reprinted with the permission of Charles Scribner's Sons.

Examples (9a), (9b): From *The Lorax*, by Dr. Seuss. Copyright © 1971 by Dr. Seuss and A. S. Geisel. Reprinted by permission of Random House, Inc.

Examples (9c) through (9g): From *I Had Trouble in Getting to Solla Sollew*, by Dr. Seuss. Copyright © 1965 by Dr. Seuss. Reprinted by permission of Random House, Inc.

Example (9h): From *Happy Birthday to You!*, by Dr. Seuss. Copyright © 1959 by Dr. Seuss. Reprinted by permission of Random House, Inc.

Example (10a): Text excerpt from *The Runaway Bunny* by Margaret Wise Brown. Copyright © 1942 by Harper and Row, Publishers, Inc. Text renewed © 1970 by Roberta Brown Rauch. By permission of Harper and Row, Publishers, Inc.

Examples (10b), (10c): Text excerpts from *Wait Till the Moon Is Full* by Margaret Wise Brown. Copyright 1948 by Margaret Wise Brown. Text copyright renewed 1976 by Roberta Brown Rauch. By permission of Harper and Row, Publishers, Inc.

Example (10d): Text excerpt from *Little Fur Family* by Margaret Wise Brown. Copyright 1946 by Harper and Row, Publishers, New York and Evanston. Renewed 1974 by Roberta Brown Rauch and Garth Williams. By permission of Harper and Row, Publishers, Inc.

Example (10e): From *Fox Eyes*, by Margaret Wise Brown. Copyright © 1952 by Pantheon Books, Inc. Reprinted by permission of Pantheon Books, a division of Random House, Inc.

Example (11a), (11b): From Beatrix Potter, *The Tale of Peter Rabbit*. 1902. New York: Frederick Warne and Co., Inc. Used with permission.

Example (11c): From Beatrix Potter, *The Tale of Two Bad Mice*. 1904. New York: Frederick Warne and Co., Inc. Used with permission.

Examples (11d), (11e): From Beatrix Potter, *The Tale of Mr. Jeremy Fisher*. 1906. New York: Frederick Warne and Co., Inc. Used with permission.

Example (12a): From Bill Peet, *Big Bad Bruce*. Copyright © 1977. Boston: Houghton Mifflin Co.

Examples (12b) through (12e): From Bill Peet, *Eli*. Copyright © 1978. Boston: Houghton Mifflin Co.

Example (13): From *A Duck Is a Duck* of the Reading 720 series by Theodore Clymer and others. © Copyright 1976, 1969, by Ginn and Company (Xerox Corporation). Used with permission.

1. For testing kindergarteners' ability to recognize literary style, we considered a number of tasks. A simple recognition task, wherein a child would be asked if a passage had been heard before, was rejected as not directly tapping the abilities we wanted to test. A 2x2 forced-choice task (matching unfamiliar (or familiar) passages with familiar authors' names two at a time) was rejected as not very informative, since making one incorrect answer practically entailed making another, and vice versa, one correct answer practically entailed making another correct answer. A 2-out-of-3 (or more) matching task, where a child would be asked to say which two passages out of a group were by the same author, was rejected as logistically unfeasible for nonreaders: the passages would have to be presented orally; and we judged that it would be asking too much to ask children to remember three or more passages and their order of presentation, in order to say which two were most alike.

We wanted to make the task as difficult as we could and still get better-than-chance performance so that it would test the limits of the children's ability and so that the results would be as informative as we could manage. For this reason, we settled on a 1-out-of-5 multiple-choice style-matching task, with the test materials containing as few non-style-related clues as possible.

2. Brown did not limit herself to 'lullaby' stories. A bizarre and aggressive picture-book called *The Steamroller: A Fantasy* (Walker Publishing Company, 1974) shows an entirely different side of her.

3. In response to perceived demands from text book selection bodies.

REFERENCES

Davison, A., R. N. Kantor, J. Hannah, G. Hermon, R. Lutz, and R. Salzillo. 1980. Limitations of readability formulas in guiding adaptation of texts. Technical Report No. 162. Urbana: University of Illinois, Center for the Study of Reading. ERIC Document Reproduction Service No. ED 184 090.
Hardiman, G., and T. Zernich. 1978. Basic research: Aesthetic behavior in the visual arts. Viewpoints 6.1:29-38.

TOPICS WITHIN TOPICS

Joseph E. Grimes
Cornell University and
Summer Institute of Linguistics.

When you and I talk, much of the time we talk 'about' something. Some of us here, myself included, are not too sure what 'about' means, but we have a few observations we can build on:

1. There are interesting properties of the form our sentences take that seem to depend on what we are talking about. Clefting would be one example.

2. Conversations and other discourses that do not succeed in establishing some agreement on what they are about do not get very far as vehicles for communicating information, though they may succeed as phatic speech acts.

3. Often, while talking about one thing, we put it aside temporarily and talk about something else for a while. After we finish with the new thing, we may come back to the first one, but we do not always do so.

4. What we talk about does not have to be a thing in the physical sense or even in the grammatical sense of being encoded as a noun. Places, times, activities, and states of affairs are also candidates.

5. Linguists use terms like 'topic', 'theme', 'focus', and 'foregrounding' for some of these things I have just mentioned, but no two linguists use the terms in the same way.

I invite you to concentrate with me on the third observation: that while talking about one thing, we often put it aside and talk about something else before we return to pick up the main point and finish whatever we set out to do regarding it.

I warn you that I am not far enough along in my understanding of this phenomenon that I can lay out very many signals for you, even for English, and that I am far from being able to give an algorithm that can recognize shifts to embedded topics or to following topics. Both are part of a total effort that a number of people are engaged in. We hope it will eventually show how referential orientation is communicated.

What I can do is to help you see that such a phenomenon is plainly there, and that even now we can discern a considerable richness in the way it works. My argument is from weaker to stronger: if we can learn this much about one aspect of language with nothing but the crude concepts I have used, we can certainly expect to get somewhere by refining them some more.

Let me illustrate concretely this setting aside and resuming of reference. Many of us studied Abraham Lincoln's Gettysburg Address of 1863 in school; we may even have memorized it. There is broad agreement that whatever we may mean by a well-formed discourse, this qualifies as one. Furthermore, it is brief enough that it is not hopeless to understand, yet the text is complex enough that our reward for doing so will be something more than a sense of having found out the obvious. Schank and Carbonell (1978) have called attention to some of the complex inferences that have to be made in order to understand this speech; I focus my attention here on different aspects.

The text itself, with the sentences numbered, is given in the appendix to this paper. The spelling and punctuation reproduced there are from Lincoln's own hand, as preserved in the Cornell University Library's copy. Asterisks indicate points of audience reaction, taken from a *New York Tribune* account reproduced in Everett (1863).

This text is typical of a large class of texts in which the things we are talking about at any point have properties of identity, place, and time, and may be indexed by any combination of these. The identities in this text are not hard to sort out. There are the speaker and around 15,000 hearers, taken as a group. There is the nation with which that group is affiliated. There are soldiers who fought during a period of war, some of whom were killed. The world, in the sense of its inhabitants, is mentioned.

Spatial reference is not as prominent in this text as it is in some. There is the continent on which the nation was established, a battlefield, and 17 acres out of that field that include the actual site of the speech. At the end there is a reference to the earth as a whole.

The most complex part of the referential system is time. Time references center around the war period already referred to, and in particular around two events within that period: a

significant battle, and the event of the speech itself four and
a half months after. In addition, there is the time when the
nation to which all the participants belong began, 'fourscore
and seven years' before the time of the speech.

Related to these are four time periods that extend without
limit into the future but share a boundary on the other end
with one of the concrete events. The first begins with the
founding of the nation and refers to the things its founders
were trying to accomplish in what to them was the future.
The second is to begin as soon as the occasion of the speech
ends and has to do with its results. The third began when
the speech did and has to do with attitudes that the speaker
and his hearers share and that the speaker is encouraging
them to continue to hold. The fourth is expected to begin
when the period of war ends.

Another unbounded period reaches back into the past by
way of gnomic or timeless reference--something that is independent of any particular time framework.

Figure 1 diagrams the topology of the time framework, using
Litteral's conventions. On that time line 'before' lies to the
left and 'after' to the right, and significant stretches of time
numbered with even numbers are separated by vertical boundary marks numbered with odd numbers, with no attempt to
represent actual duration.

Figure 1. Topology of time in Lincoln's Gettysburg
Address.

	1		3	5	7		9		11		13	15	
0		2		4	6		8		10		12	14	16
		NEW NATION 1776			BATTLE July 1-3, 1863				SPEECH November 19, 1863				
					CIVIL WAR 1861-? [1865]								

When each portion of the text is related to this overall
referential framework, its parts sort themselves into four connected subsystems. In establishing these subsystems, time
reference seems to be the most important factor, though I
cannot yet define what I mean by 'most important' with either
a structural or a quantitative measure.

The first group is in Figure 2. It consists of those references for which time is not a factor. Their time reference is
indicated by a single unbounded line that can be identified by
its first and last parts as (0,16). Sentence numbers in parentheses identify fragments that illustrate the time reference.

Figure 2. Atemporal elements in Lincoln's Gettysburg Address.

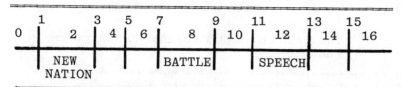

the proposition that all men are created equal (1) any nation so conceived and so dedicated (2) in a larger sense (6)

The second group is in Figure 3. It has to do with the nation: its founding (1,3), the intent of its founders (3,16), its testing (5,15), and its future (15,16). Here are a set of time references that share common boundary lines, including also the time displacement (3,11) and the possible end of the nation (3,15).

Figure 3. The NATION complex in Lincoln's Gettysburg Address.

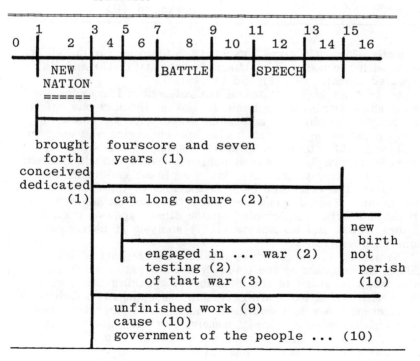

The third referential group is in Figure 4. It has to do with the battle Lincoln is speaking of (7,9), along with its short-range outcome (9,11) and its long-range consequences (9,16).

Figure 4.   The BATTLE complex in Lincoln's Gettysburg Address.

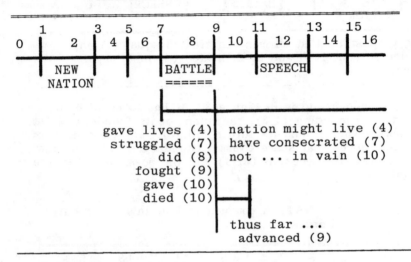

Finally, Figure 5 gives the fourth referential group. It has to do with the occasion of Lincoln's speech (11,13) and its expected outcome (11,16) and (13,16).

Now that we have an idea of the referential framework we are dealing with, we can begin to look at the way one referential complex within it is laid aside temporarily for another, then picked up again later. This speech begins and ends in what we could call the referential complex of the NATION, given in Figure 3. The first sentence makes implicit reference to the situation by speaking, via the phrase ending in *ago* that moves the reference back to the time of the founding of the nation. This displacement away from the situation of speaking has been commented on for other types of text, including Labov and Waletzky's (1967) analysis of narratives done 14 years ago.

The second sentence moves into the middle part of the referential complex of the NATION by two paths. The first is through a return to the situation of speaking using *now*, along with the situational expression *are engaged*, which is in the present tense and defines a time span broader than that of the situation of speaking, namely, the Civil War. That period had begun before the speech started, and it was not yet over when the speech was given.

Figure 5. The SPEECH-related complex in Lincoln's
Gettysburg Address.

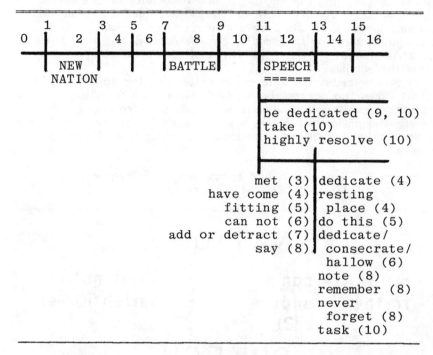

The second approach takes off from the preceding reference
to the NATION, and speaks of the possible termination of that
entity in the words *can long endure*. There is a complex process of inference that ties the termination of the Civil War
with the possible termination of the concept of the NATION;
this is the point where a precise statement of what is going
on gets sticky, but where we ordinary users of language not
unreasonably recognize that a referential connection does exist.

Following the second sentence there are only three minor
references to the NATION complex until the end. They are
all embedded grammatically within sentences whose major reference is laid out in Figure 5, associated with the SPEECH.
The three minor references: in Sentence (3), *of that war*
refers briefly to the NATION complex; in Sentence (9), *the
unfinished work* refers to the sequel to the founding of the
NATION, which Lincoln hopes will outlast the war itself; and
in Sentence (10b), *that cause* refers to the same sequel.

At the end, however, and at a point where the audience
responded overtly, the whole reference pattern shifts back
to the point in time where Sentence (2) left off. At the time
indexed by 15, which is later than the SPEECH and at which

it will be possible to confirm or deny the content of the words *can long endure* in Sentence (2), the last two segments of Sentence (10) pick up the hoped for continuity of the referential complex of the NATION and the idea behind it: *that this nation, under God, shall have a new birth of freedom--and that government of the people, by the people, for the people* [the manifestation of the NATION concept] *shall not perish from the earth.*

In other words, the referential pattern of the speech as a whole takes the perspective of the nation: its founding, its uncertain continuation, and hope for its perseverance. This referential pattern, however, is laid aside in Sentences (3) to (10c), which talk about more immediate things, as Figure 6 shows.

Figure 6.   Suspension and resumption of reference in Lincoln's Gettysburg Address.

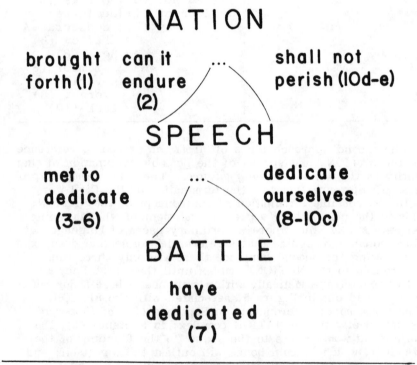

In this central section, all but one of the matrix sentences belong to the SPEECH complex of Figure 5. Sentences (3), (4), and (5) are stative and perfective in form and refer to the immediate occasion: for example, the time reference of *we are* in (3) is only part of the temporal scope that is associated with the same words in (2). Sentence (3) provides a transition from the NATION orientation of the beginning sentences. The words *of that war* in Sentence (3), which I take it have to be read as part of the tail of the intonation, in Ladd's (1980) terms, are the context within which *battlefield* and *we are met* point to circumscribed events, the BATTLE complex and the SPEECH complex of Figures 4 and 5, respectively.

Sentences (3), (4), and (5), and I think the word *but* with which (6) begins, anchor to the occasion of the speech itself. Sentence (3) places that occasion in its larger context, while (4) through (6) continue on to talk about what is to happen following the speech, which in the case of (6) also includes the activity of the speech itself.

At this point there comes what I have elsewhere called a composite operation in the progression of changes in participant orientation. The relation of the participants in Sentences (3) through (6) is 'We...are doing something about a place...for those who fought'. Sentence (7) reverses this orientation: 'Those who fought...did something about that place...regardless of us'. In the study of participant orientation systems, I have noticed a high correlation between composite shifts of orientation like this one and surprise points (Grimes 1975: 266).

Figure 7.   Changes in participant orientation, adapted from Grimes (1975:264).

srs (we...place...those who fought)
     A   B

= (those who fought...place...us)
          C   B   A

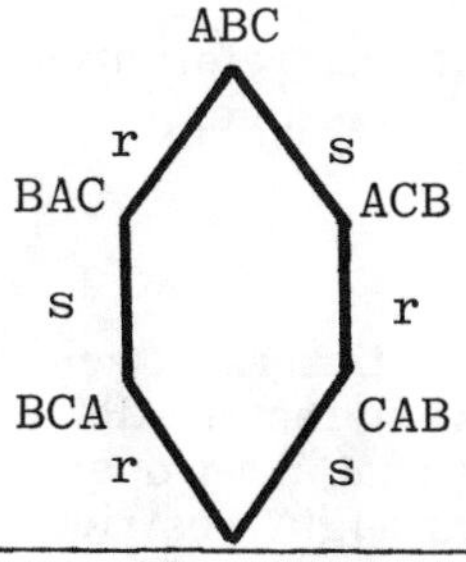

```
         ABC
          /\
       r /  \ s          r (reversal)
  BAC  /      \  ACB        (12)(3)
      |        |         ABC ——————►BAC
   s  |        |  r
      |        |
  BCA  \      /  CAB     s (switch)
        \    /             (1)(23)
       r \  / s          ABC ——————►ACB
          \/
```

The next four sentences, taking the parts of the last orthographic sentence as separate divisions, all have matrices that refer to what is likely to happen after the SPEECH.

Sentence (8) is referentially a recapitulation of (4) through (6) in its first half, and of (7) in its second half.

Sentences (9) and (10b) are parallel to each other. They organize the same referential complexes in the same relation. Each touches base with the main triple: the SPEECH and its sequel, the unbounded sequel to the founding of the NATION, and the BATTLE period. Sentence (9) also fills the gap between BATTLE and SPEECH, which is otherwise untouched, in the words *have thus far so nobly advanced*. Either of these sentences could stand as a minimal statement of the content of the speech by virtue of bringing together its three referential complexes; yet if either were taken to be the summary, that would miss the perspective of the speech because neither of these sentences has the NATION complex as its framework, and the speech as a whole has.

Sentence (10c) appears to provide the transition from the center section oriented around SPEECH references back to the outer NATION complex. It does so by having the SPEECH and its sequel be the referents for the matrix sentence, then picking up the unbounded sequel to the BATTLE. This open segment (9,16) shares its final segment, the unbounded one, with the remainder of the speech.

I have laid out a fairly complicated set of interrelationships that I have noticed so far in the referential structure of one text. I have done it without recourse to any particular theoretical model. I have found none yet that is quite rich enough to allow me to sort out what I observe, though some of the proposals of our next speaker [Teun van Dijk] offer a partial model. To me, recognizing these relationships brings up several questions that ought to be asked:

1. Is this linguistics or something else?

2. Could anybody else get a comparable analysis out of the same data?

3. What have we got when we finish?

4. Have we actually proved anything about one referential complex being laid aside while another takes over, followed by reinstatement of the first?

5. Do all texts behave this way?

Since I for one have never thought of linguistics as something sharply circumscribed, but rather as a characteristic way of thinking about language, I would say that I am operating somewhere near the edge of what others might restrict linguistics to, but I am doing so as a linguist would. Specifically, I am not making assertions about language that are not required by the kinds of forms that are actually said, nor am I making assertions for which no parallels can be found in other texts or in other languages.

As for whether other people can be brainwashed into seeing things my way well enough to get a comparable analysis out of the same data, all I can say is that I think I am closer to it than the last time I tackled this subject (Grimes in press).

The results of this kind of analysis are a more precise idea of what referential elements are being dealt with at each stage of a text, together with a notion of suspension and resumption of a set of referents, indicated in some cases (but not in all) by transitional sentences that tie one referential complex with another. Whether this hypothesis about nesting one referential complex inside another is confirmed by texts like this one is, of course, open to interpretation; one alternative would be that we simply ramble around from one sentence to another, and occasionally meander back to some referential complex we have already taken up, perhaps with some broad constraints to the effect that we ought to try to end up in the same area we started out from.

This is possible, but I think an argument for nesting can be constructed from those cases in which referential shift goes along with grammatical subordination. I would ask why any language needs to have any mechanism of subordination at all in order to carry out its communicative tasks. Most of the shifts in reference that are made within sentences in this text and others I have examined coincide with the boundaries of grammatically dependent or embedded syntactic units. I would take it, then, that subordinate structures could be thought of as one explicit means of communicating referential shift.

So far, the differences I have found among texts involve two things: the kinds of elements on which I find referential continuity or discontinuity, and the depth of nesting. In a movie review from *Time* magazine, for example, I find that all the referential shifts are on identifiable elements: the script, the actors, the color print, and so on. The only shifts that involve time or place are embedded within sentences, and have nothing to do with the text as a whole or with major sections of it. On the other hand, in Koine Greek texts I find considerable suspension of one referential complex in favor of another, and that of another, and so on until the chain of resumptions starts up in the other direction. Much of this nesting is made explicit by grammatical embedding and subordination, with the result that the average syntactic depth of Greek sentences is greater than would be natural for English.

So we are in the intriguing position of being able to recognize the temporary replacement of one set of referents by another. To a certain extent we can match this with shifts in syntax; but we have some distance to go before we can say we really understand either the mechanisms of this replacement or the part it plays in human communication.

APPENDIX

Gettysburg Address
Abraham Lincoln
November 19, 1863

(1) Four score and seven years ago (3,11 NATION related
        to SPEECH)
    our fathers brought forth, on this continent, a new
        nation, conceived in Liberty, and dedicated to
        the proposition (1,3 NATION)
    that all men are created equal. (0,16 TIMELESS)*

    (PARAGRAPH)
(2) Now we are engaged in a great civil war, testing
        whether (5,13 WAR to limited sequel to NATION)
    that nation, (3,15 NATION + limited sequel)
    or any nation so conceived, and so dedicated, (0,16
        TIMELESS)
    can long endure. (3,15 NATION + limited sequel)

(3) We are met on a great (11,13 SPEECH)
    battle-field (7,9 BATTLE)
    of that war. (5,15 WAR)

(4) We have come (11,13 SPEECH)
    to dedicate a portion of that field, as a final
        resting-place for (13,16 sequel to SPEECH)
    those who here gave their lives, (7,9 BATTLE)
    that that nation might live. (9,16 sequel to BATTLE)

(5) It is altogether fitting and proper (11,13 SPEECH)
    that we should do this. (13,16 sequel to SPEECH)

    (PARAGRAPH)
(6) But, (11,13 SPEECH)
    in a larger sense, (0,16 TIMELESS)
    we can not dedicate--we can not consecrate--we
        can not hallow--this ground. (11,16 SPEECH +
        sequel)

(7) The brave men, living and dead, who struggled
        here, (7,9 BATTLE)
    have consecrated it (9,16 sequel to BATTLE)
    far above our poor power to add or detract. (11,13
        SPEECH)*

(8) The world will little note, nor long remember (13,16
        sequel to SPEECH)
    what we say here, (11,13 SPEECH)

but it can never forget (13,16 sequel to SPEECH)
what they did here. (7,9 BATTLE)*

(9) It is for us the living, rather, to be dedicated
      here to (11,16 SPEECH + sequel)
    the unfinished work which (3,16 unlimited sequel to
      NATION)
    they who fought here (7,9 BATTLE)
    have thus far so nobly advanced. (9,11 sequel to
      BATTLE up to SPEECH)*

(10a) It is rather for us to be here dedicated (11,16
      SPEECH + sequel)
    to the great task remaining before us (13,16
      sequel to SPEECH)

(10b) --that from these honored dead we take increased
      devotion to (11,16 SPEECH + sequel)
    that cause for which (3,16 sequel to NATION)
    they here gave the last full measure of
      devotion (7,9 BATTLE)

(10c) --that we here highly resolve (11,16 SPEECH +
      sequel)
    that these dead (9,16 sequel to BATTLE)
    shall (11,16 SPEECH + sequel?)
    not have died in vain (9,16 sequel to BATTLE)*

(10d) --that this nation, under God, shall have a new
      birth of freedom (15,16 sequel to WAR)

(10e) --and that (15,16 sequel to WAR)
    government of the people, by the people, for the
    people, (3,16 sequel to NATION)
    shall not perish from the earth. (15,16 sequel to
      WAR)*

REFERENCES

Everett, Edward. 1863. An oration delivered on the battle-
    field of Gettysburg. New York: Baker and Godwin.
Grimes, Joseph E. 1975. The thread of discourse. The
    Hague: Mouton.
Grimes, Joseph E. (in press) Reference spaces in text.
    In: Nobel symposium on text processing. Edited by
    Sture Allén. Gothenburg: Språkdata.
Labov, William, and Joshua Waletzky. 1967. Narrative
    analysis: Oral versions of personal experience. In:
    Essays on the verbal and visual arts. Edited by June Helm.
    Seattle: American Ethnological Society and University of
    Washington Press.

Ladd, D. Robert, Jr. 1980. The structure of intonational
  meaning. Bloomington: Indiana University Press.
Lincoln, Abraham. [1863] The Gettysburg address of Abraham Lincoln: Holograph manuscript presented by George
  Bancroft with accompanying letter by Lincoln, February 29,
  1864. MS.
Litteral, Robert. 1972. Rhetorical predicates and time
  topology in Anggor. Foundations of Language 8.391-410.
Schank, Roger C., and Jaime G. Carbonell, Jr. 1978. Re:
  the Gettysburg address: Representing social and political
  acts. Yale University Department of Computer Science,
  Research Report 127.
van Dijk, Teun A. 1977. Text and context: Explorations
  in the semantics and pragmatics of discourse. London:
  Longman.

EPISODES AS UNITS OF DISCOURSE ANALYSIS

Teun A. van Dijk
University of Amsterdam

1. Units of discourse analysis. One of the tasks of a sound
theory of discourse is to explicate the analytical units postulated in the abstract description of textual structures at various levels. In addition to the usual morphophonemic, syntactic,
semantic or pragmatic units or categories of sentence grammars,
the theory of discourse has introduced new notions, such as
'coherence', 'cohesion', 'topic', or 'theme'--explicated in so-
called 'macrostructures', whereas the analysis of conversation
makes use of such notions as 'turn' or 'move'.
    Thus, more or less at a 'meso-level' in between the unit of
a clause or sentence on the one hand, and the unit of a text,
discourse, or conversation as a whole, the notion of 'paragraph' or 'episode' has recently been discussed in various
branches of discourse analysis (Chafe 1980, Longacre 1979,
Hinds 1979). Roughly speaking, paragraphs or episodes are
characterized as coherent sequences of sentences of a discourse, linguistically marked for beginning and/or end, and
further defined in terms of some kind of 'thematic unity'--for
instance, in terms of identical participants, time, location or
global event or action.
    In this paper I would like to contribute to a further defini-
tion of the notion of paragraph or episode, and will thereby
focus on their semantic properties. It is argued here that an
explicit account of these notions also requires a characterization in terms of semantic macrostructures, of which the various
'surface manifestations' often function as typical paragraph or
episode markers.
    For the sake of theoretical clarity, I make a distinction be-
tween the notion of 'paragraph' and the notion of 'episode'.
An episode is properly a semantic unit, whereas a paragraph
is the surface manifestation or the expression of such an

episode. Since I would like to pay attention especially to semantic issues, the discussion is mainly about episodes, rather
than about paragraphs and their grammatical properties (as
have been studied by Longacre 1979, Hinds 1979, and others).
   Although this paper has a predominantly 'structuralistic'
nature, the assumption that episodes are semantic units raises
the possibility that they also have psychological relevance, as
units in a cognitive model of discourse processing. Recent
work in that area seems to suggest, indeed, that episode-like
units have processing relevance in reading, representation,
and memorization of discourse (see, for example, Black and
Bower 1979; Haberlandt, Berian, and Sandson 1980). It is
briefly shown at the end of this paper that my linguistic/
semantic observations may indeed be relevant for a cognitive
discourse model.
   Before I begin my discussion, a methodological remark is in
order. There has been considerable controversy--mostly outside discourse analysis or text grammar, and often directed
against these--about the linguistic and in particular the grammatical status of postulated discourse categories or units. In
order to keep linguistics and especially grammar nice and
clean, not only have many linguists preferred to remain within
the seemingly safe boundaries of the sentence, but at the same
time they have tried to discredit as linguistically or grammatically 'foreign' most of the specific units, categories, or levels
used in various kinds of discourse analysis, admitting these at
most to a theory of language use, to pragmatics, to rhetoric,
or to other theories or disciplines outside their scope of responsibility.
   The style of the last sentence suggests that I do not share
that opinion. It is certainly true that many properties of discourse cannot and should not be accounted for in the format of
a linguistic grammar; for example, rhetorical or narrative structures require separate--but integrated--treatment. Yet, many
other discourse phenomena are properly linguistic or even 'grammatical', that is, they can be fully accounted for in terms of
the usual levels, categories, or units that are familiar in the
account of sentences. This does not mean, of course, as some
have suggested, that therefore a linguistic theory of discourse
can safely be reduced to that of a theory of sentences (plus
some theory of language use, a pragmatic or a cognitive model).
New notions and specific phenomena, such as coherence, macrostructure, or episode, are certainly necessary, but they can
be described in terms of familiar theoretical notions.
   Although I do think that linguistics and grammar have specific tasks and hence theories of their own, I would like to suggest more generally that the boundaries between 'grammar' and
other linguistic theories, or between linguistic accounts of language and language use, and psychological or sociological ones,
are not and should not be too sharp. In a general functional
approach to language (Dik 1978, Givón 1979a, 1979b) which is

now a central paradigm in linguistics, it is stressed that on the
one hand units, categories, rules, and structures at one level of
analysis are systematically linked with those at other levels,
and that on the other hand, all these 'linguistic' structures are
functionally linked (both ways: determining and depending on)
to the cognitive and social processing and use of language in
communicative interaction. Thus, properties of the sentence--
morphophonemic, syntactic, semantic, and pragmatic--appear
also to have functions within the discourse (Givón 1979b). The
same holds for a theory of the episode. Some properties of
episodes can conveniently be formulated within a linguistic and
even a grammatical framework; others need additional or alternative description in cognitive, interactional, and social terms.
If attention is focused on the first, it should be kept in mind
that the theory is essentially partial, and that the interdepen-
dencies with the cognitive and social processes and functions
are an indispensable further explanation of the 'grammatical'
structures of a more abstract account of episodes in discourse.

2. Intuitive notions of 'episode'. The notion of episode occurs not only in a theory of discourse, but also in everyday
discourse. We speak about an 'episode' of our life, an 'episode' during a party, an 'episode' in the history of a country,
or about episodes in stories about such episodes. In this
sense an episode is first of all conceived of as a part of a
whole, having a beginning and an end, and hence defined in
temporal terms. Next, both the part and the whole mostly involve sequences of events or actions. And finally, the episode
should somehow be 'unified' and have some relative independence: we can identify it and distinguish it from other episodes. Thus, a war can be an episode in the history of a
country, a battle an episode in a war, and some brave action
of a group of soldiers an episode during the battle. Apparently, the 'unifying' aspect of such sequences of events or
actions conceptually appears in global event or action notions,
such as 'war', 'battle', 'attack', and so on, as well as in the
identity of the participants of such events and actions (a
country, armies, groups of soldiers, individual persons, etc.),
and finally, in the temporal identification of beginning and end.
  This intuitive notion of episode corresponds to the notion of
episode in a story or account of such actions and events: one
speaks about an episode in a novel or in a history textbook,
and the meaning of that notion is similar to its corresponding
world episode: a sequence of sentences (or of propositions
expressed by such sentences) denoting such an episode, hence
with marked beginning and end and some conceptual unity. It
is this intuitive notion that has been taken over in the theory
of discourse. In this paper, then, I try to explicate this theoretical notion, and investigate whether it can be applied also to
other discourse types, that is, not only to event or action
discourse such as stories.

3. **The semantics of episodes.** Since episodes are taken to be semantic units of discourse, one must be able to define them in semantic terms, for example, in terms of propositions. I will indeed so do, and characterize an episode of a discourse as a specific 'sequence of propositions'. Just like the discourse as a whole, such a sequence must be coherent according to the usual conditions of textual coherence (van Dijk 1972, 1977). That is, the respective propositions should denote facts in some possible world, or related possible worlds, that are--for example, conditionally--related. Besides this so-called local coherence, the sequence should be globally coherent, that is, be subsumed under some more global macroproposition (van Dijk 1972, 1977, 1980). Such a macroproposition explicates the overall unity of a discourse sequence as it is intuitively known under such notions as 'theme', 'topic', or 'gist'. Macropropositions are derived from sequences of (local, textually expressed) propositions of a discourse by means of some kind of semantic mapping rules, so-called macrorules, which delete, generalize, or 'construct' local information into more general, more abstract, or overall concepts.

These macrorules are recursive, so that one may have several layers of macroproposition sequences, together forming the macrostructure of a discourse. Such a macrostructure can typically be expressed by (individually varying) summaries of a discourse. Macrorules not only have textual propositions as input, but since much of the information of a text is implicit for pragmatic reasons also need information from the 'knowledge' and 'belief' sets of language users, for example, from frames or scripts which organize this knowledge according to criteria of stereotypical usage. By definition, a macroproposition features a central predicate and a number of participants, denoting either an important or global property, event, or action and central participants in a discourse. The textual 'basis' of each macroproposition, thus, is a sequence of propositions of the discourse. It is precisely this sequence which we call an 'episode'. In other words, an episode is a sequence of propositions of a discourse that can be subsumed by a macroproposition.

Because macrorules operate recursively, and we therefore may have macropropositions at several levels of generality, there may also be episodes of varying length or scope in a discourse. Theoretically, even the discourse as a whole, as a limiting case, is an episode. The overall 'unity' we intuitively postulated for world episodes and discourse episodes is precisely defined by the subsuming macroproposition(s). The beginning and end of an episodic sequence are then theoretically defined in terms of propositions which can be subsumed by the same macroproposition, whereas the previous and the following proposition of, respectively, the first and the last proposition of an episodic sequence should be subsumed by another macroproposition.

Further on, I show that these 'breaking points' are interestingly marked by linguistic (and other) means.

Although there may be episodes of varying length or scope
in a discourse, it might be more relevant to restrict the notion
of an episode to those sequences which have some specific further properties, intuitively characterized in terms of 'importance'. That is, perhaps lowest level macropropositions do not
always define what is intuitively called a discourse episode, so
that only higher level and sometimes nonreducible macropropositions subsume textual episodes. It must be seen, therefore,
whether there are additional constraints on the identification of
episodes.

The theoretical relevance of the notion of episode first of all
lies in the fact that we now have a text-base unit corresponding to the earlier notion of macroproposition, that is, the sequence of propositions from which the macroproposition is derived. Secondly, one may assume that this textual unit has
cognitive and linguistic properties. As the theory predicts
and as has been confirmed in descriptive analysis (Chafe 1980,
Longacre 1979, Hinds 1979, and the analysis to be given further on in this paper), the following grammatical 'signals' may
be expected for the beginning of episodes:

1. pauses and hesitation phenomena (fillers, repetition) in
    spoken discourse;
2. paragraph indentations in written discourse;
3. time change markers: *in the meantime, the next day*,
    etc. and tense changes;
4. place change markers: *in Amsterdam, in the other room*;
5. 'cast' change markers: introduction of new individuals
    (often with indefinite articles) or reintroduction of 'old'
    ones (with full noun phrases instead of pronouns);
6. possible word introducing or changing predicates (*tell,
    believe, dream*, etc.);
7. introduction of predicates that cannot be subsumed under
    the same (macro-) predicate, and/or which do not fit the
    same script or frame;
8. change of perspective markers, by different 'observing'
    participants or differences in time/aspect morphology of
    the verb, (free) (in-)direct style.

Such markers signal the beginning of a new episode and hence
at the same time the end of a previous one. In other words,
as soon as there is a change of time and place (a scene), a
different cast of participants, and a different global event or
action now being initiated--according to scriptal or frame-like
world knowledge about the components of such events or actions
--one may assume that there is a beginning of a new episode.
It goes without saying that such markers play an important role
in a cognitive model for the strategies of discourse

comprehension in which the language user has to derive a
macroproposition from the propositions in the text.

In the foregoing I have assumed that perhaps not every
macroproposition would qualify as a good candidate for defining
episodes. In a story about a party, the sequence of events
and actions that constitute the beginning of the story, and
which can be subsumed under such macropropositions as 'I was
invited to Peter's party', or 'I left', or 'I arrived at Peter's
party', would not usually be qualified as episodes. Of course,
the theoretical notion of an episode could have wider application, but I prefer to explicate an intuitively relevant concept.
On the other hand, one does speak of an episode, both in the
discourse and in the denoted world, if I get drunk at the party,
or if as a consequence of getting drunk I have a car accident
afterwards. In that case, the episode seems to have a specific,
e.g. narrative, function in the discourse. In my example, for
instance, it would be the interestingness criterion defining the
Complication category of a story. The initial macropropositions
would also have a function, e.g. that of a Setting, but they
rather define the theoretical correlate of an episode, like a
scene or background of other episodes, such as place, time,
participants, and so on.

In addition, it seems that in order to be able to really define
and identify a sequence, the global events or actions should
not, as such, be stereotypical or normal--according to our world
knowledge and beliefs. And finally, those global actions or
events that are only preparations for or components of more
global and interesting actions and events, should also not be
identified as episodes. 'Leaving to go to a party' is not a goal
on its own but part of a higher level action (going to a party
and participating in it). Getting drunk or having an accident,
however, is not stereotypical and hence may be qualified as
episodic. It follows that those macropropositions have episodic
nature (i.e. define a textual episode) which are not stereotypical
according to scripts or frames, which cannot be subsumed by
higher level macropropositions, and which have a specific function in the discourse as a whole. In other words, episodes
typically require global goals of participants, or actions and
events that frustrate, thwart, or menace the realization of such
goals, so-called 'incidents'. Thus, studying psychology may be
a global goal in my life and hence the sequence of events or
actions defined by it may be an 'episode' of my life, whereas
the incident of flunking an exam or being seduced by my
teacher may be an episode within this more general episode:
this holds both for world episodes and for the episodes in the
discourses about them.

We now have a number of specific semantic criteria--and some
brief suggestions for surface manifestations of these constituting
the episode markers--for the identification of episodes in a discourse. Yet, just as intuitive episodes are usually distinguished
especially in event and action sequences, it seems that especially

event or action discourses, e.g. stories, have episodes. How about other discourse types?

I am going to show that 'newsstories' also have episodic structure: they are about (locally, nationally, or internationally) important events, feature important participants, are not stereotypical or only in part predictable, and can be identified in time and place.

Similarly, in history textbooks, parts of the discourse may be episodes because they are about important historical events and actions of a country or of the world: that is, actions or events that have broad social, economical, political, or cultural consequences, and which are characterized by the same cast of participants and limited in time and place.

Whether poems, advertisements, psychological theories, or concert programs have 'episodes' of this kind, however, remains to be seen. These certainly have (functional) 'parts', but they are not necessarily defined in terms of a global event or action, a cast of participants, or identical time or location parameters. Further research is necessary to see whether episode-like units can or should be identified for these and other discourse types. So my observations provisionally hold only for the large class of event and action discourses, of which the set of stories is only a subset.

4. **Analysis of an example: A newsstory.** To make the theoretical remarks of the previous sections more concrete, let us analyze a text sample in terms of episodic structure. I have chosen a newsstory from *Newsweek* about the American foreign policy in Latin America after the election of Reagan as president. This article (see Appendix) is mainly about the various opinions, both in the United States and in Latin America, about this assumed foreign policy. This means that one cannot simply analyze the text in terms of events and actions, but rather should also account for different 'opinions'. Since, however, different participants, different opinions, and different 'locations' are involved, an episodic analysis seems possible.

Table 1 lists the episodes, with the sentences which are part of them, and the respective segmentation criteria. Since there may be several layers of macrostructure, one may also distinguish different episodes, which are given in Tables 2 and 3, respectively. In this way the total number of episodes drops from 39 to 22 and to 13. The latter 13 episodes seem to correspond with the 13 nonreducible macropropositions of the text. Macropropositions 1 and 2 are, as usual in newsstories, the more general 'summaries', highest in the macrostructure, of which the other macropropositions are specifications.

At the level of surface structure one may observe that these 13 macropropositions and their episodes correspond more or less with the 11 paragraphs of the text.

Table 1. Episode segmentation of 'A new team's Latin test'.

Episode: lines	Sentences	Segmentation criteria
1: 4-7	Nowhere...Latin America	General thematic introduction: USA
2: 7-8	And nowhere...passion	General thematic introduction: LA
3: 8-11	Many governments... White House	Specification: attitude LA governments
4: 11-15	In Chile...friends	Specification: attitude government Chile
5: 15-20	and on a tour...found it	Specification: La capitals/Rockefeller (USA)
6: 21-23	Most human-rights... region	Specification: HR activists
7: 24-27	Leaders in Cuba... Washington.	Specification: LA left countries
8: 27-31	But for R. administration....on the list	Reagan administration policy
9: 31-35	'The most...policy'	Specification: statements Kirkpatrick
10: 36-43	*Traditional wisdom...* K. herself.	R's policymakers: the team
11: 43-51	Kirkpatrick...practices	Kirkpatrick: presentation and policy
12: 52-54	Reagan's...governments	Reagan's traditional policy
13: 55-57	'For four...Buenos Aires'	Official opinion Argentina
14: 57-68	'That will end...respect'	Opinion Kirkpatrick: better relations, respect
15: 69-72	Among the Carter... liberalize	Opinion Carter supporters in LA
16: 72-76	Said Eduardo...everywhere	Specification: Opinion Brazilian C. supporter
17: 76-92	Kirkpatrick...C.'s HR-policy.	Opinions K.: realistic HR policy
18: 93-97	*Green Light...*Meza	Foreign ministries in LA: Bolivia policy USA?
19: 97-104	'It would be...from us'	Opinion Bolivian diplomat in exile
20: 104-110	Reagan aides...nations'	Opinion aides, K. about Bolivia
21: 111-113	The real test...Caribbean	General statement: policy in Caribbean
22: 113-120	The problems...Belize	K's opinion about Caribbean
23: 120-121	Some LA officials... activist.	Opinion LA officials about Reagan

Table 1.   Continued.

Episode: lines	Sentences	Segmentation criteria
24:122-124	The presidents...region	Specification: Opinion presidents M. and P.
25:124-129	And one analyst... America	Opinion analyst in Rio about anti-communism
26:129-132	But...them	Opinion Kirkpatrick: help against communism
27:133-136	*Fourth Place...sales*	General statement: how does R. help?
28:136-144	'Our whole...demili-tarize.'	K's opinion: sell arms
29:145-151	The R. administration... conditions	General statement: will R. help unfriendly nations?
30:151-155	We must...United States	Opinion K.: only under strict conditions
31:156-157	Moderating influence... controversial	General statement: this is controversial
32:157-171	Some analysts...Soviet Union	Specification: opinion some analysts
33:172-174	Similarly...Cuba	General statement: policy about Cuba
34:174-177	Some LA experts... Havana	Specification: opinion LA experts
35:177-182	On the basis...Third World	Opinion *Newsweek*: un-likely
36:183-188	Some LA's worry... exists	Attitude in LA
37:188-191	"People...diplomat	Opinion LA diplomat
38:191-199	But Kirkpatrick...big way	Opinion K: democratic regimes get help
39:199-204	Such talk...action	Evaluation *Newsweek*

Table 2.   Second level episodes in 'A new team's Latin test'.

Episode₂: lines	Segmentation criteria
1: 4-7	General summary statement: USA foreign policy change in LA
2: 7-8	General summary statement: reactions in LA to R's election
3: 8-20	LA governments: relief
4: 21-27	Human rights activists' opinion: severe setback
5: 27-35	Insiders R's policy: priorities already set
6: 36-39	R's transition team at work on LA policy
7: 39-48	Kirkpatrick important member of the team
8: 48-68	Opinion K: traditional policy, better relations with LA
9: 69-76	Opinion Carter supporters in LA: less pressure on conservative regimes
10: 77-92	Opinion K.: more realistic human rights policy than Carter's
11: 93-104	Foreign ministries: what will happen with Bolivia, recognition?
12: 104-110	Reagan aides: different criteria for recognition
13: 111-120	R's policy in Caribbean: against unrest
14: 120-129	LA's reaction: crusade against communism will be dangerous
15: 129-132	K's opinion: we are going to help regimes against communism
16: 133-155	R's policy: sell arms, but not to leftist countries
17: 156-171	Carter's help is moderating policy in Nicaragua
18: 172-177	Plea to continue good relation with Cuba
19: 177-182	Reagan will have different policy towards Cuba
20: 183-191	LA's worries about help to democratic regimes
21: 191-199	Kirkpatrick denies this: we will nurture democracies
22: 199-204	Opinion *Newsweek*: reassurance, but how from thought to action?

Table 3.   Third level episodes in 'A new team's Latin test'.

Episode₃:
lines   Segmentation criteria

1: 4-7   General summary statement: USA foreign policy
             change in LA
2: 7-8   General summary statements: reactions in LA to
             R's election
3: 8-20   LA governments: relief
4: 21-27   Human rights activists' opinion: severe setback
5: 27-48   R's LA team for LA policy, with Kirkpatrick as im-
             portant member
6: 48-68   K's opinion: traditional policy, better relations
             with LA
7: 69-92   Opinions about human rights policies of Carter and
             Reagan
8: 93-110   Policy towards Bolivia: recognition by R
9: 111-132   Policy in Caribbean: against communism
10: 133-155 Help by selling arms
11: 156-182 No moderating help for leftist regimes like
             Nicaragua and Cuba
12: 183-199 Democratic countries will be helped
13: 199-204 *Newsweek*'s evaluation

But what are the semantic properties which define the episodes on these respective levels? Let us examine the first
(most detailed) level first (see Table 1). A first criterion for
segmentation appears to be level of description: the first sentences express rather general (macro-) propositions, which summarize the text as a whole. They are so-called thematic sentences, often appearing at the beginning of newspaper articles.
In dailies they are sometimes printed in bold characters (as the
'lead' of the story). So, the general theme is 'Change in US
foreign policy towards Latin America after Reagan's election as
president'. Then, the subsidiary main theme is: 'Various reactions to this policy in Latin America'. From there on, the
general structure of the article is as follows: some topic from
Reagan's Latin American policy is mentioned (mostly through
the mouth of his adviser Kirkpatrick), and then the reactions
(opinions, fears, etc.) to this point both by left wing (pro
Carter) officials and right wing (pro Reagan) officials, mostly
conservative governments.
    The relatively large number of episodes for this short text
comes from this recurrent switch between a policy statement by
Reagan's aides and reactions from various people in Latin America, or vice versa. In between are found the general statements of the *Newsweek* journalists, introducing a new theme or
new aspect of a theme (mostly policy points). So, if level of
description is a first distinguishing criterion--because the

statements cannot be reduced to the same macrostructure (i.e. have different participants, etc. from the subsequent sentences), we must have a change of level as a mark for the next episode. That is, we change from the general theme 'change of policy' to the more specific 'consequences of this change'.

Similarly, in the third episode, we now get the various specifications: who is reacting how? So, we first go down to the collective group of (conservative) governments, then find a specification of the reaction in Chile, then a statement by Rockefeller in Argentina. In other words, we first witness a change of participants: we go either from a general set to a member, or change between members of different sets (representatives of Carter vs. those of Reagan, left wing vs. right wing Latin American officials). This also means in our text changes in the local scene of the respective opinions being given: the various countries are passed in review. The episode change markers in many of these episodes are simply the first noun phrases (sentence topics) of the sentences: *Many governments, In Chile, Most human-rights activists, Leaders in Cuba,* etc. These may be subjects, often indicating the semantic agent, or complementizers of place or time. A further indication are the connectives: differences in opinion may be introduced with *but: But for Reagan Administration insiders-to-be...* (line 27). Another typically journalistic device is not to first introduce the next speaker or opinion, but to introduce it with a direct quotation, followed by name or function or group of the speaker. Finally, we have the usual bold printed headings, indicating new main themes, as well as the paragraph identations, as indications of episode change.

We now have, for this kind of text, the following episode (and hence episode change) criteria:

(a) Level of description (general vs. particular)
(b) Major participant(s): Reagan camp, Carter camp, Latin American left, Latin American right, *Newsweek*
(c) Place (in this text hardly time: all present)
(d) Different main themes about Latin American policy
(e) Contrasting, conflicting opinions about these themes

Also we see what kind of coherence is at work here. Besides the usual type of conditional relations between actions or events (X says p and therefore Y says q), we witness various functional relationships between sentences or between episodes (and hence between macropropositions): we have many Specification relations: a sentence or episode specifies or gives an Example of a more general point. This Specification may be a specification of a theme, a specification of a country (location), or a specification from group to members of the group. Furthermore, we have already observed that Contrast plays an important role: several spokesmen give their conflicting opinions about the respective policy items. More specifically, the Contrast may take

the form of Counterargument. Not only do the two respective
camps try to counterargue each other's opinions, but also the
reporters of *Newsweek* try to fomulate (rather moderate)
counterarguments, or at least doubts about several policy
points.

Now, if we analyze the further reduction of episodes--that is,
episodes with a larger scope, as pictured in Tables 2 and 3--
which of the criteria mentioned earlier remain, and which should
be relaxed? First of all, the General-Specific dimension, that
is, the level of description, remains: very general statements
cannot be reduced nontrivially (that is, if they are not reduced
to themselves, as highest macropropositions) and subsumed
under another macroproposition with their more specific subsequent episodes. However, we may abstract from the most particular participants: instead of talking about a Chilean official,
we may just segment an episode with respect to 'Chile' or
'Chilean government' as participant. The same holds for the
respective pro-Carter groups in Latin America. In this text,
this leaves us with the various groups with different opinions
in the respective countries.

Next, we still have the respective main themes of Reagan's
Latin American policy: better relations with conservative
regimes, more realistic human rights policy, opposition to com-
munist regimes, encouragement of 'young democracies', etc.
Again, the different groups and different or even conflicting
opinions seem to be the main cirteria for the establishment of
episode boundaries at this higher (or more embracing) level of
episode structure. The scene change is from the United States
to some Latin American countries, and the participant change is
from one camp to the other.

As a provisional conclusion, we may assume that this kind of
newspaper or weekly articles about (foreign) policy is episodically organized according to the following dimensions: (1) main
tenets of the policy; (2) opinions of those who endorse the
policy; (3) opinions of those who are against it; (4) groups of
people who are affected by the policy (positively or negatively),
and their respective contrasting opinions; (5) in relation to
these: the varying locations of the respective groups or people.
This kind of article, typical for weeklies such as *Newsweek*, is
merely a review of various opinions. It does not give an independent critical analysis; it gives little background and few
facts or good arguments, or historically motivated sketches of
prospects. This means that there are few historical explanations
(background) and hence few past tensed episodes; nor are there
prospects or predictions, and hence future tensed episodes
(there is, however, some hint of these in the last sentence of
the article, and the passage beginning with line 133); the only
future tense passages are those which are about the plans of
the Reagan camp, but *Newsweek* itself hardly mentions its own
predictions.

Similarly, in this example, the functional Contrast relations between the episodes hold between the respective opinions of the two camps, but not between these opinions, on the one hand, and critical opinions of the reporters, on the others. The weekly just reports in a more or less 'balanced' way, what the United States government's or the president's policy will be, and the global consequences of this in the respective countries, where the consequences are given in terms of opinions of officials. The article does not investigate the more important possible consequences for the social and political situation of the various peoples of Latin America, let alone give a critical evaluation of the new president in terms of these social values and norms (will the degree of suffering of more people be higher?).

This very brief and superficial characterization of a typical American weekly article also can be deduced from its episodical structures, because the kind of themes, the kind of groups of participants, the kind of functional relations (contrast between conflicting parties rather than critical counterarguments against opinions), and the role of the opinions of the reporters themselves, give a different overall picture of the episodes and their connections from the one that is presented when other participant groups, other time aspects (past, for instance), other type of opinions (criticism), etc. are given.

Most important for this analysis, however, is the fact that for rather 'static' text types also, such as policy reports in weeklies, an episodic analysis makes sense. Such an analysis specifies how macropropositions are realized in the text itself, how episodes can be unified during comprehension, how episodes and hence the (sub-)theme can change, how further organization can be assigned to the text base (e.g. by unity of place, time, participant, theme), and what kind of episode, and hence macroproposition, changes are explicitly marked in the text (new paragraphs, headings, sentence topic, etc.).

5. **Some implications for a cognitive model.** The theoretical linguistic analysis of episodes which I have given here may have interesting implications for a cognitive model of discourse processing. Black and Bower (1979) have already shown that story statements tend to cluster in episodes and that such chunking has cognitive relevance: if we add propositions to an episode, this 'total load' does not affect recall of other episodes. Similarly, if we add unimportant propositions to an episode, this in general enhances memory for the important episode propositions. And Haberlandt, Berian, and Sandson (1980) have shown that episodes are a 'macrounit' of discourse; the encoding load at the boundaries of an episode is higher than at other nodes of a story schema. In ongoing experimental research in Amsterdam (see, for example, den Uyl and van Oostendorp 1980), it was also discovered that at the beginning of one-episode stories, the comprehension time for first sentences is significantly higher

than for other sentences of the episode (say, 800 milliseconds vs. 600 milliseconds). The explanation for this phenomenon seems obvious: the reader not only must understand the sentence, but also needs to actualize relevant world knowledge, e.g. frames or scripts, which may stay 'active' in the comprehension of the next sentences. Also, as has been shown in detail in my work with Kintsch (Kintsch and van Dijk 1978; van Dijk and Kintsch 1977, 1982), the first sentence is strategically used to derive a macroproposition. This macroproposition remains in Short Term Memory for the rest of the interpretation of the same episode. As soon as propositions are interpreted that no longer fit that macroproposition, a new macroproposition is set up.

The various linguistic markers I mentioned earlier serve as strategic data for this change of macroproposition, and hence of episode: as soon as the cast of participants, time, place, circumstances, and (global) event or action seem to change, a new macroproposition can or should be formed, and these semantic changes are often expressed in surface structure: paragraph indentation, pauses, macroconnectives, full noun phrases (cf. Marslen-Wilson, Levy, and Tyler 1981).

Against this experimental and theoretical background, the episode has several cognitive functions:

(a) As an additional unit in the organization of textual sequences of propositions, it assigns further 'chunking' possibilities, i.e. further organization, to the text, which in general allows more structured representation in memory and especially better recall.

(b) Episodes are the textual manifestation of macropropositions; properly marked, they therefore strategically allow an easier derivation of macropropositions and hence allow better and faster understanding of the text as a whole, as well as better retrieval and recall.

(c) Episodes may be associated with various textual and cognitive functions, e.g. narrative categories of a story, or as the bearers of 'interestingness' or 'importance' for certain text segments, and maybe--for certain discourse types--of pragmatic functions: the Conclusion of an argument or the Coda of a story may indicate what general practical inference should be drawn, or what should be known, believed, done.

(d) Episodes may be the 'locus' for local coherence strategies: coherence relations between facts, the (re-)identification of referents by means of pronouns, the possibility to keep place or time indications implicit, may take place within the boundaries of an episode: language users therefore need to search for the relevant information not in the full preceding discourse representation in memory, but only in the representation of the current episode.

Of course, further theoretical and experimental work is necessary to specify and test these assumptions. Earlier work, however, suggests that discourse chunks such as episodes do indeed have relevant cognitive properties in terms of short-term
memory interpretation; long-term memory representation, retrieval, and recall; hierarchical differences between important
and less important information; the application of macrostructure formation strategies; the application of local coherence
strategies and their corresponding information searches in
memory; and the further organization of the discourse in terms
of functional categories.

6. Conclusions. Episodes appear to be linguistically and
psychologically relevant units of discourse structure and processing. They are taken as semantic units, which can be defined as sequences of propositions of a text base which can be
subsumed under a macroproposition. In surface structure they
are expressed by sequences of sentences which usually correspond with paragraphs, and signalled by various phonetic,
morphological, lexical, and syntactic means. Semantically, they
can be identified in terms of (changes of) global predicate, denoting a global event or action, a specific cast of participants,
and time and place coordinates. Discourse episodes are taken
to denote world episodes, that is, sequences of events or actions
of some participants in some specific period. In general, both
for world episodes and for discourse episodes, we constrain the
identification of episodes to those propositions (or actions) that
are important, interesting, or 'incidents'--that is, not stereotypical or normal. This means that especially the higher level
macropropositions which have a specific function, e.g. narrative
or pragmatic, cover episodes in a text.
In a cognitive model, episodes appear to function mainly as
further organizers of the text base in short-term processing
and long-term representation, allowing the strategic derivation
and application of a macroproposition, and restricted information
search in local coherence strategies, as well as better recall due
to this more elaborate organization of the discourse.
In addition to earlier linguistic work on episodes, we now have
a somewhat better insight into their semantic and cognitive
status. However, much additional work is necessary. First,
more work is necessary regarding episode markers in surface
structures. Second, we should try to be more explicit about
which macropropositions can be singled out as episode subsuming. Third, the internal organization of episodes needs further
attention, for example, its 'development'. Fourth, the correspondence between episodes and functions or categories of
stereotypical discourse schemata should be further investigated.
Finally, the corresponding cognitive properties need further
empirical research. In general, it remains to be seen whether
the notion of episode is also relevant for other discourse types
and not only for action or event discourse.

APPENDIX

DIPLOMACY

A New Team's Latin Test

Nowhere will U.S. foreign policy change
more abruptly—or radically—during
the Reagan Administration than in Latin
America. And nowhere did the American
election arouse greater passion. Many governments in the region have breathed a sigh
of relief at the prospect of Ronald Reagan
in the White House. In Chile last week
Interior Minister Sergio Fernandez happily
predicted that "the new United States Government will treat its friends as true
friends," and on a tour of several Latin
American capitals, Chase Manhattan Bank
chairman David Rockefeller told smiling
audiences that Reagan would be a realistic
President, that he would "deal with the
world as he found it."

Chase's Rockefeller with Argentina's President Jorge Videla: A return to 'realism'?

AP

Most human-rights activists in Latin
America viewed the election as a severe
setback for democracy in the region, and
leaders in Cuba and Nicaragua worried that
Reagan's landslide victory would preclude
any chance of improvement in bilateral relations with Washington. But for Reagan
Administration insiders-to-be, priorities
are already being shaped, and rebuilding
links with conservative regimes is high on
the list. "The most important issue is to
repair relations in the region," vows Jeane
J. Kirkpatrick, Reagan's top adviser and
designated spokesman on Latin American
policy.

Traditional Wisdom: The Reagan transition team is already at work putting together a task force to refine Latin American
policy. Among the group's likely members:
Georgetown University's Roger Fontaine,
Pedro San Juan of the American Enterprise
Institute, a Washington think tank, and
Kirkpatrick herself. Kirkpatrick, a 53-
year-old professor of government at
Georgetown—and a lifelong Democrat—
is expected to play a key role on the transition task force and in the new Republican
government itself. "The Reagan Administration," she said last week, "will have
higher regard for traditional wisdom and
traditional practices."

Reagan's foreign policy will almost certainly be "traditional" in the way it treats
many of the region's military governments.
"For four years we have been treated as
an enemy by the United States," says one
official in Buenos Aires. "That will end
in January." Kirkpatrick concurs, and ac-
cuses the Carter Administration of causing
the "rapid deterioration" of relations with
all the nations of Latin America. During
Reagan's Administration, she says, the emphasis will be on bilateral relations and
reciprocity. "We treated the Mexican Government outrageously in our negotiations
on the natural-gas contracts," Kirkpatrick

contends. "Above all, we should treat them
with more respect."

Among the Carter Administration's sup-
porters in Latin America, the greatest fear
is that more "respect" will mean less pressure on regimes to liberalize. Said Eduardo
Seabra Fagundes, president of the Brazilian
Lawyers' Association, "Reagan's election
will certainly have negative effects everywhere." Kirkpatrick denies that. "We want
a human-rights policy that is realistic and
focuses on reasonably attainable goals such
as the protection of personal and legal
rights," she says. Calling Carter policies
"more offensive than effective," Reagan's
adviser maintained that future policy will
involve a more flexible definition of human

Kirkpatrick: A vow to repair relations

Wally McNamee—NEWSWEEK

rights. "Carter's policy was concerned only
with violations of human rights that derive
from governments and no other sources—
terrorists, for instance," she argues. "What
this has meant in practical terms is that
any government that has forcibly attempted
to suppress terrorism and guerrilla action
has tended to run afoul of the Carter human-rights policy."

Green Light: Foreign ministries in Latin
America are watching attentively to see
how Reagan handles one policy choice:
whether or not to recognize the Bolivian
regime of Gen. Luis García Meza. "It
would be like a flashing green light to every
itchy Latin American general who has ever
dreamed of mounting a coup," warns one
Bolivian diplomat in exile. "It's a way of
saying, 'If you overthrow a constitutional
government, you will not hear any com-
plaints from us'." Reagan aides see it differently, and think that diplomatic recognition is inevitable. "I would not make
conformity to democratic practices a condition of our continued relations with Bolivia," says Kirkpatrick. "We do not do
that with most other nations."

The real test of Reagan's Latin American
policy, however, will probably come in Central America and the Caribbean. "The
problems in Central America must be dealt
with immediately," Kirkpatrick says. In
addition to the "near-civil war" in El Salvador and the growing insurgency in Guatemala, she sees the danger of unrest and
violence in Costa Rica, Honduras and Be-
lize. Some Latin American officials worry
that Reagan will be too much of an activist.
The presidents of both Mexico and Panama
recently issued warnings against U.S. intervention in the region. And one analyst
in Rio de Janeiro warns that "the United
States is likely to find itself isolated if it
seeks to carry out a crusade against what

NEWSWEEK/NOVEMBER 24, 1980

21

194 / Teun A. van Dijk

Michel Philippot—Sygma

Violent death in El Salvador: Under Reagan, a 'flexible' definition of human rights

it sees as the spread of Communism in Central America." But, retorts Kirkpatrick, 130 "all the countries seem to be quite vulnerable [to Communism] and we are going to have to help them."

Fourth Place: Just how the Reagan Administration intends to help is unclear. Al-135 most certainly, it will lift Carter's 1977 ban on arms sales. "Our whole military-sales and training-assistance policy is overdue for review," says Kirkpatrick. "The amount of arms acquired in Latin America 140 is at a higher level than ever while the United States has simply fallen to fourth place as a supplier behind France, West Germany and the Soviet Union. That's not progress toward demilitarization." 145 The Reagan Administration is expected

to be much less enthusiastic—and perhaps downright opposed—to aiding nations that it considers "unfriendly." Reagan will have to decide soon after taking office whether 150 to help Nicaragua—and if so, on what conditions. "We must have guarantees about where the aid will go," says Kirkpatrick. "It should *not* be used to assist in the consolidation of power in a one-party state 155 that is hostile to the United States."

Moderating Influence: That attitude is certain to prove controversial. Some analysts say the Carter Administration's offer of $75 million in aid is exerting a moder-160 ating influence on Nicaragua's Sandinista leaders. They argue that given the Nicaraguan Government's massive economic problems and the destruction left behind

by the former regime of President Anastasio 165 Somoza Debayle, Managua is going to need help from the outside world. If Reagan vetoes aid, they maintain, it would only serve to alienate the Sandinista leadership further—and probably force Nicaragua to 170 move closer to Fidel Castro's Cuba or the Soviet Union.

Similarly, the incoming Reagan Administration will have to clarify its stance toward Cuba. Some Latin American experts 175 are urging the Reagan team to continue Carter's tentative efforts to improve relations with Havana. On the basis of current readings, that is unlikely. Reagan can be expected to end any modest good-neighbor 180 policies put in place under Carter and to take a tougher line against Cuba's military and diplomatic activity in the Third World.

Some Latin Americans worry that the Reagan Administration will get so caught 185 up in its new realpolitik that it will not do enough to reinforce democracy in those countries of Latin America where it now exists. "People like President Jaime Roldos of Ecuador are going to be looking over 190 their shoulder from now on," predicts one Latin diplomat. But Kirkpatrick adamantly denies that the incoming Administration will be lax in supporting democratic regimes like the recently restored ones in Peru 195 and Ecuador. "You will see very great efforts by us to nurture democracies in the region," she insists. "That will involve both moral and economic support—and in a very big way." Such talk is bound to reassure 200 Washington's friends in the hemisphere—but it remains to be seen just how quickly and effectively the incoming Reagan Administration can translate such thoughts into action.

DOUGLAS RAMSEY in Washington with
LARRY ROHTER in Rio de Janeiro

REFERENCES

Black, John B., and Gordon H. Bower. 1979. Episodes as chunks in narrative memory. Journal of Verbal Learning and Verbal Behavior 18.309-318.

Chafe, Wallace. 1980a. The deployment of consciousness in the production of a narrative. In: Chafe (1980b:9-50).

Chafe, Wallace, ed. 1980b. The pear stories. Norwood, N.J.: Ablex.

van Dijk, Teun A. 1972. Some aspects of text grammars. The Hague: Mouton.

van Dijk, Teun A. 1977. Text and context. London: Longman.

van Dijk, Teun A. 1980. Macrostructures. Hillsdale, N.J.: Erlbaum.

van Dijk, Teun A., and Walter Kintsch. 1977. Cognitive psychology and discourse. In: Current trends in text linguistics. Edited by W. U. Dressler. Berlin/New York: de Gruyter. 61-80.

van Dijk, Teun A., and Walter Kintsch. 1982. Strategies of discourse comprehension (in preparation).

Dik, Simon C. 1978. Functional grammar. Amsterdam: North Holland.

Givón, Talmy. 1979a. From discourse to syntax: Grammar as a processing strategy. In: Givón (1979b:81-112).

Givón, Talmy, ed. 1979b. Syntax and semantics 12. Discourse and syntax. New York: Academic Press.

Haberlandt, Karl, Claire Berian, and Jennifer Sandson. 1980. The episode schema in story processing. Journal of Verbal Learning and Verbal Behavior 19.635-650.

Hinds, John. 1979. Organizational patterns in discourse. In: Givón (1979b:135-158).

Kintsch, Walter, and Teun A. van Dijk. 1978. Toward a model of discourse comprehension and production. Psychological Review 85.363-394.

Longacre, Robert E. 1979. The paragraph as a grammatical unit. In: Givón (1979b:115-134).

Marslen-Wilson, William, Elena Levy, and Lorraine Tyler. 1981. Producing interpretable discourse: The establishment and maintenance of reference. To appear in: Language, place and action. Edited by R. J. Jarvella and W. Klein. Chichester: Wiley.

den Uyl, Martyn, and Herre van Oostendorp. 1980. The use of scripts in text comprehension. Poetics 9.275-294.

DISCOURSE THEORY AND
THE INDEPENDENCE OF SENTENCE GRAMMAR

J. L. Morgan
University of Illinois

0. Introduction. During this time of remarkable growth in the study of discourse, an important question has been posed for the generative grammarian and the discourse theorist alike: what is the relation between, on the one hand, the mental systems that underlie human ability to understand and produce connected discourse, and, on the other hand, theories of grammar of Chomskyan coloration that take just sentences as their domain--what I call 'sentence grammar'.

There are a number of positions one might take on the relation between discourse competence and sentence grammar, on either prioristic or empirical grounds. A couple of these positions are potentially threatening to theories of sentence grammar, and I would like to examine some arguments that might be advanced for them, to see whether the arguments are persuasive as criticisms of sentence grammar.

The literature of discourse studies by linguists, from at least van Dijk (1972) to de Beaugrande (1980) and Givon (1980), contains a number of proposals with a common thrust: that close study of problems of discourse analysis and theory shows that sentence grammar is deficient in important respects, hence incorrect; therefore it ought to be abandoned in favor of a general theory of discourse, in whose terms sentence grammar is reformulated or entirely subsumed. But in fact, such proposals contain two major claims that are logically independent, since one can be true and the other false. The weaker of the two is the claim that certain facts about discourse show that generative sentence grammar cannot be the correct account for sentence syntax and semantics. The second, stronger position is that the right discourse theory (or complex of theories) will do the work of a generative sentence grammar, making the latter superfluous as a distinguishable component of overall linguistic ability, thus debunking

196

such important hypotheses as the autonomy of syntax, the independence of sentence grammar, perhaps even the existence of a logically independent 'language faculty'. These are not trivial issues, as one can see from the large and combative literature in several fields that has grown around Chomsky's work. So it is worthwhile to consider whether the arguments against sentence grammar that are so common in the literature of discourse theory actually are a threat to sentence grammar theory.

In this paper I want to examine both the weak and strong positions to determine the strength of the arguments for each. I try to show that arguments for the weak position have no force, since they overlook a central claim of sentence grammar theory. I argue that the strong position, though unconvincing in present forms, is more promising, and worth pursuing. I also discuss what it would take to make the strong position a more persuasive one.

1. **The weak position.** Arguments for the weak position--that is, against sentence grammar--are generally taken as arguments for the complete abandonment of sentence grammar in favor of some other theory. But it is not always clear which crucial property of sentence grammar it is that the argument is directed against. So it might be useful to list some central properties of sentence grammar. I believe that the following five properties--that is, claims about the nature of grammar-- are characteristic of more or less standard versions of generative grammar.

(1) *The independence of sentence grammar:* Linguistic competence contains as a distinguishable component a cognitive system whose domain is the sentence (and, implicitly, smaller expressions that make up sentences). The fact that this system interacts with other cognitive systems in performance is not an argument against the claim that it is an independent system. The boundaries of this system--that is, what properties of sentences fall in its domain--is an open empirical question, not determinable by a priori means.

(2) *Language uniqueness:* At least some aspects of this cognitive system--or, from the linguist's viewpoint, the conceptual vocabulary for describing it--are unique to language, not found in other cognitive systems.

(3) *Grammar is formal:* Sentence grammar is organized and, from the linguist's viewpoint, can be described, purely as a matter of form, entirely independent of questions of communication, speaker's intention, and other matters of language use.

(4) *Structure is Chomskyan:* The proper treatment of the notion 'sentence structure' is in the terms of the familiar phrase markers in the work of Chomsky and many others

before and since; that is, syntactic structure (at a given level) is reducible to relations of dominance, precedence, and syntactic category, and other notions defined in these terms.

(5) *More than one level of structure:* An empirically adequate grammar requires that each sentence be assigned at least two levels of structure. The exact number of levels is an open question.

Obviously, these five properties do not exhaust the conceptual content of generative grammar; Chomsky's more recent work on extended standard theory, to pick a single example, is far richer. And, in fact, there is not unanimity on all five properties even within the generative camp. Properties (4) and (5) are presently controversial within generative grammar, under attack by proponents of 'arc-pair grammar' (Johnson and Postal 1980), and in recent work on 'constituent structure grammar' by Gazdar (1980) and his collaborators. Abandoning or replacing these properties would indeed constitute an important theoretical shift; but the result would still count, as far as I can see, as a sentence grammar of the sort under attack from discourse theorists. Unless I am mistaken, it is properties (1) through (3) that are relevant to the criticism of generative sentence grammar vis-a-vis discourse grammar.

The question is, then: do the arguments of the weak position succeed as arguments against the first three properties?

There are two lines of argument for the weak position. The first, apparently intended as an argument against the independence of sentence grammar, is that the only 'naturally occurring unit' for linguistic analysis is the discourse, not the sentence. This argument is far from convincing. If it is taken as a rather bizarre a priori methodological restriction, then it has no bearing on the question of independence. Even accepting this restriction, there is no reason to believe that it precludes the possibility of discovering, from close analysis of discourse, motivation for an independent sentence component. Taken more seriously, as leading in some obscure way to an a priori argument against the independence of sentence grammar, again it has no force. The question of independence is an empirical one--either there is an independent sentence grammar or there is not--and cannot be decided a priori.

The second line of argument is to criticize sentence grammar as inherently incapable of providing an analysis of phenomena of various sorts. Such observations can be construed either as arguments that sentence grammar is incomplete, or as arguments against one or more of the first three properties. Van Dijk (1972:7) uses them to show, if I understand correctly, that sentence grammar is incomplete, that there are discourse phenomena that cannot be accounted for by a sentence grammar:

> As long as S-grammars cannot provide satisfactory,
> general and consistent, descriptions of the structures
> underlying discourses, by formulating the rules which
> must be mastered by native speakers to be able to per-
> form the different tasks, we have to consider them
> empirically inadequate.

But one cannot criticize an owl for not being a partridge.
This kind of criticism ignores a central thesis of sentence
grammar theory. Chomskyan generative grammar and its
descendants are based on a hypothesis of great theoretical
and empirical importance: the existence of an independent
language faculty, within which there is a sentence grammar
with rather narrow domain. Insofar as sentence grammar in
the Chomskyan spirit can offer only an incomplete account of
some language-related phenomenon, it amounts to a claim about
the nature of the phenomenon--that it is outside the domain of
sentence grammar, perhaps outside the domain of the language
faculty altogether, the product of some other cognitive system
or systems. The incompleteness is not an incompleteness by
default or omission, but a claim, correct or incorrect, about
the facts.

Thus arguments of this type against sentence grammar, on
the grounds that it cannot account for certain discourse phenomena, have no force, unless accompanied by a demonstration
that the phenomena in question must be considered to be in the
same domain as phenomena that are central to sentence grammar
theory. But such a demonstration is a very difficult task--
phenomena are not pre-sorted by nature in this way. There
is no basis from which to argue one way or the other, save to
provide support for what I have called the 'strong position':
to present an alternative theory which treats sentence phenomena and discourse phenomena in a single unified theory,
without a distinguishable sentential subcomponent. One could
then attempt to compare such a theory with a sentence grammar
as an explanation of sentential phenomena. Lacking such an
alternative, there is no ground for comparison. Along these
lines, observations taken to be arguments for the incompleteness of sentence grammar could be construed as arguments
against properties (2) and (3) (hence potentially as arguments
against independence), if it could be shown that the phenomena
in question require a uniform treatment of discourse and sentential properties, and that the sentential properties concerned
are central to sentence grammar.

One such argument is the claim that there are important
parallels between properties of discourse and properties of
sentences. In fact, there are at least three parallels one
might see between sentences and discourses. First, they
both have structure. The point has been made again and
again, and quite correctly, that one key to the understanding
of discourse is the idea that discourses have structure. Then
one might propose 'grammars' of some kind for discourses, to

generate texts and assign them structure. From here it is
only a short step to the hypothesis that one can provide a
single grammar that treats both sentence and discourse structure.

But the parallelism turns out to be rather tenuous on closer
inspection. The kind of structure commonly attributed to sentences (and not just by Chomskyans) is not the same kind of
structure commonly attributed to discourses (see Morgan and
Sellner 1980 for more discussion). What is needed is a demonstration that the system for determining discourse structure
can be extended to give a complete treatment of the syntax of
sentences, a demonstration so far lacking, though not incon-
ceivable.

A second apparent parallel is that texts, like sentences, have
'meaning' in some sense of this perniciously vague term. For
example, de Beaugrande (1980:37) points out that meaning relations that can hold within a sentence can hold between independent sentences in a discourse. He offers the following
pair from Isenberg (1971:155) as illustration of this point:

Peter burned the book because he didn't like it.
Peter burned the book. He didn't like it.

But again the observation of the parallelism is misleading, in
that it obscures an important difference between the two cases
in the illustration. In the first, sentential case, we understand the relation to hold because of the parts of the sentence
and their mode of combination. But in the second, discourse
case, as in all cases of understood relations between independent sentences in a discourse, we must infer that the relation is to be understood to hold. Two different mechanisms
are involved: in the sentential case, our knowledge of gram-
mar--of the conventional meaning of the word *because*, and of
just how the meanings of larger English expressions are related
to the meanings of their parts; in the discourse case, our
ability to make common sense inferences. The latter can be
cancelled by contextual factors, in the manner of Grice's (1975)
conversational implicature; the former cannot. It would be a
mistake to ignore the difference.

The third parallel--anaphoric relations like some antecedent-
anaphor relations, the interpretation of definite noun phrases,
and so on--is similar to the previous one, in that such relations can hold either between elements within a sentence or
between elements in two separate sentences in a discourse.
In this case, though, the evidence suggests the necessity for
a unified treatment. It is fairly clear that such matters need
to be treated in extrasentential, perhaps discourse terms.
But a perfectly coherent response to such arguments is available to the proponent of the independence of sentence grammar: namely, just to yield the territory--to conclude (correctly, to my mind) that such cases are outside the domain of

sentence grammar. Nothing in sentence grammar theory entails
that everything that can conceivably be labelled a property of
sentences must be accounted for in sentence grammar.
Another kind of criticism of sentence grammar is based on
the observation that there are discourse explanations for
apparently syntactic facts. There are a number of interesting
attempts in the literature (see Givon 1980 for some recent examples, especially the papers by Garcia and Erteschik-Shir).
But generally, the sentence grammarian can respond to such
analyses in the same way as to the previous case: by yielding
the territory, concluding that the existence of convincing discourse explanations shows that the problem was not a syntactic
one to begin with.
A related kind of argument is based on the observation that
there are expressions whose meaning and/or syntactic distribution is clearly to be given in terms of discourse or functional terms. One might conclude from the existence of morphemes that function as topic or focus markers, for example,
that a complete theory of sentence grammar must incorporate
a treatment of notions like 'focus', 'topic', and the like. But
there is no reason to accept this conclusion. It is no more
necessary than this one: since English has pronouns like *he*
and *she* whose meaning properties (hence use) are determined
in part by natural gender, the theory of sentence grammar
must contain a theory of physical gender. More plausibly,
these are instances of the interaction of sentence grammar with
other linguistic or nonlinguistic cognitive systems. The existence of such interactions in no way provides arguments for the
identity of the interacting systems.
A similar approach is available for dealing with 'optional'
rules or constructions with clear discourse value--constructions
like 'Y-movement', for example, that have different discourse
appropriateness conditions from their unmoved counterparts.
Sentence grammar need only specify which orders are possible,
i.e. grammatical. The rest should follow from language-
specific discourse rules, from general principles of communication, or from the interaction of grammar with other cognitive
systems.
In short, such empirical arguments against the independence
of sentence grammar are not convincing, taken one by one.
Conceivably, they could become persuasive cumulatively, by
gradually reducing the domain of sentence grammar to empti-
ness; but that day is hardly on the horizon. In the meantime,
the sentence grammarian can fairly comfortably continue to
take such observations as progress in the empirical determination of the domain of sentence grammar.

3. The strong position. The strong position is that the
right discourse theory will entirely subsume sentence grammar
or provide a radical reformulation of it in discourse terms.
Obviously, one persuasive way to argue for the abandonment

of a theory is to present an alternative that gives a superior
treatment of a significant portion of the domain of the theory
under attack; for example, to show how a fairly well articulated
theory of discourse provides an account of some phenomenon
that is central to sentence grammar. What would be required
of the theory of discourse, then, is that it be complete enough
to allow examination of its consequences at the sentence level
for naturally occurring or constructed discourse, with a degree of formal detail that approaches that of existing sentence
grammars. Unfortunately, there is no theory of discourse
that is that well developed. This state of affairs is hardly
surprising, given the almost miraculous complexity of the mental systems that underlie our ability to produce and understand
discourse. At this point such a comparison is impossible.
Still, it might be useful to sketch in hypothetical terms some
directions that such an enterprise might take.

To begin, I need to narrow down a bit what I mean by 'discourse theory'. I mean any theory that attempts to satisfy
two minimal conditions:

(1) It attempts at least a partial account of the most
    striking aspect of discourse comprehension: how an
    understanding of a discourse is so much greater than
    the logical sum of the parts (i.e. sentences) that make
    it up.

(2) It offers a definition or explication of indispensable
    but elusive notions like 'topic', 'focus', 'given/new',
    'relevance', 'coherence', and 'text structure'.

Such a theory might fruitfully be framed in terms of communicative actions, i.e. rules or strategies for the activity of communication, rather than rules of well-formedness. Matters of
ill-formedness would be recast either as actions that violate
rules of communication, or as inefficient or self-defeating
communicative actions, given principles of communicative
efficiency. Such a theory would also need to include (or appeal to interaction with) a theory of common sense reasoning,
and would likely include a component of language-specific
conventions of discourse and of other aspects of language use
(see Morgan 1978a,b for discussion).

If such a theory were available, then, it would be possible
to attempt to recast central aspects of sentence grammar in
terms of the independently motivated discourse theory. Again,
lacking a detailed theory of this type, discussion is necessarily
speculative. But a couple of illustrations help make clear what
kind of attempt I have in mind. The strategy would be to
determine how much of the semantics and syntax of sentence
grammar could be treated by discourse theory, leaving only
matters of morphology and the lexicon to sentence grammar.

The possibilities for semantics are rather dubious, it seems
to me. A theory whose goal is to explain discourse

comprehension must give a central role to inference, though perhaps with a language-specific, conventional component as well (by language-specific here I mean principles that differ from language community to language community, and must be learned). Then it is not out of the question that this system could provide a parallel treatment for problems of compositionality within sentences, yielding then a single uniform system for all aspects of meaning analysis, both at discourse and sentence-internal levels. But such an attempt faces large obstacles. It would be necessary to show how the compositionality that is a central tenet of sentence grammar could be dispensed with. The claim of compositionality is that any adequate theory of semantics must analyze meaning as depending not only on the elements that make up expressions, but on their syntax--on the way they are combined to make up the expression. It is hard to see how to extend an inference-based understanding system to deal naturally with the difference between *the dog bit the cat* and *the cat bit the dog* without in the process reinventing sentence syntax, let alone how to conquer the well-known problems of the relation of syntactic properties to scope of logical operators. The likelihood of success of such an attempt is very implausible, I think, though it cannot be ruled out a priori.

The attempt to recast syntax in discourse terms is perhaps slightly less implausible. Take the syntax of noun phrases, for example. Given a theory well developed enough to include treatment of the action of referring, and given that language communities can differ in their conventional rules of discourse, one could attempt to recast the syntactic rules for English noun phrases as English strategies for the act of referring. The possibility of such reformulation of syntax in terms of communicative function is tantalizing, since there are obvious correlations between syntactic form and communicative function. For example, in language after language, the unmarked position of the restrictive relative clause is adjacent to the 'head noun' that it 'modifies', as in *The woman who invented the wheel died in 70,000 B.C.* Viewed purely formally, this seems just an unexplainable (though widespread) quirk. Viewed functionally, on the other hand, it is hardly surprising, since the head and accompanying relative are uttered in pursuance of a single purpose--to pick out a referent by describing its properties. Uttering the head and the relative constitutes a single communicative act, and the temporal adjacency is unsurprising, assuming some intuitively obvious principles of efficiency. From this viewpoint, it is the cases where the relative is detached from the head that are surprising.

But this kind of analysis, though tantalizing, also faces serious obstacles insofar as form does not always follow function. For example, how could such a theory explain cases of apparent functional disunity like extraposed relatives, as in *The woman died in 70,000 B.C. who invented the wheel* or verb-particle constructions like *John put the cat out*, to say nothing of the numerous apparently purely formal conditions and constraints proposed by generative grammarians from Ross (1967) to Chomsky (1981)? The burden is clearly on the discourse theorist to show that at least a significant fraction of these problems have explanations in discourse and/or functional terms. Personally, I am skeptical that such explanations will ever be achieved. But I think the knowledge to be gained in the attempt is worth the effort.

REFERENCES

de Beaugrande, Robert. 1980. Text, discourse, and process. Norwood, N.J.: Ablex.

Chomsky, Noam. 1981. Lectures on government and binding. Dordrecht, Holland: Foris Publications.

van Dijk, Teun. 1972. Some aspects of text grammars. The Hague: Mouton.

Erteschik-Shir, Nomi. 1980. Discourse constraints on dative movement. In: Givon (1980).

Garcia, Erica. 1980. Discourse without syntax. In: Givon (1980).

Gazdar, Gerald. (to appear) Phrase structure grammar. In: The nature of syntactic representation. Edited by G. K. Pullum and Pauline Jacobson. Boston: Reidel.

Givon, Talmy. 1980. Syntax and semantics, Vol. 12: Discourse and syntax. New York: Academic Press.

Grice, H. P. 1975. Logic and conversation. In: Syntax and semantics, Vol. 3: Speech acts. Edited by Peter Cole and Jerry Morgan. New York: Academic Press.

Isenberg, Horst. 1971. Ueberlegung zur Texttheorie. In: Literaturwissenschaft und Linguistik: Ergebnisse und Perspektiven. Edited by Jens Ihwe. Frankfurt: Athenaeum.

Johnson, David, and Paul Postal. 1980. Arc pair grammar. Princeton: Princeton University Press.

Morgan, Jerry. 1978a. Two types of convention in indirect speech acts. In: Syntax and semantics, Vol. 9: Pragmatics. Edited by Peter Cole. New York: Academic Press.

Morgan, Jerry. 1978b. Toward a rational model of discourse comprehension. In: Theoretical issues in natural language processing. Edited by D. Waltz. Urbana, Ill.: University of Illinois.

Morgan, Jerry, and Manfred Sellner. Text structure from a linguistic point of view. In: Theoretical issues in reading comprehension. Edited by Rand J. Spiro, Bertram C. Bruce, and William F. Brewer. Hillsdale, N.J.: Erlbaum.

Ross, John R. 1967. Constraints on variables in syntax. MIT Ph.D. dissertation. Bloomington: Indiana University Linguistics Club. Mimeo.

STRATEGIES FOR UNDERSTANDING FORMS AND OTHER PUBLIC DOCUMENTS

V. Melissa Holland and Janice C. Redish
American Institutes for Research

Since 1978, we and our colleagues in the Document Design Center at the American Institutes for Research have been studying the problems that people have in understanding and using public documents. Our interest ranges across a wide variety of documents--for example, legal contracts, insurance policies, warranties, regulations, instructions for forms, and the forms themselves. In this paper, we are concerned with forms as discourse: how are forms similar to other types of text? how do they differ? how can we best study forms as a type of text? what have we learned in our work so far?
From other studies that we have done, we have both objective and subjective evidence that forms are critical in people's lives and that they have difficulty dealing with them. Yet very little research has been done on them. Our interest in conducting this research is threefold. We hope to (1) help writers and designers improve forms so that they better fit the skills and strategies of the target audience; (2) help educators to improve the skills and strategies of students who will have to use these forms; and (3) add to linguists' and psychologists' understanding of how people process written material.

A model for reading forms and other functional documents. Documents have pragmatic contexts and immediate consequences that the more traditionally studied texts may not have. Reading a document is a functional necessity for the reader; documents usually require immediate action rather than long-term memory storage. We, therefore, use the term 'functional reading' to contrast document-reading with reading for pleasure (stories) and reading to learn (expository prose).
The model pictured in Figure 1 is an illustration of some of the factors we see as critical to understanding 'functional

Figure 1. Critical aspects of functional reading.

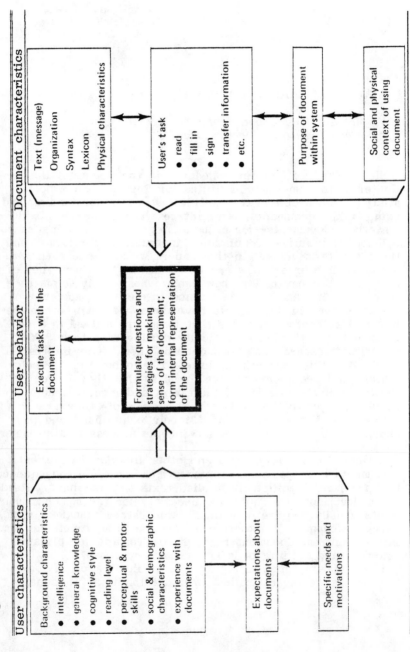

reading'.[1] As the model shows, successful use of a document is an interaction between the document's characteristics and the user's characteristics as they influence the user's behavior. The user employs strategies and processes to make sense of the document and to fulfill the required tasks. We propose that by viewing forms as discourse, we can stimulate a productive line of research--that is, we find that forms exhibit identifiable text characteristics and elicit strategies for comprehension that call on these characteristics, on context, and on the user's prior knowledge about the world--as do other types of text. We further propose that simply carrying over what we know about other types of text is not sufficient for understanding forms--that is, we find that forms have unique characteristics and that they require processes and strategies which differ in systematic ways from those needed to understand stories or textbooks.

We want, however, to bring previous research to bear on our studies of forms as discourse.

What has research on other text types shown? Linguists analyzing discourse have found a range of variables that serve as distinct levels in the description of stories, expository prose, and the more traditional forms of text. Psychologists studying text comprehension and memory have found that these variables are robust predictors of readers' performance. These variables include:

(1) Cohesion: the ties between sentences identifiable in surface structure such as ellipsis, anaphora, word repetition (Kintsch 1974, Grimes 1975, Halliday and Hasan 1976).

(2) Message structure (staging): the patterning of information in sentence sequences by theme-rheme or given-new relationships (Halliday 1967, Chafe 1970, Grimes 1975, Clark and Haviland 1977).

(3) Rhetorical predicates or coherence relations: the deeper logical and semantic connections between sentences (Grimes 1975, Meyer 1975, Hobbs 1979).

(4) Text structure: the overall organizational form, depending on the text type or genre (van Dijk 1972, 1980; Kintsch and van Dijk 1978). Grammars have been formulated to characterize the structures of texts that fit highly steroetyped cultural norms, e.g. simple stories (Rumelhart 1975, Mandler and Johnson 1977, Stein and Glenn 1979). For example, Adams and Collins (1979) suggest that to interpret a simple tale as a fable, the reader must have a schema for fable specifying that some statement will be interpreted as a moral.

(5) Content or message base: the level that draws on world knowledge, such as is represented in scripts (Shank and Abelson 1977) and frames (Minsky 1975). Scripts

represent people's knowledge about frequently encountered episodes with predictable participants and
scenes (for example, a restaurant script). Knowledge
frames define elements and relationships in more static
arrays. At the very least, the presented text, in order
to be understood, must engage some part of the reader's
prior knowledge about the world (Bransford and Johnson
1973, Bransford and McCarrell 1974). This knowledge,
as revealed by work in artificial intelligence, semantic
memory, and discourse comprehension, appears to be
organized into richly structured, global configurations--
not only scripts and frames, but looser, more abstract,
and more flexible structures known as 'schemas' (Anderson 1977) (a distinction drawn by Winograd 1977 and
developed by Rumelhart and Ortony 1977).

Tannen's work (1979) on frames in the discourse of
oral reporting fits here also; it conforms to what might
be called dynamic schemas. Tannen's work shows that
one can operate on several complex and subtly distinct
levels at once--from adopting a general rhetorical frame
(subject-of-the experiment vs. telling-a-story) to frames
for interpreting content.

(6) The cooperative contract: a pragmatic convention described by Grice (1975) in which speaker and hearer (or
writer and reader) enter into a tacit agreement to cooperate, and for each to assume that the other is cooperating
toward the purpose of communicating. Cooperating, according to Grice, means being relevant, clear, truthful,
and informative. This contract underlies all discourse.
As we show later, one of the problems that unsuccessful
form users have is that they do not assume the forms
designer had a communicative intent.

This very productive work needs to be expanded in two ways:
(1) to see how these variables affect performance with other
text types beyond expository prose and stories; (2) to delve
deeply and more directly into the box in our model labeled
'strategies' or 'processes'. We are exploring both of these
directions in studying application forms.

Forms as discourse--textual analysis. It might be objected
that forms are not text. After all, they typically consist of
numbered, fill-in-the-blank items rather than complete sentences
in a linear flow. The connections between items appear to be
largely procedural rather than logico-semantic or rhetorical.
And the cognitive result of using a form is not the construction
of an internal text base, or macrostructure, as Kintsch and
van Dijk (1978) have posited as the product of reading prose.
However, work indicates that forms do display properties of
connected prose, although the connections are looser and
sparser than in more traditional text. (On the continuum

suggested by Halliday and Hasan 1976, forms would fall somewhere between an index and a narrative.) We have both
analytical and empirical indications that forms are text. That
is, the indications can be seen in the document itself and in
the behavior of document users.

We have discussed analytical evidence that forms are text in
other papers (Charrow, Holland, Peck, and Shelton 1980; Holland 1980, 1981; Campbell and Holland forthcoming). Therefore, we only briefly review some of this evidence here. Consider the Medicaid form shown as Figure 2.

Like most forms, this one displays 'cohesion' by using word
repetition and anaphora. As an example of repetition, note
that terms like *family* and *family member* have special meanings
defined in the form. These terms can be seen in the heading
of the box on the front of the form. They are repeated
throughout the document with the same special meaning. If
form users do not keep the same special meaning in mind
throughout the form, if they do not grasp the intended cohesion, then they may make errors in filling out the form.

As an example of anaphora, note the pronouns *he(she)*,
your, and *their* connecting the separate items under Questions
3 and 4, referring to support from spouses. Anaphora is more
common in new 'plain English' forms we have designed, in
which the pronouns *we* and *you* are defined as specific parties
in the beginning of the form and then occur throughout the
document. Obviously, users must look for and recover the
special meanings of repeated terms and the anaphoric connections if they are to understand and respond accurately on the
form.

This Medicaid form also displays a 'given-new' patterning of
information. This pattern underlies local hierarchies of items
in several places on the form. For example, the items in Question 5 'Income from work' are all hierarchically related: 'Amount
Taken Out' and 'Expenses' refer to 'Income from Work'. 'Expenses', in turn, subsumes 'Transportation' and 'Other'. The
appropriate response to 'Transportation' and 'Other' is only the
expenses in these categories that are related to work--not just
any 'transportation' or 'other' expenses in one's life. Many of
the Medicaid recipients who were subjects in our study of this
form did not observe these topical links. They answered all
items as if they were independent and unconnected. Understanding the hierarchy in Question 5 requires operating under
the conventions for staging information in texts. This means
seeing each label or phrase as the 'new' information at the
level where it is introduced, and then as the implicit 'old' information for the next lower level. The hierarchy is recover-
able by applying a given-new strategy.

Analyzing forms is one of the techniques that we and our
colleagues are using to understand and improve public documents. We are also conducting empirical studies in which we

Figure 2. Medicaid form.

DHR 1209

GOVERNMENT OF THE DISTRICT OF COLUMBIA
DEPT. OF HUMAN RESOURCES

RECERTIFICATION FOR MEDICAL ASSISTANCE

CENSUS TRACT:

DATE:

SERVICE AREA:

D. C. I. D. NO:

UPON RETURN SEND TO:

IMPORTANT YOUR ELIGIBILITY FOR MEDICAL ASSISTANCE EXPIRES ON
PLEASE COMPLETE THIS FORM and return it before your Medical Assistance Card expires. If you don't we will not know if you continue to be eligible, and we will be required to take action to end your medical assistance. The information you give must be TRUE AND COMPLETE. It will be verified. You will be asked to furnish proof of information given. Those persons found to have given false information may be fined up to $500 or imprisoned for up to one year, or both.

If this form is not returned completed within 15 days your eligibility for Medical Assistance will terminate.

PLEASE PRINT CLEARLY. ANSWER ALL QUESTIONS ON BOTH SIDES OF THIS FORM. WHEN THE FORM IS COMPLETED AND SIGNED, RETURN IT IN ENCLOSED ENVELOPE. IF YOU HAVE ANY DIFFICULTIES FILLING OUT THIS FORM CALL 724-5174.

IMPORTANT: 1. Please attach 3 recent payment statements. 2. All income must be listed and verified, including children that are not in school. 3. If you are unemployed, send verification from person that supports you.

1. FAMILY MEMBERS (LIVING WITH YOU AND USING A MEDICAID CARD)				TELEPHONE NUMBERS HOME					RELATION TO YOU
LAST NAME	FIRST NAME	MI	DATE OF BIRTH	SEX	INS. CODE	SOCIAL SECURITY NO.	INDIVIDUAL DCID NO.		

IF SOME FAMILY MEMBERS LISTED ABOVE HAVE LEFT THE HOME, PLEASE CROSS OUT THEIR NAMES. CHECK THIS COLUMN IF RECV'ING WELFARE ▲

LIST ANY NEW FAMILY MEMBERS IN THIS SHADED AREA AND ATTACH BIRTH CERTIFICATES.

LIST NAME OF ANY FAMILY MEMBER WHO IS DISABLED OR BLIND:

2. WRITE IN NEW ADDRESS IF YOU HAVE MOVED: STREET: _____ CITY: _____
APT. NO. _____ STATE: _____ ZIP CODE: _____

3. Does the spouse of any person listed above live outside the family? ☐ YES ☐ NO

If yes, give name and address:

Write in the amount that he (she) gives toward your support each month $

4. Does parent(s) of any minor children listed above live at a different address? ☐ YES ☐ NO

If yes, give name and address:

Write in the amount that he (she) gives toward their support per month: $

➤ **NOW FILL IN BACK OF THIS FORM**

Figure 2.   Continued.

5. **INCOME FROM WORK**
    A. Name of person working
    Income Before Deductions: Weekly: $_____ Bi-Wkly: $ _____ Monthly $_____
    Employers Name and Address:

AMOUNT TAKEN OUT (deductions)	EXPENSES	
$_____Federal Tax	$_____	Transportation (Daily)
$_____D. C. Tax	$_____	Child Care (Weekly)
$_____Social Security	$_____	Other (Explain)
$_____Retirement		Example: Uniforms,
$_____Bonds & Credit Union		Support payments, etc.

DO NOT WRITE

IN SHADED AREA

   B. Name of person working
   Inomce Before Deductions   Weekly: $_____ Bi-Wkly: $ _____ Monthly $_____
   Employers Name and Address:

AMOUNT TAKEN OUT (deductions)	EXPENSES	
$_____Federal Tax	$_____	Transportation (Daily)
$_____D. C. Tax	$_____	Child Care (Weekly)
$_____Social Security	$_____	Other (Explain)
$_____Retirement		Example: Uniforms,
$_____Bonds & Credit Union		Support Payments, etc.

6. OTHER INCOME: Do any family members living with you and having a medical assistance
    card receive income from the following:

SOURCE	NAME OF PERSON RECEIVING INCOME	MONTHLY AMOUNT
Social Security		$
Civil Service Retirement		$
V.A. Pension		$
Military Retirement		$
Railroad Retirement		$
Rental of Property		$
Interest from Stocks or Bonds		$
Support from relatives or friends		$
Other		$

WORKER'S SSR CODE:_____
INSURANCE CODE:_____
9.   **CATEGORICALLY EXEMPT**
    (Disregarded Income)   ☐ OAA   ☐ AB
                            ☐ AFDO ☐ OTR
                                    $ _____
10.   **EXEMPT RESOURCES**_____
    TOTAL RESOURCES_____
    EXCESS RESOURCES_____

7. **RESOURCES:**
    (Name of Bank, Savings & Loan Association)   _____
    Cash on Hand . . . .
    Money in Savings . . . . $_____
    Other resources such as Stocks, Bonds, etc. . . . . $_____
    Real estate: (Other than Home in which we live) assessed value . . . . $_____

11.   **TOTAL LESS EXEMPTIONS**
    Less Health Ins. (6 months)
    FAMILY ADJUSTED INCOME
    INCOME SCALE
    EXCESS INCOME
    EXCESS INCOME (FROM 10)

8. **INSURANCE**
    A. **Life Insurance** on the following persons:
    Insurance Company _____   Policy No. _____   Date Issued _____
    Cash Value $ _____   Face Value $ _____
    B. **Health Insurance** on the following persons
    And pay $ _____ (Circle one) Weekly   Bi-Weekly   Monthly   Quarterly   Insurance   Company_____
    Policy No. _____

EXCESS INCOME AND RESOURCES
Signature of Certifying Officer
_____
Date:_____

   C. **Medicaid Information** (age 65 and over, disabled or blind) with Red, White, Blue Card is any person listed in the family group living with you receiving Medicare?
    If so, indicate in the space provided below.
    Claim No. _____   Person(s) covered _____   Kind of Coverage_____
    _____ HIB   _____ SMID
    _____ HIB   _____ SMID

   D. List names of family members who have claim(s) pending for personal injury (For example: Auto accident or on the job injury)
    _____
    _____

12. I declare that, to the best of my knowledge and belief, the information on this application for Medical Assistance, is true, correct, and complete. I understand that I may be asked to bring proof of the information I gave or that a representative of the Bureau of Eligibility Determination may get in touch with me or visit my home to request such proof. I will report promptly any changes in my income, resources, family members, needs or address change to the Bureau of Eligibility Determination. I understand that receipt of Medical Assistance will be paid for from Federal and State (D.C.) funds, and that any false claims, statements, documents or incomplete information will be prosecuted under applicable Federal or State (D.C.) Laws.

13. _____
    SIGNATURE OF APPLICANT OF "X MARK   MONTH DAY YEAR   SIGNATURE OF HUSBAND/WIFE OR "X" MARK   MONTH DAY YEAR

14. _____
    SIGNATURE OF WITNESS
    TO "X" MARK ABOVE   ADDRESS
                                                                                OF
                              MONTH YEAR YEAR   WITNESS:_____

15. Anyone who knowingly aids or encourages another person in obtaining or attempting to obtain Medical Assistance by giving false or incomplete information is punishable for fraud. He might be imprisoned, or both. (D.C. Code Section 3.3-216).

    Signature of Applicants Guardian, or person who helped fill out   Month Day Year   Telephone Number

    Street   Address   City   State   Zip Code   Relationship to Applicant

16. If for any reason you need to contact the Fair Hearings Division, the Telephone Number is 629-6701.

observe performance to locate sources and types of errors, and in which we revise and test forms to incorporate more discourse level features.

Another empirical method that we are using to understand public documents involves analyzing oral protocols of subjects 'thinking aloud' as they fill out forms. In the rest of this paper, we present some very preliminary results from a protocol study of the processes and strategies used by experts and novices to fill out an application form.

Forms as discourse--processes and strategies. Analysis of thinking-aloud protocols is not a technique that has been widely used in studying discourse. In searching for strategies that readers use to understand text, researchers have generally used recall or recognition tests and then inferred what the reader is doing from the patterns of omissions or intrusions. Kintsch and van Dijk (1978), for example, constructed a model of the way in which readers restructure a text to make it comprehensible. They acknowledge that 'the model does not specify the details of the processes' (1978:364).

Looking again at our model (Figure 1), one can see that the area we are interested in here is the box with the heavy border--the processes and strategies that constitute the user's behavior with the document. Traditional discourse studies only infer what might be in that box; protocol analysis allows us to peek inside. A thinking-aloud protocol is a record of the sequence of thoughts and behaviors a person engages in while performing a task. In a thinking-aloud protocol, the subject is asked to say whatever comes to mind as he or she does the task (in this case, filling out the form). The protocol is tape-recorded, transcribed, and analyzed by methods that assume objectivity and interrater reliability.

Developed by Newell and Simon (1972) to look at problem-solving, thinking-aloud protocols have also been a rich source of information on writing process (Flower and Hayes 1979, 1980, 1981). As colleagues on the Document Design Center's major project (funded by NIE), Flower and Hayes have used protocols to look at how people read and interpret Federal regulations (Flower, Hayes, and Swarts 1980).

We have been collecting protocols of subjects instructed to 'think aloud' as they attempt to complete the Federal government's job application form--SF 171. This form ranked very high in difficulty among 54 critical documents, selected in a scientific sampling of critical and frequently used public documents. Subjects in this study vary in education, work experience, and English language proficiency. We are particularly interested in the differences in the protocols of subjects who are successful--who complete a form that is highly likely to be well received (we call these people 'expert form users')--and subjects who cannot complete the form or whose form is not likely to be accepted by the government service agency (we call these people 'novices' or 'inexperienced form users'). In looking at this distinction, it is important to note that we judge novices as unlikely to be successful not by their inherent qualifications, but by how they represent these qualifications on the form: is it the appropriate and best representation of themselves for getting a government job?

We have only begun to analyze our protocols, but it appears that the expert form users are operating on several levels as they try to understand and complete the form--specifically, it seems that at least three levels of strategies are involved in successfully filling out this form. Figure 3 is a list of strategies we have identified from the protocols we have thus far analyzed. We have tentatively categorized these strategies into three levels, as Figure 3 shows.

Figure 3. Strategies of form users (from a preliminary protocol analysis).

1. Decoding strategies:	2. Form-using strategies:	3. Metacomments/ reality-testing:
lexicon syntax	creating examples selecting among examples creating scenarios proposing definitions calling on memory rereading instructions editing/reviewing/reflect- ing on what is already written being concerned about consistency	about forms in general about the rhetorical situation about the way to fill out forms about the writer's in- tentions

The lowest level is represented by 'decoding' statements--indicating that the user was devoting attention to deciphering the lexical and syntactic aspects of the form, attempting to figure out word meanings and to disambiguate sentences. Typical responses at this level include:

(1) Subject reads the instruction to 'estimate the amount of time in each type of work' and then says, 'That's gonna be a problem--what is a "type of work"?'

(2) Subject reads the item heading, 'lowest pay or grade you will accept', and then says, 'I don't understand about grade'.

At this level, we could say that the reader is in a word-bound frame.

At the second level are comments reflecting what we call 'form-using strategies'. These are generally text-level processes for understanding in which the user goes beyond words and sentences and attempts to relate items across the form or to draw on personal knowledge to clarify the meaning of items. Processes we have found at this level include:

(1) Instantiating: in deciding how to answer the question
    'When will you be available?' one subject commented,
    'Let's say I feel that I must have at least, must give
    my present employer 30 days notice ...' To understand
    the question and decide on a response, this subject
    conjured up a specific plausible situation.
(2) Calling on memory: 'My discharge from the reserves ...
    Let me see if I can resurrect it.'
(3) Watching for consistency: '[That answer] would cause
    me a dilemma because it sounds like I'm saying "Yeah,
    I'll take a part-time job", when over here someplace I
    said I'm not going to take a part-time job'.

It is at this level that we would also put the 'scenarios' that
Flower, Hayes, and Swarts found in studying readers trying to
understand regulations. That is, subjects trying to interpret
an abstract definition or condition would try to express it as
a concrete event in which someone does something (like a piece
of a story). The work on scenarios shows that readers create
strategies for interpreting difficult documents by borrowing
from discourse frames that are familiar and natural--here, the
narrative frame.
    At this second level of comments, we can say that the reader
is in a form-bound frame.
    Finally, we observed a third, higher level class of statements
which we call metacomments. These reflect the global strategies
that arise as the reader puts the document in a societal and
institutional context. The reader at this level is in a context-
bound frame, looking for the intention behind the questions,
predicting how answers will be interpreted, and showing awareness of the rhetorical situation and the text type. These
strategies call on a very complex set of cognitive operations
which involve taking the perspective of another--specifically,
of the agency that produced and will make use of the returned
form.
    Some of the linguistic cues to these global strategies in the
protocols of our form users are:

'I assume that if anything appears on a form it's there for
   a reason.'
'I have to stop and think and guess at what the implications
   [of different answers] are.'
'I interpret this in terms of what I think they're asking.'
'You're always gonna answer with what will get you the
   most points.'
'The intent of the question is ...'
'If I were applying to XXX, I would probably not put that
   down. If it were YYY I probably would.'

These strategies clearly invoke the rhetorical setting of the document and assume a two-party discourse between user and agency.

From this preliminary analysis, we believe that three levels of processing can be clearly distinguished in the protocols of expert form users. The protocols indicate, however, that subjects move rapidly from one frame to another; clearly, the frames are interconnected. For example, subjects call on their world knowledge for the information they use in the second-level strategy of creating examples. They use the same kind of knowledge at the top level, in predicting the purposes of the agency and the criteria by which institutional decisions are made.

Differences in processes of expert and novice form users. Of greatest interest in our preliminary results is this finding: the comments of the expert form user are far more likely to reflect the higher two levels of strategies than are the comments of the novice form user. Comments from novices are more likely to reflect the first level, decoding. Novices are likely to say, 'I don't know my Social Security number' and leave the question blank. Experts use various recall strategies or go get the card and copy down the numbers. Novices are likely to say 'this word is ambiguous' and not try to disambiguate it.

Novices are far more likely than experts to make no meta-comments at all--to ignore the rhetorical situation or intent. This failure to make metacomments is reflected in other behavior. If the expert form users have a piece of information they think will win points, they are likely to find a place to put it down. The novice is far more constrained by the individual items on the form, leaving out potentially point-winning, personal information because 'they don't ask about that'.

We are speculating that the experts are successful because they have available and use these higher level discourse strategies; and, further, that these macrolevel strategies are probably essential for coping effectively with forms--at least with complicated forms like the SF 171.

Two reasons can be suggested for the finding that novices tend to respond mainly on the first level. They may be spending all of their energy in decoding, because just dealing with the words and sentences overtaxes them. As Norman and Bobrow (1975) have pointed out, humans appear to have a limited capacity central processor which distributes a finite pool of cognitive resources to ongoing mental tasks according to need. These resources may be entirely depleted by the words and sentences for poorer readers.

Of more interest to us, a second reason for failing to operate in larger frames may be that the novice form users have not developed the appropriate strategies, or have developed them but do not apply them to forms. We hypothesize that we can take the successful strategies we uncover in our protocol analysis and teach them to the less successful form users. Direct teaching of higher level strategies has been a successful educational practice in reading (Bartlett 1978; Jones, Monsaas, and Katims 1979).

Although our analysis of the protocols in this study is not complete, we can foresee two practical outcomes of the study: (1) we can use our results to recommend or develop instruction to teach people how to approach forms; (2) we can use our results to recommend principles for designing forms.

How might the second application work? We think that forms can be designed to facilitate the use of macrolevel strategies and to exhibit more explicitly the discourse features--cohesive devices, scenarios, instantiation--that we find successful form users attending to in forms or building into their subjective structuring of forms.

For example, in the Medicaid study discussed earlier in this paper, many subjects not only failed to recognize some of the critical text-level variables in the form, but they failed to see the form as any kind of purposive communication at all. They did not appear to understand what a form is. We rewrote the introduction as a letter, on the theory that a letter format is a more familiar communicative frame for this audience. The letter frame seemed to help.

Both the analytical work we have done and the protocol studies we are conducting show that forms can be productively studied as a type of discourse. Although the work we have reported on in this paper is barely a beginning to an understanding of forms and how people use them, we believe that this research will eventually show us how to help both those who must develop forms and those who must fill them out.

NOTE

1. The model in Figure 1 is a refinement of an earlier model developed by Robbin Battison and Melissa Holland of the Document Design Center. Brown, Campione, and Day (1981) have recently presented a similar model for thinking about problems that students have in learning from instructional text.

REFERENCES

Adams, M. J., and A. Collins. 1979. A schema-theoretic view of reading. In: New directions in discourse processing. Edited by R. O. Freedle. Norwood, N.J.: Ablex.

Bartlett, B. J. 1978. Top-level structure as an organizational strategy for recall of classroom text. Unpublished doctoral dissertation. Arizona State University, Tempe, Ariz.

Bransford, J., and M. Johnson. 1973. Considerations of some problems of comprehension. In: Visual information processing. Edited by W. G. Chase. New York: Academic Press.

Bransford, J., and N. McCarrell. 1974. A sketch of a cognitive approach to comprehension: Some thoughts about what it means to comprehend. In: Cognition and the symbolic processes. Edited by W. Weimer and D. Palermo. Hillsdale, N.J.: Erlbaum.

Brown, A. L., J. C. Campione, and J. D. Day. 1981. Learning to learn: On training students to learn from texts. Educational Researcher 10.14-21.

Campbell, L. J., and V. M. Holland. (in press) Understanding the language of public documents, because formulas don't. In: Linguistics and the professions. Edited by R. Di Pietro. Norwood, N.J.: Ablex.

Chafe, W. 1970. Meaning and the structure of language. Chicago: University of Chicago Press.

Charrow, V. R., V. M. Holland, D. G. Peck, and L. V. Shelton. 1980. Revising a Medicaid recertification form: A case study in the document design process. Washington, D.C.: American Institutes for Research.

Clark, H. H., and S. E. Haviland. 1979. Comprehension and the given-new contract. In: Discourse production and comprehension, I. Edited by R. O. Freedle. Norwood, N.J.: Ablex.

Flower, L. S., and J. R. Hayes. 1979. A process model of composition. Document Design Project Technical Report No. 1. Pittsburgh: Carnegie-Mellon University. [Also published in: Cognitive processes in writing. Edited by L. W. Gregg and E. R. Steinberg. Hillsdale, N.J.: Erlbaum. 1980.]

Flower, L. S., and J. R. Hayes. 1981. The pregnant pause: An inquiry into the nature of planning. Paper presented at Annual Meeting of AERA, Los Angeles.

Flower, L. S., J. R. Hayes, and H. Swarts. 1980. Revising functional documents: The scenario principle. Document Design Project Technical Report No. 10. Pittsburgh. Carnegie-Mellon University.

Grimes, J. E. 1975. The thread of discourse. The Hague: Mouton.

Halliday, M.A.K. 1967. Notes on transitivity and theme in English: II. Journal of Linguistics 3.199-244.

Halliday, M.A.K., and R. Hasan. 1976. Cohesion in English. London: Longman.

Hobbs, J. 1979. Coherence and coreference. Cognitive Science 3.67-90.

Holland, V. M. 1980. Revising a government document: The case of the Medicaid recertification form. Paper presented at the Symposium on Writing and Designing Documents: Research and Practical Solutions, Carnegie-Mellon University, October.

Holland, V. M. 1981. Psycholinguistic alternatives to readability formulas. Explanations from psycholinguistics. Document Design Project Technical Report No. 12. Washington, D.C.: American Institutes for Research.

Jones, B. F., J. A. Monsaas, and M. Katims. 1979. Improv-
ing reading comprehension: Embedding diverse learning
strategies within a mastery learning instructional format.
Paper presented at Annual Meeting of AERA, San Francisco.
Kintsch, W. 1974. The representation of meaning in memory.
Hillsdale, N.J.: Erlbaum.
Kintsch, W., and T. A. van Dijk. 1978. Toward a model of
text comprehension and production. Psychological Review
85.363-394.
Mandler, J. M., and N. S. Johnson. 1977. Remembrance of
things parsed: Story structure and recall. Journal of
Verbal Learning and Verbal Behavior 9.111-151.
Meyer, B.J.F. 1975. The organization of prose and its effect
on recall. Amsterdam: North-Holland.
Minsky, M. 1975. A framework for representing knowledge.
In: The psychology of computer vision. Edited by P. H.
Winston. New York: McGraw-Hill.
Newell, A., and H. Simon. 1972. Human problem serving.
Englewood Cliffs, N.J.: Prentice-Hall.
Norman, D. A., and D. G. Bobrow. 1975. On data-limited
and resource-limited processes. Cognitive Psychology 7.44-
64.
Rumelhart, D. E. 1975. Notes on a schema for stories. In:
Representation and understanding: Studies in cognitive
science. Edited by D. G. Bobrow and A. M. Collins. New
York: Academic Press.
Rumelhart, D. E., and A. Ortony. 1977. The representation
of knowledge in memory. In: Schooling and the acquisition
of knowledge. Edited by R. C. Anderson, R. J. Spiro, and
W. E. Montague. Hillsdale, N.J.: Erlbaum.
Schank, R. C., and R. P. Abelson. 1977. Scripts, plans,
goals, and understanding: An inquiry into human knowledge
structures. Hillsdale, N.J.: Erlbaum.
Stein, N. L., and C. G. Glenn. 1979. An analysis of story
comprehension in elementary school children. In: New directions in discourse processing, Vol. 3. Norwood, N.J.:
Ablex.
Tannen, D. 1979. What's in a frame? Surface evidence for
underlying expectations. In: New directions in discourse
processing. Edited by R. O. Freedle. Norwood, N.J.:
Ablex.
van Dijk, T. A. 1972. Some aspects of text grammars. The
Hague: Mouton.
van Dijk, T. A. 1980. Macrostructures: An interdisciplinary
study of global structures in discourse, interaction, and
cognition. Hillsdale, N.J.: Erlbaum.
Winograd, T. 1977. Discourse. In: Cognitive processes in
comprehension. Edited by M. Just and R. Carpenter.
Hillsdale, N.J.: Erlbaum.

SPEECH ACTIONS AND REACTIONS
IN PERSONAL NARRATIVE

William Labov
University of Pennsylvania

Through the better part of this century, linguists have taken
as their major focus the internal relations of linguistic structures, and they have drawn considerable profit from this en-
gagement.[1] There is no indication of a weakening of the focus
on internal structure in the last several decades. Yet there
are several critical issues where linguistic analysis is necessarily brought into confrontation with physical reality. I am not
speaking here of speech acts that work on the social understandings of speakers and listeners, where people can be seen
to suffer embarrassment, boredom, or insult. I am considering
rather the interrelations of language with violent acts that can
terminate conversational turns abruptly and bring an end to
any and all linguistic analysis.

In recent months, the Philadelphia newspapers have run accounts of several violent events, where people have been killed
by their fellow-citizens without any apparent reason. Three of
these incidents took place on the highways. One case involved
James Harkins, a Philadelphia policeman of 20 years' standing.

Camden police said that Harkins drove from a downtown
Camden parking lot into the path of a Philadelphia-bound
Transport of New Jersey bus at about 10:15 p.m.

Harkins' car cut in front of the bus, and driver Enrique
Cardona honked his horn, police said. Harkins then
stopped his car in the middle of the street, in front of
the bus, and demanded that Cardona open the door, they
said. When Cardona refused, Harkins walked to the other
side of the bus, drew a gun and fired, police said. Two
Camden police officers, Albert Ruderow and Howard Cad-
well, reportedly heard the gunshot and rushed to the bus,
where they encountered Harkins holding a gun. Harkins

allegedly aimed the gun at them when they ordered him to drop it. The officers opened fire and wounded Harkins in the chest, abdomen and arm.

--Philadelphia Inquirer, 3/12/81, B:1-2.

In another incident, a man shot and killed a truck driver after an argument on the Schuylkill Expressway. Everyone who has heard about these cases wonders what could be the cause of this sudden and apparently senseless violence. People suggest that there is a general climate of violence, a sense of frustration and despair in American life, or that Americans are simply going crazy these days. There may be far-reaching sociological or economic factors that go beyond the details of face-to-face interaction. But there are also causal sequences that are embedded in the structure of the immediate confrontation of one person and another. And in all the cases reported here, words were exchanged in that confrontation. Things were said, and immediately after, things were done--a close connection between speech acts and actions that implies a causal relation. (Though speech acts are, of course, kinds of actions, I refer throughout to nonverbal physical actions as 'actions' and refer to verbal actions as 'speech acts'.[2])

We do not know just what was said in any of these cases, so as linguists we are in no better position than anyone else to guess at the relations between language and action from the newspaper accounts. But we can draw inferences from comparison with a wider range of data concerning similar incidents, drawn from narratives of personal experience obtained in various studies of the speech community.

In this discussion I draw on three narratives of events where speech acts alternate with violent physical actions. Each of these narratives has been observed to hold the attention of listeners to a remarkable degree. I analyze the sequential structure of these narratives in order to get at the general principles that underlie the relations of speech and action and the particular sequences where speech leads to violence. In doing so, I try to keep in the foreground the fact that we are dealing with reports of events, not observations of the events themselves. The complexity of the many-layered relationship between reality and reported reality cannot be overestimated. I have already indicated some of the ways in which narratives are thoroughgoing transformations of reality (Labov 1972: Chapter 9). How then, can narratives of personal experience be used to illuminate relations of speech and action in the world reported by narrative?

Goffman (1974) gives us the most sophisticated view of the many-sided relationship between reality and reports of reality. On the one hand, reports of events are framed in ways that are highly conventionalized. On the other hand, behavior itself incorporates imitations and replayings, strips derived from those conventional representations (Goffman 1974:560-562).

Narrative accounts are not unreal accounts in the sense of being unrelated to reality. They are framed accounts, and with
proper attention to those frames and the rules of transformation, we can begin to reconstitute their relations to the wider
frames outside of the narrative context.

Attention to the social setting of the narrative is then an
essential part of this analysis. All of the narratives to be discussed here are drawn from tape-recorded interviews. They
therefore include the effects of formal observation, as speakers
adjust their speech to the norms appropriate for such observation. At the same time, all of our field work indicates that
these effects are minimal in narratives of personal experience,
highly dramatized and objective accounts of events actually ex-
perienced by the speaker. For this reason, many of our field
methods (Labov 1981) are concerned with techniques for eliciting such narratives. In face-to-face interviews, they yield the
closest approach to the phonology and syntax of the vernacular,
the form of language used among intimate peers when the mini-
mum degree of attention is given to superposed norms of speech.
As we will see, they also yield information on vernacular norms
of behavior; not in the normative rules or explanations that are
consciously reported, but in the unstated assumptions that
govern sequences of reported events. [3]

1. **Narratives of violent events.** In a discussion of violence
and the danger of death, Harold Shambaugh of Cleveland gave
me an account of something that had happened to him in Buenos
Aires, when he was in his early twenties and in the Merchant
Marine. He was 31 at the time I talked with him.

(1)

(What happened in South America?)

1　Oh I w's settin' at a table drinkin'.
2　And--uh--this Norwegian sailor come over
3　an' kep' givin' me a bunch o' junk about I was sittin'
　　with his woman.
4　An' everybody sittin' at the table with me were my
　　shipmates.
5　So I jus' turn aroun'
6　an' shoved 'im,
7　an' told 'im, I said, 'Go away,
8　I don't even wanna fool with ya.'
9　An' next thing I know I'm layin' on the floor, blood
　　all over me,
10　an' a guy told me, says, 'Don't move your head.
11　Your throat's cut.'

There are many things that might be said about Shambaugh's
narrative in the attempt to explain its powerful impact on

audiences, in the concise use of language, in its extraordinary shift of visual perspective. For my present purpose, the most important feature is the pattern that relates speech acts to actions.

This narrative shows the intimate relations of speech acts and actions that is the main focus of this discussion. In this case, speech and action are simultaneous in lines 5 and 6, associated more or less like word and gesture. Shambaugh's refusal to deal with the Norwegian sailor is conveyed by the imperative, 'Go away', the statement 'I don't even wanna fool with ya', and the action of shoving the other away. There is nothing problematic about this association: it is normal for words to be reinforced by gestures. The problem in understanding Shambaugh's narrative is to account for the sudden increase in the level of violence from line 8 to line 9. The linguistic question is then whether there are any properties of the speech acts reported that can contribute to this explanation.

Among the various narratives that I have dealt with over the last decade, one stands out in its strong effect on listeners. It is an account given to me by Jacob Schuster, a retired postman from New York City, of a sudden and violent conflict that broke out in his family just after his father's death. In a hundred retellings, to audiences of one or one thousand, the result is the same: after the first few sentences, the small movements, whispers and coughs that establish the normal noise level of an audience come to an end, and there intervenes the total silence that marks the undivided attention of listeners.

(2)

(What happened?)

1 My brother put a knife in my head.
2 Like kids, you get in a fight,
3 and I twisted his arm from behind him.
4 This was just a few days after my father had died,
5 and we were sitting shive.[4]
6 And the reason the fight started,
7 --this was in Coney Island--
8 a rat ran out in the yard,
9 and he started talk about it,
10 and my mother had just sat down to have a cup of coffee.
11 And I told him to cut it out.
12 'Course kids, you know, he don't hafta listen to me.
13 So that's when I grabbed him by the arm
14 and twisted it up behind him.
15 When I let go of his arm,
16 there was a knife on the table,
17 he just picked it up

18 and he let me have it.
19 And I started bleed like a pig.
20 And naturally, first thing was, run to the doctor,
21 and the doctor just said, 'Oh just about this much more,'
22 he says, 'and you'd a been dead.'

An understanding of this narrative and its effect on audiences
demands a study that goes beyond the scope of this analysis.
Here I am primarily concerned with the relations of speech acts
to action. The escalation of violence in Schuster's narrative,
Example (2), follows the same pattern as that outlined for
Shambaugh in Example (1).
In this case, the first physical action is not simultaneous
with a speech act, but follows in sequence. Line 14 is a response to 12, which does not report a speech act directly, but
implies one. Again, the problem is to explain the escalation of
the level of violence from 14 to 18. We might say for both
Shambaugh's and Schuster's narratives that it is appropriate
for one action to follow another; but in the absence of a grammar of action, we can say from our own knowledge of American
culture that stabbing someone with a knife is not a typical response to having an arm twisted. The challenge for us then
is the same: are there any characteristics of the speech acts 9,
11, and 12 that would motivate or explain the passage from 14
to 18?
The third narrative that deals with a sudden outbreak of violence was told me by Joanna Williams, 31, of Morgantown, West
Virginia. We were not talking about the danger of death, but
about this very subject, the level of violence in Appalachia.

(3)

They didn't believe in calling the law or anything like that.
They just took things in their own hands. (Did you ever
see any shooting of that sort?)

1   Oh yes, I can remember real well.
2   I was just a girl.
3   In fact, it stayed with me quite a while.
4   Well there w's a fellow, his name was Martin Cassidy and
    Bill Hatfield.
5   Mr. Hatfield's mother give him some money
6   and told him to go get a bushel of peaches.
7   And he went down to Martin's house.
8   And Martin had some moonshine there.
9   Back down there they make their own liquor, you know.
10 So--we call it moonshine.
11 Today they call it white lightnin'.
12 But at that time we called it moonshine.
13 And--I remember real well what happened.
14 Bunch of us kids was out there playin'.

15 And no one meanin' any harm about it.
16 but anyway Mr. Hatfield--Mrs. Hatfield come down
17 And took away her money from Mr. Hatfield,
    y'know, for the peaches,
      'cause she know that--
      he was gonna buy drinks with it.
18 And Mr. Cassidy was layin' out there in the yard.
19 And Mr. Cassidy just looked up
20 and he said to Bill, just--just jokin', just in a kiddin'
    way, he said,
    'Ah hah,' he says, 'that's another dollar bill you
      won't get to spend for a drink, hah.'
21 And Bill said, 'I'll fix you, you so-and-so.'
22 So he walked to Martin Cassidy's HOUSE, his own house,
23   come out with a double-bitted axe,
24   hit him down across the head once,
25   turned over
26 and hit him again,
27 then throwed the axe down
28 and run down through the woods.
29 Just over two dollars
    that he was sent for peaches with.

This account is from a third-party witness of the violence rather than one of the main actors. But the effect on a young girl was profound. Through her eyes we can isolate an alternation and combination of speech acts and action. Joanna Williams' account does not give us a direct view of the speech act implied in line 5, but by inference there must have been a verbal request with the transfer of money. There may have been a speech act when the money was taken away in line 17, but it is not reported. The speech acts of 20 and 21 are reported in clear detail, and the final action, lines 22-28, as well. Here the analytic problem is to account for the escalation of violence in response to a speech act: the insult (20), interpreted as a joke by the observer, does not seem in any way enough motivation to explain the killing. We do not know the past history of Hatfield and Cassidy. But the question for us is whether there are any characteristics of the speech acts involved that would make the whole sequence part of an understandable pattern instead of incomprehensible violence.

The patterns presented so far have been independent of any theoretical framework. To advance further, it is helpful to review briefly the characterization of narrative that has been presented in previous publications, and to develop a further framework that facilitates the connection between the rules for speech acts of Labov and Fanshel (1977) and the analysis of narrative as a means of recapitulating and transforming experience. The approach to speech acts as forms of action that is characteristic of Goffman (1976) is followed throughout. The more abstract interpretation of speech acts and their sequences then yields some insight into the relation between speech and action, the emergence and escalation of violence.

2. **The structure of narrative.** The view of narrative structure that is used here begins with the definition of narrative developed in Labov and Waletzky (1967), their analysis of the temporal organization of narrative, and the role of evaluation in narratives of personal experience. The concept of REPORTABILITY presented there is developed further, and the notion of a MOST REPORTABLE EVENT is introduced as the generating center of narrative structure. I then analyze more closely the other events that make up the complicating action, with the help of the distinction between OBJECTIVE and SUBJECTIVE events. A sequence of objective events is isolated. This leads in the following section to the recognition of speech acts as elements in the narrative sequence, and the analysis of the higher level interpersonal actions that operate on social identity and social status.

2.1 **Temporal organization.** As conceived by Labov and Waletzky (1967), NARRATIVE is a technical term, referring to one of many linguistic devices available to speakers for the recapitulation of past experience. Narrative does this through the basic rule of narrative sequencing (Labov and Fanshel 1977), which allows the listener to infer the reported temporal order of past events from the temporal sequence of clauses in the report of those events.

2.1.1 **Temporal juncture.** If two clauses occur in a given order, and a reversal of that order leads to a change in the semantic interpretation of the order of the reported events, they are said to be separated by a TEMPORAL JUNCTURE.

2.1.2 **Narrative clauses.** Only a limited number of clause types participate in temporal juncture and so serve as NAR-RATIVE CLAUSES. Subordinate-independent pairs like 'When I let go of him arm ... he picked it up' (Schuster, in Example (2), lines 15,17) may occur in the same temporal order as the original events, but reversal of that order produces no change in the order of semantic interpretation, e.g. 'He picked it up when I let go his arm'. Narrative clauses are independent clauses with verbs in the indicative mood and (in English) one of three tenses: the preterit, the historical present,[5] or the past progressive. Beyond the test of temporal juncture, narrative clauses can be identified by the criterion that they are appropriate answers to the criterial question, 'And then what happened?' The sequence of narrative clauses forms the COMPLICATING ACTION.

2.1.3 **Definition of narrative.** A NARRATIVE is then a sequence of two or more narrative clauses, that is, a sequence
of clauses separated by one or more temporal junctures.

2.2 **Orientation.** Most narratives give orienting information
on four types of data: the time, the place, the participants in
the action, and their general behavior before or at the time of
the first action. This information is usually concentrated at
the beginning, in an ORIENTATION section--Shambaugh,
Example (1), line 1; Schuster, Example (2), lines 4-7;
Williams, Example 3, line 4. But some orienting information
can be placed later in the narrative. The location of the knife
in Schuster's story is not given until line 16. In the Williams
narrative, Cassidy's behavior is not described until line 18.
Though the displacement of orientation can sometimes be accounted for on simple cognitive grounds, it often appears to
serve an evaluative function.

2.3 **Evaluation.** Narratives of vicarious experience and
narratives of young children are often limited to complicating
action. Such narratives are often heard as not having a point.
As narrators mature, they use an increasing number of evaluative clauses that do not refer to an event that occurred, but
rather to one that did not occur (Labov 1972). The contrast
between what did occur and what did not but might have
occurred serves to evaluate the narrative. Negatives, futures,
modals, and comparatives thus enter into narrative structure.
Other evaluating devices group several actions or behaviors in
the same time unit, using participles and other nonfinite verbs.
 The main point or focus of the narrative, as told, is often
indicated by the concentration of a number of evaluating clauses
in an EVALUATION SECTION directly before a particular narrative clause.
 In Examples (1) and (2), the evaluation section is placed at
the end of the narrative, and merged with the final action or
RESOLUTION. In Shambaugh, lines 8-9, we observe the suspension of the action (with progressive and adverbial phrase).
The seriousness of the situation is then stated by a negative
imperative: 'Don't move your head'. In Schuster, line 21, we
find a comparative ('this much more') and a complex modal
('would have been'), evaluating the seriousness of the situation
by comparison with what might have taken place.

2.4 **Abstracts.** Many narratives are preceded by a brief
summary statement of the substance of the narrative as viewed
by the narrator. The focus of the abstract is normally the
same as the point of the narrative, but not necessarily, since
it is more closely linked with the preceding utterance of the
other person and the insertion of the narrative in the conversation. An ABSTRACT of this kind is given in Schuster,
lines 1-3.

2.5 Analysis of the complicating action. Much of the attention of previous analyses has focused on the elaboration of narrative beyond the fundamental sequence of narrative clauses. The main thrust of this discussion is in the other direction: to reduce the narrative to its skeletal outline of narrative clauses, and to outline the generating mechanism that produces the narrative backbone.

2.5.1 Reportability. When people tell narratives, they occupy a larger portion of social time and space than in most other conversational turns. There have been various discussions of how narrators alert listeners to the impending narrative. Here one must be concerned with the other end of the question: AFTER the narrative is finished, do listeners accept this occupation of conversational time as justified? If the response to a narrative is 'So what?' or 'What are you getting at?', it must be considered a failure, and much of narrative is organized to forestall such a response. The evaluation section can contribute a great deal to this end, but the fundamental burden of achieving acceptability is on the character of the events being reported.

We can classify all narrative clauses into two types in terms of the appropriateness of complementary sets of responses from listeners:

In response to Type A, expressions of ordinary understanding: 'I see', 'Uh-huh', 'Naturally' ... [6]
In response to Type B, expressions of ordinary surprise:
   'Really?', 'Is that so?', 'You don't mean it!', 'No kidding!',
   etc.

Thus, Williams' first clause, line 1, is Type A:

1   Oh I w's settin' at a table drinkin'.
    (I see.)

And the same holds true for the clause in line 2, but not for line 3, which is Type B:

2   And--uh--this Norwegian sailor come over
    (Uh huh.)
3   An' kep' givin' me a bunch o' junk about I was sittin'
    with his woman.
    (I see.)

Here, a response of 'Really?' would be more appropriate. Shambaugh's last sentence, in line 11 of (1), is even more clearly Type B. After 'Your throat's cut', it would be out of the question to say, 'Naturally', 'I understand', or 'Uh-huh'. Ordinary expressions of surprise like 'Really?' are not strong enough here. A good number of listeners respond with an ingressive gasp of breath. My response on tape is, in fact, a devoiced 'Wow!' Evidently, reportability is not a binary dimension but a scalar one.

These reactions are not to expressions but to the report of events. Events of Type B are REPORTABLE events. If a narrative contains such an event, it is not possible for someone to respond at the end with 'So what?' A normal narrative, then, which has succeeded in the tasks of holding the attention of an audience and justifying the time taken to tell it, contains at least one reportable event. The reportability of a narrative is equivalent to that of the maximally reportable event in it.

The assessment of REPORTABILITY does not rest on the objective grounds that I would like, first, because it is evidently relative to the culture of the narrator. For cultures very different from our own, we may have only a dim view of what is reportable. The relativity of this concept is also obvious when we listen to children's narratives. Second, reportability is relative to the social occasion. Higher degrees of reportability are required to hold the floor when other reportable matters are on hand than when nothing else is happening.[7] Third, the judgments on reportability that I use here are intuitive. Though I have some objective evidence from participant-observation and the reactions of audiences, I am primarily using my own reactions in judging the appropriateness of responses.

Against this subjectivity of response there is the generalization that death and the danger of death are among the two or three major themes of human concern and interest for all of the cultures that we know. It is for this reason that these themes play an important role in our interviews. The central events of the three narratives given here are highly reportable; they are far from the margins of reportability where the subjective character of such judgments becomes a problem. It is only under very special and terrible circumstances that someone's death is not reportable: where we would agree with Macbeth that 'there would have been a time for such a word'.

2.5.2 Credibility. Reportable events are almost by definition unusual. They are therefore inherently less credible than nonreportable events. In fact, we might say that the more reportable an event is, the less credible it is. Yet credibility is as essential as reportability for the success of a narrative. A narrative that is judged entirely false, 'nothing but a big lie', does not have the impact or acceptability of a narrative that is considered essentially true. And except for certain special storytelling traditions,[8] the reputation of the narrator suffers if he or she is judged to be a liar. For narratives of personal experience, this situation raises the question of whether there is an inherent contradiction between reportability and credibility.

There are two main directions in which we can look for the resolution of this question. One has to do with the credibility of the evaluation provided in the narrative, and the scale of objectivity of evaluation (Labov and Waletzky 1967). In this discussion, I look in the other direction: at the construction of the complicating action that precedes the reportable event. Credibility is seen to rest on a series of causal relations that lead from the initial situation to that maximally reportable event.

2.5.3 **The generation of a narrative.** Every narrative is about something. The abstract, if there is one, tells us what it is about. It is usually about the maximally reportable event, though the relocation of the evaluation section can alter this perception on the part of listeners (Labov and Fanshel 1977). When someone decides to tell a narrative, he or she has normally decided to tell a story about that event. Though that decision has not yet created a narrative by my definition (Section 2.1.3), the reportable event holds a central position in any formal characterization of a narrative. One can write $N \to E(r)$, where E is a series of ordered events in temporal sequence and r is the index number of the most reportable action. The basic solution to the problem of achieving credibility of $E(r)$ is to provide an account of the events that led up to it, that is, the real-world conditions that gave rise to this unusual event. It might be possible to construct a narrative by a series of adjuncts to $E(r)$, each one answering the question 'How did that come about?', of the form $E(r) \to E(r-1) + E(r)$, where each $E(r-1)$ would be an event that led to the simple or complex series of events that follow. Yet the major problem is to know where to stop in this process, often expressed by the phrase, 'Where should I begin?' The selection of the orientation section by the narrator is one of the crucial steps in the construction of the narrative and the theory of causality that supports it. In general, the speaker searches for the first set of general conditions where the question 'How did that come about?' might be appropriately answered by, 'That's the kind of thing that we usually did then'. Thus, Shambaugh's story begins with him sitting with his shipmates at the table in Buenos Aires drinking, the kind of thing they usually did in port.

Given these initial conditions, the speaker has to find a credible way to bridge the gap between them and the reportable event with a series of intervening actions. This suggests a set of four rules:

(1) $N \to Or + E(r)$
(2) $Or \to Or + E(1)$
(3) $E(i) \to E(i) + E(i+1)$
(4) $E(i) \to E(i-1) + E(i)$

These rules have no intrinsic order. They register the fact
noted earlier, that the first decision in forming a narrative is
to select the orientation that ultimately makes understandable
the reportable event. An orientation is frequently coupled with
or superimposed on a first event. Then there is no control
over whether actions are picked as consequences of previous
actions by Rule (3) or as the causes of later events by Rule
(4). At first glance, it might seem necessary to impose an external condition that no $E(i)$ can be earlier than an $E(i-1)$, but
there is no need for such a condition. If $E(i)$ precedes $E(i-1)$
in time, the past perfect tense is used, as the result of just
such an overlap in the construction of a chain of events.

2.5.4 **Objective and subjective events.** The process I have
described characterizes the generation of a skeleton of events
that forms the complicating action of a narrative, each event
separated by temporal juncture from the other. Each event
can be thought of as the answer to a question, 'And then what
happened?' or 'How did that come about?' Up to this point,
the process can be thought of as relatively neutral to the many
transformations of these events that are characteristic of narratives as delivered. Narratives often show the insertion of
evaluative material throughout the text, not only in the evaluation section, additions that are not directly related to the
business of telling what happened. But other functions of
narrative--the presentation of self, the maximization of the
position of the narrator, the polarization of antagonist and
protagonist, are also facilitated by the selection of orientation
and the arrangement of narrative clauses.
   In completed narrative, one can distinguish two kinds of
events, which I call OBJECTIVE and SUBJECTIVE EVENTS.
The distinction can be seen most clearly if we refer to potential
testimony in a court of law. A report of an objective event
can be contradicted by a witness who was present at the time;
a report of a subjective event cannot. Things that narrators
feel or say to themselves are then subjective ('I had this feeling that ...', 'I said to myself, "There'll be times I can't put
up with this ..."'). What is said aloud to others is objective.
Most physical events are objective, but there are subjective
ones. The report, 'I took this girl and started to move her
away' cannot be contradicted, since the mere intention to move
is enough to justify 'start + FOR/TO + Verb', as opposed to
'I started moving her away', which demands some physical
motion.[9] Actions of turning and orientation are often subjective.[10]
   The three narratives considered here show a remarkably high
proportion of objective events. Subjective events that can be
identified are Shambaugh, line 5, 'I jus' turn aroun", and
Williams, lines 1, 13, 'I (can) remember real well (what
happened)'.

2.5.5 **Instrumental events.** The sequence of narrative
clauses that appears in the surface text of a narrative often
shows events that are predictable means of implementing other
events. Thus Schuster, line 13, '... I grabbed him by the
arm' is an inevitable antecedent of line 14, '(I) twisted it up
behind him'. Such instrumental events are not appropriate
responses to the generating question, 'How did that come
about?' If that question is addressed to 'I twisted it up behind him', the answer would be line 12, 'He didn't listen to
me'.

2.5.6 **The basic sequence of complicating action.** This mode
of analysis can be used to reconstitute the complicating action
for the three narratives as an objective event sequence (OES),
leaving aside evaluative clauses, subjective events, and instrumental events. Events located as simultaneous, between
the same two temporal junctures, are restated as a single compound event. Each event is then separated from the others
by a temporal juncture. This OES then represents the cognitive framework that is provisionally accepted as a true representation of the events reported in the narrative. If the sequence is then coherent, each event will be an appropriate response to the criterial question addressed to the preceding
event, 'What happened then?' (forward sequencing) and the
criterial question addressed to the following event, 'How did
that come about?' (causal sequencing).
  We can now see whether an OES constructed for each of the
three narratives is more coherent than our original reading of
the text. I represent each of the events by the independent
narrative clause(s) with preterit heads.

OES for Shambaugh narrative, Example (1):

Or	1	
E(1)	2	A Norwegian sailor come over
E(2)	3	he kep' givin' me a bunch o' junk
		about I was sittin' with his woman.
E(3)	6,7	I shoved 'im an' told 'im, 'Go away'
E(r)	11	A guy says, 'Your throat's cut.'

Certainly, E(1) through E(r) answer the first test of forward
sequencing, but the causal sequence fails in the same way when
we address the question 'How did that come about?' to E(r).

OES for Schuster narrative, Example (2):

Or	4-7	
E(1)	8	A rat ran out in the yard,
E(2)	9	My brother started to talk about it,
E(3)	11	I told him to cut it out.

```
E(4)    12    (brother refuses)
E(5)    14    I twisted his arm
E(r)    18    He let me have it with the knife
E(7)    19    I started bleeding
E(8)    20    We ran to the doctor
E(9)    21    The doctor said, 'just that much more,
                    and you'd a been dead.'
```

Again, the forward sequencing is a coherent series of events, but the causal sequence seems no more coherent when we ask if E(r) is a likely outcome of E(5).

OES for Williams narrative, Example (3):

```
Or      4
E(1)    5     Mrs. Hatfield gave Hatfield money
        6     and told him to get a bushel of peaches
E(2)    7     He went down to Cassidy's store
E(3)    16    Mrs. Hatfield come down
E(4)    17    She took her money away from Hatfield
E(5)    20    Cassidy said, 'That's another dollar ...'
E(6)    21    Bill said, 'I'll fix you'
E(r)    24    He hit Cassidy with an axe
E(8)    26    He hit him again
E(9)    28    He run down through the woods
```

Here again the causal sequence fails when we address the question 'How did that come about?' to E(r). The interpretation of E(6), of course, depends on the seriousness of the offense E(5). The narrator interprets E(5) as a joke. Accepting this, we would interpret E(6) as a joking threat. If Hatfield had returned with a bucket of water and thrown it on Cassidy, we might understand that as an appropriate fulfillment of his threat. But as it is, we are left with the same sense of shock and wonder that Joanna Williams expresses: people behaved in violent and incomprehensible ways in those days.

It would seem therefore that the construction of an objective event sequence has not so far advanced our understanding of the violent reactions in these narratives. The sense of strangeness remains: these people did not behave as we expect people to behave. This effect is not due to the transformation of the narrative through the insertion of interpretative or evaluative material, but seems inherent in the events themselves. In Section 3, I use that event structure to move to a higher level of abstraction, examining the sequencing of speech acts and actions, to see if further comprehension is to be gained at that level.

3. Action and reaction. The preceding sections have confirmed the general principle that there are no (necessary) connections between utterances (Labov and Fanshel 1977).

Though there are tying relations between sentences--anaphoric, elliptic--the coherence of discourse is not established at this level but at a more abstract level of representation. Ultimately, the cohesion of the three narratives that we are examining does not depend on the sequence of narrative clauses but on the sequences of speech acts and actions that the narrative presents.

The first step in the analysis of the reported actions is to translate the quoted speech acts into their least abstract representation at the level of action. All three narratives, like most accounts of human interaction, center around REQUESTS FOR ACTION and sequential responses to them. In the Shambaugh and Schuster narratives, these are followed immediately by violent action; in the Williams narrative, there intervenes another kind of speech act, an INSULT.

3.1 **The rule of requests.** Most of the apparatus that is needed for the analysis to follow is contained in the basic rule for requests for action formulated in Chapter 3 of Labov and Fanshel (1977).[11] It is a rule of interpretation that states the conditions that lead the addressee to believe that a request for action has been made. The rule is presented here in a somewhat simplified form, omitting details that are not relevant to the analysis to follow.

Rule of Requests:

If A addresses to B an imperative specifying an action X at a time T, and B believes that A believes that

(conditions based on needs and abilities)
‹1› X should be done,
‹2› B has the ability to do X,

(conditions based on rights and obligations)
‹3› B has the obligation to do X, and
‹4› A has the right to tell B to do X

then A is heard as making a valid request for action X.

If we now turn to the objective event sequence or OES of Williams' narrative, given at the end of Section 3, we can begin to establish the series of actions represented by the reported objective events. It is not difficult to identify E(1)

Mrs. Hatfield gave Hatfield some money and told him to get a bushel of peaches.

as a request for action made by Mrs. Hatfield of Billy Hatfield. E(1) implements condition ‹ 2 ›. We can infer that Mrs. Hatfield is the head of the household and is therefore an authority on the need for peaches ‹ 1 ›. It is also apparent that her son has

‹ 3 › the obligation and she has ‹ 4 › the right to tell him to get peaches. We can therefore write the first of a series of actions as an indexed A series at the higher level of abstraction than the event sequence:

A(1) Mrs. Hatfield makes a request for action of
Billy Hatfield to buy a bushel of peaches.

Events (2) and (3) are Hatfield's and Mrs. Hatfield's descent to Cassidy's house. They are simple locomotions that are essential to show that the participants in the interaction were in contact and the audience present. No audience is indicated for E(1), but Cassidy and the children are witnesses to E(4), Mrs. Cassidy taking back the money. This action can be considered the cancellation of the request A(1) since one of the conditions--Hatfield's ability to buy peaches--is removed. The remark E(5) of Cassidy is an insult that can be reconstructed using the principle of conditional relevance of negation:

That's one more dollar you won't spend for drink because your mother took the dollar away.

It presupposes

You would have spent that dollar for drink if your mother had not taken the dollar away.

This leads by inference to the general proposition, 'You are the kind of person that spends every dollar that comes into his hands for drink'.

Rules for threats and promises (Searle 1969) allow us to identify E(6) as a threat, and the reportable actions E(r,8) do not need deeper analysis to be identified as killing or manslaughter.[12] We then have derived the sequence of reported actions:

A(1) Mrs. Hatfield makes a request of action of Billy Hatfield to buy a bushel of peaches.
A(2) Mrs. Hatfield cancels the request by taking back the money.
A(3) Cassidy insults Hatfield as an irresponsible alcoholic.
A(4) Hatfield threatens Cassidy.
A(5) Hatfield kills Cassidy.

This reduction of the narrative text to actions does not yet illuminate the fundamental problem of the passage from A(3) to A(5). But given this more abstract characterization of the events, we can turn to the rule of requests for a further understanding of what is reported to have taken place.

By A(1) it is established as shared knowledge that Mrs. Hatfield has the right to request Billy Hatfield to go to buy peaches, and he has the obligation to do so. It is further evident that she is the head of the household, since by A(2) it appears that he has no money of his own. He is then in the relationship of dependent member of the household to head of the household, though he is a grown man. That a grown son should have no regular income and that his mother should have to scrape together a few dollars for food is a normal situation in Appalachia. The important thing to note is that it is an asymmetrical status well understood by others in the community.

In the most probable interpretation of the reported event, the action of taking back the money A(2) represents a cancelling of the request A(1). But the reason given for this by the narrator and by the insult of A(3) is that even when Hatfield has the money he does not have the ability to carry out that request: that he is not a dependable person. The reported action A(2) reduces his status from dependent member of the household to something lower: a no-account person. Furthermore, this act is performed publicly. If we continue to accept provisionally the objective event sequence as an account of events that did occur, we are in a position to clarify the causal sequence of actions involved.

The act of cancelling the request has a social meaning at a higher level of abstraction. It is a CHALLENGE: an assertion of a condition that, if true, lowers the esteem of a person in a status or removes him or her from that status (Labov and Fanshel 1977). The sequential response to a challenge is a DEFENSE and often a COUNTER-CHALLENGE. But Billy Hatfield apparently had no options open to him for defense or counter-challenge, and the result is a profound and predictable state of rage.

The fact that this rage found a violent outlet against Martin Cassidy is not predictable. Nor can we say under what conditions violent rage will result in such violent action. But it seems from an analysis of the conditions governing the request and withdrawal of the request that the controlling dynamic of this situation is one of social status and challenge to social status. Whatever verbal sequence was available for Billy to deal with his mother had come to an end, and the route to violent action was then taken.

I have less information on the social and cultural background of the participants in the Williams story than in the other two cases. The Shambaugh narrative deals with an encounter between strangers in a bar. The pattern of actions is easy to establish with the help of the Rule of Requests and the auxiliary Rule for Indirect Requests, as given in Labov and Fanshel (1977:Chapter 3).

Rule for Indirect Requests:

If A makes to B a Request for Information or an assertion to B about

⟨a⟩ the existential status of an action X to be performed by B,
⟨b⟩ the consequences of performing X,
⟨c⟩ the time T that X might be performed by B, or
⟨d⟩ any of conditions for a valid request for X given in the Rule of Requests

and all other conditions are in effect, then A is heard as making a valid request of B for the action X.

The substance of event E(2) can then be understood as a request for action made indirectly.

(he) kep' givin' me a bunch o' junk about I was sittin' with his woman.

In Example (1), the Norwegian sailor has explained to Shambaugh that he is sitting with his woman. It can be easily inferred that he believes that Shambaugh should not be sitting with his woman but sitting somewhere else. Under subsection ⟨d⟩, this is an indirect assertion of one of the conditions of the Rule of Requests, ⟨1⟩ the need for an action to correct this situation. It is evident ⟨2⟩ that Shambaugh has the ability to do so. The crucial questions under dispute concern ⟨3⟩ the obligation of Shambaugh to move and ⟨4⟩ the sailor's right to make the request.

There are ways and means for putting off or refusing requests in an accountable manner, which recognize the rights and obligations of the other, and I deal with these later in the Rule for Putting Off Requests. But Shambaugh does not report himself using any of these means. He does not even dispute the Norwegian sailor's rights. Instead, he refuses to hear the sailor's talk as a valid request and says that he does not want to fool with him. How can we account for this mismatch of social perception between the Norwegian sailor and Shambaugh?

The situation in the Buenos Aires bar is not unique. I have found a number of parallel narratives from Philadelphia, from Scotland, and elsewhere where working-class people meet in bars, at dances, at celebrations of various kinds. Most of the narratives about the fights that break out give only a partial view of the overall situation, and I did not understand it myself until it was explained to me by Joe Dignall, a 23-year-old man from Liverpool. As a natural ethnographer, he was able to lay out for me the sequence of events that often follow when single men walk into a pub and 'try to cop off a few birds'.[13]

A lot of fellas, if they're with a gang, they let their
birds sit with their mates, while he stands at the bar with
his mates, talkin' about things. And you could go up,
start chattin' this bird up, an' next thing--y'know, you're
none the wiser. An' she's edgin' yer on, on, you're a nice
fella, you've got a few bob. Great! And--you're chattin'
it up there, you're buyin' her a few shorts ... Nex'
thing, eh, a fella comin' there over there, 'Eh ay lads ...
what are ya doin?' Well YOU don't know he's goin' with
her, so you tell HIM to push off. Nex' thing he's got his
friends--his mates on to you, an' uh ... you're in lumber!
You've either got to run, or fight!

This, then, is the situation of mismatched information that
Shambaugh found himself in, though even in his account given
years after, he does not see it that way. He had evidently sat
down with his friends at a table where there was a girl who
had been with the Norwegian sailor. But to Shambaugh, the
Norwegian sailor had no standing at all. Shambaugh refused
him the right to enter into an argument. There was no verbal
sequence open to the Norwegian sailor: a violent reaction
followed.
Shambaugh's response can be characterized as an unaccounted
refusal. Goffman has outlined the sequences of actions involved here as in Figure 1.[14]

Figure 1.

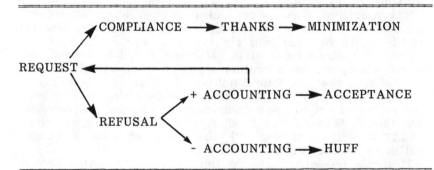

This schema indicates that a request can be followed by com-
pliance, which is normally followed by expressions of thanks on
the part of the requester and an expression of minimization on
the part of the complier. A request can also be followed by a
refusal. This can then be followed by an accounting as to why
the request cannot be complied with (and can then be classed
as a way of putting off the request). There are then two further routes. The requester can accept the refusal and the sequence comes to an end. Or he can by various mechanisms put
the request again, setting up a recursive sequence. If, on the

other hand, the refusal is not followed by an accounting, there is no further verbal sequence. In polite society, the termination of verbal exchange can be called a 'huff'. In many circumstances, this leads to a situation where individuals or families do not talk to each other. In others, it leads to the kinds of violent reactions we have been looking at.

We can then rewrite the event sequence of the Shambaugh narrative as follows:

A(1) The Norwegian sailor makes a request for action of
      Shambaugh: to move away from his woman.
A(2) Shambaugh refuses without an accounting.
A(3) The Norwegian sailor cuts Shambaugh's throat.

Shambaugh's refusal to recognize the right of the Norwegian sailor to make the request led naturally to his failure to give an accounting. He followed a sequence that did not leave room for any further verbal exchange. The moral that he drew for himself from the event is that the next time he shoves someone, he will stand up and hit them. Others who know these situations have drawn the opposite conclusion: that the proper thing to do when someone says you are sitting with their woman is to excuse yourself, get up, and move.

The Norwegian sailor cut Shambaugh's throat, but he missed the jugular vein. One of Shambaugh's shipmates hit the Norwegian on the head with a chair and he died. When Shambaugh got out of the hospital, they gave him the knife; he still has it with him in Cleveland.

The narrative of Schuster is also centered about a request for action. In E(2), his brother started to talk about the rat, and in E(3), Schuster tells him to 'cut it out'. This is reported as a direct imperative. If it was heard as a valid request, then Schuster's brother must have believed that Schuster believed that the four conditions for this rule held true: ‹1› that there was a NEED: that he should stop talking about the rat so as not to upset their mother; ‹2› that his brother had the ABILITY to stop talking; ‹3› that Schuster had the RIGHT to tell him to stop; ‹4› that his brother had the obligation to do what Schuster told him.

It should be underlined that this does not mean that Schuster's brother himself believed that these conditions held, but only that in order to hear the remark 'cut it out' as a valid request for action (and not a joke or a suggestion), it is essential that he believed that Schuster believed this. Once a valid request is recognized, the consequences for further sequencing are well defined, as we have seen, and quite different from the situation that prevails if the other person is seen as joking or less than serious.

Given his recognition of the validity of the request, Schuster's brother had a number of options for rejecting it. These are sketched out in the following rule from Chapter 3 of Labov and Fanshel (1977).

Rule for Putting Off Requests:

If A has made a valid request for an action X of B and B addresses to A:

   ‹a› a positive assertion or request for information about the existential status of X,
    ‹b› a request for information or negative assertion about the time T, or
   ‹c› a request for information or negative assertion about any of the four conditions of the rule of requests,

then B is heard as refusing the request until the information is supplied or the negative assertion is contradicted.

Schuster's brother's response is not given directly, and in E(4), the refusal is indicated in parentheses. Schuster says something that can be interpreted not as a report of an act but as an excuse for it:

(2)12 'Course kids, you know, he don't hafta listen to me.

It is not uncommon in family narratives for someone to substitute an excuse for an action ('Kids will be kids') for the report of the action itself. I originally thought that this is what Schuster had done here. But on further consideration of the central problem of this narrative, that of accounting for the violent reaction of his brother, I came to believe that line 12 contains an indirect quotation that can be reconstructed as the direct quotation:

'I don't hafta listen to you.'

This would follow option ‹c› of the Rule for Putting Off Requests, and in that option, selects the negative assertion about the third condition: his obligation to do what Schuster says. In denying that obligation, he refuses the request.
   Labov and Fanshel point out that there is a great difference in the interactive consequences of putting off or refusing a request by reference to ‹ 1 › needs or ‹ 2 › abilities, on the one hand, and ‹ 3 › obligations and ‹ 4 › rights, on the other. References to needs and abilities are mitigating. If his brother had denied the need to stop talking, saying 'Oh that won't bother Mom', we can imagine that Schuster's response would have been quite different from what it was. But the act of refusal by denying an obligation to listen produced a violent response on Schuster's part.

The central actions in Schuster's narrative can then be summarized:

A(1) Schuster makes a request of action of his brother:
to stop talking about the rat.
A(2) His brother refuses by denying his obligation to do
what Schuster said.
A(3) Schuster tries to enforce his request by physical
force: he twists his brother's arm.
A(4) His brother stabs Schuster.

So far, we have advanced in our understanding of the situation by seeing that his brother's refusal was made in an
aggravating form. This might explain for us the violence
that Schuster used. But it does not explain the terrible increase in the level of violence on the part of his brother.
It is an important and yet curious fact that no one who
hears the story thinks of Schuster's brother as a bad person.
'Uncontrolled' is the most common adjective that is applied to
him. Some social or emotional force had driven him out of
control. We think immediately of the folk theory that great
grief often produces violent reactions: that we do not expect
someone who has suffered the loss of a father to behave
rationally.
It is evident that something was said that made Schuster
angry with his brother, and that his brother was even angrier
with him. What is the source of this violent anger? If we reflect on the conditions for the rule of requests, it clearly has
to do with the rights and obligations involved. If Schuster's
brother believed that Schuster believed he had the obligation to
obey him, and he rejected that claim, it is probable that he believed that his brother was assuming rights he did not have.
The inference that I have drawn here rests on my own personal
interpretation of the reported events, the result of many years
of familiarity with the narrative. In this interpretation, the
substance of what Schuster's brother said to him goes beyond
the indirect quotation of line 12:

'I don't have to listen to you. You can't take my father's
place and you never will.'

It seems to me that the violence of his reaction can only be
explained by his belief that Schuster was unjustly assuming
his father's place a few days after his father had died.

4. The defense of rights and the struggle for status. Reviewing the analysis of actions of the three narratives, two
common themes emerge. First, violent reactions are found when
the sequence of speech acts leads in a direction where speech
stops. Secondly, each of these situations is associated with a
dispute over the social status of the participants.

This consideration leads me to renew the emphasis put by Labov and Fanshel on the role of social rights and obligations in the dynamics of the Rule of Requests. As one might expect, the philosophical literature on speech acts deals with needs and abilities and rarely touches on these dimensions of social relations. In imagining conversations, one rarely imagines the kinds of social situations that discourse is embedded in. In the analysis of these three narratives, I have tried to show, among other things, the importance of an understanding of that social context.

Table 1 is an analysis of the origins of violent conflicts in narratives of personal experience.

Table 1. Origins of violent conflict given in 60 narratives of personal experience.

| | Age of protagonist | | |
	Pre-adolescent	Adolescent	Adult
Bothering	5	2	
Play	8	4	
Defense against aggression			
of persons	4	1	1
of property	3	1	1
against unjust accusation	1		
Status (gang, nongang)		4	1
Unknown		4	1
Women who were insulted or			
who claimed to have been	3	2	2
Defense of rights			
to a seat		1	
to a cigarette		1	
to the right of way		1	
to walking space			2
to a piece of cake			1
to women		2	4
Total	24	23	13

These are not drawn from a random sample of a closed population of narratives, but from 300 narratives that I have drawn from a wide range of interviews for the study of narrative structure. The causes of conflict are classified on the vertical dimension, and the 60 narratives are broken down into three columns by the age of the protagonist at the time of the action.

Table 1 shows a striking differentiation by age. For preadolescent narrators, there is a heavy concentration in narratives where someone was 'bothering' another, where play led to fighting and defense against physical aggression. Adolescent protagonists show a much wider range of origins of conflict, including those just mentioned, but with a heavier concentration on gang status and a number of cases where the origins were unknown. There are six cases of fights that broke out over the defense of rights: the right to a certain seat, to the loan of a cigarette, to the right of way on the sidewalk, to being with a certain woman. Narratives of adult conflicts show an even heavier concentration in this area: 7 of the 12 adult narratives of violent conflict deal with the defense of rights, and 4 of these over the rights to women.

Looking more closely at this struggle over rights, it appears that it is not the right itself that is at issue, but the general status that the right pertains to. Following the general argument of Labov and Fanshel (1977), I would say that the fundamental cohesion of discourse is not at the level of speech act but at the more abstract level of interaction where status and role are negotiated. The arrays of actions outlined here are therefore not the level of analysis that advances our understanding of the relation of violent reactions to speech acts, but a more general characterization that Goffman has called MOVES.

In my own conception, a MOVE is an interaction that alters or threatens to alter the relative social positions of the interactants. These include challenges, defenses, retreats, counterchallenges, supports, and reinforcements (Labov and Fanshel 1977). A CHALLENGE is an assertion which, if true, lowers the esteem of someone in a certain status: asserting that someone is not a fit mother, or an effective employee, or a responsible partner in a game. Challenges may also be more categorical, putting into question the right of a person to hold a given status: of parent, adult, employee, or friend. SUPPORTS or SECOND DEFENSES do the contrary, raising the esteem given to someone, reinforcing that person's right to hold a given status. COUNTER-CHALLENGES and RETREATS do more complicated work which ultimately covers the same range of effects. REINFORCEMENTS preserve and maintain the status quo.

Within this framework, the moves that led to violence in the three narratives can be summarized in this way:

Moves of the Shambaugh narrative, Example (1):

M(1) The Norwegian sailor challenges Shambaugh's right to sit with his woman.
M(2) Shambaugh makes a counter-challenge to the Norwegian sailor's status as a person.

Moves of the Schuster narrative, Example (2):

M(1) Schuster challenges his brother's status as a responsible member of the household.
M(2) His brother makes a counter-challenge to Schuster's claim to take the role of his father.

Moves of the Williams narrative, Example (3):

M(1) Mrs. Hatfield reinforces the status of her son as a dependent member of the household by sending him to buy peaches.
M(2) Mrs. Hatfield challenges the status of her son as a responsible adult by taking her money away.
M(3) Martin Cassidy challenges Billy Hatfield's status as a responsible adult by rehearsing this fact in public.

Throughout this analysis, I have tried to keep in the forefront of attention the fact that we are dealing with reported events, not the events themselves. The objective event sequence is a sequence of reported events; the arrays of actions are reported actions; and the moves are reported moves. It is therefore even more interesting to note that the moves analyzed here do not necessarily coincide with the presentation of the self that emerges when we consider the evaluative material and the subjective events added by the narrator. For the three narratives studied here, the interpretation of events presented by the narrator, and the main point or focus of evaluation are quite different from the series of moves that are derived from this analysis. This observation suggests that we may have bypassed some of the transformations of reality that are the inevitable accompaniment of the narrative work.

The results of this further analysis are then three series of moves that form the preconditions for violent reactions in the narratives we have studied. We have seen that one route to violence is a sequence of speech acts that comes to a termination: where there are no further verbal moves to be made. One general principle that is well known to those who negotiate violent and difficult situations is: keep talking. To do this, negotiators have to have a good knowledge of the sequences that engage the other in verbal interaction, and the ability to follow the patterns that lead to further talk rather than those that lead to the termination of talk. The central core of these techniques is the recognition that the other is a responsible person in a structured social status. No matter what violent or irrational behavior the other has shown, the negotiator acts at all times as if the other knows the rights and duties appropriate to that status. Once the recognition of social status is withdrawn, the expectation of violent reactions is greatly increased.

I am not suggesting that we can predict or control violent reactions by this analysis. In no way would I claim to have described the conditions that are sufficient or even necessary for such violence. I have tried to reduce the strangeness and inhuman quality of this violent behavior by showing its relation to the general principles of social structure. I have also tried to show that in the reports of violent conflict, we can hope to find some comprehension of the conflict itself. By following this line of analysis further, we may reach the point where our analysis of discourse will be useful for those who have to deal professionally with destructive and antisocial violence. At the least, I hope to have brought Billy Hatfield, Jacob Schuster's brother, and the Norwegian sailor within the range of our human understanding, so that they no longer appear to us as strange and terrifying creatures, but rather as people who acted as we ourselves might act, if we too had been suddenly deprived of our rightful place in the social world.

NOTES

1. The question which first raised the analytical questions discussed here was posed by Michel Fournel, who raised the issue of the relationship between the analysis of speech acts in Labov and Fanshel (1977) and the ongoing analysis of narrative that I have been developing for the past several years. I am much indebted to him for that insight. I gratefully acknowledge here my indebtedness to Erving Goffman, whose contributions to my thinking are noted at several points in the text. Teresa Labov has been an invaluable companion in these explorations: her insights and corrections are to be found throughout. I am particularly indebted to her for any concept of social structure that I may have acquired over the years.

2. The philosophical and formal literature sometimes uses the term SPEECH ACT in a more limited way, specifying a limited number of performative categories or a subset of utterances that appear to have a particular set of properties like requests or promises. In the use of Labov and Fanshel (1977), all utterances are analyzable as acts, and frequently as hierarchically organized or parallel sets of acts. As will be evident, I use the term in that latter sense, referring to that abstract level of analysis where a verbal action is categorized as an action.

3. The question is often raised as to the relation of narratives given in interviews to narratives told in unmonitored conversation. In an initial interview, the speaker has an ideal audience: a listener who is interested in everything that is said and who rarely interrupts. We therefore tend to get fully formed narratives, without interruptions from others who may have shared some of the same experience or have other points of view. Some adjustments of reference are made: some people are identified who would not have to be identified among intimates, other identifications are left out because they are irrelevant. But studies of unmonitored conversations show many examples of such fully formed narratives, told without interruption from beginning to end: narratives that can be retold to general audiences with near-perfect understanding. Narratives given in interviews are subsets of the whole set of personal narratives. As Goffman has pointed out (personal communication), narratives given in interviews tend to be about

those experiences that are best suited for interviews: events of the most general interest that can be understood by anyone. This subset is obviously well suited to the present inquiry into the general conditions that relate speech acts and violent actions.

4. The word *shive* [ʃɪvə] is derived from the Hebrew word for 'seven'. 'Sitting shive' refers to the Orthodox Jewish mourning practice of commemorating a member of the nuclear family for seven days. Family members stay at home without doing any work and receive visits from friends and members of the extended family.

5. See Schiffrin (1981) for the role of the historical present as an organizing feature of narrative.

6. Many of these expressions take the form of feed-back or back-channel signals when they do occur in response to narratives. It is not their positive role in facilitating communication that is at issue here, but simply their appropriateness as opposed to expressions of surprise.

7. I was able to observe directly this kind of competition among events one evening in West Philadelphia, when the normal conditions for reportability were shifted by a serious public event. Black and white members of the local community had gathered to observe a crisis in the relations of the police with MOVE, a local group with its own life-style and ideology. MOVE members were being pressed hard by police and other authorities, and had appeared with submachine guns and rifles on the front porch of their house. They were surrounded by police cars and troops, and everyone expected that there would be a bloody assault on the house at any moment. I was one of four bystanders who were strangers to each other, all anxious to serve as witnesses in case the police got out of hand. One man started to tell a narrative of a run-in he had had with the police after an accident. It was very long and repetitious, and after five minutes one of the other men said in a very angry tone of voice, 'Well what's the hang-up of the story? What's the hang-up of the story?' The narrator said, 'I was just getting to it', but the other had already turned his back and walked away.

8. Richard Bauman (1981) has called my attention to the existence of such traditions, as in dog stories told in the Southwest where the narrator is expected to lie. These stories are part of a pattern of traditional storytelling which is quite distinct from the kinds of personal narratives I am dealing with. The narratives of personal experience discussed here are told by ordinary people who have no reputation as storytellers, and in many cases (e.g. Schuster) there is internal evidence that the story has not been heard before by members of their own family. Whereas the traditional storyteller takes ordinary events and elaborates them to the status of reportable events, the ordinary narrator begins with reportable events and tells them in a simple and straightforward manner. The traditional story

is usually humorous; the ordinary story I am dealing with here is serious. The traditional story is expected to be part fiction; the ordinary story is expected to be true.

9. Note that Schuster uses two forms of embedding with zero complementizer, (9) 'started talk' and (19) 'started bleed'. Though not common, they are possible colloquial forms.

10. At first glance, it may seem that turning the head or body is an objective physical act. But turning does not always mean a 90 or 180 degree turn, and there is no minimal reorientation that corresponds to the expression, 'So I turned to him and said ...' In many narratives, such expressions amplify the activity attributed to the narrator without risk of contradiction.

11. In many ways, the Labov and Fanshel rules are parallel to the rules formulated in Gordon and Lakoff (1975). The most important difference is the absence of any reference to right and obligation in the latter.

12. The legal metaphor used here to distinguish objective from subjective events reminds us that the interpretation of the acts involved here is indeed problematic: a violent physical action can be represented legally as an assault, an attempted murder, manslaughter, premeditated murder, and so on.

13. 'Bird' is the regular Liverpool term for 'young woman'; 'mates' are close friends of the same sex; to 'cop off a few birds' is to meet up with and spend the evening with; to be 'in lumber' is to be in serious trouble.

14. The schema presented here is my adaptation of one presented to a class by Goffman.

REFERENCES

Bauman, Richard. 1981. 'Any man who keeps more'n one hound'll lie to you': Dog trading and storytelling at Canton, Texas. In: 'And other neighborly names': Social process and cultural image in Texas folklore. Edited by Richard Bauman and Roger D. Abrahams. Austin: University of Texas Press. 79-103.

Goffman, Erving. 1976. Replies and responses. Language in Society 5.257-313. Reprinted in: Forms of talk. Philadelphia: University of Pennsylvania Press, 1981.

Goffman, Erving. 1974. Frame analysis. New York: Harper and Row.

Gordon, David, and George Lakoff. 1975. Conversational postulates. In: Syntax and semantics, Vol. 3: Speech acts. Edited by Peter Cole and Jerry Morgan. New York: Academic Press. 83-106.

Labov, William. 1981. Field methods of the project on linguistic change and variation. Working Papers in Sociolinguistics, No. 81. Austin, Texas: Southwest Educational Development Laboratory.

Labov, William. 1972. Sociolinguistic patterns. Philadelphia: University of Pennsylvania Press.

Labov, William, and David Fanshel. 1977. Therapeutic discourse. New York: Academic Press.

Labov, William, and Joshua Waletzky. 1967. Narrative analysis: Oral versions of personal experience. In: Essays on the verbal and visual arts. Edited by June Helm. Seattle: University of Washington Press. 12-44.

Schiffrin, Deborah. 1981. Tense variation in narrative. Lg. 57.1:45-62.

Searle, John R. 1969. Speech acts. London and New York: Cambridge University Press.

IDEAL READERS AND REAL READERS

Charles J. Fillmore
University of California, Berkeley

1. For the past year and a half I have been working on a research project which investigates the ways in which school children interact with standardized tests of reading comprehension. The children in the study are skilled and medium-skilled readers chosen from third and fifth grade classes in two schools in Berkeley and Oakland, California.[1] The tests we have been examining are selected from those currently given in American schools to children at our subjects' grade level.[2]

An example of the kind of material the team is working with is the following passage, taken from the Metropolitan Achievement Tests and intended to be administered to third-grade students.[3]

> The carpenter was astonished that such a weird, weak-looking creature as Nasrudin was applying for a job.
> 'Okay, I'll give you a chance,' said the doubtful carpenter finally. 'Take this ax and chop as much lumber as you can.' At dusk Nasrudin returned.
> 'How many trees have you felled?' questioned the carpenter.
> 'All the timber in the forest,' Nasrudin replied.
> Shocked, the carpenter glanced out his window. There were no trees standing on the hillside. Nasrudin had destroyed the entire forest. 'Where did you learn to chop lumber?' asked the astonished carpenter.
> 'In the Sahara Desert,' answered Nasrudin.
> 'That's ridiculous!' shrieked the carpenter. 'There aren't any trees in the desert!'
> 'There aren't any, NOW,' said Nasrudin calmly.

The passage is followed, of course, by a series of test questions. Item (1) gives the first question.

(1) The carpenter told Nasrudin to
    (a) look for another job
    (b) cut down as many trees as he could
    (c) go back to the Sahara Desert
    (d) plant as many seeds as he could

The children confronting this question, presented as it is immediately after the reading passage, are expected to understand that they are not here being asked to continue the narrative. That is, they have to sense that the story they have just read has been finished, as far as they are concerned, and that they are now being asked to show how well they understood it. Should they by mistake construe their task as one of advancing the narrative beyond the point where Nasrudin made the boastful claim about creating the Sahara Desert, they might find it quite reasonable that the carpenter should advise Nasrudin to look for another job (since he was no longer needed here), tell him to go back to the Sahara Desert (as a kind of 'get-out-of-my-life' remark), or indeed, order him to plant as many seeds as he could (to make sure that something could get growing on the bared hillsides). The test-takers must first keep in mind the test-taking maxim, that if two answers appear to be equally good, both are probably wrong, but they must then realize that they are probably not being asked to advance the narrative. What they must remember is that in Nasrudin's probationary period, he had been given the ax and told to 'chop as much lumber' as he could. They had to figure out that 'chop lumber' is our author's unusual way of saying 'cut down trees', and they must sense that it was the early conversation between the carpenter and Nasrudin with which the question is concerned.

The second question is shown in (2).

(2) How long did it take Nasrudin to complete the job?
    (a) one day
    (b) three days
    (c) thirty days
    (d) three years

In order to answer this question correctly, the children are required to realize that in the sentence 'At dusk, Nasrudin returned', the phrase 'at dusk' refers to the dusk of that same day, and they must also realize that there is nothing in the story that could back up any answer with the number 'three' or 'thirty' in it. Those children who are uncommonly sensitive to language will wonder what it might mean to 'complete the job' under these circumstances, since the only task Nasrudin had been given was to 'chop as much lumber' as he could.

The third question is stated in (3).

(3) Nasrudin suggested that there were no trees in the
Sahara Desert because
(a) trees can't grow in the desert
(b) no one had ever planted any there
(c) they had been destroyed by fire
(d) he had chopped them all down

The answer is that Nasrudin had chopped them all down.
This was 'suggested', to use the question's word, by Nasrudin's
answer, 'There aren't any, NOW', said after Nasrudin had explained that the Sahara Desert was the place where he had
'learned' to 'chop lumber'.
The fourth question is given in (4).

(4) After Nasrudin finished work, he
(a) left for the Sahara Desert
(b) told the carpenter what he had done
(c) applied for a new job
(d) yelled at the carpenter

The expected answer is that Nasrudin told the carpenter
what he had done. The ordinary scene a reader might construct based on that description, however, is probably a bit
different from what we saw in the story, so a certain amount
of construing is necessary. The carpenter, it will be recalled,
asked Nasrudin, 'How many trees have you felled?', to which
Nasrudin replied, 'All the timber in the forest'. This utterance,
an elliptical answer to a question which presupposed an understanding of what he had done and speaks only to the question
of how much he had done, has to be construed as an instance
of Nasrudin telling the carpenter what he had done. The
tempting possibility that the correct answer is 'yelled at the
carpenter' is presumably introduced to take advantage of the
printer's decision to put the word 'now' in capital letters, in
the sentence, 'There aren't any, NOW'. The capitalized word
suggests shouting, so what is being tested with this foil is the
child's ability to notice that what followed 'There aren't any,
NOW' in the text is 'said Nasrudin calmly'.
The fifth question appears in (5).

(5) The carpenter had not expected that Nasrudin
(a) had ever seen the Sahara Desert
(b) really needed a job
(c) would be so rude
(d) could do the job so quickly

In this item the pluperfect form, 'had not expected', plays
an important role. The sentence has to be situated in the text
at some time point where it serves an explaining role. The
text reveals that something was unexpected in the place where

it shows the carpenter surprised. Being 'shocked' is an extreme form of being surprised. The text describes the carpenter as 'shocked', through a grammatical device whose function may not be transparent to most third grade readers, and backs this up by showing that the carpenter spoke from then on only in sentences ending in exclamation points. He had been shocked when he learned--and hence he had not expected that it had been possible--that at the end of the first day on the job Nasrudin had conquered the entire forest.

2. It is of interest to our group how young readers construct an understanding of reading passages of the kind we have just seen, and how well that understanding can be appealed to in finding 'best answers' to test questions about those passages.

There are two intended goals in our research, and a third that we have taken on against our will. Our first goal is to analyze reading-test items, both the passages and the test questions, in such a way as to be able to isolate and describe the kinds of background knowledge and the kinds of interpreting and integrating skills which a reader must bring to the passages in order to get out of them what their creators intended. The second goal is to find out, by interviewing our young subjects, whether they have that knowledge and those skills. We begin by analyzing tests and devising a system of annotations for them which can serve three purposes: it represents our view of the comprehension process of someone who understands the passage with no difficulty, it provides the material for our choice of the interview probes, and it gives us a framework or checklist against which we can evaluate the children's performance with the texts. The second part of our work involves close observation of the children's experiences with the texts, with free retellings, interviews, and metacognitive probes, looking for the presence or absence of the kinds of knowledge and skills which seem to us to be necessary for understanding them.

The third and unwelcome task which fell to us is due to the nature of the corpus we had chosen. Oddly enough, in view of the time and expense that goes into the construction of reading test items, we are dealing in this research with seriously flawed texts, texts which frequently require of their readers an uncommon degree of tolerance and cooperation. The testing industry, we have come to realize, has created a new genre for English written language, a genre whose characteristics are determined by very unnatural requirements of lexical choice, grammatical structuring, and synonym alterations, these dictated, I presume, by the intention to test knowledge of particular vocabulary items, the need to produce something which fits accepted readability formulas, which avoids gender or ethnic stereotyping, and which satisfies copyright laws with respect to the percentage of material that needs to be modified

in the case of passages taken from the trade literature. This
third goal of ours, then, is to understand some of the consequences of the development of this special genre, to show why
it introduces complications that interfere with the ability of
these tests to measure what they are designed to measure, and
to see how well young children are able to master this particular genre through their repeated experiences with it. [4]

3. We need, in our work, to be able to compare real readers in their experience of these texts with the kind of reader
who gets out of them everything that is needed. For this
comparison we had to develop a particular kind of abstraction,
something we call the 'Ideal Reader'. It is this invented Ideal
Reader who sees the connections, creates the expectations,
performs the inferences, and asks the questions which our
annotation is designed to represent. It is with this Ideal
Reader that our flesh-and-blood readers are to be compared.

My purpose in this paper is to explain the nature of this
idealization and to show how we think we can decide on its
characteristics.

Our notion of the Ideal reader is localized to given texts and
to given interpretations of those texts. That is, we do not
speak of 'an ideal reader' in the abstract, but of 'the Ideal
Reader' of a given text on a given interpretation. We see before us a written text; we determine what we take to be a
'correct' or somehow necessary interpretation of it; and we
then project, from the text and the interpretation, to an invented Ideal Reader: that individual who has exactly what it
takes to get from the text to the interpretation via the usual
principles of compositional semantics, schema building, inferencing, goal and plan detection, and so on. (I should point out
that the notion is a technical one, designating an abstraction
that is of limited utility. It is not necessarily a desirable
thing to be an Ideal Reader in our sense.) [5]

Once we have decided on the characteristics of an Ideal
Reader (for a given text on a given interpretation), we can
then ask certain important empirical questions about the text
and its living readers. If, for example, we find ourselves
convinced that there are in the world no real readers who
match certain essential characteristics of our invented Ideal
Reader, then we can believe that we have on our hands a useless text. It is not written for anybody. If we find among
our young subjects that the only real readers who match the
conditions we have specified for the Ideal Reader are those
children who have had experiences not shared by the others,
especially if those experiences are distributed among the children in patterns that follow social, economic, or ethnic differences, then we have learned something about the fairness of
the item or the representativeness of the test results as these
are affected by the item. With items that we believe are
reasonable and fair, we can examine in detail the nature of

the gaps between particular real readers and our projected Ideal Reader, and ask how such gaps can be filled. Discovering such gaps is a matter of reading failure diagnosis; instituting measures for bridging the gaps by providing children with new experiences, facts, or skills, or by helping them become aware of the gaps, is a matter of improving children's reading abilities.

4. Simplifying a little, the Ideal Reader is someone who knows, at each point in a text, everything that the text presupposes at that point, and who does not know, but is prepared to receive and understand, what the text introduces at that point. Real readers, then, can differ from the text's Ideal Reader in two directions. With respect to any given point in the text, they may be underqualified, in that they do not know what the text assumes they know at that point, or they may be overqualified, in that they already know what the text introduces. [6]

(A passage in a linguistic textbook which uses the term 'contrast' without explanation but which defines, explains, and exemplifies the notion 'neutralization', is addressed to a reader who already understands 'contrast' in its technical linguistic sense, but who does not yet know how linguists use the term 'neutralization'. The Ideal Reader for this text, then, is in part described as someone who knows, at this point, about contrast, but who does not know about neutralization. In this respect, at least, such a text appears to be perfectly reasonable. There are, we can be sure, any number of readers who meet perfectly this pair of conditions. A text in which the opposite choice had been made, however--one which explained 'contrast' but presupposed knowledge of 'neutralization'--would be a pedagogically defective text, since only readers with very unusual educational histories would be likely to satisfy just those conditions.)

5. Linguists will have noticed that I have been talking about readers and written texts, whereas it is much more common in linguistic circles to talk about hearers and spoken language. Our idealization is possible for written language more than for spoken language because of the fact that written texts are more characteristically monologic and closed: in a word, they tend to be 'composed'. By contrast, we find in conversational language situations in which the interlocutors need to negotiate a common background as the conversation progresses, we find texts in which the linguistic part of an interaction is insufficient for constructing anything that could be called the intended interpretation, and we find, in dialogue between people communicating at cross purposes, texts that lack any discernible point or structure.

6. While I have said that the Ideal Reader is defined with respect to a text that is composed--that is, to a text that is fixed and in some sense complete--I do not intend to imply that composed written texts can be interpreted statically. The interpreter's experience always has a clear dynamic aspect, to which our work has to pay close attention. We need to show, for example, that a text can create expectations in the reader's mind at one point which it then satisfies or subverts at a later point. The recognition of structure, development, or point; of suspense, surprise, or closure; of the interruption and resumption of a 'thread', etc., all make up part of a reader's experience with a written text.

It is, in fact, just this dynamic aspect of the reading experience which is the most important part of our analysis, and the most difficult part of our interview process with the children. What I mean by that is that in the interview process, we have had to be particularly sensitive to the difference between asking questions which will reveal the dynamics of the text-understanding process as it occurs naturally, and questions which themselves guide and advance that process.

We are pleased if we find a child, who, on reading the seventh sentence in a text, spontaneously says, 'Oh, now I see what's going on!', because we have just had revealed to us the workings of the comprehension process in that child. We have learned not to be pleased when a child says something like that in response to one of our interviewers' questions. Our job is to track the child's coherence-creating process, not to shape it for him.

In order to present the dynamic aspect of a reader's experience with a text, we have developed a method of text analysis which takes the text one segment at a time, asking ourselves at each point in this unrolling of the text something like, 'Having read this far, what would it have figured out, or be puzzled by, or be expecting?' In order to make our analytic task reasonably finite, we have found it useful to keep the analyst's point of view distinct from that of both the Ideal Reader and the real readers. In particular, we, the analysts, have the advantage of knowing the whole text, knowing the point of the text, knowing how everything comes out in the end. We might know that the point of a particular passage is that it introduces a surprise. For example, if we know that the point of a particular line in a story is to reveal, for the first time, that the characters we have been reading about live in a tree, and if we feel sure that the reader is expected at this point to be surprised, that assumption imposes specific requirements on our annotation of earlier parts of the text. We have to make the Ideal Reader assume, throughout some earlier part of the text, that the people in the story do not live in trees, and at the same time we have to make sure that this assumption is known not to be explicitly bound to the actual material of the text. That is, we need an annotation which will show, at the point when the surprising information is introduced, that the reader is supposed to feel surprised but not cheated. If we ourselves, in preparing the annotation for the text, had to examine it only one segment at a time, ignorant at each point of what was going to come up next, we would have no basis for including or excluding any part of the probably boundless number of things that ordinary readers would assume in the world of the unrolling text. That is, knowing the nature of the surprise that is coming up gives us a reason to ignore many aspects of the normal reader's envisionment of what's going on.[7]

7. The analyst sees the text as a whole. The Ideal Reader and the real reader see it one segment at a time. It is necessary for us, then, if we wish to explore the real readers' experience of the text, to present it to them one segment at a time. The general method we use works like this: we show the readers the first segment, then ask our first batch of questions; then we show them the second segment, asking them our next batch of questions; and so on. At each point, we make sure that the previously exposed part of the text is still available for scanning, rereading, consultation, etc.

The mechanics of this kind of presenting and interviewing proved to be interestingly difficult. Since some of these difficulties shed light on the process of text understanding, I believe they are worth discussing here.

At first our method was to decide on a particular segmentation of a text, type it out with each segment on a separate line, and have the subjects slide a piece of cardboard down over the text one line at a time during the interviewing process. This method introduced two major difficulties. First, as the card got lower on the page, the exposed piece of text at the top ended up looking more like verse than prose, and that, we felt, could affect some people's interpretations of what they were reading. Second, the method did not make it obvious to the subject how much of the text was left, and we felt that subjects might use different strategies for interpreting a sentence if they thought it was the closing sentence in a text than if they thought more was coming. This uncertainty made the experience quite unlike normal reading; in normal reading, we almost always know how close we are to the end, and that knowledge plays a large part in shaping our expectations and putting our interpretative faculties to work.

Our current method is more expensive and troublesome, but it has eliminated both of the difficulties presented by the sliding card method. We type the text on a sheet of paper, in the normal way, double-spaced. If the text has been given n segmentations, we make $n+1$ xerographed copies of it, and construct a booklet. Page 1 of the booklet has the entire text blocked out with a marking pen. Page 2 has everything blocked out but the first segment. Page 3 has everything blocked out but the first two segments. And so on. (Having found that some children have trouble finding quickly the place where they left off, we have begun using a small red dot at the beginning of the increment to help them.) With this method, then, as the text gets exposed, it looks like ordinary printed prose, and it is very clear to the subject how much of the passage is left before the end is reached. (The passages we use all fit on one page.)

The interview works something like this. The child who turns the first page sees

    Once upon a time xxxxxxxxxxxxxxxxxxxxxxxxxxxxxxxxx
xxxxxxxxxxxxxxxxxxxxxxxxxxxxxxxxxxxxxxxxxxxxxxxxxxxxxxxx
etc.

exposed at the top of the second page. Our interviewer asks something like, 'What can you tell me about this passage so far?' The subject answers, 'Well, it's going to be a story. Most likely a fairy tale.' 'How do you know that?' 'You only say "Once upon a time" when you're telling a fairy tale.' 'Do you have any guesses about what we're going to read when we get to see more of the story?' 'Well, maybe something about a poor old lady who lived in the woods, or maybe a rich king with a beautiful daughter. I don't know.'

The child then turns the page to expose the next increment, and sees

    Once upon a time there was a rich king xxxxxxxxxxxxxx
xxxxxxxxxxxxxxxxxxxxxxxxxxxxxxxxxxxxxxxxxxxxxxxxxxxx
etc.

The interviewer says, 'Say, you were right, weren't you? The sentence isn't finished yet, is it? Do you want to stick to your guess about the beautiful daughter?' 'Yeah.' The child turns the page and sees

    Once upon a time there was a rich king who had three
sons.   xxxxxxxxxxxxxxxxxxxxxxxxxxxxxxxxxxxxxxxxxxxx
etc.

And so on through the text.

The new method of presentation solved some of our problems in exploring the reading experiences of real readers, but there remain a number of very serious problems connected with the piecemeal presentation, no matter how it is adapted. One difficulty with our method comes from the fact that the talk produced by the interviewer is itself a text which the children have the right to believe has a point and a direction. If, in connection with the text about the people who lived in trees, we were to ask a question like, 'Do you think these people live in houses like everyone else?', in order to be able to predict whether our young subjects were going to be surprised when they found out the truth, the children would quickly catch on to our purposes. If we tried to balance this by asking dozens of questions about normal readers' default assumptions ('Do you think they grow hair on their teeth?', 'Do you think they sleep at night?'), our questions would be intolerably distracting.

A second problem produced by the interviewer's own text shows up when we are exploring the reasons for the choice of particular test question answers. With some young children, the question, 'Why did you choose this answer?' suggests powerfully that the answer was wrong.

One source of difficulty, then, resides in the character of the conversation with the interviewer. Another is the pacing. A paragraph that takes less than a minute to read in normal circumstances can take half an hour to go through in the segment-by-segment presentation. The interview brings so many things into the subjects' consciousness that the simple thread that is our text can get completely lost. Using the method with adult readers on adult texts, we learned that passages that are humorous when read all at once are not humorous when given out piece by piece. I am not merely saying that the passages do not seem funny; sometimes their humorous intent is not even discerned. Furthermore, if a text takes a digression and then returns to the main theme, the re-turn to the theme can seem very striking. In natural fast reading, by contrast, the digression itself would hardly be noticed.

With young readers, the factor of interest works against us both ways. If the story is interesting, the reader wants to get to the end to see how things turn out, and becomes impatient with all these boring questions. If the story is un-interesting, the reader wants to get the whole experience over with as soon as possible, and becomes impatient with all these boring questions. A lot depends, in short, on the warmth and charm of the interviewers, and on whatever rewards children might feel in knowing that an adult is paying very close atten-tion to their words and thoughts.

The upshot is that while we are leading children through our kind of micro-analysis of a text, we may indeed be learning a lot about whether they are prepared to understand the text we are examining--which is, after all, our purpose--but the method itself might be preventing them from actually understanding it. A control is obviously needed, and for our control we have a second group of children who are exposed to the text in a different way. These children read the passages, answer the test questions, retell what they have read in their own words, and only then submit to the piecemeal presentation. The ques-tions for this group are somewhat differently formulated: 'What were you thinking when you read this?', 'Do you remember what the next sentence is?', and so on.

8. As we see it, the main dynamic aspect of the reading
experience is that of constructing and revising an Envisionment
of the 'world of the text', some coherent 'image' or understanding of the states of affairs that exist in the set of possible
worlds compatible with the language of the text. We do not
intend the word Envisionment, which we have borrowed from
John Seely Brown (personal communication), to suggest too
strongly the visual aspects of a text world, but at the same
time, we recognize that in the kinds of texts we are dealing
with, the visual aspects do, in fact, predominate.

We have found it useful to distinguish various confidence
levels of material in the Envisionment, according to whether
such material is explicitly justified by the linguistic material of
the text, whether it came into being by inferences which the
text is seen as clearly inviting, or whether they represent
interpretations which result from schematizations brought to
the text to situate its events in common experience, but which
do not follow necessarily from anything the text has provided.
In our discussions of real readers, we need still another level
of Envisionment: ways in which the world of the text has
been shaped by the idiosyncratic experiences and imaginings
of individual readers.

To illustrate the theory of levels of Envisionment, we can
consider the following three-line text, borrowed from Marcelo
Dascal (personal communication).

The princess ate some jam.
The queen slapped her.
The princess cried.

At what we call the E^0 level of Envisionment, there are only
those states of affairs that have to hold in the world of the
text for the individual sentences to be separately true. In our
case, the Envisionment at E^0 has three disjoint parts: somebody who is a princess eats some jam; somebody who is a queen
slaps a female being; and somebody who is a princess cries.

At the second level in the Envisionment, which we call E^1, it
is assumed that we are dealing with a cohesive text, rather
than with three independent statements, and so the princess
in Sentence 1 is the same as the princess in Sentence 3, and is
the *her*, the one who is slapped, in Sentence 2. The queen in
Sentence 2 is furthermore taken to be the princess's mother.

We have here the workings of a kind of Parsimony Principle
in text comprehension. If, in constructing an understanding
of the first sentence, we had to instantiate a Royal Family
schema, we find it parsimonious to use that same schema instantiation for identifying the queen, too. Hence the queen
and the princess are mother and daughter. If at the beginning
of the second sentence ('The queen slapped her.') we have two
people 'on stage', the princess and her mother the queen, then
the *her* of this sentence must refer to the princess. The

Parsimony Principle is a text-interpretation maxim that says something like: Don't bring more people or props into the text world than are needed to make the text cohere.

In the example just given, the difference between E^0 and E^1 amounted to a difference between individual sentences and sentence sequences. It was when we put the sentences together that we began needing interpretations at the E^1 level. The difference between E^0 and E^1 can also be illustrated with single sentences.

The favored kinds of sentences used in psycholinguistic experiments typically have only an E^0 interpretation. In a sentence like 'The actress sold a fish to the carpenter', the kind of sentence you might be expected to learn or shadow or associate something with in a psycholinguistic experiment, we find that there is nothing we know about either actresses or carpenters that we can call on to motivate the scene of the one selling a fish to the other. If we compare that with a sentence like 'The cobbler sold a pair of boots to the mountain climber', we find that the latter invites more interpretative work. The Parsimony Principle would induce us to make the hypotheses that the cobbler sold boots that he had made in his shop, and that the mountain climber was buying boots that he would use in mountain climbing. That is, we tend to assume that it is as a cobbler and as a mountain climber that the two participants were engaged in this particular commercial event.

These assumptions are made at the E^1 level, rather than at the E^0 level, because we could, without contradiction, immediately find out that these hypotheses were completely wrong. It could turn out that the cobbler was sitting in for his wife, a shoe store clerk, while she was at the dentist's, and that the person described here as the mountain climber was buying the boots to give to his mother for Mother's Day.

The sort of 'default' interpretations that we assign to the Envisionment at the E^1 level remain tentative for a very brief time. Knowing that we are dealing with a composed text, we somehow believe that if we were not meant to give this interpretation, the author owes us an explanation very soon. If the text does not very quickly turn us away from the E^1 interpretation, the normal reader quickly converts it to an E^0 confidence level. [8]

At the third level of the Envisionment, which we call E^2, we 'situate' elements of the passage in terms of our knowledge of goals and institutions and folk theories of human nature. With the story of the princess and the jam, we make sense of what is going on by assuming that the queen's act of slapping the princess was in punishment for the princess's having eaten the jam, and we assume that the princess's tears are in response to the queen's slap, showing pain, remorse, or shame.

The next higher level, E^3, contains particular real readers' embellishments of the text world, the filling in of details not motivated by the text itself. For our story we might find, in particular readers' experiences of it, the assumption that the queen had wanted the jam for herself and was very selfish, or maybe that the princess had recently been made to promise to stay on a diet until she found a husband. In our annotation for the Ideal Reader, we obviously do not need such a level; but in our representations of the subjects' interpretations of our texts, we definitely do.

My co-workers and I have no stake in the proposed number of levels, and we will not be surprised to find out that the phenomena we are concerned with do not at all lend themselves to a description in terms of discrete ranked tentativity levels. What we are sure of--and this is the main practical purpose of the levels theory--is that a child who is not able to do the kind of inferencing or 'reading between the lines' that is necessary for filling out material at what we are calling E^1 and E^2 is not a good reader, nor is the child who fills in lots of E^3 material and immediately assumes that it was in the text. A child who reads very slowly, figures out the meanings of the sentences in the text one at a time but never puts them together into a cohesive whole, is a poor reader in the first sense. Such a reader cannot go beyond E^0. Poor in a different way would be the reader who, in reading our story about the princess with the sweet tooth, would unhesitatingly answer 'Strawberry' to the question, 'What kind of jam did the princess eat?' Such readers overtrust their own E^3 embellishments of a text.

9. The lexical and grammatical material of the unfolding text creates or identifies for the reader the conceptual tools needed for constructing the Envisionment. The main kind of tool I have in mind is the construct (or set of constructs) variously known as 'scripts', 'frames', 'schemata', 'folk theories', 'cognitive models', and the like. These constructs are intended to represent the knowledge structures with which our experiences with the world are held together. Sometimes in a given portion of the text such tools are merely activated, merely made available for later use. At other times they are actively used in constructing and maintaining the Envisionment. In our annotation we make a great deal of use of labeled schemata, with which we appeal, informally, to structured knowledge that the Ideal Reader is believed to have and which real readers may or may not have, may or may not be able to use, or may or may not know when to use.

Two applications of such schemata have already been illustrated: the Royal Family schema, which allowed us to see instantly how the princess and the queen were related to each other, and the schemata we used in bringing coherence to the sentence about the cobbler and the mountain climber. A slightly more complicated one-sentence example is: *The defendant had forged the will.* Somebody called the *defendant* is seen as a person who plays a particular role in a Criminal Trial schema, that of the Accused; the object called the *will* in our example is the Legal Instrument in an Estate Inheritance schema; and the act of forging is the central act in a Forgery schema. The character of each of these schemata could be spelled out in considerable detail. The Parsimony Principle would invite us, at perhaps an E^2 level (the level at which we seek to bring in outside explanations) to imagine that the act of committing the forgery was one of the acts for which the defendant was currently involved in the judicial process, and to imagine that the will that got forged had the defendant named as a beneficiary.

The schemata just mentioned have all been brought into the Envisionment by virtue of particular lexical items that are keyed to particular roles or steps in their associated schemata. In the comprehension process, the interpreter activates the schema connected with such lexical items and works at building an Envisionment out of knowledge derived from these schemata. This is done partly by combining primary schemata into larger assemblies or networks, sometimes, as we have seen, by bringing in schemata not explicitly indicated by material in the text but needed for holding the other schemata together.

There are various ways in which schemata can be linked together. Some are linked in semantic memory by what can be called Knowledge Links (K-links), connections between schemata provided by general knowledge, independently of any information provided by the actual present text. For our forgery sentence, K-links bring to play our knowledge that all of the schemata lexically introduced by that sentence somehow fit into a larger schema that could be called Judicial Process, and make us aware that a defendant in the criminal trial has been accused of a crime, and that forgery is a crime.

The text itself, which tells us about some 'world', links together instantiations of schemata by anchoring them to each other in that world. These can be called Text Links (T-links). An E^0 T-link in our forgery sentence establishes, through the grammar of the sentence, that the person who is the defendant in a criminal trial is also the perpetrator in an act of forgery, and that the product of that act of forgery was (or has been put forth as being) a legal instrument in a matter of estate inheritance.

The schemata that we have been considering so far are schemata that operate in what with many others we have come to call the Content domain. We distinguish three domains for the Ideal Reader's speculations, puzzlements, and conclusions: the domain of 'Content', by which we have in mind the properties and events in the world of the text; the domain of 'Text', with its schemata of grammatical structure and text structure; and the domain of 'Genre', where we have in mind those structures of expectation that come with knowing that one is dealing with a folk tale, a detective story, an obituary, a reading test, or the like.

Within the Text domain, our forgery sentence has, in addition to the grammatical structurings which aided us in providing the T-links, a number of features which mark it as 'text-internal'. We recognize that a sentence like *The defendant had forged the will* is not likely to be the first, and certainly not likely to be the only sentence in a text. This judgment we base on the use of the definite article (*the defendant, the will*) and the use of the pluperfect (*had forged*). The text-schematizing necessarily associated with them shows that there must be a presupposed temporal reference point in the part of the larger text where this sentence can occur (the point on which the pluperfect is semantically anchored) and a pre-established setting within which the descriptions *the defendant* and *the will* are uniquely identifying.

Genre schemata arise from structured expectations created by familiarity with particular genres. If we read in a folk tale that the king's two older sons have both failed to slay the dragon, we are filled with hope when we learn that the king's third and youngest son has set out to try his hand. Were the story to end with the third son being slain by the dragon, we would feel that we had just been exposed to a new and cynical derivative genre, not that we were wrong in forming the expectations we had formed. When we read questions in a reading test, we know that we are not being asked to figure out a clever way to finish the passage we have just been reading, but rather that we're being asked what we remember, or what we can now figure out, about what the passage told us.

10. There is one more device that we need for our complete annotation, and that is a representation of Point of View. It has played a relatively small role in the work we have done so far, so I will say little about it. For some texts, especially texts involving histories, descriptions of objects or terrains, and narratives, the text world not only has the properties it has in some objectively describable way, but its properties are presented to us from a particular point of view: there is an observer, an experiencer, or a camera's eye, and perhaps always a temporal reference point.

I illustrate the notion merely by showing that some sequences of sentences in a text can be seen to cohere only when they are taken as sharing a single point of view. The sequence

He was coming up the steps. There was a broad smile on his face.

is coherent in the sense I have in mind, since the position from which his ascending the stairs can be described as 'coming' is also the position from which it would be natural to see his smile. Analogously, a sequence like

He was going up the steps. There was a wad of bubble-
gum on the seat on his pants.

is also coherent, given a constant viewpoint. By contrast, a
sequence like

??He was coming up the steps. There was a wad of
bubble-gum on the seat on his pants.

seem quite bizarre if taken as a visual description, and the
sequence

He was going up the steps. There was a broad smile on
his face.

seems to require us to imagine a side view. The recognition
of Point of View figures in any complete account of lexical semantics (with respect, for example, to such words as *come* and
go), the semantic role of grammatical categories (involving, for
example, tense and definiteness), and the cooccurrence or sequencing of sentences in a text.

11. The descriptive framework we have ended up with includes: a streamlined record of the grammatical parsing of the
sentence; the schemata of Content, Text, and Genre which are
introduced by lexical and grammatical form, in the first instance, and from the interpreter's repertory of schematizing
devices, in the second instance; the questions and expectations
raised in the reader's mind concerning the still unrevealed por-
tions of the text; the growing and changing Envisionment of
the world of the text, with changes in the levels of tentative-
ness as the text develops; and point of view.
Given such machinery and the goals of our project, we seek
to annotate texts in a way which represents the Ideal Reader's
processing of them and which provides the basis for the construction of probing devices designed to assess a real reader's
experience of the text.
I would like to return to the passage I started out with, the
story about the uncommonly gifted woodcutter, to show something about how this annotation is used in our work.
The method requires an initial segmentation of the text,
since we are assuming, for theoretical purposes and contrary
to fact, that readers bring their full armament of interpreting
skills to each piece of text without peeking at the next one.
The segmentation we provide is, of course, arbitrary; since we
are not equipped to carry out the kind of research it would
take to find out what natural segmentations real readers would
make, we have to be arbitrary. In general, our segmentation
procedure amounts to taking one clause at a time.

In my demonstration I am going to do the first segment of the Nasrudin story with some degree of completeness, and then just briefly touch on a few other aspects of the passage. The first segment is

The carpenter was astonished XXXXXXXXXXXXXX

The Ideal Reader will take note that this is the first segment of the text, that it is not a complete sentence (since there is no following punctuation), that it has a definite noun phrase as its subject, a passive factive complement verb as its predicating element, and the simple past as its tense.

The lexical item *carpenter* introduces a Carpentry schema, which is merely another way of saying that when we understand the noun *carpenter* we do so by knowing something about what carpenters do. (It is a word for which one would be hard put to distinguish semantic information about what the word means and practical information about what carpenters do.) The person designated as the carpenter is the practitioner in a work schema, the other elements of which include the tools, the materials, and some notion of the products of a carpenter's work. Our schematic knowledge about carpentering could be spelled out in great detail, with, for example, different types of activities associated with particular tools; but since we, the analysts, know how the story develops, we know that what we need for our Ideal Reader is a mere skeleton of the whole schema, with only certain aspects drawn out in detail, these involving the carpenter's need for wood. From that we get the K-links that connect wood with trees and the cutting and milling of lumber.

The next major lexical item in the segment is *astonished*. This word, we allow ourselves to say, introduces an Astonishment schema. To understand what it means to be astonished is to have an outline knowledge of the kind of scenario that could lead a person to have the experience which this word describes. In this schema there is at least the experiencer of the emotion, a perception on the experiencer's part which triggers the emotion, the event which was responsible for that perception, and a history or set of expectations against which this causing event stood out in sharp conflict. (One is astonished when one notices that something very unexpected has occurred.)

There are no K-links between Carpentry and Astonishment. There is, of course, a T-link: it is the workman in an instantiation of the Carpentry schema who is the experiencer in an instantiation of the Astonishment schema.

In addition to the Content schemata of Carpentry and Astonishment, we recognize in this segment certain schemata in the Text domain. These include the grammatical knowledge that the verb *astonish* is a factive complement verb, giving rise to the expectation that what follows is going to be a description or mention of the event which, in the world of the text, caused the astonishment experience. When the next segment is exposed, the Ideal Reader is prepared to integrate the information it provides into the Content domain of the text-world as the cause of the carpenter's astonishment. More superficially, knowledge of the kind of word *astonish* is primes the Ideal Reader to expect that the very next segment will be *at*, *to*, or *that*, followed by a nominal, verbal, or clausal description of the causing event.

The expectation that what follows is to be an account of the causing event comes not simply from the form of our segment, but is further informed by the knowledge that the segment is not a complete sentence. There could be a text which read

The house collapsed. The carpenter was astonished.

where our segment was a complete sentence. But that is not what we have here.

There are also Text-domain schemata associated with the definite article and the simple past tense, and their activation invites the Ideal Reader to hypothesize that what we have here is the beginning of a particular type of narrative, one in which characters and props can be introduced with definite noun phrases or proper nouns, and in which a presupposed time point can be presented without explanation. These schemata, and the conditions in which they are introduced, invite the Ideal Reader to activate a particular schema from the Genre domain. There are kinds of third-person narrative in which such in medias res textual features are common and proper. (I am only pretending, of course, to have access to a theory of genres. Since our collection of texts is made up mostly of narratives, expository prose, personal letters, and simple poems, there are not really many distinctions of genre that we have had to worry about. If we are to choose from that limited inventory of genres, we are already fairly safe, after even this first short segment, to guess that we are in a narrative.)

After exposure to this simple segment, *The carpenter was astonished ...*, the Ideal Reader has two Content schemata instantiated, has T-links between them provided by the grammatical relations present in the segment, has expectations about both the content and the form of what the next piece of the sentence is likely to be, and has an active hypothesis about what kind of a text it is dealing with. Questions the interviewer might ask of a real reader, on the presentation of this first segment, to see how closely this real reader matches the accomplishments of the Ideal Reader, include the following:

Do you know what a carpenter does?
What does it mean to be astonished?

When we turn the page and look at the next part of the
paragraph, what do you think we're going to find out
about?
Can you guess what the next word is going to be?
That's a pretty good guess. Can you think of anything
else?

So much for the first segment. With third graders we tend
to postpone questions about the genre until at least one or two
complete sentences have been exposed.
In the next segment, Nasrudin is described as *weak-looking*.
A Physical Strength schema, or scale, has to be introduced
into the Ideal Reader's awareness, with the knowledge that
weak and strong are the two extremes, and the associated
knowledge that somebody who is strong can do more work and
heavier work than somebody who is weak. This, of course,
turns out to be related to the carpenter's surprise, since Nasrudin looked weak but was asking for work that required
strength. The second part of the word *weak-looking* raises in
the Ideal Reader's mind the question of whether somebody who
is described as weak-looking really is weak. A predication of
appearance naturally invites a question about reality. That
question, you will recall, gets answered very soon in the story.
We can clearly put the Parsimony Principle to work with the
first full sentence, which is: 'The carpenter was astonished
that such a weird, weak-looking creature as Nasrudin was
applying for a job.' Without the Parsimony Principle, we could
imagine the carpenter peeking in the door of a personnel office,
or an employment bureau, and seeing Nasrudin standing in line.
With it, we try to use the characters in our scene maximally for
filling out the introduced schemata. In the applying-for-a-job
scene, we make Nasrudin the applicant and the carpenter the
interviewer. In the work for which Nasrudin is applying, we
make Nasrudin the potential employee and the carpenter the
potential employer.
These T-linking assumptions can be wrong, so we will put
them in E^1 and keep them there until we see whether or not
they get immediately corrected. Not only do they not get corrected: the next sentences cannot be made intelligible unless
they are true. The next words of the carpenter are, 'Okay,
I'll give you a chance. Take this ax and chop as much lumber
as you can.' The relationship between interviewer and interviewee is suddenly transformed into a relationship between employer and employee.
The text offers the Ideal Reader a number of places to 'read
between the lines'. The first sentence, we have seen, is
apparently about the carpenter's inner life: it reports that
he was astonished at what he saw. The very next sentence
is a record of the carpenter's words: 'Okay, I'll give you a
chance.' The first word, 'Okay', can count as a signal of
assent; but a signal of assent does not follow naturally a

statement about that person's mental experiences. The first sentence has to be understood as introducing, by presupposition, the first move in the narrative. We then construe Nasrudin's 'applying for a job' as an act of asking the carpenter something like 'Will you give me work?' It is to that appeal, not explicitly present in the text, to which the utterance, 'Okay, I'll give you a chance', is a response.

Similar cooperation is required of the reader in the transition between the following two sentences, the first one in quotes:

'Take this ax and chop as much lumber as you can.'
At dusk Nasrudin returned.

To make this sequence cohere, the Ideal Reader has to build into its picture of the story the information that the carpenter held in his hands or otherwise indicated the ax, that he spoke the quoted sentence to Nasrudin, that Nasrudin took the ax and went off to the forest to cut down trees with it, and that it was at dusk of the same day that Nasrudin returned to the place where the carpenter was. The text tells us none of that, but we have to believe it. The Parsimony Principle would have us believe that the carpenter's order was obeyed, since the author does not tell us that it was ignored or defied. We are, in short, not free to believe that Nasrudin might have stared at the ax all afternoon, giving up his ambitions as a carpenter's helper and returning at dusk to Istanbul.

The patterns of inferencing in this story reach great complexity, especially in the place where the reader figures out that Nasrudin has claimed responsibility for creating the Sahara Desert, and where the reader realizes in the domain of Genre that our narrative is a joke.

The reader of my text will have figured out (with relief or disappointment, I cannot guess which) that the few remaining pages are not going to provide a complete account of the Nasrudin story.

12. I explained earlier that one of our project's unwelcome problems was that of coping with flawed texts. The Ideal Reader abstraction works out most satisfactorily and most straightforwardly with well-constructed texts, texts in which the author's plans are discernible and in which the author's assumptions about the text's readers are reasonable. Almost all of the texts we have examined in our work are seriously flawed in one way or another.

Here is one, picked almost at random:

In 1877 a machine appeared which surprised many people. Can you guess the name of this strange new machine? As you spoke into the mouthpiece and turned the handle, a tube covered with a thin piece of tin moved around. As

the tube moved a needle pressed deep lines into the tin.
As you turned the handle once more, the needle touched
against the same lines and played back your words. This
was the first phonograph. How different from the hi-fi of
today! [9]

Not only do our third-grade subjects have difficulties with
this text; so do many very literate adults. Our subjects had
a much worse time of it, however. Although these children
knew the words *recordplayer* and *stereo*, not one of them knew
the word *phonograph*. Where the text tells us that *the tube
moved,* those adults who know what the antique roll-type phonograph looked like are able to picture a cylinder rotating. The
children knew about toothpaste tubes and video tubes, but that
knowledge did not help them at all. Not one child was able to
create anything remotely resembling the intended image. The
pictures they were induced to draw of the machines they
imagined ranged from tractors to microphones to Coca-Cola
machines.

One attitude we could take toward such a passage, is that it
is merely difficult, and that nobody has a right to complain
about finding difficult items in a test. Our interview protocols
on this item convince us, however, that it simply does not belong in a reading test. The one child (out of 30 subjects) who
figured out that the machine was a record-player could answer
very few of the questions correctly, largely because she became confused by the word *phonograph*, which she said was
unfamiliar to her. (She pictured it as a record player until
she came upon the word *phonograph*, and then she became uncertain.) By contrast, a boy who misread the word *machine*
as *magician* and who performed the wildest sort of mental
acrobatics in order to preserve that part of his Envisionment,
was able, by absolutely absurd reasoning plus a certain amount
of test-taking know-how, to choose mainly correct answers to
the test questions.

The Ideal Reader for such a test has to be, quite simply, a
person who happens to know what the oldest phonograph looked
like and who can be cooperative enough with the text, once the
information that it is a phonograph is finally provided, to realize that the description of the machine is some author's poor
attempt to describe what the Ideal Reader already knows it
should look like. For a text like this, the concept of the Ideal
Reader is workable, but pointless. In the usual case, we as
readers have to know something about the real world in order
to build on that to construct an Envisionment of the world of
the current text; in a case like this, however, what we have
to know in order to understand the text exhausts what the
text tells us. [10] That, in my mind, is a clear case of a bad
text, most assuredly a bad test item.

13. Forthcoming from the project on which I am reporting are an analysis of the interview data from our subjects and a critical study of the worst of the test items. Here I have merely tried to give an informal account of the goals and methods of the project and a survey of the problems one has to face when trying to monitor closely the reading experience, and to show the relevance to this enterprise of the Ideal Reader abstraction.

NOTES

The work reported here has been supported by the National Institute of Education under Grant No. G-790121 Rev. 1, 'Text semantic analysis of reading comprehension tests'. Co-PIs are C. J. Fillmore and Paul Kay; others on the project are reading specialist Judith Langer and a team of Berkeley graduate students from Anthropology, Education, and Linguistics (Karen Carroll, Linda Coleman, Katharine Kovacic, Thomas Larsen, Mary Catherine O'Connor); the project has received good advice from Patrizia Violi, Mary Sue Ammon, and Haj Ross.
 1. The schools in which we have been allowed to do our work are Cragmont Elementary School in Berkeley and Sequoia Elementary School in Oakland. The principals of the two schools, Dr. Benton Ng and Mr. Alfred C. Valdix, have our gratitude.
 2. These have included CTBS Comprehensive Tests of Basic Skills, Level 1, Form S, Complete Battery, Expanded Edition, CTB/McGraw-Hill, Inc., copyrights 1968, 1969, and 1973; and the Metropolitan Achievement Tests: Reading Instructional Tests, Form JI, Elementary, The Psychological Corporation, Division of Harcourt, Brace, Jovanovich, copyright 1978; and (not cited in this report) the California Achievement Tests, the Stanford Achievement Tests, and the Gates-McGinnitie Reading Tests.
 3. Form JI, page 15.
 4. One part of each interview is the genre question, which generally takes some such form as 'Where do you think you might read a passage like this? In a story book? In a letter from a friend? In the Weekly Reader?' One answer we received, in connection with an intendedly humorous narrative passage, was 'in a CTBS test'.
 5. Research applications of the Ideal Reader concept must make use of a large and unarticulatable common sense component. We all know that there are situations in which texts communicate new information by presupposition, and very many situations in which a text develops its argument by reminding its readers of things they already know. The Ideal Reader who has the subtlety we need it to have will be able to convert, by Peircean abduction, information that is formally presupposed into information intended to be derived from the text, and will

be able to recognize situations in which old information is being introduced mainly as a link in the chain of an argument or a narrative.

6. It will seem, to many readers of this text, that my colleagues and I have a hopelessly naive view of the nature of the reading experience. People find pleasure in reading texts they only minimally understand, there are often rhythms and patterns in texts that can only be detected on repeated rereading, readers can experience suspense and surprise in a narrative even if they know, as in a thoroughly familiar text, exactly how it's all going to end, and quite frequently texts are designed precisely to invite idiosyncratic imaginative responses in their readers--a situation for which the notion of a 'correct' interpretation is thoroughly unwelcome. It should be remembered that the simplistic view of the reading experience which we adopt for our research purposes is aimed at a level of understanding for which readers can be reasonably expected to choose 'best' answers to multiple-choice questions.

7. It is this criterion, in conjunction with the decision to define the Ideal Reader as relativized to given texts, which simultaneously makes our work do-able (by defining a stopping place) and guarantees that the Ideal Reader offers only limited predictability to 'good' readers. There is obviously no reason whatever for a reader to create only those inferences and embellishments which the current text will build upon.

8. The Parsimony Principle is found in essentially the form suggested here in such works as Harvey Sacks (1972), 'On the analyzability of stories by children,' in J. Gumperz and D. Hymes (eds.), *Directions in Sociolinguistics*, Holt, Rinehart and Winston, Inc.; and Yorick Wilks (1973), 'Preference semantics,' in E. Keenan (ed.), *Formal Semantics of Natural Language*, Cambridge University Press, and (1973), 'Understanding without proofs,' in *Proceedings of the Third International Joint Conference on Artificial Intelligence*, Stanford Research Institute, Menlo Park, California. The Wilks references were brought to my attention by Robert Kirsner.

9. From Comprehensive Tests of Basic Skills, Form S, Level 1, page 8. Reproduced by permission of the publisher, CTB/McGraw-Hill, Del Monte Research Park, Monterey, California 93940. Copyright © 1973 by McGraw-Hill, Inc. All rights reserved. Printed in the United States of America.

10. The case has been slightly overstated. One does learn in this passage that the first phonograph appeared in 1877.

LITERATURE: WRITTEN AND ORAL

William Bright
University of California, Los Angeles

My title suggests a topic more appropriate for a large book
than for a half-hour talk, so I should say at the outset that
my main goal is to discuss some recent research, by Dell Hymes
and others, in which American Indian oral narratives are analyzed as having the form of verse or poetry; and I want to express a word of caution about some of that work. However, for
the sake of orientation, I would like first to mention briefly my
personal background in the field, and then to clear some terminological underbrush by discussing the problems of defining
the crucial terms 'literature' and 'poetry'.
   My own linguistic training was originally in the post-Bloomfieldian school of the 1940s and 1950s--even though it was, to
my good fortune, more post-Sapirian than post-Bloomfieldian,
and was specifically in the tradition of American Indian anthropological linguistics. In the context of the present Georgetown
University Round Table on Discourse, I am thus aware of being in a somewhat paradoxical position: on the one hand, I
can remember when descriptive linguistic analysis of American
Indian languages, starting from the phonetic level, rarely went
beyond the level of the word, much less to that of the sentence.[1] On the other hand, it was emphatically borne in upon
the academic heirs of Boas, Kroeber, and Sapir that the collection and analysis of texts were absolutely essential parts of
their linguistic field work; thus, for me to receive my Berkeley
doctorate in 1955, I not only had to file a grammar of Karok as
my 'official' dissertation, but simultaneously to submit two other
comparably weighty but 'unofficial' volumes: a Karok dictionary,
and a copious collection of Karok texts. The matched sets of
grammars, dictionaries, and texts which were thus produced
over several decades have quite regularly been issued in the
University of California publication series in linguistics, continuing the Boasian tradition manifested in publications of the

Smithsonian Institution and elsewhere. So the reality of languages as consisting of connected discourse remained part of
the consciousness of many American linguists for years; yet
all those volumes of native American texts on our library
shelves, though consulted by the occasional anthropologist or
folklorist, have tended to be neglected by linguists--and even
more so by scholars of literature. But now things are changing. Owing in particular to the efforts of Dell Hymes and of
Dennis Tedlock, the study of American Indian narrative is
having a revival, from both linguistic and literary viewpoints. [2]
   However, much work remains to be done, not the least of
which is that of terminological clarification. How should we define the differences between formal and informal language,
written and spoken language, literary and colloquial language
(cf. Tannen 1980)? How do we define the term 'literature' itself? Is it appropriate to speak of 'oral literature'? If so,
what are its distinctive characteristics? Within the framework
of 'literature', how can we define 'poetry'? And what about
'oral poetry': how is it to be distinguished from song or
chant on the one hand, and from prose on the other? I touch
on these problems only briefly, and then go on to a more specific question, raised specifically by the work of Hymes--
namely, what are the distinctive characteristics of Native
American oral narrative as poetry?
   I would like first of all to remove from discussion the words
'formal' and 'informal'. I prefer to use these to refer to contrasting sociolinguistic registers--or as poles on a sociolinguistic continuum--described by Ferguson (1959) under the rubric
of 'Diglossia'. [3] A more relevant pair of terms is 'written language', i.e. writing, vs. 'spoken (or oral) language', i.e.
speech. These terms too are useful, as referring to media of
transmission, but still are not directly applicable to defining
'literature'. The point is that much written material--e.g. most
of the content of newspapers--is not generally considered to
be literature; yet other materials originally produced in oral
form--e.g. the Homeric epics--are universally considered literary
works, whether recited aloud or reproduced in printed form. [4]
   We are then confronted with the terrible question of how to
define literary language. [5] I merely suggest here that 'literature' refers, roughly, to that body of discourses or texts
which, within any society, is considered worthy of dissemina-
tion, transmission, and preservation in essentially constant form.
In our society, we typically associate literature with the written
medium; however, works originally composed in writing can of
course be performed orally, as when parents read aloud to children, or when poets give public 'readings'. A further question, however, is the appropriateness of the term 'oral literature'--a phrase which for some people probably still constitutes
an oxymoron: how can something consist of *litterae.* and yet be
oral? Still, the term has been widely used for literature which
is composed, transmitted, and performed orally; well-known

examples are the *Iliad* and *Odyssey* in their original forms, and the much longer epics of Ancient India--the *Mahābhārata* and the *Ramāyana*--as well as the Vedas and a whole huge corpus of ancient Hindu literature. In modern times, the term 'oral literature' has been applied to the body of myths and legends existing in nonliterate societies of, for example, Native America and Africa; witness book titles such as Ruth Finnegan's *Oral Literature in Africa* (1970). 'Oral literature' even covers the large number of jokes, riddles, song texts, etc. which exist primarily in the oral traditions of literate societies like our own: the term 'folklore' is, of course, often applied to such material, but it suggests a different level of evaluation which I would prefer to avoid. In any case, it is clear that texts which were originally oral may be transcribed and transmitted in the written medium; examples would include printed versions of the *Iliad* as well as the contents of the *Journal of American Folklore*. Finally, if I read such printed materials aloud to a child or a friend, the text passes back into the oral medium. It must be recognized, then, that the difference between speech and writing is not necessarily basic to a definition of literature.

A secondary problem is that of possible distinctive qualities in literature whose origin is oral. Finnegan argues persuasively that a typical oral literature may differ in quantity, but not in quality, from a typical written literature. Oral literatures have developed a variety of genres from the epic to the love song (1973:116); they display the same types of content as written literatures, including intellectual perception and aesthetic expression (1973:118-124).

A question that arises here, however, is whether oral literature involves verbatim memorization, so that texts can be preserved in the unchanging form characteristic of written literature. Here we find some controversy: Jack Goody (1977:116-120) has emphasized that many oral literatures show constancy only in overall structure and in the recurrent use of formulaic expressions, rather than in word-for-word repetition; yet other writers have reported many cases in which high value has been attached to exact memorization. A remarkable case is known from Ancient India; once the Vedic hymns had been orally composed (in strict meter), it was considered that their religious effectiveness depended on their being transmitted without the slightest change, and elaborate methods of teaching and memorization were established to ensure this--culminating in the celebrated grammar of Pāṇini. But since the early Sanskrit linguistic texts date from the fifth to the late fourth centuries B.C., and since our earliest evidence of written Sanskrit dates from the mid-third century B.C. (cf. Basham 1954:387-388, 394), we have reason to believe that Pāṇini's grammar itself-- which not only described but standardized a language--was composed and initially transmitted without the use of writing, i.e. in the oral medium alone. This belief is supported by the form of *sūtras* or rules used by Pāṇini and other early Hindu scholars, in which memorization was facilitated by extraordinary brevity.[6] Even after writing was introduced to India, memorization of sacred texts such as the Vedas by purely oral means has continued down to modern times. For us Westerners, who have leaned for so long on the crutch of writing, it is hard to realize the capacities of the human memory! In a very different context, Joel Sherzer (1980) reports that perfect memorization of oral texts is still practiced by the Cuna Indians of Panama. Our conclusion, then, must be that some oral literature can be and is transmitted verbatim, though much is not. On the other side of the balance, we should recall that written literature has not always been transmitted without variation. Finnegan (1973:140) has, in fact, suggested that it is printing rather than writing alone which is responsible for our Occidental ideas about the fixity of literary texts.

Yet if all the foregoing is accepted, we come to a still more terrible question: How can we define 'poetry'?[7] A concept which is traditional in our society, and still held by many individuals, is that 'poetry' refers exclusively to texts organized in regular phonological patterns of meter, and often of rhyme as well. By this definition, it is clear that many oral texts have been composed in well-defined meters; examples include the *Iliad*, the *Mahābhārata*, or Anglo-American folksongs of recent centuries; but such texts were originally chanted or sung, and we may wish to exclude from consideration oral literature in which meter is imposed by a separate rhythmic pattern. Of greater current relevance is the fact that, among the literary texts of our own society--at least since the time of Walt Whitman--there has been increasing recognition of 'free verse', or poetry without well-defined metrical structure. At the present time, most new poetry published in English lacks recognizable meter. The question then arises of how it can be distinguished from prose--along with the subsidiary problem of defining the so-called 'prose poem'. Many poets don't seem to worry much about how to define poetry: they simply know a poem when they meet one. However, a rough definition that appeals to me is this: a poem is a text in which linguistic form--phonological, syntactic, and lexical--is organized in such a way as to carry an aesthetic content which is at least as important, as regards the response of the receiver, as is the cognitive content carried by the same text. Finnegan (1977: 89) says something like this when she states that, in poetry, 'style and structure are a kind of end in themselves...' In traditional English poetry, both oral and written, a large part of the aesthetic content was carried by well-known phonological patterns of meter and rhyme. In more recent English poetry, phonology still plays an important part, insofar as sound is still used for aesthetic effect; but grammatical and lexical structures are also exploited extensively for poetic ends.[8]

Given the recognition of nonmetrical poetry in our own modern society, can we recognize similar poetry in older or more traditional cultures? In fact, it has long been realized that parts of the Hebrew Bible--the so-called 'poetic' books, such as the Psalms--are examples of nonmetrical poetry, presumably of oral composition; linguistic features other than meter, e.g. syntactic parallelism, carry much of the aesthetic content. By contrast, the historical books of the Bible lack these special linguistic features, for the most part, and are thus identified as prose. But what about the works of oral literature which have been transcribed in preliterate societies of our own century, by linguists and anthropologists? Can a distinction between prose and poetry be recognized in, for instance, American Indian materials?

In many older writings on American Indian literature (e.g. Day 1951), one finds the implicit viewpoint that song texts are poetry--but that everything else, such as myths, are prose. This view perhaps derived from the traditional notion, in English literature, that poetry must be metrical; and a musical performance would, of course, associate a song text with a particular meter. By contrast, since American Indian myth texts were normally not sung, they were classified as prose. More recently, this view has been eclipsed, and modern collections of American Indian literature translated into English, such as Jerome Rothenberg's *Shaking the pumpkin* (1972), contain numerous examples of myths which are presented typographically as poems--i.e. in 'lines' of verse. However, as Finnegan warns us (1977:25):

> ... written literary poetry is normally *typographically* defined ... [but] obviously this particular rule will not, by definition, work for oral poetry. One is thus forced to look for other, apparently more 'intrinsic' characteristics ...

We need to ask, then, whether a poetic structure exists in the original text, or whether it has been imposed by the English translator. In fact, although the translators have often been skilled poets, they have just as often been totally ignorant of the native languages concerned; their procedure has simply been to take literal English translations published by linguists and anthropologists, and to rewrite them in more poetic form. In such cases, we have no assurance that the native-language texts are in any way recognizable as poetry rather than prose.

A long-standing concept of 'poetry' (as suggested, for example, by de Groot 1946) is that it can be defined minimally as 'discourse organized in lines'--i.e. strings defined not arbitrarily, by the width of a page, but structurally; such a view was also stated by Dell Hymes in 1960. A step toward demonstrating the existence of such lines in American Indian narratives was taken by Tedlock (1972) in his translations from

Zuni. Here we have a translator who knows the original language, and who has scrupulously tape-recorded the expressive
features of pitch, loudness, rhythm, timbre, and--above all--
of pause as used in the oral performances of Zuni storytellers.
Thus, although Tedlock does not explicitly point out many linguistic features which would identify Zuni narratives as poetry,
his organization into lines on the basis of pause strongly points
to a poetic structure in the Zuni originals. [9]
    Another approach, however, has been taken by Hymes (1976,
1977, 1980a,b), who has focused not on features of live performances, but rather on patterns that can be observed in published
texts--namely, the ways in which vocabulary, word formation,
syntax, and semantics are used to create literary structures. [10]
In his own research, Hymes has shown that Chinookan texts,
transcribed and published years ago, can be divided into
verses--defined not by meter or rhyme, but by other types of
structural features. As he has written (1976:153-156),

> Verse having a defining phonic numerical regularity is
> typically in view in discussion of 'meter' ... Chinookan
> oral narrative is at quite the opposite pole: it has a
> characteristic grammatico-semantic repetition within a frame
> as its base ... One might introduce the term 'measure' for
> verse that answers to the second pole ... The Shakes-
> pearean sonnet is metrical; Louis Simpson's 'Deserted Boy'
> [a Chinookan narrative] is measured.

In seeking a basis for the analysis of measured verse, Hymes
has put great emphasis on the use of sentence-initial particles,
translatable into English as 'and', 'so', 'then' etc. With this
concept of the verse as basis, Hymes finds it possible to recognize other structurally defined units, both smaller--such as the
line, defined typically in terms of its unity as a grammatical
predication--and larger, such as the scene and act, often de-
finable in terms of actors present or shifts of locale. Building
on the work of both Tedlock and Hymes, I myself have attempted
(Bright 1979, 1980a,b,c) to identify structures of measured
verse in the myths of the Karok tribe of California, and to
produce English translations in a corresponding poetic form.
Studying a tape-recorded text both with the approach of Ted-
lock--focusing on the expressive features of performance--and
with the approach of Hymes--identifying verses, etc. in terms
of linguistic structure--I find (Bright 1979) that the two approaches coincide 90 percent of the time in their identification
of basic units. [11]
    Hymes is very positive in his identification of American Indian
narratives as 'verse' or as 'poetry'. [12] Yet he admits that the
recognition of this poetic structure cannot be carried out in
any mechanical way. For example, although sentence-initial
particles provide the primary cue for the recognition of verse

patterning in languages as widespread as Chinookan, Karok, and Tonkawa, Hymes notes (1977:439-440):

Once such patterning has been discovered in cases with such markers, it can be discerned in cases without them. The Clackamas [Chinookan] narratives of Mrs. Victoria Howard do not regularly make use of initial particles ... To determine the organization of her narratives, one has to recognize and abstract features that *co-occur* [emphasis added] with the use of initial particle pairs in the [Wishram Chinookan] narratives of Louis Simpson ... The discovery of such pattern is not arbitrary, because it is governed by the coherence and articulation of the particular narrative, by a rhetorical pattern that pervades Chinookan texts.

Hymes has shown great skill in carrying out such analysis; and other researchers have begun to identify line and verse structures, formally marked not necessarily by initial particles, but by other phenomena such as grammatical and semantic parallelism, in other Native American literatures.[13] Yet the more subtle are the devices which mark verse structure, the more cautious the researcher must be--especially when dealing with dead and moribund languages, where it is impossible to validate one's analysis with members of a living and creative speech community. The delicacy of the task is recognized by Hymes, but at times I feel that he relies more on his own intuition as an English-language poet than on objective characteristics of his Native American data. Thus, in justifying his verse analysis of a Wasco Chinookan text, as told by Hiram Smith, in which initial markers are scarce, he writes (1980a: 77):

In sum, pervasiveness of the meaning dimension of rhetorical patterning asks for such an analysis, [Hiram Smith's own] English retelling provides for it, and the concord relations in the Wasco text seem to require it.

Here the statement that 'the English retelling provides for it' is what disturbs me, even though the English is that of Hiram Smith himself: we risk falling into the error against which we were so often warned by Boas, and more recently by Hymes himself--that of imposing English-based categories on linguistic data from other cultures.

The possibility remains open, in fact, that some Native American cultures--or culture areas--simply told their narratives as prose--or, to put it more properly, that they lacked a distinction between prose and poetry in their literary discourse. An area that concerns me in this regard is Southern California. When I look at the Cahuilla texts published by Hansjakob Seiler (1970), or at the delightful Diegueño text collected by Leanne Hinton under the title 'Coyote baptizes the chickens' (1978), I find neither initial particles nor grammatico-lexical parallelism; I find, in fact, nothing like the clearly recognizable structures of measured verse which we see in the Pacific Northwest and in Northern California. To be sure, I may simply be missing something; other scholars should certainly examine the Southern Californian materials. But linguists have already in recent years tended to postulate too many poorly founded universals: let us not assume that the poetry/prose distinction must exist everywhere.

Other questions that arise are these. Consider a culture like that of the Karok, where traditional narratives show abundant characteristics of measured verse. But if Karok poetry (apart from song texts) is what we find in myths, what are the characteristics of Karok prose? Does a distinction in fact exist, in the literature of the Karok (or the Chinookans), between prose and poetry? Or should we say, as was perhaps the case in some early Indo-European societies, that all literature was poetic, and that prose was used only for nonliterary discourse?

Data now available on Karok are inadequate to answer these questions.[14] But many other native American speech communities continue in full function, and deserve study in terms of all aspects of Hymes' 'ethnography of communication'. Tedlock can probably tell us for Zuni, or Sherzer for Cuna, a great deal about the actual formal distinctions between different types of poetic vs. nonpoetic and literary vs. nonliterary discourses. In fact, we recently have a tantalizing report from Anthony Woodbury concerning the Central Yup'ik Eskimo of Alaska: he suggests that 'lines' and 'verses' are characteristic of all Central Yup'ik discourse, and that his identification of these units is readily verifiable by native speakers--but that 'lines' and 'verses' are used differently in distinct types of discourse, ranging from 'poetry' to ordinary conversation. I look forward eagerly to learning more about Woodbury's findings.

In the meanwhile, returning to the topic of oral literature, I wish to add my voice to those of Tedlock, Hymes, and others who have emphasized that Native American oral narratives must be taken seriously as literature. We should learn, for a broad range of Native American societies, how to differentiate prose and poetry--and possibly other genres; we should learn the defining characteristics of each genre; we should learn the social function of each; and we should attempt to understand the nature of written literature as it develops in Native American languages. Students of these topics have much to gain, not only in increased appreciation of the richness of literary traditions in the Western Hemisphere, but also in improved comprehension of the nature of literary discourse among human societies in general.

NOTES

Thanks for suggestions and encouragement to Linda Arvanites, M. B. Emeneau, Paul Friedrich, Dell Hymes, and Ken Lincoln.

1. One widely admired 'grammar' of the 1940s barely went past what we might now call the morphophonemics. Against that background, it is encouraging to realize that a conference devoted exclusively to American Indian syntax has been held in Calgary this spring.

2. Indeed, the lead article in a 1977 issue of that bastion of literary scholarship, the *Publications of the Modern Language Association*, was Jarold Ramsey's study of an Oregon Indian myth.

3. To be sure, Ferguson uses the terms 'H(igh)' and 'L(ow)' instead of 'formal' and 'informal'; but these labels invite confusion with the social dialects of higher vs. lower social classes or castes. Furthermore, although formal varieties, in countries like India, are often written, they need not be--as when they are used in impromptu political speeches or sermons; and in the same connection, they may lack any of the aesthetic quality which would prompt us to label them as 'literary utterances'. By contrast, 'informal varieties' are not usually written, but sometimes they are--as, increasingly, in some types of popular fiction and comic books--which might or might not be considered forms of 'literature'.

4. The possible confusion that results from use of these terms is illustrated when Ochs (1979) refers to 'writing' as planned vs. 'speech' as unplanned; or when Chafe (1979) sees 'writing' as integrated and detached, but 'speech' as fragmented and involved. Without denying the validity of these labels, I would suggest that they apply not strictly to the media of 'writing' and 'speech' as such, but more properly to the contrast between literary and colloquial language.

5. As Ruth Finnegan (1973:118) has said, 'The whole area of "What is literature?" is of course a controversial and unending one.'

6. Thus the famous last *sūtra* of Pāṇini is *a a*, the interpretation of which is: 'The long low vowel [a:] has, as its short counterpart, the raised vowel [ə]' (Renou 1954:144).

7. Finnegan (1977:24), with the length of an entire book at her disposal, says, 'I cannot here enter into deep discussion of the question "What is poetry?"'

8. On a cross-cultural basis, Finnegan raises another important point about prose vs. poetry: 'the local classification of a piece as "poetry" [is] in one sense ... the most important [factor], but it is by no means simple. For one thing, the relatively neat formal differentiation we make in our own culture between poetry and prose is not recognized everywhere ...' (1977:25). 'It emerges, then, that any differentiation of "poetry" from "prose", or indeed of "poetry" as a specific literary product or activity, can only be approximate ... the

whole delimitation of what is to count as "poetry" necessarily
depends not on one strictly verbal definition but on a series
of factors to do with style, form, setting and local classification, not all of which are likely to coincide' (27).

9. He states, indeed, that 'prose has no real existence outside the written page' (1972:xix).

10. Regarding the poetic 'line' defined merely in terms of
pause, Hymes comments (1977:453-454): 'there remains the
problem of differentiating pause that is motivated, that
heightens the organization of lines, from pause that is inherent in the spoken medium ... one cannot be content with
a purely definitional victory for the claim of the pervasiveness
of poetry as lines ... Pausing may itself be culturally shaped,
but if it is, one needs evidence beyond the fact of its occurrence.'

11. This gives me confidence that occasional ambiguities of
one approach can be resolved by reference to the other: thus
linguistic sequences which have two possible grammatical interpretations can be disambiguated by reference to phenomena of
pitch and pause; and conversely, accidental hesitations which
create 'false' pauses in performance can be recognized because
they are interruptions of normal sentence structure.

12. As he has recently stated (Hymes 1980b:34-35): 'the
study of Native American languages has yet to take its materials seriously enough ... It now appears that we have misled
ourselves as to the myths and tales we have thought long
known. We have allowed to stand a perpetuation of the cardi-
nal sin, the distortion of another cultural reality through impo-
sition of categories of our own. We have thought that Native
American myths and tales are prose and have printed them as
such ... All the collections that are now in print must be re-
done. They do not show the structure of the texts they represent ... Hidden within the margin-to-margin lines are poems,
waiting to be seen for the first time.'

13. See Karttunen and Lockhart (1979) for Classical Nahuatl,
Tedlock (1979) for the colonial Quiché of the *Popol Vuh*, Norman (1980) for modern Quiché, and Sherzer (1980) for Cuna.

14. During my major period of field work on Karok, in 1949
and 1950, the texts which I transcribed were mainly limited to
narratives--because I was interested in the myth literature, because 'stories' were an easy type of text to elicit, and because,
except for a few days at the end of my work, I had no tape-
recorder. So I never obtained any conversational texts. I
did transcribe--from dictation, not from tape--some nonnarra-
tive, ethnographic texts (Bright 1957:282-301), and they show
a structure of sentence-initial particles similar to that found in
narratives. Does this mean that I was actually getting ethnographic poetry? Probably not; the situation in which a Karok
speaker dictated texts to me, word by word, was analogous to
the native situation in which stories were told to children for
piece-by-piece repetition, and so the style of narrative may

have artificially been extended to descriptions of salmon-fishing
and sweathouses. To be sure, elderly speakers of Karok are
still living, and it may still be possible to tape-record more
natural samples of Karok discourse. However, no functioning
Karok speech community exists now, and so conditions are not
ideal for resolving these matters.

REFERENCES

Basham, A. L. 1954. The wonder that was India. New York:
Grove.

Bright, William. 1957. The Karok language. University of
California Publications in Linguistics, 13. Berkeley and Los
Angeles.

Bright, William. 1979. A Karok myth in 'measured verse':
The translation of a performance. Journal of California and
Great Basin Anthropology 1.117-123.

Bright, William. 1980a. Coyote's journey. American Indian
Culture and Research Journal (UCLA) 4.21-48.

Bright, William. 1980b. Coyote gives salmon and acorns to
humans. In: Coyote Stories II. Edited by Martha Kendall.
IJAL-NATS Monograph 6. Chicago: University of Chicago
Press. 46-52.

Bright, William. 1980c. Poetic structure in oral narrative.
In: Spoken and written language. Edited by Deborah
Tannen. Norwood, N.J.: Ablex.

Chafe, Wallace L. 1979. Integration and involvement in
speaking, writing, and oral literature. In: Spoken and
written language. Edited by Deborah Tannen. Norwood,
N.J.: Ablex.

Day, A. Grove, ed. 1951. The sky clears. New York:
Macmillan. [Reprinted, Lincoln: University of Nebraska
Press, 1964.]

de Groot, A. Willem. 1946. Algemene versleer. The Hague:
Servire.

Ferguson, Charles A. 1959. Diglossia. Word 15.325-340.

Finnegan, Ruth. 1970. Oral literature in Africa. Oxford:
Clarendon.

Finnegan, Ruth. 1973. Literacy vs. non-literacy: The
great divide? Some comments on the significance of 'litera-
ture' in non-literate cultures. In: Modes of thought:
Essays on thinking in Western and non-Western societies.
Edited by Robin Horton and Ruth Finnegan. London:
Faber and Faber. 112-144.

Finnegan, Ruth. 1977. Oral poetry: Its nature, significance,
and social context. Cambridge: University Press.

Goody, Jack. 1977. The domestication of the savage mind.
Cambridge: University Press.

Hinton, Leanne. 1978. Coyote baptizes the chickens (La
Huerta Diegueño). In: Coyote stories. Edited by William

Bright. IJAL-NATS Monograph 1. Chicago: University of
Chicago Press. 117-120.
Hymes, Dell. 1960. Review of: Ob-Ugric metrics, by Robert
Austerlitz. Anthropos 55.574-576.
Hymes, Dell. 1976. Louis Simpson's 'The deserted boy.'
Poetics 5.119-155.
Hymes, Dell, 1977. Discovering oral performance and measured
verse in American Indian narrative. New Literary History
8.431-457.
Hymes, Dell. 1980a. Verse analysis of a Wasco text: Hiram
Smith's 'At'unaqa'. IJAL 46.65-77.
Hymes, Dell. 1980b. Tonkawa poetics: John Rush Buffalo's
'Coyote and Eagle's Daughter'. In: On linguistic anthro-
pology: Essays in honor of Harry Hoijer, 1979. Edited by
Jacques Maquet. Malibu: Undena. 33-87.
Karttunen, Frances, and James Lockhart. 1979. The struc-
ture of Nahuatl poetry as seen in its variants. In: Estudios
de Cultura Nahuatl, Mexico City.
Norman, William M. 1980. Grammatical parallelism in Quiché
ritual language. In: Proceedings of the 6th Annual Meeting,
Berkeley Linguistic Society. 387-399.
Ochs, Elinor. 1979. Planned and unplanned discourse. In:
Discourse and syntax. Edited by Talmy Givón. New York:
Academic Press. 51-80.
Ramsey, Jarold W. 1977. The wife who goes out like a man,
comes back as a hero: The art of two Oregon Indian narra-
tives. PMLA 92.1:9-18.
Renou, Louis. 1954. La grammaire de Pāṇini, fasc. 3. Paris:
Klincksieck.
Rothenberg, Jerome, ed. 1972. Shaking the pumpkin: Tra-
ditional poetry of the Indian North Americans. Garden City,
N.Y.: Doubleday.
Seiler, Hansjakob. 1970. Cahuilla texts, with an introduction.
Language Science Monographs, 6. Bloomington: Indiana Uni-
versity.
Sherzer, Joel. 1980. Tellings, retellings, and tellings within
tellings: The structuring and organization of narrative in
Cuna Indian discourse. Paper presented at the conference
on 'Oralità: Cultura, letteratura, discorso', Centro Inter-
nazionale di Semiotica e Linguistica, Urbino, Italy.
Tannen, Deborah. 1980. Spoken/written language and the
oral/literate continuum. In: Proceedings of the 6th Annual
Meeting, Berkeley Linguistics Society. 207-218.
Tedlock, Dennis. 1972. Finding the center: Narrative poetry
of the Zuni Indians. New York: Dial. [2nd ed., Lincoln:
University of Nebraska Press, 1978.]
Tedlock, Dennis, 1979. Las formas del verso quiché, de la
paleografía a la grabadora. Paper presented to the Primer
Congreso sobre el Popol Vuh, Santa Cruz del Quiché,
Guatemala. To be published in its Actas (Guatemala City:
Piedra Santa.)

Woodbury, Anthony C. 1980. Rhetorical structure in Central Yup'ik Eskimo narrative. Paper presented at the LSA Annual Meeting, San Antonio. [Abstract in Meeting handbook, p. 79.]

MEANING, RHETORICAL STRUCTURE, AND DISCOURSE ORGANIZATION IN MYTH

Sally McLendon
Smithsonian Institution and
Hunter College of City University of New York

The role of texts in language.   Linguists have increasingly come to appreciate the centrality of discourse and texts in language and communication.   In a recent book examining the organization of discourse in English, Halliday and Hasan have gone so far as to propose that 'A text ... can be thought of as the basic unit of meaning in language' (1976:25) or as 'the basic semantic unit of linguistic interaction' (1976:295).

The characterization of a text as the basic semantic unit of linguistic interaction suggests that the text is the form taken by the particular meaning(s) communicated in a linguistic interaction, and that the ability to produce and comprehend texts requires a shared understanding on the part of speakers of how meanings are to be associated with texts (or how meanings are to be created by texts) in a language.   Halliday and Hasan (1976:299) assume that 'what creates text is the TEXTUAL or text-forming component of the linguistic system of which cohesion is one part'.   Unfortunately, they do not specify what this text-forming component consists of besides the phenomenon of cohesion which is the topic of their book, and their study focuses on written texts to the virtual exclusion of oral texts.

The rhetorical structure of texts.   It has been clear for a long time that a text involves the simultaneous manipulation of several formal systems of language: the sound system, the lexical system, and the grammatical system.   Linguists have largely left to literary critics, however, the investigation of what seems appropriately called the rhetorical system, which may well be the most important aspect of the organization of form in a text to convey meaning (and is probably to be identified with what Halliday and Hasan refer to as the 'text-forming component'). The rhetorical system establishes in a text relations among sounds, among lexical items, among grammatical patterns, and among discourse units, which structure a discourse and signal its organization and meaning.

Traditionally, the most commonly studied rhetorical devices in addition to figures of speech have been those which involve repetition of some sort and which establish cohesion, such as alliteration and rhyme in the sound system and parallelism in the grammatical system. The rhetorical system of a language, more importantly, however, establishes relations of disjunction as well as continuity or cohesion between elements in a text.

Repetition is only the most obvious device for establishing continuity. Continuity can also be achieved through the sorts of cohesive devices discussed by Halliday and Hasan, like pronominalization, anaphora, and lexical implicature, as well as by the lack of clitics and particles which have disjunctive discourse function, the suppression of pauses and junctures at constituent boundaries, and other grammatical and prosodic phenomena.

Disjunction can be signaled by pauses, junctures, phrase, clause, and sentence boundaries, the use of substantives rather than pronouns, the use of clitics and particles signaling larger narrative units, and the presentation of material as an independent sentence rather than as a dependent clause or phrase.

The cohesion in English which Halliday and Hasan discuss involves devices for establishing continuity, but patterns of continuity and cohesion take on significance only by contrast with breaks in that continuity, signaled by disjunction of some sort. Both cohesion and disjunction are equally important in the shaping of a text.

Written forms of oral texts. In written discourse, rhetorical organization is reflected by punctuation and indentation, while in oral discourse, the actual oral delivery of the text, the pauses, junctures, and pitch changes, combine with patterns of grammatical and lexical cohesion and disjunction to organize a text rhetorically into a coherent whole. This organization is often missed or obscured when oral material is, as it is often too aptly put, 'reduced to writing'. An example of the traditional scholarly presentation of an oral text is given in Figure 1. In part, this is probably because we have all been trained to attend primarily to the phonology of words, although we also know that sentences have characteristic intonational patterns associated with them. However, we also lack easy to use and read conventions for representing in writing the rhetorical function of intonational phenomena.

Dell Hymes (1976, 1977, 1980a,b, 1981) has recently published several stimulating attempts to recover the rhetorical organization of Chinookan texts recorded by Sapir and Jacobs before the easy availability of tape recorders which offer an alternative to the traditional text presentation in Figure 1. By close

Figure 1. KU·NÚ·LA-BÙ·ČIKE AND HIS BROTHER, CʰI·MÉW, AT KU·ŠÁ·-DA·NÒ·YÒW [Told by Ralph Holder, May, 1973.]

1. yú xa na·pʰó·le, cʰi·Méwqay, ku·nú·la-bù·čikeqay, ma·dú·xačiMaǩ, ku·šá·-da·nò·yòw.

1. They were living there, Wolf and Old man Coyote, him and his brother, at ku·šá·-da·nò·yòw.

2. mí·n ʔíkkiliday xa cʰi·Méw mí·pal ya·ʔó qa·múkk·le; bá· kʰi ḍa·lál mé·rklile, ma·ʔáy qa·wá·lakʰùy. 3. *[míl] ka·té· xa ku·nú·la-bú·čikehe·ʔmì·p̣ yó·-qa·qo·yal kákkllle, ma·ʔáy hí·p̣, báyawa kʰi tu·nú, lámi, mí·n ʔá·m kál-kʰi·díkkllle. 4. báyawa káluhun xa kʰi ma·ʔáy hí· kálkʰi·dìʔba· cá·rdu·bákin, ǫo·díy du·bákin, ...

2. Well, been long like that Wolf had a toothache, then he lay there sick, he never eat. 3. Then (Nevertheless) Old Man Coyote go to Big Valley to get some food; from there he bring home them digger squirrel; from there he bring home field mice and gopher. 4. When he come home that food that he bring he clean ...

*Mr. Holder inserted when transcribing.

attention to the placement of discourse particles and clitics in
the text, and the structure and content of the sentences they
mark off, he attempts to reflect systematically what was probably the rhetorical structure intended by the narrators, utilizing the written conventions developed largely for poetry in
western European languages. These in fact reflect rhetorical
structure visually through placement in terms of lines and
verses on the page. William Bright (1979a,b, 1980) has represented Karok texts similarly, but using the prosodic features available on tape recordings of these texts, as has Joel
Sherzer, I understand. Anthony Woodbury (in press) has used
a line and verse format which reflects rhetorical structure indicated in prosodic as well as syntactic features for a whole
series of Inuit oral narratives which he has converted to written
form for the Alaska Native Language Center.

Hymes has suggested that the success of the approach indicates that at least some Native American narrative is poetry
rather than prose. It is not clear that it is useful to impose
such a distinction on the literature of societies that do not
traditionally make such a distinction. It also seems likely that
the communicative value of a line and verse presentation of
narrative material has more to do with the responses of audiences literate in European languages to the format of poetry
than necessarily with the nature of the narrative itself. As
Hymes (personal communication) has said, 'it slows the eye
and hence feeds the mind.'[1]

For the past five years, I have been experimenting with the
same use of written conventions to reflect the rhetorical structure and discourse organization signaled in the actual oral
delivery of texts in Eastern Pomo, a Hokan language of native
North America, spoken in northern California.

In 1973, I was fortunate to have the opportunity to begin
research with a remarkably talented speaker of Eastern Pomo,
Ralph Holder of Upper Lake, California. Mr. Holder was a
monolingual speaker of Eastern Pomo until he went to school
around the age of seven. From the age of six on, he lived
primarily with elderly grandparents who had been adults before serious white settlement began in this area. They apparently preferred to use Eastern Pomo in all communicative contexts until their deaths when Mr. Holder was 16. Mr. Holder's
grandfather, Jim Bateman, was a master myth teller. He is, in
fact, mentioned by several Eastern Pomo in the turn of the century fieldnotes of A. L. Kroeber as a person to be consulted
about myths and traditional precontact ways. Mr. Holder spent
his childhood and youth listening to his grandfather recount
both myths and his own experiences of childhood and youth,
a great many of which Mr. Holder has recorded in Eastern
Pomo with me over the past nine years (McLendon 1977a,b,
1978).

Continuing work with the 14 long, complex, and rich traditional narratives called *ma·rû·* 'myth' which Mr. Holder recorded

in Eastern Pomo has revealed that a close analysis of pauses, pitch, rise and fall of voice, relative speed or deliberateness of delivery and the location of breath taking, in conjunction with a consideration of the form and content of the utterances associated with these intonational features, permit the nonsubjective recognition of both the rhetorical structure and the discourse organization of a text. This organization, once recognized, can then be reflected visually in a line format such as Hymes has developed.

This new presentational format has the additional advantage of making it possible to use the narrator's original words in both the native language and the translation versions of the text. When the rhetorical structure is reflected visually, the original words seem to take on heightened dramatic potential and meaning in ways that seem highly appropriate from the point of view of English literary standards. Thus, this line format has the additional advantage of eliminating, or at least making less pressing, the need (or temptation) to edit and retell the English translation of a Native American myth in order to make it more accessible to an English-speaking audience (which increasingly even the Eastern Pomo, themselves, are). One can then simultaneously provide both a more scholarly version and a more immediately available one, using such a presentational format.

Features of the oral delivery of Eastern Pomo myths which are useful in recognizing their rhetorical structure. In myths, Eastern Pomo sentences must be in the hearsay evidential mode. This means that the inflected verb of the main or matrix clause must be suffixed with the hearsay suffix --*le*, and that the hearsay clitic *xa* must be postposed to the first constituent of that clause (cf. McLendon 1975, 1979). Thus, in Sentence 1 in Figure 1, the main clause is:

yú   xa   na·pʰó-·*le*
perfective   they   dwell plurally-they say
              say

The inflected verb is *na·pʰó·le* 'dwell plurally', and the hearsay clitic *xa* follows the initial constituent, *yú*.

In myths, Eastern Pomo sentences consist of one or more phonological phrases. Phonological phrases are characterizable as having one primary word stress associated with a significant rise in pitch. Each phonological phrase has a pitch norm throughout which reflects (1) the relative location of the phrase within a sentence, (2) its degree and type of syntactic relatedness to the surrounding phrases, and (3) the communicative importance within the sentence of the semantic content of that phrase.

Eastern Pomo sentences begin on a higher pitch than they end. When a sentence is complex in syntactic structure and includes several phonological phrases, successive phrases drift down in pitch, rather like the phenomenon known as downstep in many West African languages. However, when a sentence contains one or more phonological phrases which are syntactically in apposition, the pitch of these phrases stays at the same level.

Boundaries between phonological phrases and, ipso facto, between sentences, are signaled by perceptible pause or its lack (suppression seems a more accurate term), plus changes in the pitch of the phonological phrase on either side of the pause.

Nonsuppressed pauses are of two main types: (1) one in which the breath is held back by audible glottal stricture, and (2) one in which breath is audibly exhaled at the end of a phrase and/or audibly inhaled at the beginning of the next. Glottal stricture seems to draw attention to the cohesion intended by the speaker between the two phonological phrases it separates, while inhalation and exhalation mark a greater disjunction. As one might expect, suppression of pause seems to signal greater cohesion intended between the two phrases linked by it, and so far has mainly been observed when the two phrases are syntactically clauses in apposition. Not all apposed clauses are linked by suppressed pauses, however.

Sentence boundaries in Eastern Pomo myths, thus, are signaled by a combination of syntactic and prosodic phenomena.

The recognition of sentence boundaries is indispensable to a correct understanding of rhetorical structure but is far from a mechanical process. A myth consists observationally of a succession of fully independent main clauses (having the hearsay clitic *xa* plus the -·*le* suffix), separated by other material of varying degrees of dependency, ranging from formally subordinated to potentially independent (but marked as apposed by the absence of the hearsay clitic *xa*). These structures are grouped prosodically into phonological phrases by patterns of pause and pitch change. One recognizes sentence boundaries as much by what follows as by what precedes. A sentence consistently begins on a higher pitch than that on which the preceding sentence ended, and the beginnings of sentences are marked syntactically by characteristic features. Discourse particles are sentence initial, and adverbial particles occur either sentence initially or as the second constituent of a sentence.

The generalizations presented here about Eastern Pomo sentences describe the regularities which are observable when one breaks a text into sentences in this way. Since these regularities are the basis for recognizing sentence boundaries, the process is unavoidably circular. The correctness of the sentence boundaries determined in this way is supported by the semantic cohesion which holds within each sentence and which is greater than that which holds between adjacent sentences.

The rhetorical organization of a portion of an Eastern Pomo myth. The beginning portion of the Eastern Pomo text presented in Figure 1 in traditional run-on prose format is represented in Figure 2. The prosodic structure of the actual delivery is visually represented by presenting phonological phrases as separate lines, except when two phrases are linked by suppressed pause preceded by a fall in pitch.

The type of pause and pitch changes are indicated by the following mnemonic abbreviations printed above the line.

EX	Exhalation
IN	Inhalation
CLD LIPS	Closed Lips
GSTR	Glottal Stricture
P	Rise in pitch accompanying one primary stress in a phrase
1/2P	Flattened pitch rise
↓	Drop in voice and pitch
→	Steady pitch without change
↓^	Drop in pitch with suppression of pause

Traditional English punctuation--commas, periods, quotation marks, etc.--are used to signal the sentential organization reflected by the interaction of syntax and prosody.

Within a sentence, successive phonological phrases closed by EX and introduced by IN are, after the initial phrase in a sentence, placed one directly below the other, as in Sentence 1 in Figure 2. Phrases separated by glottal stricture are indented, as in Sentence 2 in Figure 2. The second of two phrases separated by suppressed pause which is preceded by a steady pitch (→) is dropped one line below the first, but at the same point at which the preceding phrase ends. Phrases with suppressed pause plus a falling pitch are written on the same line, separated by a comma.

It is easiest to follow the discussion if one has heard the text. This is unfortunately not possible in a written format. Without the oral performance, it is particularly important to read through the text which follows using the line divisions, diacritics, and punctuation to imagine what the text sounds like.

The visual presentation of the text in terms of lines makes the prosodic features easier to hear, even if one is unfamiliar with the language. More importantly, it also makes clearer the patterns of cohesion and disjunction which organize the material rhetorically.

For example, in the first sentence of Figure 2, which sets the stage, as first sentences always do in well-formed performances of Eastern Pomo myths, the protagonists are named, their kin relations specified, and their residence at a real, known site established. Each of these three types of information is given in a distinct phonological phrase (the naming of the

Figure 2.

1. They were living,

   Wolf and Old Man Coyote,

   him and his brother,

   at ku·šá--da·nò·yò.

2. Well, been long like that

   Wolf

   had a toothache;

   then he lay there sick, he never eat.

```
          1/2P      ↓EX CLD LIPS
1.  yú xa na·ɣhó·le,
    PERF  they-say dwell-PL

      1/2P   ↓^       P       ↓EX
    c̓hi·Méwɣày,  ku·nú·la·bù·c̓ikeɣày,
    Wolf-and Coyote-Old Man-and

    1/2IN P        ↓EX
    ma·dú·xacíMaǩ,
    his-own-younger-brother-with

    1/2IN P       ↓EX
    ku·šá--da·nò·yòw.
    (village site on Scott's Creek)

(higher pitch)
    IN   P       ↓ EX CLD LIPS
2.  mí·n ʔíkkiliǎay xa
    like-that was-HAB-SR they-say

    IN   P   →GSTR
    c̓hi·Méw
    Wolf

              P      ↓EX
    mí·pal ya·ʔó qa·múk̓h·le;
    3p-PAT-MASC tooth vise-like-hold

    IN   ↓^          P        ↓^   1/2P         ↓EX
    bá·khi ɣa·lál mé·rkille, ma·ʔáy ɣa·wá·lakhuy.
    then 3p-CL sick lay-HAB food eat-not
```

3. Then (Nevertheless)
   Old Man Coyote
   go to Big Valley
   to get some food;

   from there he
   bring home them digger squirrel;

   from there he

   bring home field mice and gopher.

4. When he come home

   that food that he bring

(higher pitch)
IN
    P →
3. *[míl] ka·té· xa
   [that previously beside they-say ku·nú·la·bu·čikehe·ʔmì·p̓ →
   mentioned action]   Coyote- Old Man-AG
                                     yó··qa·qòˑyal kákkille, →
                                     South-Valley-towards run-habitually
                      P ↓EX
                      ma·ʔáy hí·p;
                      food collect

(higher pitch)
IN
      P →
   báyawa kʰi qu·Mar
   there-from 3p-CL ground-squirrel   kálkʰi·dìkkille; ↓EX
                                      homewards-bring-carrying-HAB

(no
IN) PAUSE GSTR
   báyawa kʰi;
   there-from 3p-CL
     P ↓EX
     tu·nú,
     fieldmouse
   IN
   lami mì·n ʔa·m   P   ↓EX CLD LIPS
   gopher like-that things   kálkʰi·dìkkille.
                                      homewards-bring-carrying-HAB

(higher pitch)
IN
   P →   EX
4. báyawa káluhun xa kʰi
   there-from homewards-go-CoR they-say 3p-CL
   IN
      P   GSTR
   ma·ʔáy hí· kálkʰi·dìʔba.
   food 3p-CoR homewards-bring-that

P ↓⌢ , P ↓EX
cá·rdu·bàkin, ŕo·díy du·bàkin,
clean-make-CoR good-make-CoR
he clean that, fix it good,

IN P GSTR
ma·tólqàkilin xa kʰi
cook-cause-HAB-CoR they-say 3p-CL
then he cooks that

P ↓EX
ma·dúxaȼal si·xákʰ·le.
his-own-younger-brother-PAT give
and gives it to his brother.

(higher pitch)
IN
5. bá· xa ȼàikị·ya·lkilịe̅→ GSTR
then they-say refuse-do-HAB
5. Then he refused:

IN P ↑
"ma·ʔáy ku·hú·ba·ʔkʰùy P↗ wi tǎ.
food eat-to-not 1p-PAT feel ya·ʔóhe? P GSTR
tooth-specific
'I don't feel like eating

qa·mùqa·mù·lin. ↓EX
vise-like-hold-extended-CoR
because my tooth ache.

(higher pitch)
IN P ↓EX
bá· wi ma·bóya."
that 1p-PAT swell-up
That (my jaw) is swell up.'

ní·n xa kʰi P ↓CLD LIPS GSTR
Né·le,
that they-say 3p-CL say
that's what he say,

P ↓EX
**(xa:) cʰi·Mèwhe?mì·p̣.
Wolf-AG
the Wolf.

(BREATH)
(higher pitch)
IN
6. bá· xa yu·ke·hél qa·wá·iklille, (hK̲) ʔín ká·ya ku·ʔémkílle; ↓EX
   then they·say-PERF alone eat-HAB CoR after sleep-PL-HAB
   CLD LIPS GSTR
   (ʔê:)

6. Then he eat alone, then they sleep;

xa·ʔása khi yúpʰa kákkílle, bá·ka khi ye·hé·lle. ↓CLD LIP
dawn-because-SR 3p-CL again run-HAB that-only 3p-CL do

Next morning he run down (to Big Valley), that's all he been doing.

(higher pitch)
IN
7. mí·n ka·nkʰ kʰi ye·hé·liday xa
   like-that long-time 3p-CL do-SR they·say

mí·p ba· pʰi·qótʰke·le ↑
he-AG that suspect

ma·dú·xacal,
his-own-younger-brother-PAT

7. Been that way for a long time and he had suspicion of his brother,

GSTR
cʰíi,

chí·n ʔín mí·p ba.
what CoR he-AG that

what he been doing

(higher pitch)
IN P GSTR
ma·ʔáy qa·wá·lakʰúy mé·rhe?
food eat-not lay-specific

never eat, laying down

qa·wás ma·bó·. ↓EX
jaw swell-up

his jaw swell up.

(higher pitch)
IN P
8. "há·ʔ ba· ku·ʔába?è," ↓
   I that search-for-SUBJ

8. 'I'm gonna find out,'

ní·n xa kʰi baik·le. ↓EX CLD LIPS
that they·say 3p-CL think-REFL

that's what he's thinking to himself.

(higher pitch)

IN P   ↓⌢   P

9. bá· xa ḳʰi, xa·ʔáɢan xa ḳH̄i   P   EX   du·wéMi
    then they–say 3p-CL dawn–SR they–say 3p-CL   early-in-the-morning

IN P

   wáɖu·kè·łe   yó·qa·qòyàl̄
   go–begin   South-Valley towards   ma·ʔáy hi·p̣.   P   ↓EX
                                  food collect

9. Next morning he
   early in the morning

   starts to go
   to Big Valley
     to get some more
      food.

---

*Mr. Holder inserted when transcribing.
**Mr. Holder deleted when transcribing.

KEY: PL = plural; SR = switch-reference; CoR = co-reference; HAB = habitual; AG = agent; PAT = patient; p = person; MASC = masculine; CL = clitic; SUBJ = subjunctive; REFL = reflexive; PERF = perfective [Grammatical abbreviations]

IN = inhale; EX = exhale; GSTR = glottal stricture [Intonational abbreviations]

protagonists is actually in two phonological phrases linked by
suppressed pause). The termination of the phrase presenting
each of these three types of information ends with the same
falling intonation and exhalation. The second and third types
of information, the specification of kin relation and the identification of residence, are introduced by partial inhalation. A
prosodic parallelism is thus established which reflects both the
equal weight assigned these three pieces of information and
their discreteness. It also underscores the syntactic parallelism established by the fact that they are all three in apposition
to the main clause, *yú xa na·pʰó·le*.

Pause phenomena simultaneously separate and connect syntactic
material. The suppressed pause in line 2 of the first sentence
between *cʰi·Méw-qay* 'Wolf-and' and *ku·nú·la-bù·čike-qay* 'Coyote-Old Man-and', while separating them, also signals the
greater cohesion between the naming of the two protagonists in
comparison with the specification of kin ties and residence. The
exhalation following *ku·nú·la-bù·čike-qay*, by contrast, functions
disjunctively to signal the distinction between the naming of the
protagonists and the specification of their kin relations, but in
the larger context of the succession of phrases closed by exhalation, also creates cohesion. In the second sentence, the
pause with glottal stricture separating line 2 *cʰi·Méw* 'Wolf' from
the rest of its clause both establishes a disjunction which fore-
grounds 'Wolf' and signals the grammatical and semantic cohesion of 'Wolf' with what follows.

In Eastern Pomo myths, significant discourse units larger than
sentences are distinguished by the use of a small number of
sentence initial particles and phrases, very much like what
Hymes (1976, 1977, 1980a,b) has drawn attention to in Chonookan
and other Native American languages. There is, in fact, an important disjunction between the first and second sentence in
this text which is signaled syntactically by the initial phrase in
Sentence 2: *mí·n ʔíkkiliday* ... 'Well, been long like that ...'

At least two levels of discourse unit seem to be distinguished
by these elements. Smaller units, analogous to paragraphs, can
be marked off by *bá·* ... 'Then ...'. Discourse sequences similar to episodes are marked off by *mí·n* plus a verb suffixed
with *-iday*, as in Sentence 2. These episodes show a consistent,
clear-cut, thematic cohesion, as in Sentences 2 through 6 in
this text. They can also include sequences distinguished by
bá·, as in Sentences 5 and 6.

As Hymes (1980a:10-11) has also pointed out, it seems to
facilitate the appreciation of the text by a nonnative speaker if
the thematic cohesion within an episode is reflected by an episode title in the written version of the text. Figure 3 presents
the same portion of an Eastern Pomo myth with lines representing phonological phrases separated by pauses (as described
earlier) and English titles added to suggest the focus of each
episode. Traditional English punctuation is used to signal
sentential organization, as in Figure 2.

In an earlier Georgetown University Round Table paper (McLendon 1977a), I proposed that one must understand the cultural presuppositions which a narrative presumes if one is to appreciate fully the drama, point, and organization of a narrative. Here the two named protagonists are specified to be older and younger brother, and associated with two mammal predators whose range of prey overlaps and who therefore are potential competitors for the same food supply. They are predators who also competed with the Eastern Pomo in the pre-contact period for some of the same prey--small mammals, fish and fish eggs, birds and wildfowl and their eggs. Thus the sibling relationship is associated with potentially competitive animals who are similar in size, type, and habits.

In the second episode of this myth, which begins with Sentence 2, Wolf is described as lying passively, sick with a toothache and not eating--in fact, refusing the quite delicious food that his brother, Old Man Coyote, is described as going to considerable trouble to acquire and prepare for him.

To refuse food is an unusual and deviant thing to do in Eastern Pomo society. It is impolite unless one is too sick to eat, or ritually prepared for doctoring, gambling, or ceremonial activity (all of which involve contact with supernatural forces). When one is ritually prepared, one must abstain from eating a number of foods, particularly meat and fat. If one refuses food and is not sick, then members of the society usually assume the refusal is motivated by exigencies of ritual preparedness, and often become suspicious that the ritual preparedness might be intended to bring them harm. The acceptance or refusal of food is thus a highly charged issue in the traditional society presupposed by the myths. Wolf, it will later be revealed, is actually catching deer magically in a fish net but not sharing his catch with Coyote Old Man (a reprehensible thing to do) and seems likely, in fact, to be ritually prepared.

In this second episode, succinct though it seems, the narrator takes the time to establish the desirability of the food being offered by Coyote, and the care and attractiveness with which it is being prepared, presumably to emphasize and highlight Wolf's refusal to eat, since Wolf's refusal to eat the food which Coyote offers is the point of this episode. Each of the five sentences in the episode makes a distinct and indispensable contribution to making this point through a distinct manipulation of the rhetorical system.

Sentence 2 prepares for Wolf's refusal, and establishes Wolf as of dominant interest in this episode, by naming Wolf with a substantive, in a separate phonological phrase at the beginning of the sentence, set off by the glottal stricture pause, rather than referring to him with a pronoun or kinship term. Wolf's passivity is emphasized by the fact that the noun $c^{hi \cdot} M\acute{e}w$ 'Wolf' is the patient of the main clause verb $qa \cdot m\acute{u}k^{h \cdot} le$. In terms of informational content, it would be equally acceptable to make $m\acute{e}rkille$ 'lie (sick)' the main verb, as in 'Wolf lay there

Figure 3.

SETTING THE STAGE

1. yú xa na·pʰó·le,
   cʰi·Méwqay, ku·nú·la-bù·čikeqày,
   ma·dù·xadiMàɫ,
   ku·šá--da·nò·yòw.

WOLF'S TOOTHACHE

2. mí·n ʔikkiliday xa
   cʰi·Méw
       mí·ɽal ya·ʔó qa·múkʰ·le;
   bá· kʰi qa·ìal mé·rkìlle, ma·ʔáy qa·wálakʰùy.

3. *[míl] ka·té· xa
       ku·nú·la-bù·čikehe·mì·ṗ
       yó·-qa·qò·ɣal kákkìlle,
           ma·ʔáy hí·ṗ;

   báyawa kʰi qu·Mar
       kálkʰi·dìkkìlle;
   báyawa kʰi::
       tu·nú,
       lami mí·n ʔa·m
           kálkʰi·dìkkìlle.

4. báyawa káluhun xa kʰi
   ma·ʔáy hí· kálkʰi·dìʔba·
       cá·rdu·bakin, qo·dɪ́y du·bákin,
       ma·tòlqàkìlin xa kʰi
           ma·dùxacal si·xakʰ·le.

5. bá· xa čaíki·ya·lkìlle:
   "ma·ʔáy ku·hú·ba·ʔkʰùy
       wi ta.
           ya·ʔóhe?
               qa·múqa·mù·lin.

   bá· wi ma·bòya."
   ní·n xa kʰi Né·le,
       **[xa:] cʰi·Mewhe·mì·ṗ

1. They were living,
   Wolf and Old Man Coyote,
   him and his brother,
   at ku·šá--da·nò·yò.

2. Well, been long like that
   Wolf
       had a toothache;
   then he lay there sick, he never eat.

3. Then nevertheless
       Old Man Coyote
           go to Big Valley
               to get some food;

   from there he
       bring home them digger squirrel;
   from there he
       bring home field mice and gopher.

4. When he come home
   that food that he bring
       he clean that, fix it good,
       then he cooks that
           and gives it to his brother.

5. Then he refused:
   "I don't feel
       like eating
           because my tooth
               ache.

   That (my jaw) is swell up."
   that's what he say,
       the Wolf.

6. Then he eat alone, then they sleep;

   Next morning he run down, that's all he been doing.

7. Been that way for a long time
   and he had suspicion
                        on his brother.
         what
         what he been doing
   never eat, laying down
         his jaw swell up.

8. 'I'm gonna find out,'
         that's what he's thinking to himself.

9. Next morning he
         early in the morning
   starts to go
         to Big Valley
                  to get some more food.

OLD MAN COYOTE'S SUSPICIONS

6. bá· xa yu ḱe·hél qa·wá·lkiłle, (hǎ) ʔín ḱá·ya ku·t̓emḱiłle;
   (ʔě:)
   xa·ʔása kʰi yúpʰa ḱákkiłle, bá·ḱa kʰi ye·hé·lle.

7. mí·n ḱa·nkʰ kʰi ye·hé·liday xa
   mí·p̓ ba· pʰi·qotʰke·le
                        ma·dú·xacal,
   čʰi
         čʰí·n ʔín mí·p̓ ba·
   ma·ʔáy qa·wa·lakʰuy mé·rheʔ
         q̓a·wás ma·bó·.

8. "há· ba· ku·t̓ába ʔè,"
   ní·n xa kʰi bálḱ·le.

9. bá· xa kʰi, xa·ʔáqan xa kʰi
                        du·wéMi
   wádu·ḱe·le
         yó·-qa·ǵóyal
                  ma·ʔáy hí·p̓.

*Mr. Holder inserted when transcribing.
**Mr. Holder deleted when transcribing.

sick, not eating, with a toothache'. However, this would have required that Wolf be marked as the agent of the verb, and would have displaced the emphasis from the toothache and Wolf's passivity. The syntactic and prosodic organization of the information in Sentence 2 focuses on Wolf and his toothache, as the result of which he lies sick and does not eat.

Sentence 3 juxtaposes and contrasts intensive activity on Coyote Old Man's part with Wolf's passivity, compressing into a single sentence Coyote Old Man's going hunting in Big Valley (where he apparently has traps set), and his bringing home tasty, tender small mammals to roast on the coals--digger squirrels, field mice, and gophers.

Sentence 3 consists of three independent clauses: (1) Old Man Coyote goes to Big Valley to get some food; (2) from there he brings home digger squirrel; (3) from there he brings home field mice and gopher. These clauses could have been presented as independent sentences without a loss of information, but have been combined into a single sentence presumably because Coyote's hunting activities are not the topic of this episode, but rather provide a background against which Wolf's subsequent behavior will be all the more marked. To present these three independent clauses as separate sentences would give them too much rhetorical weight.

Similarly, $ku \cdot n\acute{u} \cdot la$-$b\grave{u} \cdot \check{c}ike$-$he\,?m\grave{\imath} \cdot \acute{p}$ 'Coyote-Old Man-agent' is not foregrounded in Sentence 3 with a glottal stricture pause as Wolf was in Sentence 2. This is Wolf's episode, although Coyote is doing all the running, and the different prosodic treatments of the names of the two protagonists underscore this fact.

Sentence 4 shifts the focus to the food which Coyote brings back. Greater semantic cohesion between Sentences 3 and 4 than between Sentences 2 and 3 is signaled by the parallelism of $b\acute{a}yawa$ 'from there' introducing three successive clauses. Two of these are adposed to the main clause of Sentence 3, while the third is the first constituent in the main clause of Sentence 4. This intrasentence cohesion is reinforced by the recurrence of the preverb $k\acute{a}l$ 'homewards' preposed to the verbs of all three clauses. However, the fact that the third clause occurs in a separate sentence, and with its verb marked as dependent (with the switch reference suffix $-in$), constitutes a disjunction signaling a change of focus from the action of collecting the game to the game itself, and its careful preparation for eating.

The third parallel clause is followed by the only nominalized clause in this whole sample:

ma·?áy	hi·	kál-kʰi·dî-?bà· ...	'that food that he bring ...'
food	3pCo-Ref.	homewards-bring-that	

This stands out both syntactically and prosodically as one must assume it was meant to do, since it would have been equally possible to convey the propositional content of this clause by a clause embedded with the switch reference suffix *-in*, parallel to the following three clauses on the next two lines, i.e.:

ma·ʔay hi   kal-k^{h}i·din
food 3p Co- homewards-bring-Co Ref
      Ref

giving the sequence:

From there he come home
    he bring home food
        he clean that, fix it good,
           then he cooks that
                and gives it to his brother.

Such a sequence would have left the focus on Coyote and his activities, however. The use of a nominalized clause shifts the focus to the food Coyote is bringing home and thereby builds a transition to the next sentence, in which Wolf rejects this food, which also heightens the impact of the rejection, keeping the focus of attention firmly on Wolf and his behavior.

Sentence 5 presents Wolf's refusal of the carefully prepared food, highlighted by a direct quote. The climax could be intensified, although Mr. Holder did not chose to do so, by using a dramatic voice for Wolf, one which would emphasize the humorousness of the scene, since everyone knows that Wolf has a small pestle in his mouth to simulate the appearance of a swollen jaw caused by an abscessed tooth, which could make him talk oddly.

Once again, it seems significant that only Wolf is given a direct quote in this episode. In terms of information, it would seem equally plausible to report a conversation between Wolf and Coyote over the food. However, direct quotes always carry a potential for heightened dramatic effect and limiting this potential to Wolf is another device for making Wolf dominant in this episode. The fact that Coyote has direct quotes in the next episode signals a shift in focus between these episodes.

Sentence 6 returns to Coyote again, compressing several independent clauses into a single sentence. Once again, Coyote is far more active than Wolf, but the compression of so many independent clauses into a single sentence, with pairs of clauses linked by suppressed pauses and with no explicit arguments expressed in the first two, deemphasizes this activity. Once again, Coyote's activity is backgrounded, providing a coda to the climax of Wolf's refusal, and a transition to the next episode in which Coyote's suspicions are finally aroused. It also emphasizes Coyote's persistence in the praiseworthy and appropriate behavior of hunting for his brother and sharing food with him, even in the face of his brother's deviant and suspicious behavior.

The next episode begins with Sentence 7, which opens with the episode marker *mí·n* plus a verb suffixed with *-iday*. Neither Coyote nor Wolf is named. It is, in fact, not necessary to re-identify the protagonists with nominals from episode to episode, and this is the neutral, unmarked pattern. Wolf's behavior is recapitulated with an interesting shift in emphasis. The putative toothache is no longer mentioned. Instead, only the features observable by Coyote are mentioned: the fact that Wolf is always lying down, does not eat, and has a swollen jaw. This episode is going to provide another explanation for this cluster of observable traits, and the shift in the characterization of Wolf's behavior prepares the listener for the new explanation. Perhaps the most striking change from the preceding episode, however, is that Coyote's activities are no longer compressed several to a single sentence (compare Sentence 9 with Sentence 3) and Coyote now has a direct quote.

Space does not permit a detailed examination of the interlocking and overlapping patterns of cohesion and disjunction which organize this entire text rhetorically. I hope, however, that these few examples suggest how much meaning is conveyed by this process, which a native speaker must be presumed to respond to, at least subliminally, but which a written presentation of the traditional sort given in Figure 1 makes much more obscure.

I think it also suggests that just as a text is a creative, semantic unit and not merely the sum total of a string of sentences, a sentence is also a creative construct, imposed by a speaker on the syntactic and lexical resources of the language by means of the rhetorical system, with a meaning at least partially unique to its occurrence in that particular text.

In fact, a discourse involves a speaker imposing a point of view and a frame of reference on events, thoughts, actions, plots. Imposing a point of view involves choosing the significant components of the experience, event, etc. to be described, presenting them with sufficient communicative competence, background and contextualization to make it possible for one's audience to share one's point of view. This process of selective emphasis and down-playing involves what the Prague School (in the translation of Garvin 1964) has referred to as foregrounding and automatization. Sentences within a discourse are creative constructs within which the speaker manipulates the syntactic, lexical, and phonological resources of the language to assign relative discourse prominence to the phenomena described. This seems to be one of the means by which the individual voices alluded to by Becker (this volume) are achieved.

I hope that these examples have also suggested the desirability of basing syntactic description at least in part on the sorts of sentences which naturally occur in discourse if one is ever to understand fully syntactic structures and their role in language. For example, in the portion of the text presented here, one can see that apposition is one of the most frequently occurring

devices for combining clauses and phrases into sentences in
Eastern Pomo, even clauses which are morphologically also
marked as dependent, as in lines 3 and 4 of Sentence 4, which
translates 'He clean that, fix that good, cooks that ...' The
verb in each of these three clauses is suffixed with the switch
reference suffix -in, but the clauses are juxtaposed without an
intervening clitic xa, signalling that they are in apposition to
each other.

The single nominalized clause in this entire sample, which
also occurs in Sentence 4, stands out both syntactically and
prosodically, as discussed earlier. Nominalized clauses are
rare in Eastern Pomo and always seem to have a disjunctive,
topic-shifting rhetorical function, as in Sentence 4. Although
one can translate this nominalized clause with a relative clause
in English, it seems clearly to differ from English relative
clauses in function as well as structure. This difference would
be hard to recognize were one to study clause nominalization in
Eastern Pomo only through sentences elicited as translations of
English sentences with relative clauses. Such a technique, in
fact, usually elicits switch reference embedded adverbial
clauses rather than nominalized clauses, perhaps because the
topic-shifting function of nominalized clauses is hard to make
clear without a discourse context.

The rhetorical system of a language, then, is not simply a
matter of style or optional choices. It is the communicative
principle which organizes discourse, determining sentence
boundaries, paragraphs, and episodes. It is the means through
which speakers impose a point of view on what they say. When
systematically reflected in the written form of oral texts, it
makes transparent the organization of a discourse and the art
inherent in all literature, but rarely studied if the language is
unwritten.

NOTES

It is a pleasure to acknowledge that the research on which
this paper draws was supported at various periods by NIMH
grant R01 MH 22887, a Guggenheim Fellowship, a City University of New York Faculty Research Award, and a Fellowship
from the Smithsonian Institution. Versions of this paper were
also read at the Conference on American Indian Languages at
the 1980 American Anthropological Association Meetings in
Washington, D.C., the March meeting of the Albert Gallatin
Philological Society, and the 1981 Hokan-Penutian Conference
held at Sonoma State University, Rohnert Park, California; I am
grateful for the comments and discussions provided on these
occasions. This paper has also profited a great deal from discussions with Anthony Woodbury, as well as with William Bright
and Joel Sherzer. My greatest debt is to Dell Hymes, who
both through his own pioneering research and in conversation

and correspondence, encouraged and urged me to attend to the meaning in narrative form.

1. Erickson and Scollon in their papers in this volume draw attention to the metrical organization of talk. The metrical structure which Dell Hymes so convincingly finds may reflect the fact that talk is metrical as much as that Native American oral literature is poetry.

REFERENCES

Bright, William. 1979a. A Karok myth in 'measured verse': The translation of a performance. Journal of California and Great Basin Anthropology 1.117-123.

Bright, William. 1979b. Coyote gives salmon and acorns to humans. In: Coyote Stories II. Edited by Martha Kendall. International Journal of American Linguistics, Native American Texts Series, Monographs. Ann Arbor, Mich.: University Microfilms.

Bright, William. 1980. Coyote's journey. American Indian Culture and Research Journal 4(1-2).21-48.

Garvin, Paul. 1964. A Prague School reader on esthetics, literary structure, and style. Washington, D.C.: Georgetown University Press.

Halliday, M. A. K., and Ruqaiya Hasan. 1976. Cohesion in English. London: Longman.

Hymes, Dell. 1976. Louis Simpson's 'The deserted boy'. Poetics 5.119-155.

Hymes, Dell. 1977. Discovering oral performance and measured verse in American Indian narrative. New Literary History 8.431-457.

Hymes, Dell. 1980a. Tonkawa poetics: John Rush Buffalo's 'Coyote and Eagle's daughter'. In: On linguistic anthropology: Essays in honor of Harry Hoijer. Edited by Jacques Maquet. Malibu, Calif.: Undena Publications for the UCLA Department of Anthropology. 33-88.

Hymes, Dell. 1980b. Particle, pause and pattern in American Indian narrative verse. American Indian Culture and Research Journal 4(4).7-51.

Hymes, Dell. 1981. In vain I tried to tell you. Studies in Native American Literature, 1. Philadelphia: University of Pennsylvania Press.

McLendon, Sally. 1975. The Eastern Pomo language. University of California Publications in Linguistics, 74. Berkeley: University of California Press.

McLendon, Sally. 1977a. Cultural presuppositions and discourse analysis: Patterns of presupposition and assertion of information in Eastern Pomo and Russian narrative. In: Georgetown University Round Table on Languages and Linguistics 1977. Edited by Muriel Saville-Troike. Washington, D.C.: Georgetown University Press. 153-190.

McLendon, Sally. 1977b. Bear kills her own daughter-in-law,
Deer. In: Northern Californian texts. Edited by Shirley
Silver and Victor Golla. International Journal of American
Linguistics, Native American Texts Series 3.26-65.
McLendon, Sally. 1978. Coyote and the ground squirrels.
In: Coyote stories. Edited by William Bright. International
Journal of American Linguistics, Native American Text Series,
Monograph 1.87-111. Ann Arbor, Mich.: University Micro-
films.
McLendon, Sally. 1979. Clitics, clauses, closure and dis-
course in Eastern Pomo. In: Proceedings of the Fifth
Annual Meeting of the Berkeley Linguistics Society. 637-646.
Berkeley, Calif.: Berkeley Linguistics Society.
Tedlock, Dennis. 1971. On the translation of style in oral
narrative. Journal of American Folklore 84.114-133.
Tedlock, Dennis. 1972. Pueblo literature: Style and
verisimilitude. In: New perspectives on the Pueblos.
Edited by Alfonso Ortiz. Albuquerque: University of New
Mexico Press. 222-224.
Tedlock, Dennis. 1977. Towards an oral poetics. New Literary
History 8.507-519.
Tedlock, Dennis. 1978. Finding the center: Narrative poetry
of the Zuni Indians. From performances in the Zuni by
Andrew Peynetsa and Walter Sanchez. Lincoln: University
of Nebraska Press. New preface. (First published, New
York: Dial Press, 1972).
Tedlock, Dennis. 1979. Beyond logocentrism: Trace and
voice among the Quiche Maya. Boundary 2.8.321-333.
Woodbury, Anthony. (in press) Narratives, stories and tales
from Chevak, Alaska. Fairbanks: Alaska Native Language
Center, University of Alaska.
Woodbury, Anthony. (1980). Rhetorical structure in Central
Yup'ik Eskimo narrative. Paper presented at Winter Meetings
of the Linguistic Society of America, San Antonio, Texas.

THE INTERPLAY OF STRUCTURE AND FUNCTION
IN KUNA NARRATIVE, OR:
HOW TO GRAB A SNAKE IN THE DARIEN

Joel Sherzer
University of Texas at Austin

This paper is intended as a contribution to a discourse-centered approach to the study of the language-culture-society relationship. One aspect of the recent interest on the part of several disciplines in the detailed and precise analysis of discourse is a focus on structure and style in such a way that it seems difficult if not incorrect to make a distinction between ordinary language on the one hand, and literary and poetic language on the other. All discourse has features that have characteristically and traditionally been considered to be literary, and analysis of poetic structure is often what discourse analysis is all about. So rather than shove off the study of metaphor, foregrounding, cohesion, line and verse structure, dramatization, and grammatical aspects of style on literary critics, we find that attention to such matters is basic to the work of linguists, anthropologists, and folklorists.

In fact, as has recently been stressed in a series of papers by Dell Hymes, analysis of the poetic organization of discourse, especially narrative, is a logical continuation of the Boas, Sapir, Whorf tradition in anthropology and linguistics. The concern is not with the relationship between grammar, conceived in a narrow abstract sense, and thought, as one limiting and probably dead-ended interpretation of the Sapir-Whorf hypothesis would have it, but rather with the poetic and rhetorical organization of discourse as an expression and actualization of the intimate intersection of language and culture. As but six of many quite distinct manifestations of this trend toward consideration of poetic, literary aspects of and approaches to discourse as central to the study of language and speech, we can point to Bauman's (1977) focus on culturally and socially situated performance as the locus of verbal art; Friedrich's

(1979) studies of the symbolic and poetic potentialities of grammar; Gumperz' (1971) studies of code-switching and contextualization, in which such poetic processes as foregrounding and
metaphor are shown to be at the heart of everyday communication; Hymes' (1977, in press) grammatical/cultural/rhetorical
analyses of North American Indian narrative, in which it is
argued that narrative is central to the creative expression of
what culture is all about; Labov's (1972b) analysis of the structure of the quite literary personal narratives that occur within
everyday conversational interaction; and the work of Tedlock
(1978) in the analysis and especially the translation of American
Indian performance style. A somewhat related approach is
Geertz' (1973) thick description of cultural texts, which, while
not texts in the sense that the term text is usually used by
linguists, are approached in a literary way.

In addition, my approach in this paper involves another important aspect of the analysis of discourse--attention to and
indeed focus on the intersection and interplay between structure and function. I examine in some detail a single narrative
in use among the Kuna Indians of Panama, a magical chant used
to grab a dangerous snake and raise it in the air. An investigation of this chant from phonological details to overall narrative organization reveals a constant and dynamic interplay and
intersection of structure and function. Attention to this interplay is crucial to an understanding of each of the devices in
the text, the meaning of the text as a whole, the role of the
text in the event in which it occurs, and the significance of
the text in Kuna culture and society more generally. It is not
my purpose here to try to clarify or elaborate on the different
meanings and uses that have been given to the concept of
function. My use of this concept is in keeping, in a general
sense, with the way it has been used by the various researchers who take a multifunctional approach to the study of language use. [1]

The Kuna are a society of more than 25,000 agriculturalists,
most of whom inhabit a string of islands along the northeast
coast of Panama, known as San Blas. While there are literate
Kuna, their discourse is essentially oral. The Kuna have a
rich, complex, and varied system of language and speech, which
can be viewed in relation to Kuna politics, religion, curing,
magic, and puberty practices, but which can also be studied
in and for itself, in terms of textual, discourse, and literary
properties. It is important to stress that there is no single
feature which characterizes Kuna discourse as a whole, but
that there is rather a set or complex of such characteristic
features. Furthermore, it is not possible to use these features to identify Kuna language and speech diagnostically as
oral rather than as written. While some of these features may
turn out to be more characteristic of oral than of written language and speech, others are clearly found in written discourse.
And much more cross-cultural research is needed before it can

be determined if there is a set of features which uniquely
characterize oral language, speech, literature, and culture.
The text I discuss here is one of the many quite diverse examples of Kuna discourse.

I am going to set the scene for my discussion with a very
brief overview of the types of Kuna narrative. One useful way
to classify Kuna narratives is as either first person narratives
or third person narratives. First person narratives can in
turn be grouped into, on the one hand, new information narratives, characteristic of informal occasions and especially informal conversations and greetings, and, on the other hand,
retellings, in which personal experiences are retold in a formal
and often ritual language and style, characteristic of the speaking and chanting of the Kuna gathering house, the public,
political, and social meeting place. Third person narratives
are also quite common and appreciated among the Kuna. They
are the form used for the performance, in a ritual language,
of tribal traditions, myths, legends, history, and stories.
Public performances of these tribal traditions in third person
narrative form are typically used as models of good or bad
behavior by narrators. They are part of the exhortative
rhetoric of Kuna public politics and oratory. In a certain
sense, then, these third person narratives are understood to
be embedded within a first person form: 'I exhort you to do
X.' In addition, one of the salient devices of third person and,
indeed, all narration among the Kuna is the incorporation of
direct quotations, including reported conversations, into the
narration. This is so common in Kuna speech that the actual
speaker is often not the main narrating voice of the narrative
he is telling. In these dramatizations, first person narratives
are embedded into third person narratives. This interplay of
first and third person narrative, including especially the embedding of narrator within narrator, is a basic characteristic
of Kuna discourse (see Sherzer in press).

Another type of third person narrative is the magical *ikar*
'way' or 'text' which is the central and crucial act in Kuna
curing and magical events. Magical *ikars* are memorized chants
in the esoteric ritual language of the spirit world.[2] They are
performed by specialists, *wisits* 'knowers' of them, and addressed to particular representatives of the spirit world. Kuna
magic operates in the following way. The spirit addressees of
a magical *ikar* are convinced by means of the *ikar* that the performing specialist is able to control them, that he knows their
language and every aspect of their essence and existence--the
location and nature of their origin, their present abode, their
physical and behavioral characteristics, and their names. After
the demonstration of this potential to control, the *ikar* describes
precisely what action the specialist wants to occur--for example, the curing of a disease or the grabbing and raising of a
snake. Ideally, the spirits, upon hearing and understanding
the narrative, and because of hearing and understanding the

narrative, do what is described in it. Kuna magical texts are thus dramatic scripts for action performed by a live narrator and played out by spirit actors. [3] Because the spirit world underlies and animates the real, actual physical world, what occurs in the spirit world is subsequently played out in the actual world. In this sense, the third person narratives of Kuna magic can be understood to be embedded within a first person command of the form: 'I tell you, that is, I command you X.' Magical *ikars* are performative in the sense that their performance is essential to the successful completion of a magical action; saying is doing in that correct narration not only describes an action or event, but actually accomplishes it by causing it to occur. Kuna magic contains no hocus pocus or abracadabra. [4] Rather, it is based on a highly intelligible language. This language is intelligible in two senses. First, although it is not understandable to most human nonspecialists, it is completely and necessarily understandable to the spirit addressees. Second, it is analyzable, in the sense of linguistic analysis, phoneme by phoneme, morpheme by morpheme, word by word, and line by line.

I turn now to an exploration of one magical *ikar*, *nakpe ikar* 'the way of the snake', used to grab and raise a dangerous snake on the performing specialist's arm, in terms of the interplay of structure and function. This chant is one of a set of magical *ikars* known as *kaeti*, literally 'grabber'. Other *ikars* in this set are used to attract bees and wasps and to grasp a hot iron rod. *Kaetis*, like other magical *ikars*, are performed in a variety of contexts. They are performed in the actual act of control--for example, raising the snake. And they are performed for practice, for learning and teaching, for pleasure, and to remind the ever present and listening spirits that the specialist has the potential to control them. The public, verbal display of knowledge and potential power, to both the human and spirit worlds, is as important as, if not more important than, the physical act of grabbing the snake. The particular performance of *nakpe ikar* that I discuss here was a practice session by a specialist-knower.

Why snakes? The Darien jungle in which the Kuna walk, farm, and hunt is the site of some of the most dangerous snakes in the world. This is reason enough to be worried about snakes and to want to be able to control them. In addition, according to Kuna belief, snake spirits are among the most evil of spirits and, like other animal spirits, have the potential to cause serious disease, without the actual, physical animal necessarily biting or even coming into contact with the victim. [5] It is no wonder that, in addition to *nakpe ikar*, there is a complex of magical chants whose purpose is to calm and control various snakes and snake spirits. Let us now examine the text of *nakpe ikar* itself.

The performance of *nakpe ikar* that I recorded lasts eight minutes. It opens with the setting of the scene: as the specialist is working in his jungle farm, the snake appears.[6]

The specialist [is] at the edge of his field.
The specialist is surveying his farm.

When the sun is halfway up in the sky.
The specialist is surveying his farm.
At the edge of his field.

The specialist is sharpening his little knife.
He is sharpening his little knife.
With a file.

When he finishes sharpening his little knife.
When he finishes sharpening his knife.
Then the specialist moves.
Then the specialist advances.

When the sun is halfway up in the sky.

The specialist is working with his little knife.
He is working with his little knife.

He is cutting small bushes.
He is clearing small bushes.

As he is cutting small bushes.
As he is clearing small bushes.
Machi oloaktikunappi nele [the snake's spirit name][7] is present.

   The snake is described.

Machi oloaktikunappi nele raises his chin.
His chin seems white.
Under the grass cuttings.

Machi oloaktikunappi nele sticks out the point of his tongue.
He sticks out the point of his tongue.
It looks like the dark blue of the koka plant dye.
The point of his tongue salivates.
Machi oloaktikunappi nele is present.

Indeed Machi oloaktikunappi nele is present.
In his abode under the grass cuttings.

   The snake verbally challenges the specialist.

Machi oloaktikunappi nele calls.
'How well do you know the abode of my origin?'
Machi oloaktikunappi calls.

And the specialist responds to the challenge.

The specialist counsels Machi oloaktikunappi.

'Indeed [I] know the abode of your origin.
Indeed [I] have come to play in the abode of your origin.
Indeed [I] have come to encircle the abode of your origin.'
He counsels Machi oloaktikunappi.

The snake prepares himself for the contest.

Machi oloaktikunappi nele.

He prepares his silver hooks.
He moves his silver hooks across his mouth.
He moves his silver hooks up and down.
Machi oloaktikunappi nele is present.

The specialist in turn prepares himself by applying special
medicines.

Indeed the specialist fortifies his purpa [soul].
Indeed he augments his purpa.
He gives nika [strength] to his hand.
He puts a lake of medicine on his hand.

The specialist competes with Machi oloaktikunappi nele.
He is counseling Machi oloaktikunappi nele.

The specialist is calling to Puna olotuktutili [name of bland
medicine].
He is calling to Puna olotuktutili.
He is calling to Oloputi nolomakke tule [name of medicine which
renders blowgun weak].
He is calling to Oloputi nupyasae tule [name of medicine which
causes blowgun to double up].

Indeed the specialist is ready for Machi oloaktikunappi nele.
Indeed his purpa [soul] is augmented.
Indeed his purpa is strong.
He competes with Machi oloaktikunappi nele.

Then comes the verbal display of power. The specialist
shows that he knows the snake initimately by listing the
parts of the snake's body in a series of lines.

He is counseling Machi oloaktikunappi nele.

Indeed Machi oloaktikunappi nele is present.

'The specialist knows well your purpa [soul]'
The specialist is saying.
'He captures your purpa.'
The specialist is saying.

'Indeed how your lips were placed on.
The specialist knows well.'
The specialist is saying.

'How your chin was put in place.
How your lower chin was formed.
The specialist knows well.'
The specialist is saying.

Indeed the specialist is saying.
'How your pupils were formed.
The specialist knows well.'
The specialist is saying.

The specialist is saying.

'How the point of your tongue was put in place.
The specialist knows well.'
The specialist is saying.
He counsels Machi oloaktikunappi nele.

Indeed the specialist.
'How your golden arrow was put in place.
How your golden arrow was buried in.
The specialist knows well.'
The specialist is saying.
He counsels Machi oloaktikunappi nele.

Indeed he counsels Machi oloaktikunappi nele.

Indeed Machi oloaktikunappi nele.
'How your necktie was hung on.
The specialist knows well.'
The specialist is saying.
He counsels Machi oloaktikunappi nele.

Indeed the specialist.

'How the venom of your golden arrow was put in place.
The specialist knows well.'
The specialist is saying.
He counsels Machi oloaktikunappi nele.

The specialist.
'How your flat head was formed.
The specialist knows well.'
The specialist is saying.

Indeed the specialist.

The specialist is saying.
'How your spinal cord was put in place.
How your spinal cord was made flexible.
The specialist knows well.'

Then there is a description of the desired magical action itself, the raising of the snake.

Machi oloaktikunappi is under the grass cuttings.
The vine [euphemism for snake] is dragging [in horizontal position].
The vine is turning over [in horizontal position].

The specialist is signalling toward his hand.
Toward his hand.
The vine has almost arrived, almost arrived.
He wags his golden blowgun.
Indeed on the specialist's hand.

The uttering of the performative formula:

'"Simply I raise you" I am saying.'

And the act is done.

He counsels Machi oloaktikunappi.

On his hand.
The vine is dragging [in hanging position].
The vine is turning over [in hanging position].

The snake admits defeat.

Machi oloaktikunappi calls.
'My specialist, [you] know well my purpa [soul]' he says.
Machi oloaktikunappi calls.

And he expresses his fear.

Indeed Machi oloaktikunappi is calling [in hanging position].
'My specialist, what will [you] do to me, will [you] kill me?'
Machi oloaktikunappi is calling [in hanging position].

Having won the contest and controlled the snake, the specialist shows himself to be friendly and compassionate.

Indeed the specialist counsels Machi oloaktikunappi.

'How indeed could [I] kill you? We have just become good
  friends.
How indeed could [I] kill you?'
He counsels Machi oloaktikunappi.

This is the text of *nakpe ikar*. I turn now to an examination of the various devices which are used to structure this
text. *Nakpe ikar* is in a linguistic variety and style which is
shared by Kuna magical specialists and the spirit world and
differs from everyday colloquial Kuna along several dimensions.
The most salient and diagnostic phonological characteristic of
this magical language is that many vowels which are deleted in
everyday, colloquial speech are not deleted in the ritual chanting of magical *ikars*. As a result, various consonantal assimi-
lation processes that automatically follow vowel deletion do not
occur in these chants (see Sherzer 1973). Thus *palitak-
kekwichiye* 'he is surveying' in *nakpe ikar* would be *partayk-
wisye* in colloquial Kuna; *osamakkenaiye* 'he is clearing' would
be *osamaynaye*; and *sokekwichiye* 'he is saying' would be
sokkwisye. Both the presence of these underlying vowels
(from a generative point of view) and the melodic patterning
of the chanting contribute to the phonological marking, in a
sociolinguistic sense, of this ritual magical variety and style.
They are also an important aspect of the esthetic, verbally
artistic quality of Kuna magical texts. In addition, melodic
shapes contribute to the marking of the poetic line structure
of the text.
  With regard to morpho-syntactic structure, *nakpe ikar*, like
all magical chants, is marked by the use of a particular set of
nominal and verbal prefixes and suffixes. These forms have
several functions, which operate simultaneously. They are
part of the structural apparatus of the grammar of the magical
linguistic variety, serving as nominalizers, stem formatives,
and tense-aspect markers. They are sociolinguistic markers of
this particular linguistic variety, distinguishing it from other
Kuna linguistic varieties and styles. They contribute to the
esthetics of magical texts in three ways--they increase the
length of words, especially in terms of the number of morphemes
per word; they are ornamental embellishments; and they are
one of the devices used to mark poetic lines.
  There are also morphemes which, while they occur in colloquial Kuna, have a greater frequency and a different and
wider range of meanings and functions in magical chants such
as *nakpe ikar*. An excellent example is the suffix *-ye*, which
is used in colloquial Kuna as an optative and emphatic with
verbs and an emphatic and vocative with nouns. It is also

used as a quotative marker. It occurs with great frequency in the language of magic, perhaps stressing the optative mood of magical chants. But it is also a place filler, giving the performer time to remember the next line of these memorized chants. *-Ye* can be viewed as a verbally artistic embellisher as well; it is sometimes repeated two or three times. And, since it often occurs at the ends of lines, it serves, along with other devices, as a poetic line marker.

Morphological structure is directly involved in the magical functioning of *nakpe ikar*. A set of four optional verbal suffixes can be used in Kuna to specify the position of the subject of the verb, as either *-kwichi* 'standing', *-sii* 'sitting', *-mai* 'lying' or 'horizontal', or *-nai* 'hanging, as in the air'. This optional grammatical category is crucial to the climactic moment of *nakpe ikar*, the actual raising of the snake in the air. In this section of the text, the snake is first described as dragging and turning over in a *-mai* 'horizontal' position, that is, free on the ground. After the performative formula, '"Simply I raise you" I am saying,' during which the snake is raised in the air, it is again described as dragging and turning over, but this time in a *-nai* 'hanging' position. That is, while the text never explicitly and specifically states that the specialist has actually succeeded in grabbing and raising the snake, the simple, economic shift in verbal suffixes, from *-mai* 'horizontal' to *-nai* 'hanging', on the same pair of verbs, dragging and turning over, quite poetically and powerfully signals that the snake is in the air, on the specialist's hand.

The process of moving from *-mai* to *-nai* involves the projection of a paradigm syntagmatically, the classic Jakobsonian definition of poetry. And this occurs as the magical, powerful climax of the text, addressed to the spirit of the snake itself, and thus precisely convincing it that it has been controlled, grabbed, and raised, and causing all of this to occur in actuality. This is a true case of poetry in action. [8] The poetic-magical potential of Kuna grammatical structure is actualized in these crucial lines of *nakpe ikar*, in which grammar becomes poetry and poetry becomes magic. [9] A number of scholars have recently argued that a most fruitful way to conceive of the Sapir-Whorf hypothesis is not in terms of a matching up of language and culture as abstract separate entities, but rather as a dynamic, integrated actualization of language in culturally meaningful and socially situated discourse (see especially Friedrich 1979 and Hymes in press.) The actualization of the poetic-magical potential of the Kuna suffixes of position in *nakpe ikar* provides an excellent example.

Another salient aspect of *nakpe ikar*, which must be approached in terms of the interplay of structure and function, is lexicon. Like all magical chants, *nakpe ikar* uses the vocabulary of the linguistic variety particular to the spirit world. In fact, this vocabulary is the most diagnostic marker of this linguistic variety. Many words in *nakpe ikar* are

entirely different from the corresponding words in colloquial
Kuna and have no meaning at all in colloquial Kuna. Thus,
'knife' is *esa* in colloquial Kuna and *ipetintuli* in *nakpe ikar*;
'kill' is *opurkwe* in colloquial Kuna and *kunnukke* in *nakpe
ikar*; 'small' is *pippikwa* in colloquial Kuna and *totokkwa* in
nakpe ikar. In addition, there are words in *nakpe ikar* which
have a different meaning in colloquial Kuna, resulting in a
figurative, metaphorical effect. Thus, the fangs of the snake
are described as *mananswelu* 'silver hooks', *olosiku* 'golden
arrow', or *oloputi* 'golden blowgun'; and the stripe along the
snake's body is described as his *mussue tukku* 'necktie'.

While this comparison of colloquial Kuna and spirit Kuna seems
to reveal a metaphorical structure in the lexicon of *nakpe ikar*,
according to Kuna belief, personal, creative metaphor is not involved here, although such metaphor is highly developed in
other styles of Kuna discourse, most notably in political oratory.
Rather, in the spirit world, snakes, like humans, have arrows,
blowguns, and neckties. This knowledge, and especially its
expression in the text of *nakpe ikar*, is an important aspect of
the specialist's verbal demonstration to the snake spirit that he
knows all there is to know about snakes, and especially, snake
spirits. In addition, the associated metaphorical effect, like all
the other poetic features in the chant, is pleasing to and appreciated by the spirit world and plays a significant role in the
magical, controlling power of the text.

Related to the lexical structure of *nakpe ikar* and also essential to its magical power is the use of names. A crucial element
in controlling an object is knowing its spirit name. Constantly
labelling the snake *Machi oloaktikunappi nele*, its spirit name,
is another aspect of the specialist's demonstration to the spirit
that he has intimate knowledge of it and can thus control it.
It is interesting that at the climactic moment of the raising of
the snake, the snake is no longer labelled *Machi oloaktikunappi
nele*, but rather by the colloquial metaphorical euphemism *kali*
'vine'. This is an intriguing insertion of everyday language
into a magical text. The names of the medicines used by the
specialist to protect himself against the snake involve still another type of verbal magical power. Like the snake's name,
they are the medicines' spirit names and knowledge of them is
essential to being able to control and thus use them. But in
addition, the text, by means of the creation of names, endows
the spirit medicines with properties which are encoded in these
names. Thus, *oloputi nolomakke tule* (literally: 'weak blowgun
medicine') renders the snake's fangs ineffective and *oloputi
nupyasae tule* (literally: 'double up blowgun medicine') takes
the strength out of the fangs. To describe an action in the
spirit language causes that action to occur; to name an object
causes the object to exist and to have the properties encoded
in the name.

Another feature of the vocabulary of *nakpe ikar*, which is
very characteristic of Kuna magical chants in particular and

all Kuna discourse more generally, is a reflexive and meta-communicative focus and oriéntation. *Nakpe ikar* is constantly pointing inward to itself, situating itself as a communicative event, and specifying what is happening within this event at the very moment that it occurs. In particular, the text is literally punctuated by the verbs *uanae* 'counsel' and *soke* 'say', as the performer-specialist insistently informs the snake's spirit that he is counseling it and telling it to do certain things. In addition to their intersecting referential and metacommunicative function, these two verbs, *uanae* and *soke*, occurring as the last word in a line, contribute to the formal marking of poetic lines and structured groups of lines. And they are also place fillers and holders, giving the performer time to think of his next memorized line.

I turn now to a pervasive feature of the structural organization of *nakpe ikar* and indeed of all Kuna magical chants, which is also extremely common in both oral and written ritual and poetic discourse around the world--syntactic and semantic parallelism. There are various types of parallelism operating in *nakpe ikar*.

There are certain crucial lines which are repeated identically, or almost identically,[10] throughout the text, punctuating it by marking the boundaries of sections within it. Examples are the lines: *Machi oloaktikunappi is present; the specialist counsels the snake; the specialist is saying; the specialist knows well.*

Adjacent lines are linked by several types of parallelism.

Two lines are identical, with the exception of the deletion of a single word:

Machi oloaktikunappi nele sticks out the point of his tongue.
            sticks out the point of his tongue.

Two lines differ in nonreferential morphemes (in addition to the possible deletion of a word):

The specialist is sharpening (*nuptulu-makke-kwichiye*) his little knife.
         is sharpening (*nuptulu-sae-kwichiye*)   his little knife.

in which the verb stem formative *-makke* of the first line is replaced by the verb stem formative *-sae* of the next line.

Two lines are identical except for the replacement of a single word, the two words being slightly different in meaning and within the same semantic field:

He is cutting small bushes.
He is clearing small bushes.

The specialist moves.
The specialist advances.

Another parallelistic pattern involves not single pairs of
lines, as in the preceding examples, but rather an entire set
of lines, a stanza-like frame which is repeated, each time with
a change in the word used to fill a particular slot. In the long
section of the text in which the specialist demonstrates his intimate knowledge of the parts of the snake's body, the following
frame is repeated:

'How your [body part] was formed in its place.
The specialist knows well.'
The specialist is saying.

In this way, all of the body parts of the snake are listed.
It seems worth noting here, since one of the themes of this
Georgetown University Round Table is the differences between
oral and written discourse, and since Goody (1977) and others
have pointed to the list as a characteristic of written discourse,
that this example of the use of parallelism to perform orally a
list of items is but one of the many such cases in Kuna and
other nonliterate societies. In fact, one of the functions of
this kind of frame-parallelism in oral discourse seems to be
precisely the memorization and performance of lists.[11]
Parallelism thus serves a set of intersecting and overlapping
functions in *nakpe ikar*. It often involves the syntagmatic
projection of a paradigm or taxonomy (of body parts, medicines, or movements). In addition to its poetic function, this
process of projecting taxonomies onto a fixed line, verse, or
stanza enables the generation of a long text or portion of text.
Length is an important aspect of the magical power of chants
like *nakpe ikar*. The more recalcitrant the snake, the longer
the specialist will make the text, precisely by generating more
lines by means of parallelistic structures. At the same time,
the performer's intimate knowledge of the nature of the spirit
world, especially its parts and taxonomic classification, is also
displayed by parallelistic structures and processes. And since
specialists must memorize these texts, parallelistic line, verse,
and stanza frames seem to provide mnemonic aids to memorization. Finally, this extensive parallelism aids in actual performance, providing both time and procedures for moving from line
to line, narrative description to narrative description. It is
no wonder, given these various functions, that parallelism is
so pervasive in *nakpe ikar*.
The last aspect of the structure of *nakpe ikar* that I have
chosen to examine is the crucial interplay of first, second, and
third person within the narrative. *Nakpe ikar*, like all Kuna
magical chants, is a third person narrative. Although the
actual performer is the specialist who will raise a snake, the
text describes the spirit world in which both specialist and
snake are third persons. But at various points in the text,
the dialogue between the specialist spirit and the snake spirit
is quoted and the pronouns 'I' and 'you' are used. 'You' is

used in many lines of quoted dialogue to refer to the specialist spirit and the snake spirit, and 'I' is used in several lines of quoted dialogue to refer to the snake spirit. However, 'I' is used to refer to the specialist spirit in only one line, the climactic moment of the text, the performative formula within the performative text, the actual moment of the grabbing and raising of the snake, the crucial line, '"Simply I raise you" I am saying', in which the double quotation marks within single quotation marks indicate that the actual specialist is quoting the specialist spirit who is quoting himself.[12] In this climactic moment of *nakpe ikar*, the grammatical category of person, like other features in the structure of the text, serves several functions, including especially poetic and magical ones. Once again, grammar becomes poetry and poetry becomes magic.

In this paper I have explored the structure of a single Kuna narrative, *nakpe ikar*, a magical chant used to grab and raise a dangerous snake. At one level my approach has been analogous to the linguistic analysis of a poem. And this is part of my point in this exercise, since analysis of *nakpe ikar* requires recognition of its poetic properties.[13] But at the same time, examination of this magical narrative is intended as an example of one kind of ethnographic approach to discourse. Attention to the constant and dynamic interplay of structure and function in *nakpe ikar* reveals a complex web of relations within Kuna language, culture, and society, which involves the strategic importance of snakes in Kuna culture; the relationship between humans and animals and plants; the use of language and speech to display knowledge, respect, and control; the relationship between the world of humans and the world of spirits, mediated by the poetic-rhetoric of memorized oral chants; the role of grammar, parallelism, metaphor, and narrative structure in this poetic rhetoric; and the belief in the power and ability of language to solve specific problems.

NOTES

I am most grateful for the comments of the following individuals on earlier versions of this paper: Richard Bauman, Mac Chapin, James Howe, Dina Sherzer, and Anselmo Urrutia.

1. See, for example, Givón (1979), Grossman, San, and Vance (1975), Halliday (1973), Hymes (1974), Jakobson (1960), and Silverstein (1976). My use of the term function in relation to structure is not intended to indicate an adherence to the way these notions have been related by certain schools of social anthropology, especially British. Rather, I refer here to an emerging focus on the interplay of structure and function in recent research in the analysis of discourse.

2. In the performance of magical *ikars* for curing and disease prevention, slight variations of an essentially nonreferential nature are tolerated, involving very superficial aspects of the phonology and morphology of noun and verb suffixation.

The magical texts performed for Kuna girls' puberty rites by
contrast are completely fixed. Not the slightest variation in
phonology or morphology is tolerated. The degree to which
Kuna puberty rites texts are fixed in form is reflected in a
personal experience. In 1970 I made a tape recording of a
puberty rites specialist teaching a text to several students.
Between 1970 and 1978 I never discussed this text with him.
In March of 1979, nine years after the original recording, I
brought him a transcription I had made of the text, in order
to translate it into ordinary colloquial Kuna, from which it
differs considerably. Since he does not read or write, he
asked me to read him the text. I did so line by line and he
translated each line into colloquial Kuna. Typically, I barely
began a line and he finished it, never missing a morpheme or
even a phoneme from my transcription. In a few cases where
I misread a tiny detail of my own writing, he corrected me.
The Kuna thus provide still another counterexample (for many
others see Finnegan 1977) to the view (see Goody 1977, Lord
1960, Ong 1977) that there is no pure, verbatim memorization
of fixed texts in nonliterate, oral societies.

3. I am indebted to Chapin (1981) for the comparison of
Kuna magical texts with dramatic scripts.

4. That is, the magical *ikars* described here. Another form
of discourse sometimes used in magic is the *sekretto*, a short
verbal charm which involves a considerable amount of non-
intelligible, nonanalyzable language.

5. Such quasi-metaphorical disease causation theories, involving animal spirits, are found in other societies, for example, the Ainu (see Ohnuki-Tierney 1977). For the details of
Kuna theories and practices in relation to disease and curing,
see Chapin (1981).

6. *Nakpe ikar* was performed by Pranki Pilos of Mulatuppu
on March 2, 1971. In this translated presentation, lines are
determined by melodic shape and pauses. In Pilos' performance, groups of lines (verses in Hymes' 1977 terminology) were
marked by a cough and an extra long pause. I have represented this structure here by leaving an extra space between
lines.

7. The ordinary Kuna word for this snake is *tappa*, a small
pit viper.

8. It is interesting to compare this case of poetry in action
with the sequence of increasingly powerful sounds (ritual insults) reported by Labov for a group of Harlem Blacks (Labov
1972a: 349):

Junior: I'll take your mother.
Rel: I took your mother.

Both the Kuna magical text and the Harlem sounding bring
about their results with what Labov terms the 'minimax' solution: 'striking semantic shifts with minimal changes of form.'

Labov's comments after the oral presentation of my paper at
The Georgetown University Round Table called my attention to
the similarities between these otherwise very different forms
of discourse.

9. See Rosaldo (1975) and Tambiah (1968) for studies of the
role of poetry in the magic of other societies.

10. I include identical repetition as a type of parallelism
here, although other students of parallelism might not, because
of its role in the overall parallelistic patterning and structuring
of Kuna magical texts.

11. Erickson (this volume) examines another, quite different,
function of listing, in an American conversational setting.

12. I have used [I] within brackets in other lines within
the text where I felt that the English translation required it.
The brackets are intended to indicate that the original Kuna
version did not have the Kuna word *ani* 'I'.

13. For a more general discussion of Kuna poetics, see
Sherzer (1977).

REFERENCES

Bauman, Richard. 1977. Verbal art as performance. Rowley,
Mass.: Newbury House.

Chapin, Mac. 1981. Medicine among the San Blas Kuna.
Ph.D. dissertation. University of Arizona.

Finnegan, Ruth. 1977. Oral poetry. Cambridge, England:
Cambridge University Press.

Friedrich, Paul. 1979. Language, context, and the imagination. Stanford, Calif.: Stanford University Press.

Geertz, Clifford. 1973. The interpretation of cultures. New
York: Basic Books.

Givón, Talmy, ed. 1979. Discourse and syntax. Syntax and
semantics, Vol. 12. New York: Academic Press.

Goody, Jack. 1977. The domestication of the savage mind.
Cambridge, England: Cambridge University Press.

Grossman, Robin E., L. James San, and Timothy J. Vance,
eds. 1975. Papers from the Parasession on Functionalism.
Chicago: Chicago Linguistic Society.

Gumperz, John. 1971. Language in social groups. Stanford,
Calif.: Stanford University Press.

Halliday, M.A.K. 1973. Explorations in the functions of language. London: Edward Arnold.

Hymes, Dell. 1974. Foundations in sociolinguistics: An
ethnographic approach. Philadelphia: University of
Pennsylvania Press.

Hymes, Dell. 1977. Discovering oral performance and measured verse in American Indian narrative. New Literary
History 8.3:431-457.

Hymes, Dell. (in press) Particle, pause and pattern in American Indian narrative verse. American Indian Culture and
Research Journal.

Jakobson, Roman. 1960. Concluding statement: Linguistics and poetics. In: Style in language. Edited by Thomas A. Sebeok. Cambridge, Mass.: MIT Press. 350-377.

Labov, William. 1972a. Rules for ritual insults. In: Language in the inner city: Studies in the Black English vernacular. By William Labov. Philadelphia: University of Pennsylvania Press. 297-353.

Labov, William. 1972b. The transformation of experience in narrative syntax. In: Language in the inner city: Studies in the Black English vernacular. By William Labov. Philadelphia: University of Pennsylvania Press. 354-396.

Lord, Albert B. 1960. The singer of tales. Cambridge, Mass.: Harvard University Press.

Ohnuki-Tierney, E. 1977. An octopus headache? A lamprey boil? Multisensory perception of 'habitual illness' and world view of the Ainu. Journal of Anthropological Research 33. 245-257.

Ong, Walter J. 1977. Interfaces of the word. Ithaca and London: Cornell University Press.

Rosaldo, Michelle. 1975. It's all uphill: The creative metaphors of Ilongot magical spells. In: Sociocultural dimensions of language use. Edited by Mary Sanches and Ben G. Blount. New York: Academic Press. 117-203.

Sherzer, Joel. 1975. A problem in Cuna phonology. Journal of the Linguistic Association of the Southwest 1.2:45-53.

Sherzer, Joel. 1977. Cuna *Ikala:* Literature in San Blas. In: Verbal art as performance. By Richard Bauman. Rowley, Mass.: Newbury House. 133-150.

Sherzer, Joel. (in press) Tellings, retellings, and tellings within tellings: The structuring and organization of narrative in Kuna Indian discourse. Proceedings of conference on 'oralità: cultura, letteratura, discorso,' Urbino, Italy, 1980.

Silverstein, Michael. 1976. Shifters, linguistic categories, and cultural description. In: Meaning in anthropology. Edited by Keith H. Basso and Hugh A. Selby. Albuquerque: University of New Mexico Press. 11-55.

Tambiah, S. J. 1968. The magical power of words. Man 3.2: 175-208.

Tedlock, Dennis. 1978. Finding the center: Narrative poetry of the Zuni Indians. Lincoln: University of Nebraska Press.

THE LINGUISTIC BASES
OF COMMUNICATIVE COMPETENCE

John J. Gumperz
University of California, Berkeley,
and Princeton University

Let me begin with a reminiscence which may serve to introduce the point I wish to make. This is the third paper on
conversation I have given at the Georgetown University Round
Table on Languages and Linguistics. My first on this topic,
which reflects an initial attempt to come to terms with the semantic complexities of verbal interaction processes, was given
in this room in 1972, at a session which included Harold Garfinkel, Erving Goffman, and Harvey Sacks (Shuy 1972). Sacks
gave his well-known paper on puns and punning, which by
now has become a classic of conversational analysis. Yet if
audience response counts as a measure of success, his presentation was far from successful.

The room was only partly filled and, in fact, several listeners
walked out muttering that they could not understand the
speaker. Sacks' unorthodox style of presentation seemed to
jar the audience of linguists. He introduced basic theoretical
notions by means of descriptive phrases such as: 'sequential
ordering', ' positioning of utterances', 'the interactional job
that utterances do', 'what they (i.e. speakers) need to do is
exhibit understanding', 'the use of the performance rule'. In
all of these expressions, verb constructions like 'ordering',
'positioning', 'understanding', and 'using (or for that matter
also violating) rules' are consciously employed to suggest that
reference is being made to acts that speakers perform by means
of their talk and not to givens of language usage.

Today such interactive approaches to speaking and the expressions Sacks introduced have become familiar. It almost
seems as if we are witnessing a change in paradigm. Whereas
nine years ago discourse was one of many possible sociolinguistic topics, secondary perhaps in theoretical importance to

problems of variation, language and social stratification, bilingualism and language planning, today it has become the main topic of this three-day national conference, and basic issues of discourse coherence which Sacks was among the first to raise are now of central concern to sociolinguists and linguists alike.

The issues I want to discuss today are questions of linguistic theory that arise from this new perspective and that to my knowledge have not been seriously posed. What have we learned over the last decades by applying micro-conversational analyses to conversational data such as have only recently become available for systematic study through innovations in audio and video technology? What does the interactive approach to communication, which sees communicating as the outcome of exchanges involving more than one active participant, imply for the way we look at linguistic data and for our theories of grammar and meaning? What do conversational exchanges tell us about the interplay of linguistic, sociocultural and contextual presuppositions in interpretation?

A key concept we need to reconsider is the notion of communicative competence. The term is a familiar one, coined by Dell Hymes to suggest that as linguists concerned with communication in human groups we need to go beyond mere description of language usage patterns to concentrate on aspects of shared knowledge and cognitive abilities which are every bit as abstract and general as the knowledge that is glossed by Chomsky's more narrowly defined notion of linguistic competence. Among European social scientists the term has become familiar through the writings of Jurgen Habermas, who argues that an understanding of communication is basic to a more general theory of social and political processes. He calls for a theory of communicative competence that would specify what he terms —'the universal conditions of possible understandings'. But it is far from clear exactly what facts of human interaction such a theory must account for and how we can characterize the knowledge speakers must have and the socioeconomic environments that can create these conditions.

Habermas (1970) in his informal discussion relies on notions of what he calls 'trouble free communication' and assumptions about sharedness of code which recall Chomsky's ideally uniform communities, as if understanding depended on the existence of a unitary set of grammatical rules. Yet sociolinguistic research during the last decade has demonstrated not only that all existing human communities are diverse at all levels of linguistic structure, but also that grammatical diversity, multifocality of linguistic symbols, and context dependence of interpretive processes are essential components of the signalling resources that members rely on to accomplish their goals in everyday life (Gumperz in preparation).

Other empirical findings that by now have become generally accepted are: that generalization about ongoing processes of language change must build on empirical data on everyday speech in a range of natural settings; that basic issues of language acquisition can best be explained by reference to the behavioral facts of mother-child interaction; that the grammaticality judgments which furnish the data for syntactic analysis depend on speakers' ability to imagine a context in which the sentence could occur; and that, as several speakers in this Georgetown University Round Table have pointed out, discourse consists of more than the sum of component utterances. The theoretical linguists' insistence on maintaining a strict separation between linguistic and extralinguistic phenomena has thus become untenable in many key areas of linguistic research.

Yet even though these points are by now gaining acceptance, and context and sociocultural presuppositions are beginning to be brought into our explanatory models, our ideas of what is rule governed about speaking and about how meaning is conveyed continue to be based on concepts deriving from sentence-based grammatical analysis. We talk about language and culture, language and context, as if these were separate entities, which stand outside the actual message and which, like the ideas in the conduit metaphor (Reddy 1979), can be likened to bounded concrete objects. Moreover, and more importantly perhaps, our methods for analyzing contextual and social aspects of communication rest on procedures of taxonomic categorization and on statistical distribution counts which are quite distinct from the introspective, interpretive methods of linguistic analysis. Many sociolinguistic studies of communicative competence, in fact, aim at little more than statements of regularities that describe the occurrence of utterances or verbal strategies isolated by traditional methods of linguistic analysis in relation to types of speakers, audiences, settings, and situations. This leads to a highly particularistic notion of competence, which some psycholinguists claim has little relevance for basic cognitive processes; they argue that lexical and syntactic measures are the only valid indices of verbal skills.

I believe that we can avoid the difficulties that this raises by integrating the sociolinguistic findings on variability with Habermas's call for a theory of possible human understanding. What is needed is an approach which can relate the specifics of situated interpretation to the panhuman ability to engage others in discourse. I propose therefore that we redefine communicative competence as 'the knowledge of linguistic and related communicative conventions that speakers must have to initiate and sustain conversational involvement'. Conversational involvement is clearly a necessary precondition for understanding. Communication always presupposes some sharing of signalling conventions, but this does not mean that interlocutors must speak a single language or dialect in the sense that linguists use the term.

Code-switching studies over the last ten years have documented a variety of speech situations in societies throughout the world where speakers build on the contrast between two

distinct grammatical systems to convey substantive information
that elsewhere in equivalent situations can be conveyed by the
grammatical devices of a single system. Moreover, participants
in a conversation need not agree on the specifics of what is
intended. People frequently walk away from an encounter feeling that it has been highly successful only to find later that
they disagree on what was actually said. Studies of communicative competence, therefore, must deal with linguistic signs
at a level of generality which transcends the bounds of linguists' grammatical system and must concentrate on aspects of
meaning or interpretation more general than that of sentence
content. It is furthermore evident that the perceptual cues we
must process in conversational exchanges are different from
those that apply to decoding of isolated sentences.

The following example of a brief recorded exchange between
two secretaries in a small university office serves to organize
my discussion of relevant interpretive processes.

1. A: Are you going to be here for ten minutes?
2. B: Go ahead and take your break. Take longer if
      you want.
3. A: I'll just be outside on the porch. Call me if you
      need me.
4. B: OK. Don't worry.

Brief though it is, this exchange nevertheless contains in itself much of the data we need to determine what participants
intended and how it was achieved. Setting aside for the moment our natural tendency to concentrate on the meanings of
component utterances, we note that B interprets A's opening
move as a request to stay in the office while she takes a break.
By her reply in line 3, A then confirms B's interpretation and
B's final 'OK. Don't worry' both reconfirms what was agreed
and concludes the exchange.

Given this evidence showing that both speakers have actively
participated and have proffered and agreed on (for the moment
at least) interpretations, we can proceed to employ the linguist's interpretive, introspective methods of analysis to seek
hypotheses as to what knowledge participants rely on and what
signalling cues they perceive to accomplish what they do.

Note that B's interpretation is an indirect one which responds
to more than the referential meaning or the illocutionary force
of A's utterance. The inferential process here seems to have
some of the characteristics of Gricean implicature. That is, we
assume that B assumes A is cooperating, that her question must
therefore be relevant, and that since there is no immediately
available referent she searches her memory for some possible
context, i.e. some interpretive frame that would make sense.
But this begs the question how B arrives at the right inference. What is it about the situation that leads her to think A
is talking about taking a break? A common sociolinguistic

procedure in such cases is to attempt to formulate discourse rules such as the following: 'If a secretary in an office around break time asks a co-worker a question seeking information about the co-worker's plans for the period usually allotted for breaks, interpret it as a request to take her break.' Such rules are difficult to formulate and in any case are neither sufficiently general to cover a wide enough range of situations nor specific enough to predict responses. An alternative approach is to consider the pragmatics of questioning and to argue that questioning is semantically related to requesting, and that there are a number of contexts in which questions can be interpreted as requests. While such semantic processes clearly channel conversational inference, there is nothing in this type of explanation that refers to taking a break.

Note that all the foregoing arguments rely on sentence-based views of language which assume that the cues that conversationalists process are basically those covered in traditional phonological, syntactic, and semantic analysis. I believe that conversational inference relies on additional types of linguistic signalling and that an understanding of how these signs work to channel interpretation is basic to a theory of communicative competence.

Some of these contextualization cues (Gumperz 1977, Cook-Gumperz and Gumperz 1978, Gumperz and Tannen 1979) have to do with what, following sociological work in conversational analysis, have come to be called sequencing or turn-taking processes. Sacks, Schegloff, and Jefferson (1974) argue that speaker change is a basic conversational process and that turn-taking mechanisms are organized about transition relevance places, which determine when a next speaker can take the floor. But they give no data on how such transition relevance places are signalled. Conversations, unlike sentences, do not come pre-chunked. Conversationalists must process verbal signs to determine when to take turns without interfering with others' rights. For example, B's utterance in line 2 comes in immediately at the end of A's sentence, while A in line 3 waits long enough to allow B to produce not one but two sentences. How is this negotiated?

Moreover, responses in this exchange, as well as in most verbal encounters, are rhythmically organized in such a way that--as Erickson and Scollon have pointed out in this Georgetown University Round Table--moves follow each other at regular time intervals. This rhythmicity is important in maintaining conversational involvement (Erickson and Shultz 1981). Halliday (1967), in discussing problems of segmentation in longer passages, argues that language is chunked into semantically holistic information units, but his discussion focuses largely on written texts and on the role of syntax in chunking. Chafe (1980) proposes the notion of idea unit to deal with related issues and points to the role of tempo and pausing in segmentation. These problems are treated in considerable detail in recent work on intonation. Ladd's (1980) comprehensive review of the relevant literature indicates that chunking cannot be described in terms of a single phonetically determined set of signalling cues. Chunking is an act of interpretation involving simultaneous processing of signs at several levels of signalling: prosodic, phonological, syntactic, lexical and rhythmic, which, like the process of phonemic categorization described by structural linguists, depends on learned conventions which differentially highlight or ignore some cues at the expense of others. Chunking or phrasing of speech, moreover, does more than just signal transition relevance places; it also serves to indicate relationships among items of information and to set off or foreground others. A's utterance in line 1 could have been split by a tone group boundary, while B's line 4 could have been grouped together under a single clause contour.

Another process of key importance for conversational inference is the signalling of utterance prominence to indicate which of several bits of information is to be highlighted or placed in focus. In our English rhetorical tradition this is done partly through syntax and lexical choice and partly through placement of prosodic accent. Given a particular choice of words, we have certain expectations about normal accent placement. These can then be systematically violated to convey additional information not overtly given in the message. If in line 1 'you' had been accented rather than 'be here', B might have thought the question referred to whether she, as opposed to someone else, was going to stay in the office. She might not have recognized it as a request. As it is, the interpretation B actually does make relies in large part on the fact that 'be here' is emphasized by primary stress, 'ten minutes' carries secondary stress, and the two phrases come under the same contour. We assume that B perceived the question as focusing on her being (i.e. remaining) for a period equivalent to that normally associated with the morning break, and that this led to her inference. Other rhetorical traditions rely on information signalled through a different combination of signalling channels or subsystems. What is important is that perception of focus always relies on expectations of how these channels cooccur, and these expectations are not dealt with in our usual grammatical analyses, which tend to focus on one subsystem at a time.

A final signalling cue of relevance here is the choice of discourse strategy. Note that A could have achieved her end by simply asking 'Can I take my break?', in which case a simple one-word or one-phrase answer like 'yes' or 'OK' would have been sufficient to complete the exchange. But given her choice of words, our experience with similar situations tells us that more talk is expected. There is something of a formulaic nature about exchanges such as these which affects our interpretations.

This discussion suggests that conversational inference is best seen not as a simple unitary evaluation of intent but as involving

a complex series of judgments, including relational or contextual assessments on how items of information are to be integrated into what we know and into the event at hand, as well
as assessments of content. This is a point that has been made
several times during this Round Table. Agar and Hobbs[1] distinguish between global and local assessment. Livia Polanyi,
in her comment on Coulthard's paper, suggested that we need
to distinguish between discourse and sentence level inferences.
Fillmore's (this volume) approach to reading also reflects a
similar perspective.

One can visualize the process as consisting of a series of
stages which are hierarchically ordered so that more general
relational assessment serves as part of the input to more specific ones. Perception of contextualization cues, moreover,
plays a role at every stage.

It is assumed that the initial assessment in an exchange concerns the nature of the activity being proposed or performed.
This sets up expectations about what likely outcomes are, what
topics can be covered, what can be put in words and what
must be conveyed indirectly; and what counts as suitable styles
of speaking and thereby provides the motivation for entering
into the interaction in the first place. At the next lower level,
decisions are made about the more immediate communicative or
discourse tasks such as narrating, describing, requesting,
which together make up particular activities. Such discourse
tasks have some similarity to the linguists' speech act, but
they differ in that they typically consist of more than one
utterance and in that they are described in terms of primary
semantic relationships that tie together component utterances,
rather than in terms of illocutionary force.

Note that whereas activities are often culturally or situationally specific, discourse tasks are universals of human interaction. An understanding of how relational signs function to
signal these tasks can provide basic insights into how interpretations are agreed upon and altered in the course of an interaction by differentially foregrounding, subordinating, and
associating various information carrying items. If conversational involvement is to be maintained, higher level relational
signs must be shared although participants may disagree on the
meaning of words and idioms. On the other hand, however
participants may agree on what sentences mean in isolation,
yet when relational signals differ, conversational cooperation is
likely to break down. Cross-cultural analysis of how discourse
tasks are signalled--that is, how focusing, phrasing, coreferentiality and other aspects of cohesion are signalled--can form
the basis for empirical investigations of pan human features of
communicative competence.

It must be emphasized that verbal strategies for negotiating
conversational interpretations are for the most part indirect.
Information is not overtly expressed in surface content, but

must be inferred on the basis of tacit presuppositions acquired through previous interactive experience. Indirect signalling mechanisms differ from lexicalized signs in that, like nonverbal signals, they are inherently ambiguous. Any single utterance is always subject to multiple interpretations. One decides on what interpretation to accept by examining what Austin has called uptake, that is, the conversational process through which lines of reasoning are developed or altered.

Given the nature of the signalling system, participants, in order to be able to develop their arguments, are constantly required to test and display the tacit knowledge on which they rely to make inferences in the first place. Wherever conversational cooperation is maintained over time, that is, wherever we find evidence that conversationalists actively react to and work with each others' responses to establish cohesive themes, we can assume at least some sharing of tacit contextualization strategies.

Failure to achieve this type of cooperation, on the other hand, may in some cases, although certainly by no means in all, indicate undetected differences in signalling systems. In the midst of an exchange, when conversationalists are faced with the need to respond in time and have little opportunity to reflect, such difficulties tend to go undiagnosed. The fact that they exist must be discovered through post-hoc empirical analysis. It is here that the new audiovisual technologies which for the first time in human history enable us to freeze and preserve for systematic study samples of naturalistic exchanges can provide truly novel insights into the workings of communicative processes.

Our recent empirical studies in ethnically diverse urban settings indicate that miscommunications attributable to undetected systematic differences in signalling conventions occur considerably more frequently than casual observations would lead one to suspect. A possible linguistic reason for this is that contextualization conventions are distributed along areal networks which do not necessarily coincide with language or dialect boundaries as established through historical reconstruction or typological comparison of grammatical categories. Such conventions are created through prolonged interactive experience in family, friendship, occupational, or similar networks of relationships. Typically, they affect the signalling of contextual and interutterance relationships through formulaic expressions, phrasing or chunking, focusing, anaphora, deixis, or other grammatical cohesive mechanisms. Once established through practice, they come to serve as communicative resources which channel inferences along particular lines. Knowledge of how they work becomes a precondition for active participation in verbal encounters. The knowledge is of a kind which cannot easily be acquired through reading or formal classroom instruction. Personal contact in situations which allow for maximum feedback is necessary.

Potential language learners thus face a real dilemma. They must establish long-lasting intensive person-to-person contacts in order to learn, yet their very lack of the necessary strategies makes it difficult for them to establish such contacts. In real life situations, learning of discourse strategies is most successful when outside conditions exist which force interlocutors to disregard breakdowns and stay in contact or to give the learner the benefit of the doubt. This is the case in mother and child interaction or in apprenticeship situations at work. But conditions in modern urban societies are hardly favorable to informal experiential learning. Here contact with others of different background is often the norm in public affairs, while friendship circles are limited by similarity of background. Public situations, moreover, most frequently revolve around evaluation of ability or intent to cooperate and, given the nature of the tensions of urban life, rarely provide the conditions where breakdowns can be disregarded. The result is that the ability to achieve one's goals--that is, to get things done in face-to-face public settings--is often a matter of shared background. Outsiders who enter the urban scene may learn a new language or dialect well at the level of sentence grammar or lexicon, and this knowledge is sufficient for the instrumental contacts with outsiders that fill up much of the working day. But situations of persuasion, where what is evaluated is the ability to explain, describe, or narrate, are often difficult to manage. Here breakdowns tend to lead to mutual stereotyping and pejorative evaluations.

To be sure, not all problems of interethnic contact are communicative in nature. Economic factors, differences in goals and aspirations, as well as other historical and cultural factors, may be at issue. But we have reason to suspect that a significant number of breakdowns may be due to inferences based on undetected differences in contextualization strategies, which are after all the symbolic tip of the iceberg reflecting the forces of history. The existence of communicative differences must, of course, be demonstrated. It cannot be presupposed or inferred from grammars or the usual ethnographic descriptions. Here conversational analysis becomes a diagnostic tool to determine whether the linguistic prerequisites of possible communication exist.

How do we go about documenting the functioning of contextualization strategies? One way to accomplish this is to concentrate on naturally occurring events such as court proceedings, job interviews, medical diagnoses, and committee meetings, where discourse strategies play a key role in the evaluation of performance. Let me present some data from transcribed testimony of a Navy hearing held in connection with a perjury trial. The accused was a Navy physician born in the Philippines, who had been indicted for perjury in connection with statements he had made concerning a burn injury he had treated.

A principal goal of the hearing was to document his professional qualifications. He had spent many years in the United
States and speaks English well. The questioning deals with
his training in burn treatment.

Q.1. Any other sources of burns that you've observed?
A.2. Occasionally from gasoline and kerosene burn because
     as far as the
  3. situation there, most of the houses don't have any
     natural gas or electric
  4. stove as here. They use kerosene instead as a means
     of fuel for cooking.
  5. The reason why I'm saying this also is because this
     hospital where I
  6. had my training is a government hospital, so most of
     the patients that
  7. go there are the poverty stricken patients unlike you
     going to a medi-
  8. cal center, it's usually the middle class who go where
     you don't have
  9. this problem.

In the preceding parts of his testimony dealing with his
training in the Philippines, the witness has repeatedly compared
conditions there with those in the United States. His argument
in lines 2-4 rests on such a contrast, and from the way he begins the second part of his answer, starting in line 5, one
would expect a similar comparison of 'there' with 'here'. But
the content of his sentences does not seem to bear out these
expectations. If one examines what he says, starting with:
'most of the patients who go there are the poverty stricken
patients unlike you going to a medical center...', one is unsure
what is being compared: poverty stricken patients with middle
class patients, or medical centers in the United States with
government hospitals in the Philippines?
    Participants in an interaction, as well as most casual observ-
ers, are likely to see such conflicts as reflecting on the witness's credibility, but our experience with similar types of
interethnic situations leads us to suspect that in situations
like this, <u>where expectations signalled at one level of generality</u>
<u>are not born out by lower level signalling processes, systematic</u>
<u>processing difficulties ultimately attributable to grammatical</u>
<u>presuppositions may be at work.</u>
Note that the passage is too long to be processed as a whole.
A reader will have to rely on syntactic and prosodic knowledge
to sound it out and chunk it into relevant information units.
Native speakers of English who do this will have difficulty in
assigning the word 'unlike' in line 7 to either the preceding or
following clause. The first reading yields the clause 'poverty
stricken patients unlike you'. This not only conflicts with expectations signalled through the preceding context but also

renders the remaining passage unintelligible. Speakers of Filipino English who were consulted tended to assign 'unlike' to the following clause and had no difficulty in recognizing the speaker's intent to contrast 'there' with 'here'. Yet native speakers of English are likely to have difficulty in fitting a clause such as 'unlike you going to a medical center' into the surrounding discourse frame.

The problem is a complex one, requiring more detailed analysis than can be presented here. But the most likely explanation lies in the discourse conventions for signalling co-referentiality. To make sense of the 'unlike' clause, an English speaker would have to recognize it as a syntactically incomplete clause in which 'this is' had been deleted or left unexpressed immediately preceding 'unlike'. To recover such unverbalized information, English speakers look for a pronoun or noun phrase that could signal coreferentiality. It is our inability to locate such a phrase in the foregoing passage that leads to processing difficulty. My hypothesis, which will, of course, have to be tested through systematic research, is that Filipino English speakers, even though they speak grammatical English at the sentence level, nevertheless employ discourse principles influenced by Tagalog and similar Austronesian languages, where coreferentiality is signalled by means other than overtly lexicalized pronouns or noun phrases. The same passage can thus be differently interpreted by listeners who process it with different presuppositions.

Investigation of such multilevel signalling processes, and of the role played by contextualization as well as by linguistic and sociocultural presuppositions in the multilevel inferences necessary to sustain verbal exchanges, could lay the foundation of a universal theory of communicative competence capable of providing new insights into the communicative problems that affect our urban societies.

NOTES

Research on this paper was supported by grants from The Institute of Advanced Studies in Princeton, N.J., and the National Institutes of Health.
1. Editor's note: This is a reference to Michael Agar and Jerry Hobbs, who participated in a preconference session, 'Toward adequate formal models of discourse', before the 1981 Georgetown University Round Table on Languages and Linguistics.

REFERENCES

Chafe, Wallace L. 1980. The deployment of consciousness in the production of a narrative. In: The pear stories: Cognitive, cultural, and linguistics aspects of narrative production. Edited by Wallace Chafe. Norwood, N.J.: Ablex.

Cook-Gumperz, Jenny, and John Gumperz. 1978. Context in children's speech. In: The development of communication. Edited by Katherine Snow and Natalie Waterson. London: Wiley.

Erickson, Frederick, and Jeffrey Shultz. 1981. Talking to the man. New York: Academic Press.

Gumperz, John. 1977. Sociocultural knowledge in conversational inference. In: Georgetown University Round Table on Languages and Linguistics 1977. Edited by Muriel Saville-Troike. Washington, D.C.: Georgetown University Press.

Gumperz, John. (in preparation) Discourse strategies.

Gumperz, John, and Deborah Tannen. 1979. Individual and social differences in language use. In: Individual differences in language ability and language behavior. Edited by C. J. Fillmore, W. Kempler, and W. S.-Y. Wang. New York: Academic Press.

Habermas, Jurgen. 1970. Toward a theory of communicative competence. In: Recent sociology II. Edited by H. P. Dreitzel. London: Macmillan.

Halliday, M.A.K. 1967. Notes on transitivity and theme in English, Part 2. Journal of Linguistics 3.2:199-244.

Ladd, Robert. 1980. The structure of intonational meaning. Bloomington: Indiana University Press.

Reddy, Michael. 1979. The conduit metaphor: A case of frame conflict in our language about language. In: Metaphor and thought. Edited by Andrew Ortony. Cambridge: Cambridge University Press.

Sacks, Harvey, Emanuel Schegloff, and Gail Jefferson. 1974. A simplest systematics for the organization of turn taking for conversation. Lg. 50.696-735.

Shuy, Roger, ed. 1972. Georgetown University Round Table on Languages and Linguistics 1972. Washington, D.C.: Georgetown University Press.

THE RHYTHMIC INTEGRATION
OF ORDINARY TALK

Ron Scollon
University of Alaska

Rhythm, timing, tempo, pace. Rhythm, timing, tempo, pace. These notions have appeared from time to time in our discourse about discourse. Recently, Erickson (1980; Erickson and Shultz 1977; in press) has shown that some notion of rhythmicity is central to our understanding of such very different face-to-face interactions as junior college counseling interviews and elementary school examinations. Much earlier, Chapple (1939) pointed out the centrality of time in exchanging turns between speakers in interviews. Householder was one of the first linguists to take rhythmicity seriously in his thinking about accent, juncture, and intonation (1957). He said:

> The fact is, we can't hear noises repeated with fair regu-
> larity at more than a certain average frequency without
> grouping them rhythmically (as every subway-rider can
> testify), and once a given pattern is established we will
> hear it over and over till some new irregularity breaks
> the rhythm and starts another pattern (1957:238).

Many of us, in reading Lenneberg (1967), were caught by the notion of the critical period for language development and missed his assertion that rhythm was the organizing principle of speech and language. In 1970, it was still possible for non-linguists such as Jaffe and Feldstein, working on face-to-face interaction, to say that linguists had not taken rhythmic phenomena seriously. Jaffe and Feldstein could say with confidence (1970) that when linguists began looking at connected speech (that is, at discourse), they would necessarily find themselves wanting to address rhythmic issues. Now one sees that linguists are indeed finding rhythmic phenomena of interest. As a recent example, phonologists such as Ladd (1980)

335

and Liberman and Prince (1977) have extended the work of
Bolinger (1964) to build notions of sentential stress and intonation around rhythm and timing. In short, while notions of
rhythm, timing, tempo, and pace have been around for some
time in our discourse about discourse, I believe that a point
has been reached where rhythmicity needs to become a more
central concern.

My purpose in this paper is to show how I have found the
idea of tempo to be useful in my thinking about discourse and
to try to clarify one or two confusions that seem to crop up
wherever people have wanted to use this notion in their discourse about discourse.

Before getting to my main point, though, I think it is useful
to clarify my reasons for an interest in discourse. While I
take my audience here to be primarily an audience of linguists,
I need to point out that I do not see myself as doing linguistic
work so much as using linguistic work to do other things. I
am interested in coming to understand how 'institutions' are
constituted in discursive practices. In this I rely heavily on
the thinking of Foucault (1976, 1977, 1980a, 1980b). Although
his use of the term 'discourse' is broader than the use made by
many linguists, it is not incompatible with linguists' use. I
think in this regard of the comment made by John Gumperz
(personal communication) that 'discourse is the key to historical process'. My interest, not unlike Chapple's (1980), is to
understand the constitution of our institutions in the process
of face-to-face interaction.

More specifically, in my work in Alaska I am involved with
a number of institutions--schools, from pre-school to post-
secondary institutions (Scollon 1981a), the criminal justice
system, the judicial system, resource development corporations,
federal regulatory agencies, and Alaska Native corporations--in
their relationships with a particular population, Alaska Natives,
who do not share institutional assumptions nor assumptions
about the nature of discursive practices within those institutions. Let me emphasize that the preceding clause is intended
to be a restrictive clause. I mean to speak of the population
of Alaska Natives who do not share institutional assumptions.
There are many who do share those assumptions and I want to
be careful not to include those in this general concern. My
concern with these institutions is that many Alaska Natives find
participation blocked by ordinary processes of face-to-face
interaction. Building on the work of Erickson (1980; Erickson
and Shultz 1977; in press) and Gumperz (1977a; 1977b; 1978;
Gumperz, Jupp, and Roberts 1979; Gumperz and Roberts 1978;
Gumperz and Tannen 1979), I am concerned with understanding
how in these cases institutions fail to constitute themselves in
a way that includes these Alaska Natives.

The problem with face-to-face interaction. I started with the
idea that face-to-face interaction was discourse, and I have had

problems with that. My reasons for wanting to consider discourse to be face-to-face interaction were various. I have
been interested in the discourse of one-year-old children
(Scollon 1976), as well as the discourse of elderly tradition
bearers in nonliterate traditions (Scollon and Scollon in press
a). In looking at gatekeeping encounters, I have been interested in those critical few minutes of face-to-face interaction
in which major life choices are made. I have also kept in mind
Bateson's constant reminders that human communication is
originally and primarily mammalian communication and that means
face-to-face communication (Bateson 1972, 1979). The problem
is that much of our institutional communication is carried out in
print, by telephone, on audio- and videotape, on film, and now
increasingly by computer. Studies of face-to-face interaction
can tell us relatively little about such mediated forms of communication. Hence our interest in 'literacy' research. Suzanne
Scollon and I have been engaged in a series of studies in which
we have tried to argue that children in a particular speech community are socialized into discourse conventions that are compatible with (if not actually determinative of) the preferred
medium of communication of that speech community (Scollon and
Scollon 1979; in press a; in press b; S. Scollon in preparation).
Throughout that work we have felt, somewhat uneasily, that
some critical element was missing, some concept that would considerably simplify our discourse about these quite varied forms
of discourse. The notion of tempo is the key to the concept
we were looking for; the concept itself, borrowed from my
chamber music-playing past, is ensemble.

Tempo. My interest in tempo began with an interest in pausing in oral narrative traditions. As I tried to think about ways
of representing Athabaskan oral narratives in a written medium,
the work of Tedlock (1972) and Hymes (1975, 1976, 1977) called
to my attention the great importance of the pause as an element of style and even metrics. Other writers have also been
concerned with pausing and rhythms in oral traditions. Scheub
(1977) speaks of the centrality of repetition in oral narratives
as a means of establishing rhythms and Perkins (1980) has
written of the matching of rhythms between speakers in the
Hawaiian oral tradition, this matching being a means of mutually
attesting the degree of agreement among the participants.
I was not, myself, interested in rhythm so much as in pausing. My concern was with understanding the interaction between a storyteller and his or her audience and the pause appeared to be a critical moment for the interchange between participants. This led me to look into quite another literature on
pausing. A number of researchers have had an interest in
pausing as a cognitive issue. In this research, pauses in
speaking have been argued to relate to cognitive processing
(Goldman-Eisler 1968; Pawley and Syder n.d.; Chafe 1979,
1980; Sabin, Clemmer, O'Connell, and Kowal 1979; Welkowitz,

Cariffe, and Feldstein 1976). It has been argued that pauses are the result of difficult lexical items, complex syntactic or discourse structures, or limitations on processing because of immaturity.

Another body of research has been more concerned with affective domains. Chapple (1939) and more recently, such researchers as Siegman (1979; Siegman and Pope 1972) have argued that the length of the pauses taken by speakers in interviews is an accurate indicator of states of anxiety, comfort, or interpersonal attraction. This research was of particular interest to me because of the finding that the pausing mechanism was apparently tied to a process of attribution. One group of researchers (Feldstein and Welkowitz 1978; Feldstein, Alberti, and BenDebba 1979) found that a group of negative stereotyped attitudes was attributed to speakers who take longer pauses in speaking. These individuals were stereotyped as cold, withdrawn, or even hostile while speakers who take shorter pauses were stereotyped as warmer, outgoing, or socially concerned. It was of particular interest to me that just these stereotypes tend to be attributed in social interactions between Athabaskans and non-Athabaskans, and I have had an interest in seeing to what extent this attribution of qualities is tied to pausing phenomena (Scollon and Scollon in press a; Scollon 1981b).

In these three bodies of research there were three different kinds of phenomena being addressed: cognitive, affective, and aesthetic. These were all being addressed at the same point, the pause or silence in face-to-face interaction. As a further complication, there was not only disagreement on definitions of what might constitute a pause; there was absolute disregard for other views. I was concerned with finding a way to begin to speak in a coherent manner of all three of these kinds of phenomena without stumbling over confusions in our notions of what we might mean by a pause.

Erickson's work on rhythmicity in interpersonal interaction provided the necessary insight. It was his insight that not only is talk timed, not only are pauses critical in negotiating turn exchange, but talk itself is rhythmically timed to a regular underlying metric or tempo. Erickson has shown that in ordinary talk, people speak to each other in a regular meter of regular beats, and time their entrances and exits to the rhythm of these beats.

Building on the work of Erickson, I have begun to sample a wide range of talk, at first to see if talk was really as metrical as he had argued, and then to begin a closer examination of the phenomenon of tempo itself. Since I have prepared the details of the data I have used in another paper (Scollon 1981c), here I merely summarize my findings. My sample of situations includes breakfast table talk, a family gathering with three generations (including a newborn infant) present, several university lectures, a radio symphony broadcast announcer, a radio baseball game, Groucho Marx, Athabaskan tradition bearers telling traditional narratives in both Athabaskan and English, potlatch songs, and third grade reading lessons in rural and urban Alaska and in Hawaii.

The central finding is that talk in apparently all contexts is timed to an underlying tempo. This tempo is most easily represented by a simple duple measure. I use 2/4 time as the representative measure. One might want to ask why this measure should be duple time and not something else. Hopkins (1979), in a book on music for nonspecialists, argues that the fundamental tempo is duple and that this is related to the duple rhythms of such basic activities as walking, or perhaps the human heart beat, or perhaps primitive rhythms such as the in and out of the canoe paddle. Householder's comment quoted earlier might be a preferable explanation: this tempo is heard as duple because it is regular and it is the nature of human perception to hear regular tempos as duple. In a moment I return to the issue of whether this regularity of tempo is 'real' or 'perceived'.

As in music, the underlying tempo is not to be confused with the rhythmic patterns superimposed on it. Some speakers superimpose a pattern of relatively few syllables per beat while others superimpose a pattern of a very high density. It came as a surprise to me to find that Groucho Marx, in performing on his radio show, 'You Bet Your Life', spoke in a very slow tempo (75.9 beats per minute). What gives the impression of rapid speech is the very high density of 4.62 words per measure. To trade on the parallel with music, it can be said that some speakers speak in quarter notes while others, such as Groucho Marx, speak in 32nd or even 64th notes. I find it useful to refer to this phenomenon as 'density' and to treat it as quite distinct from tempo.

A third phenomenon of relevance is the relative amount of silence. In my work I am defining silence as beats on which speech does not occur. Again, I find that our intuitive impressions of 'lots of talk' relate more to the density and the relative amount of silence than to the tempo. I have further found it useful to distinguish among silent beats. Basing my analysis on the work of Gumperz and his colleagues (e.g. Gumperz and Roberts 1978, Gumperz and Tannen 1979), I have used the tone group as a unit of analysis. I argue that silent beats which follow the closure of a tone group are qualitatively different from those which occur within a tone group, and suggest that it is the silent beats following tone group closure which are interactively and cognitively useful. I have been tentatively calling these silent beats 'useful silences', that is, silences useful for speaker interchange or for hearer processing.

In this paper it is not my purpose to elaborate on the notions of density or silence, whether useful or not. I am concerned with the idea of tempo. What is most striking about tempo is

its negotiability. In my whole sample, the range of mean
tempos is from 115.4 beats per minute in a radio spot announce-
ment to 70.2 beats per minute also in a radio program. Within
15 minutes of a conversation around a breakfast table there is
a range in tempos from 103.4 beats per minute to 60.9 beats
per minute. In other words, there is a highly variable range
of tempos both within situations and across situations. It is
also impossible to characterize individual speakers as having a
unique tempo. The variability within speakers is as great as
across situations. While density and silence do to some extent
characterize individual speakers, tempo appears to be used as
the means of negotiating the interaction between speakers. As
in music, it is the tempo that keeps the participants in touch
with each other. It is through the tempo that the performers
integrate their ensemble.

And so I find in ordinary talk, as in music and literary
metrics, there is syncopy (beats anticipated), hemiola (two
different rhythms built upon the same underlying tempo),
tempo rubato (arbitrary lengthening or shortening of the beats
with compensatory changes in the length of neighboring beats),
and anacrusis ('pick up' syllables or unaccented syllables preceding the downbeat). There is no reason to expect ordinary
speech to be less variable and more metronomic than the conventionalized meters of music and poetry.

Processes of acceleration and retardation are central to the
integration of the rhythmic ensemble of two or more speakers.
Speakers time their entrances according to the tempo set by
preceding speakers. After entering in that rhythm, speakers
often accelerate or retard their tempo to establish what is in
effect a new tempo. It is very rare that any speaker will independently and arbitrarily begin speaking without first con-
firming the established tempo. Children at breakfast bang
their spoons in the prevailing tempo. Radio emcees make their
announcements in the tempo of their theme songs. Sometimes
teachers time their instruction to the tempos of their students
and sometimes they require their students to follow the teacher's tempo.

Not only do stressed syllables express this rhythmic matrix;
conversationalists also cough, sneeze, clear their throats, blow
their noses, and laugh in rhythmic ensemble. Often after a
long silence someone clears his or her throat in a gesture
which predicts the following tempo as accurately as a conductor's silent 'one-two' before the orchestra's entrance.

Before picking up the notion of ensemble there are two points
that need to be considered, the question left hanging of how
'real' these tempos are, and a related question of how my use
of tempo relates to that of Chapple and those who have pur-
sued rhythmicity in that tradition of research. In trying to
address the first issue, we have found that in making transcriptions our ability to 'hear' the tempo seems to wax and
wane. Some situations are very easy to hear while others are

much more difficult. In some situations, certain parts are more easily transcribed than others. It is our perception that it is the rhythmicity itself that is waxing and waning. As a test of interjudge reliability, we have made multiple transcripts of single events and found that across judges it is the same points that are easily transcribed and the same points in which difficulty is encountered. While our work at this point is tentative, we can now suggest that it appears to be at the boundaries of events that rhythmicity is more difficult to perceive. We now also believe that it is at points where the original participants themselves are negotiating tempo adjustments that our own ability to perceive rhythms suffers. Our degree of interjudge reliability gives us reason to believe that the tempos we are speaking of are 'really there', while the waxing and waning of our confidence in our accuracy leads us to believe that the tempos themselves are waxing and waning in their degree of regularity.

Chapple (1980) has provided us with an excellent overview of his some 50 years of the study of rhythmicity. The concern of Chapple, begun in the thirties, to introduce a high level of objectivity into his recording has been consummated in the work of Jaffe and Feldstein (1970), who have used the computer in conjunction with voice-activated microphones to achieve a standard of completely automated recording, as they say, 'without human intervention'.

It is important now to consider Chapple's (and his followers') use of the notion of rhythm, or as they sometimes call it, tempo. This body of research is looking at the exchange of speaking turns between two or more participants. Chapple points out in his recent overview that the model he is using is that of a relaxation oscillator. This type of rhythmicity, which is characteristic of biological rhythms from the firing of neurons to circadian potassium secretions, consists of two phases, an active phase and a latent phase. During the latent phase, some form of energy is built up until it reaches some threshold. When the threshold is reached, there is a triggering of the release of this stored energy. This release of energy constitutes the active phase. Chapple very accurately points out the difference between such relaxation oscillators and harmonic oscillators.

Harmonic oscillators such as clocks and musical strings do not have a latent and an active phase. These oscillators depend on a steady input of energy to produce some form of periodic oscillation, usually represented by a sine wave. To couple these two types of oscillation is for me an interesting issue. The pendulum of the clock is a harmonic oscillator but the spring that runs it is a relaxation oscillator. When it runs down it must be wound up again. In other words, a clock succeeds by virtue of the coupling of a relaxation oscillator and a harmonic oscillator.

To get from clocks back to Chapple, Chapple argues that
the give and take of conversational interaction operates as a
relaxation oscillator, the speaker being in the active phase and
the hearer being in the latent phase. The tempo of which
Chapple speaks is the pattern of active, latent, active, latent
in the exchange of speaking turns. It should be clear that
this is a very different use of the notion of tempo from mine.
Tempo as I use the notion is a harmonic oscillation. Chapple's
use of the term 'tempo' is an analogy to music but my use
claims that tempo in ordinary talk is the same phenomenon as
tempo in music. I believe that this difference is what has led
to such radically different methodologies. Chapple's concern
is based on tying social interaction to biological rhythms.
These relaxation oscillators are most appropriately studied by
objective means. The notion of tempo as I am using it requires
methods much more akin to those of musical criticism than of
biological science.

To use a musical analogy, one might make the observation
that Toscanini's tempo in the first movement of the Brahms
First Symphony is much quicker than the tempo taken by
Bruno Walter. The question is: where does one go from that
observation? An interest in the psychophysics of music might
take you into the conductor's biological rhythms or into the
acoustic properties of the hall in which it was performed. An
interest in the quality of the performance would take you into
a very different domain in which the absolute tempo would not
be of nearly as much interest as the relative adjustments of
that quick opening tempo as the movement progresses. It is
in this latter direction that my work is leading me. The idea
of tempo can lead into either the biological foundations of social
interaction, as it has for Chapple and others, or it can lead
into the idea of social ensemble, as it has for me. For what I
am interested in doing, the concept of ensemble provides the
most useful direction. While these two views of social interaction are conceptually very different, I do not see them as
any more incompatible than the clock's pendulum and its
spring. The trick will be in learning how to build an escape-
ment.

Ensemble. What I have written to this point is really a pre-
amble to allow me to say a few words about ensemble. As
musicians use the term, ensemble refers to the coming together
of the performers in a way that either makes or breaks the
performance. It is not just the being together, but the doing
together. And so a performance of a string quartet can be
faulted, no matter how impeccably the score has been followed,
if a mutual agreement on tempos, tunings, fortes, and pianos
has not been achieved. Ensemble in music refers to the extent
to which the performers have achieved one mind, or--to favor
Sudnow (1979a, 1979b), one body--in the performance of their
work. Of the elements which contribute to the achievement of

ensemble, tempo is the guiding element. While the note you are now playing tells me about the loudness and tuning of what I am now playing, it is the tempo that tells me when you and I will play our next notes. Tempo is the temporal bond that allows us to move together in real time. It gives us an account of the immediate past and a basis for predicting the immediate future. The ensemble of either musical performance or face-to-face talk depends on this bond of immediate temporal predictability. Ensemble is what is 'real' about real time.

This gives me a vocabulary for talking about differences among forms of communication. Such forms as face-to-face and telephone conversation happen in real time. That is, the participants must mutually attend to tempo to achieve their ensemble. Other forms such as unedited audio- and videotaped communications preserve the real time predictabilities of the original event but are not heard or seen in that real time. The listener or viewer may observe the ensemble but not participate in it. Still other forms such as writing, whether of words or musical scores, do not preserve real time predictabilities except to the extent these become conventionalized.

And this is my interest now. What is the relationship between a musical score and its performance? What is the relationship between a book and its performance? I find it helps me in thinking about reading and writing to think about that other form of Western literacy, musical notation. It interests me that in musical notation there is an elaborate set of conventions by which the composer's intentions about real time performance are represented. It also interests me that these elaborate conventions in music developed during the period in which the idea of 'prose' developed. Do we want to think of prose as being a nonreal time genre of communication, a genre in which the width of the page is a more central consideration than the rhythms of the line? In any event, my interest in ensemble leads me to ask: how does ensemble become conventionalized in nonreal time communication?

Institutions and ensemble. Now it remains for me to sketch in the outlines of how I think this vocabulary of tempo, ensemble, and conventionalized rhythms helps me to think about the constitution of institutions in practices of discourse. To do this I need to make reference to Bateson and Gumperz. In a number of places Bateson has argued that it was important to recognize a kind of learning, his 'learning II' or 'deutero learning' (1972, 1979). This is the sort of learning we recognize as insightful or creative. This is learning that looks beyond the situation as given and looks into the context. In its pathological forms, according to Bateson, it is also recognizable in schizophrenia. What I am interested in is the idea that deutero learning is learning about learning, learning about the contexts of learning.

Bateson tied his ideas about deutero learning to his ideas about the double bind. In his view, it takes some form of double bind to produce deutero learning.[1] Briefly, a double bind is a situation in which one receives two simultaneous and contradictory messages from someone along with a third constraint: that one cannot leave the situation. It is this sort of bind, according to Bateson, that drives the learner to look into the context of the situation. In its productive forms this looking beyond is seen as insight or creativity, in its pathological forms it is seen as schizophrenia.

I want to combine Bateson's perspective with that of Gumperz' notion of contextualization cues (Gumperz 1977a, 1977b, 1978). Gumperz, referring to Bateson's notion of metacommunication, has introduced the idea that the contexts in which communication takes place cannot be taken as given but are constructed by the participants in the act of communicating. As people talk, they must give attention not only to the 'message' but to its contextualization as well. This perspective of Gumperz has proved highly productive in looking at issues of miscommunication between members of different groups and is, I believe, a major insight into the nature of face-to-face communication.

The question I have had, however, is: how does contextualization actually work? What learning mechanism drives people to pay attention not only to the message but also to the metamessage? I think now the answer lies in looking back to Bateson's double bind. If he was right in arguing that insight into the contexts of communication comes out of some form of double bind, and if Gumperz is right that communication critically depends on some looking into contextualization cues, I would argue that all communication must then depend on some form of double bind.

For this to be the case two elements would be needed: a double and contradictory message, and a bonding that makes it difficult to leave the situation. For the double and contradictory message, I believe the work of Lakoff (1977) and Brown and Levinson (1978) has suggested the source in the polarity between two aspects of face. In any communication, the participants are faced with the dilemma of respecting the other's right to be left alone (negative face) and the other's right to be accepted as a participating member of society (positive face). This work on politeness phenomena has suggested that any message must be a carefully concocted blend of the right amounts of deference and solidarity (Scollon and Scollon in press a).

What remained was to isolate the bond that ties participants into the situation to produce the double bind. I believe the temporal bond of ensemble completes the picture. In the view I am now taking, it is ensemble which holds participants together in a mutual attention to the ongoing situation, and it is the polarity of positive and negative face that forces the attention to the communication of relationship. These in consort produce a double bind which is the mechanism by which conversants learn to learn.

This allows me to talk about real time communication and learning, but what about the communication and learning that takes place out of real time? Where do insight and creativity (as well as schizophrenia) come from in such nonreal time communications as prose? The answer that I am now pursuing is that it comes out of learned conventions for the production of ensemble. In music, ensemble is conventionalized in scores and in conventions for performance. In my current view, institutions are best regarded as conventionalizations of ensemble. Institutions in this view are the necessary bond to make non-face-to-face communication work. You do not get literacy without binding social institutions.

Olson (1977, 1980) has argued for the intimate relationship of literacy and schooling. My current view leads me to believe that it could be no other way. Literacy as a means of achieving insightful learning may well be fundamentally inseparable from the binding social institutions that direct, manage, and prescribe its use.

Finally, to return to my most general concern, the constitution of institutions in discursive practices, I believe that the concept of ensemble will ultimately allow me to argue that our institutions are not structural entities that impinge on our achievement of ensemble in face-to-face interaction. These institutions might better be seen as the conventionalization of that ensemble itself.

NOTE

A number of colleagues, students, and friends have worked with me in our studies of tempo and ensemble. I would like to thank Richard Dauenhauer, Suzanne Scollon, Carol Barnhardt, Cecilia Martz, Bob Maguire, and Meryl Siegel for their help and hasten to point out that none of them should be implicated in what I have presented here.

1. It is unfortunate that the double bind has become so strongly tied to situations of pathological communication. As Bateson has argued more recently (1979), there are no monotonic values in biology. That is, in Bateson's view, the double bind must be viewed as a situation that with optimal values produces insight and creativity but with maximized values produces such pathological forms of communication as schizophrenia. It is critical in my view that we view 'normal' communication and 'pathological' communication as different states of the same phenomenon, as Bateson's double bind allows us to do.

REFERENCES

Bateson, Gregory. 1972. Steps to an ecology of mind. New York: Ballantine Books.

Bateson, Gregory. 1979. Mind and nature: A necessary unity. New York: E. P. Dutton.

Bolinger, Dwight. 1964. Around the edge of language: Intonation. Harvard Educational Review 34.282-296.

Brown, Penelope, and Stephen Levinson. 1978. Universals in language usage: Politeness phenomena. In: Questions and politeness: Strategies in social interaction. Edited by Esther Goody. New York: Cambridge University Press.

Chafe, Wallace. 1979. The flow of thought and the flow of language. In: Syntax and semantics, Vol. 12: Discourse and syntax. Edited by Talmy Givon. New York: Academic Press.

Chafe, Wallace. 1980. The deployment of consciousness in the production of a narrative. In: The pear stories: Cognitive, cultural, and linguistic aspects of narrative production. Edited by Wallace Chafe. Norwood, N.J.: Ablex.

Chapple, E. D. 1939. Quantitative analysis of the interaction of individuals. Proceedings of the National Academy of Sciences 25.58-67.

Chapple, E. D. 1980. The unbounded reaches of anthropology as a research science, and some working hypotheses. Distinguished lecture for 1979. American Anthropologist 82.4: 741-758.

Erickson, Frederick. 1980. Timing and context in everyday discourse: Implications for the study of referential and social meaning. Sociolinguistic Working Paper Number 67. Austin, Texas: Southwest Educational Development Laboratory.

Erickson, Frederick, and Jeffry Shultz. 1977. When is a context? Institute for Comparative Human Development Newsletter 1(2).5-10.

Erickson, Frederick, and Jeffry Shultz. (in press) Talking to 'the man': Organization of communication in school counseling interviews. New York: Academic Press.

Feldstein, Stanley, Luciano Alberti, and Mohammed BenDebba. 1979. Self-attributed personality characteristics and the pacing of conversational interaction. In: Of speech and time. Edited by Aron W. Siegman and Stanley Feldstein. Hillsdale, N.J.: Lawrence Erlbaum Associates.

Feldstein, Stanley, and Joan Welkowitz. 1978. A chronography of conversation: In defense of an objective approach. In: Nonverbal behavior and communication. Edited by Aron W. Siegman and Stanley Feldstein. Hillsdale, N.J.: Lawrence Erlbaum Associates.

Foucault, Michel. 1976. The archeology of knowledge. New York: Harper and Row.

Foucault, Michel. 1977. Discipline and punish. New York: Pantheon Books.

Foucault, Michel. 1980a. The history of sexuality, Volume I: An introduction. New York: Vintage Books.

Foucault, Michel. 1980b. Power/knowledge: Selected interviews and other writings 1972-1977. Edited by Colin Gordon. New York: Pantheon Books.

Goldman-Eisler, F. 1968. Psycholinguistics: Experiments in spontaneous speech. New York: Academic Press.

Gumperz, John. 1977a. Sociocultural knowledge in conversational inference. In: Georgetown University Roundtable on Languages and Linguistics 1977. Edited by Muriel Saville-Troike. Washington, D.C.: Georgetown University Press. 191-212.

Gumperz, John. 1977b. The conversational analysis of interethnic communication. In: Interethnic communication. Edited by E. Lamar Ross. Proceedings of the Southern Anthropological Society, University of Georgia. University of Georgia Press.

Gumperz, John. 1978. The retrieval of sociocultural knowledge in conversation. Paper presented at the American Anthropology Association, November, 1978.

Gumperz, John, T. C. Jupp, and Celia Roberts. 1979. Cross-talk: A study of cross-cultural communication. A film and notes. London: BBC and the National Centre for Industrial Language Training.

Gumperz, John, and Celia Roberts. 1978. Developing awareness skills for interethnic communication. Middlesex, England: National Centre for Industrial Language Training.

Gumperz, John, and Deborah Tannen. 1979. Individual and social differences in language use. In: Individual differences in language ability and language behavior. Edited by Charles J. Fillmore, Daniel Kempler, and William S-Y. Wang. New York: Academic Press.

Hopkins, Antony. 1979. Understanding music. London: J. M. Dent.

Householder, Fred. 1957. Accent, juncture, intonation and my grandfather's reader. Word 13.234-245.

Hymes, Dell. 1975. Folklore's nature and the Sun's myth. Journal of American Folklore 88.350:345-369.

Hymes, Dell. 1976. Louis Simpson's 'The deserted boy'. Poetics 5.119-155.

Hymes, Dell. 1977. Discovering oral performance and measured verse in American Indian narrative. New Literary History 8.431-457.

Jaffe, Joseph, and Stanley Feldstein. 1970. Rhythms of dialogue. New York: Academic Press.

Ladd, D. Robert. 1980. The structure of intonational meaning: Evidence from English. Bloomington: Indiana University Press.

Lakoff, Robin. 1977. Language and society. In: A survey
of applied linguistics. Edited by R. Wardaugh and H. Brown.
Ann Arbor: University of Michigan Press.
Lenneberg, Eric. 1967. Biological foundations of language.
New York: Wiley.
Liberman, M., and A. Prince. 1977. On stress and linguistic
rhythm. Linguistic Inquiry 8.249-336.
Olson, David. 1977. The languages of instruction: On the
literate bias of schooling. In: Schooling and the acquisition
of knowledge. Edited by R. C. Anderson, R. J. Spiro, and
W. E. Montague. Hillsdale, N.J.: Lawrence Erlbaum Associ-
ates.
Olson, David. 1980. Some social aspects of meaning in oral
and written language: In: The social foundations of lan-
guage and thought: Essays in honor of Jerome S. Bruner.
Edited by David Olson. New York: W. W. Norton.
Pawley, Andrew, and Frances Syder. (n.d.) Sentence formu-
lation in spontaneous speech: The one-clause-at-a-time hy-
pothesis. Unpublished MS.
Perkins, Leialoha Apo. 1980. Toward a modern Pacific
aesthetics for poetry. In: Kingdoms of the heart. By
Leialoha Apo Perkins. 2322 Maile Way, Honolulu:
Kamalu'uluolele.
Sabin, Edward J., Edward J. Clemmer, Daniel C. O'Connell,
and Sabine Kowal. 1979. A pausological approach to speech
development. In: Of speech and time. Edited by Aron W.
Siegman and Stanley Feldstein. Hillsdale, N.J.: Lawrence
Erlbaum Associates.
Scheub, Harold. 1977. Performance of oral narrative. Paper
presented at the Annual Meeting of the American Association
for the Advancement of Science, February, 1977, Denver,
Colorado.
Scollon, Ron. 1976. Conversations with a one year old: A
case study of the developmental foundation of syntax.
Honolulu: University Press of Hawaii.
Scollon, Ron. 1981a. Gatekeeping: Access or retention?
Working Papers in Alaska Native Studies, No. 1. University
of Alaska, Fairbanks: Alaska Native Studies Program.
Scollon, Ron. 1981b. The machine stops: Silence in the
metaphor of malfunction. Paper presented at the session,
The functions of silence. Georgetown University, March
1981. To appear in: The functions of silence. Edited by
Muriel Saville-Troike and Deborah Tannen.
Scollon, Ron. 1981c. Tempo, density, and silence: Rhythms
in ordinary talk. University of Alaska, Fairbanks: Center
for Cross-Cultural Studies.
Scollon, Ron, and Suzanne B. K. Scollon. 1979. Linguistic
convergence: An ethnography of speaking at Fort Chipewyan,
Alberta. New York: Academic Press.

Scollon, Ron, and Suzanne B. K. Scollon. (in press a)
Narrative, literacy, and face in interethnic communication.
Norwood, N.J.: Ablex.

Scollon, Ron, and Suzanne B. K. Scollon. (in press b)
Cooking it up and boiling it down: Abstracts in Athabaskan
children's story retellings. In: Spoken and written language: Exploring orality and literacy. Edited by Deborah
Tannen. Norwood, N.J.: Ablex.

Scollon, Suzanne B. K. (in preparation). Reality set, social
interaction, and linguistic change. Doctoral dissertation.
University of Hawaii.

Siegman, Aron W. 1979. The voice of attraction: Vocal
correlates of interpersonal attraction in the interview. In:
Of speech and time. Edited by Aron W. Siegman and Stanley Feldstein. Hillsdale, N.J.: Lawrence Erlbaum Associates.

Siegman, Aron W., and B. Pope. 1972. The effects of ambi-
guity and anxiety on interviewee verbal behavior. In:
Studies in dyadic communication. Edited by A. W. Siegman
and B. Pope. New York: Pergamon Press.

Sudnow, David. 1979a. Ways of the hand. New York:
Bantam Books.

Sudnow, David. 1979b. Talk's body. New York: Alfred A.
Knopf.

Tedlock, Dennis. 1972. On the translation of style in oral
narrative. In: Toward new perspectives in folklore. Edited
by Americo Paredes and Richard Bauman. Austin: University
of Texas Press.

Welkowitz, J., G. Cariffe, and Stanley Feldstein. 1976. Conversational congruence as a criterion of socialization in children. Child Development 47.269-272.

HARD WORDS: A FUNCTIONAL BASIS
FOR KALULI DISCOURSE

Steven Feld
Bambi B. Schieffelin
University of Pennsylvania

0. Introduction. This paper is concerned with cultural constructions that frame appropriate Kaluli discourse and with some kinds of discourse that operate within that frame. We begin with ethnographic and metalinguistic materials scaffolding the Kaluli notion of 'hardness', the Kaluli conception of language and speech, and the specific idea of 'hard words'. These constructs illustrate the pervasive character of a Kaluli distinction between 'langue' and 'parole'. Based on these systematic notions of language form, socialization, and behavior we analyze some situated discourse examples that indicate both how these cultural constructions are learned and how they operate in everyday interactions.

0.1 People and place. The Kaluli people are part of a population of about 1,200 who live in several hundred square miles of tropical rain forest just north of the slopes of Mt. Bosavi, on the Great Papuan Plateau of Papua New Guinea (E. L. Schieffelin 1976). They are one of four culturally identical but dialectically different subgroups who collectively refer to themselves as *Bosavi kalu* 'Bosavi people'. The Kaluli reside in longhouse communities made up of about 15 families (60-90 people), separated by an hour or so walk over forest trails. Subsistence is organized around swidden horticulture, the processing of wild sago palm to make a staple starch, and hunting and fishing. In broad terms, Kaluli society is highly egalitarian, lacking in the 'big man' social organization characteristic of the Papua New Guinea Highlands. Men and women utilize extensive networks of obligation and reciprocity in the organization of work and sociable interaction.

Kaluli is one of four dialects of Bosavi, a non-Austronesian verb-final ergative language. Most speakers are monolingual.

While Tok Pisin (Neo Melanesian), is known by some younger men, it is almost never heard in daily discourse. Recently introduced literacy programs have affected few people.

Kaluli everyday life is overtly focused around verbal inter- action. Talk is thought of and used as a means of control, manipulation, expression, assertion, and appeal. It gets you what you want, need, or feel owed. Extensive demarcation of kinds of speaking and speech acts further substantiate the ob- servation that Kaluli are energetically verbal; talk is a primary way to be social, and a primary indicator of social competence (B. B. Schieffelin 1979; B. B. Schieffelin and Feld 1979).

More generally, the realm of sound yields the most elaborated forms of Kaluli expression. In the tropical forest and village longhouse it is difficult to find auditory privacy or quiet. Greetings, comings and goings, announcements, arguments, meetings, and all soundings are projected into aurally public space. No comparable variety, salience, or exuberance exists for Kaluli visual or choreographic modes of expressions.

1. 'Hard', 'words', 'hard words': Putting a construction on life and language

1.1 *Halaido* 'hard'. *Halaido* 'hard' is a pervasive Kaluli notion that applies broadly in three cultural-semantic domains. The first is growth and maturation, where the socializing inter- actions in the acquisition of language are what 'makes (it) hard' (*halaido domɛki*); the development of strong teeth and bones in the uncoordinated infant who is 'without understanding' (*asugo andoma*) is a process of 'hardening' (*halaidan*). In these cases, the process of becoming 'hard' is a literal and metaphoric con- struct for physical and mental development and for cultural socialization. A second domain for *halaido* is the fully adult consequence of this maturation process. A *kalu halaido* or 'hard man' is one who is strong, assertive, and not a witch; a major component in this person's projection of his 'hardness' is the acquisition and command of *to halaido* 'hard words', the fully developed capacity for language.[1] The final area in which *halaido* is prominent is dramatic style. In ceremonial perform- ance, songs are intended to be evocative and make the audience weep. The climax in the development of aesthetic tension, where the manner of singing and the textual elements coalesce, is what promotes the 'hardening' (again, *halaido domɛki*) of a song. A performance that does not 'harden' will not move listeners to tears and will not be considered successful. Furthermore, the ability to 'harden' a song is an important compositional (particularly in textual craft) and performative skill.

The cultural construction and prominence of *halaido* in Kaluli growth, adulthood, and presentational style can in part be traced to an origin myth which tells how the world was once muddy and soft; a megapode and Goura pigeon together stamped

on the ground to make it hard. Like the hardening of the
land which symbolizes the necessity of physical and geographi-
cal formation, the hardening of body, language, character, and
dramatic style symbolizes the necessity of human socialization
in order to develop cultural competence.

One term used in opposition to *halaido* is *taiyo* 'soft'. Within
this oppositional frame, *taiyo* is 'soft' in the senses of: mushy
foods, things which decay and rot, or debilitation. It signifies
a stage in the process of decay, and all connotations with this
state are unpleasant. Food taboos constrain the eating of certain soft substances (such as eggs) while young lest one not
'harden'. Children, moreover, do not eat the meat of certain
birds who have 'soft' voices or redundant and otherwise strange
calls, lest their language not harden and they grow up to
speak unintelligible sounds. (On the topic of children's food
taboos vis-à-vis hardness, see B. B. Schieffelin 1979:62-65,
and Feld 1982:Chapter 2.) Similarly tabooed are all animal and
vegetable foods which are yellow; like the leaves of plants,
things yellow as they decay. Witches are said to have yellow
soft hearts, while the hearts of 'hard men' are dark and firm
(E. L. Schieffelin 1976:79, 128). In short, the passage from
'hardness' to 'softness' is undesirable, synonymous with debilitation, vulnerability, and decay, states which must be avoided.
The desired progression in all things is from softness (infant)
to hardness (adult); once hard in body, language, and dramatic style, Kaluli must stay that way.

Another term utilized in opposition to *halaido* is *halaidoma*
'unhard', 'without hardness', formed by the word 'hard' plus
the negative particle *-ma*. Something which is potentially hard
--or which should be, but is not--is 'unhard'. For instance,
when one of us was learning the Bosavi language (SF), his
verbal behavior was judged as *to halaidoma* and his mistakes
greeted assuringly with *towɔ halaidɛsɛge* 'when your language
has hardened'. Never was this speech ability referred to as
*to taiyo 'soft words', a construction which was laughed at
when suggested. 'Soft words' is neither an appropriate nor
utterable phrase; language is either 'hard' or 'unhard', i.e.
in the process of hardening, or in the state of becoming unhard, as in sickness or delirium.

1.2 *To* 'words/language'. Kaluli observe a langue/parole
distinction. This is marked by the distribution of the terms
to and *tolɛma* 'words', 'language' and imperative 'talk words/
language' (langue) and *sama* imperative 'speak' (parole).[2]
To and *tolɛma* refer to the systematic form of language or its
capacity; in contrast, *sama* refers to the manner or act of
speaking. To illustrate langue we examine the items in (1).

(1) Bosavi to   Bosavi language
    bali to   'turned over words' = systematic linguistic
                 irony/euphemism, metaphor, or obfuscation

malolo to   'narrated/told words' (= myths and stories)
mugu to   'taboo words'

In these examples, the noun *to* refers to the system or form of talk. All of these nominal forms can be followed by the habitual verbs *salan* 'one speaks/says', *asulan* 'one understands', or *dadan* 'one hears'. These indicate that one may speak, understand, or hear any of these systems of talk or different languages. The use of *tolɛma* contrasts with constructions using *sama* ('parole'), for instance; (here with *sama* in the present habitual form *salan*).

(2) wɔnoli-salan   one speaks secretly, stealthily
     tɛde-salan   one speaks in a deep voice
     hala-salan   one speaks with mispronunciations

In these instances (and a multitude of similarly constructed ones), *salan* concerns the behavior of speaking, or some description of how speaking is performed.

From our analysis the Kaluli theory of language and speech is one in which *to* 'words' are the prime substance of language; *tolɛma* is the doing or speaking of words.

Figure 1.

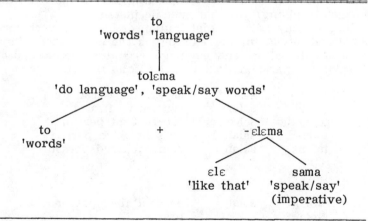

As can be seen in Figure 1, *tolɛma* is formed by adding *to* 'words' and *-ɛlɛma*, imperative 'do/say/speak like that'. The item *ɛlɛma* is the contracted form of *ɛlɛ sama*, 'like that' plus the imperative 'say/speak'. Many Kaluli verbs are formed in this way, by adding a substance or onomatopoeic root to *-ɛlɛma*. For instance, the verb for 'weep' is *yɛlɛma*, composed by contracting the onomatopoeic representation of the sound of weeping, *yɛ*, and the imperative 'say/speak like that' (Feld 1982:Chapters 3 and 4 contain materials on these formations in

Kaluli metalinguistics; B. B. Schieffelin 1979:Chapter 3 contains materials on ɛlɛma and ɛlɛ sama in interaction).

Everyday interactions make clear that the contrast between these two notions is salient for Kaluli. To take a simple instance, SF was once questioning some men about the fact that certain birds are claimed to speak some Bosavi words. He asked about bɔlo, the friarbird in the Kaluli myth about how birds received human tongues.

(3a) Bɔlo-wɔ, Bosavi to salano?
'As for bɔlo, does he *speak* Bosavi words/language?'

Two answers followed:

(3b) Bosavi to salan.
'He *speaks* Bosavi words/language.'

Mugu tolan.
'He *talks* taboo language.'

The first response is the usual specific one ('parole'), while the second was a response from a Christian referring to the way the systematic form of bɔlo's talk consists of words Christians consider taboo ('langue'). Yet in the context of listening to a tape recording of specific calls by bɔlo, the same man noted, *mugu to salab* 'he is speaking/saying taboo words/language', implying: in that specific instance.

In everyday talk the distribution of inflected verb forms for *sama* and *tolɛma* further exemplifies the importance of speaking as a situational act and language as a fundamental capacity. Part of the paradigm includes the items in (4).

(4)
tolɛma	sama	imperative immediate
tolɛbi	sɛlɛbi	imperative future
tolomɛno	sɛlɛmɛno	future first person
tolab	salab	present third person
tolan	salan	habitual third person

but:

*tolɔl	sɔlɔl	present first person
*tolɔ	siyɔ	past

The fact that the present first person form and past form are blocked for *tolɛma* is consistent with the general nature of *to* as 'words/language' and *tolɛma* as 'talk'. Moreover, *tolɔl* contrasts with:

towɔ sɔlɔl 'I speak/say words/language'
towɔ mɔtolan 'It doesn't talk words/language' (can be
said only about animals whose communication is assumed

to be a system based upon a substance other than
'words'.)
*ɛlɛ tolɔ
*ɛlɛ tolɛma
ɛlɛ siyɔ 'said like that'
ɛlɛ sama 'say like that'

Use of 'like that' is also blocked with to and tolɛma because of
lack of reference to a specific situation or context.
    The metalinguistic area provides further examples of the
distribution and further evidence for the cohesiveness of ways
of describing related modalities of soundmaking. In one example across modalities, gese, the root of gesema 'make one feel
sorrow or pity' is only blocked for tolɛma as illustrated in (5).

(5) gese-salan   one speaks sadly (plaintively; with descend-
                  ing intonation)
    gese-yɛlan   one weeps sadly (plaintively; with descend-
                  ing intonation)
    gese-holan   one whistles sadly (plaintively; with de-
                  scending intonation)
    gese-molan   one sings sadly (plaintively; with descend-
                  ing intonation)

    but:

    *gese-tolan   inappropriate because gese describes the
                  manner of speaking and is not applicable
                  to the system or capacity of talk

In these cases the verbs deal with modes of soundmaking while
the adverbs describe the manner of performance; like other
verbs of soundmaking, sama refers to the behavioral aspect of
speech; to and tolɛma refer to its form and capacity.
    A major area of metalinguistic denomination is marked by use
of sa. By itself, sa means 'waterfall'; the term also prefixes
all verbs of soundmaking to indicate that the sound has an 'inside' or text. This usage derives from the metaphor that texts
are composed 'like a waterfall flowing into a waterpool'; the
sound is 'outside' and the text, like a waterfall, is the part
that flows down and inside. Verbs of soundmaking turn into
musical or compositional terms when prefixed by sa in this way,
as in (6) (with verbs all in a present habitual form).

(6) salan 'one speaks'   sa-salan 'one speaks inside the
                             words/one speak poetically'
    yɛlan 'one weeps'   sa-yɛlan 'one weeps with text'
    holan 'one whistles'   sa-holan 'one whistles with words
                             in mind'
    molan 'one sings'   sa-molan 'one sings inside' i.e.
                             'one composes'

but:

tolan 'one talks'   *sa-tolan inappropriate because
                                      one cannot have an inner text
                                      to language capacity

Sa-salan, sa-sama, and *sa-siyo* all indicate an intention to mean
more than what is said. *To* and *tolɛma* do not participate in
this paradigm; **sa-to* and **sa-tolɛma* are blocked because there
cannot be an 'inside' or inner text to the capacity or system of
language. 'Insides' are specific and contextual, related to
situated performances only.

1.3 *To halaido,* 'hard words/talk/language'. Given the cultural importance and pervasiveness of 'hardness' as a construct
underlying mature social process and capacity, and the role of
'hardness' in the distinction Kaluli observe between langue and
parole, we turn to the specific importance of 'hard words'. In
the most general sense, *to halaido* is the system of and capacity
for grammatically well-formed and socially appropriate language.
It is the substance of what Kaluli adults know and act upon in
their verbal behaviors. It is what is normally acquired, the
competence to perform, what Kaluli should 'have in mind' when
they speak. The opposite of *to halaido* is not **to taiyo* 'soft
words'; when language is in the process of forming, it is *to
halaidoma* 'unhard words'.
Nevertheless, when asked if there is any language which is
neither hard nor in the process of becoming hard, Kaluli indicate that such is the situation for the language of song.[3] This
is a special poetic system called ɔbɛ gɔnɔ *to* 'bird sound
words'. Songs are said to be composed and sung from a bird's
point of view, and not a human one. They achieve their plain-
tive quality and ability to move people to tears in this way because birds are the spirit reflections of Kaluli dead. Song
language is thus not human and hard, but birdlike, sad, senti-
mental, reflective.
The contrast between *to halaido* 'hard words' and ɔbɛ gɔnɔ *to*
'bird sound words' is basic. 'Hard words' are assertive and
direct language forms which engage speakers in face-to-face
talk that is interactive and mutual, and are intended to get
speakers what they want or need out of social situations. On
the other hand, 'bird sound words' are reflective and nostalgic,
and are supposed to make a listener empathize with a speaker's
message without necessarily or generally responding to it
verbally. 'Bird sound words' involve linguistic means that
communicate affect by revealing the speaker's state of mind
and moving a listener to feel sympathy for that state.
It is not the case that the difference between these two constructs is simply one of referential/expressive or ordinary/
nonordinary. Certain message forms and contents can appear
in either; the different way that messages are interpreted

depends on judgments about intention deriving from contextual constraints, as well as from placement in an ongoing textual chain. Consider example (7).

(7) Dowɔ ge oba hanaya?
    'Father, where are you going?'

There are numerous daily contexts in which this might be uttered by a person to someone called 'father'. Depending on the intonational contour, the utterance could be a request for information, a challenge, or a rhetorical question--all of which might be benign or threatening. However, when we shift from conversation to song usage, the implications shift radically and the audience immediately knows that the message is that a father has died and left someone behind. The person asking the question is in the resultant state of abandonment and appealing to the audience for sympathy. The form of the words is 'hard' in the sense that they are well formed and could be uttered in appropriate daily situations. However, in a song context the words show their 'inside', *sa*, and this is why they are 'bird sound words'. What is implied in the saying context and manner of saying is more important than the referential equivalents of the words which are said.

2. Learning and speaking 'hard words'

2.1 Imperatives. To exemplify how the process of learning the model for discourse is the learning of 'speaking' and 'hard words', we turn to some discourse examples from tape-recorded family interactions. While these examples involve much adult-child speech, the same forms are used among adults (though perhaps not as frequently or with the same concentration in an episode, since child-adult speech involves more direction and repetition). Imperatives form an important class of examples since they provide major instances of learning by instruction. In addition to indicating specific rhetorical strategies for getting what one wants, imperatives teach directness, control, speaking out, sequencing, and cohesion in the flow of talk.[4] This is further strengthened by the unambiguous relation of speaker/addressee in imperatives, as evidenced by frequent deletion of the optional subject pronoun or a vocative. Moreover, imperatives are favored forms for requesting both actions and objects because Kaluli does not express requests indirectly with forms like 'would you, could you'. Additionally, language structure provides great flexibility, range, and specificity for imperatives. For example, Kaluli morphologically differentiates present and future imperative, marking iterative and punctual action, with various degrees of emphasis or seriousness, all of which can be indicated for single, dual, or plural subjects.

In the examples that follow, *sama*, *ɛlɛma*, and *to/tolɛma* clearly distribute according to whether specific instances of speaking or general prescriptions to talk are encouraged.

For the Kaluli infant, involvement in verbal interactions starts about a week after birth. A mother holds her infant so that it faces another child; she moves the infant as one might a ventriloquist's dummy, speaking for it in a nasalized falsetto voice. Her speech is well formed and clearly articulated, with the complexity of a 4-year-old's speech. The child to whom the baby is 'speaking' engages in conversation directed to the baby for as long as interest can be maintained. Through these verbal interactions the baby is presented as a person, an individual, and is made to appear more independent and mature than it actually is, largely through the mother's speech and her manipulation of the infant's body. These 'three-party' interactions, as well as the much less frequent direct talk between mother and infant, are said to 'give words/language understanding or meaning' (*to samiab*).

The use of language and rhetoric in interaction are the major means of social manipulation and control in Kaluli life. Thus, one of the most important achievements in childhood is to learn to speak Kaluli effectively to a variety of individuals with whom one participates in everyday activities. Kaluli say that language (*to*) has begun once the young child uses two critical words, *nɔ* 'mother' and *bo* 'breast'. Children who only name other people, animals, or objects are said to do so 'to no purpose' (*ba madali*); they are not considered to have begun to use language. This is evidence for the essentially social view of language taken by the Kaluli, a view which emphasizes not only the learning and using of words per se, but the use of specific words to express the first social relationship a person has, namely, the mother-child relationship mediated by food from the breast. This is a basic theme in Kaluli social life. The giving and receiving of food is a major way in which relationships are mediated and validated (E. L. Schieffelin 1976; Feld and B. B. Schieffelin 1980).

Once a child has begun to use the words 'mother' and 'breast', Kaluli begin to 'show language' (*to widan*). Kaluli say that children must be 'shown language' by other Kaluli speakers, principally by the mother. Kaluli use no baby talk lexicon as such, and claim that children must hear *to halaido* 'hard language', if they are to learn to speak correctly. When a Kaluli adult wants a child to say something in an ongoing interaction, a specific model is provided for what the child is to say, followed by the imperative 'say like that' *ɛlɛma*. The word *ɛlɛma* is a contraction of *ɛlɛ* 'like this/that' and *sama* 'say/speak' present imperative. While the adult occasionally asks the child to repeat utterances directly back to him or her, correcting the child's language or initiating a game, the vast majority of these directives to speak concern instructions to the child to say something to someone else. [5] An example of this type of interaction is given in (8).

(8) Mɛli (female, 25 months) and her mother are in the house. Mother has tried to get Mɛli into an ɛlɛma routine, and Mɛli has been distracted. Finally, she settles down. Grandfather is not in sight. [6]

   1. Mother→Mɛli: Sit on this. (Mɛli does)
now speak words.
<u>ami to ɛna sama</u>

   2. Mother →Mɛli ⟶⟶ Grandfather:

Grandfather! <u>ɛlɛma</u>

(softly)   3. Grandfather/

   4. Mother →Mɛli:
speak more forcefully/loudly.
ogole <u>sama</u>

(louder)   5. Grandfather! /

   6. Mother →Mɛli ⟶⟶ Grandfather:
I'm hungry for meat! <u>ɛlɛma</u>

              7. I'm hungry for meat! /

(This continues for 14 turns, which consist of requests to grandfather to get different foods.)

In line 1, Mɛli's mother encourages her to 'speak words/language' (to sama), to engage verbally with someone. She has the addressee and utterances in mind, which she will provide followed by the imperative 'say like that' ɛlɛma. The addressee is named, but Mɛli does not call out loudly enough, and in line 4 her mother tells her how to speak, using sama. This is followed by a specific utterance, and another directive to speak, with which Mɛli complies. Thus, to sama refers to the activity of speaking and saying, where a sequence of utterances are followed by ɛlɛma. While in this episode the addressee, Grandfather, is not in the vicinity and therefore does not respond to Mɛli's requests, the majority of such episodes involve responses from a third person to the child's directed utterances. These sequences often involve extensive and cohesive turns of talk. This 'showing the language' helps the language 'harden' (halaido domɛki) and thus is consistent with the general goals of socialization and development: the achievement of 'hardening' which produces an individual who is in control of himself or herself, and who is capable of verbally controlling others.

Directives to speak, using the imperative, occur in a variety of speech situations, but are most frequent in those involving shaming, challenging, and teasing. The interactional sequence in (9) illustrates several of the rhetorical strategies used in such situations, and demonstrates the sensitivity young children develop about the consequences of what they say.

(9) Wanu (male, 27 months), his sister Binalia (5 years), cousin Mama (3½ years), and Mother are at home. The two girls (Mama and Binalia) are eating salt belonging to another child.

1. Mother → Wanu ⟶ Mama / Binalia :
    Whose is it?!   ɛlɛma

2. Whose is it?! /

3. Is it yours?!   ɛlɛma

4. is it yours?! /

5. Who are you?!   ɛlema

6. who are you?! /

7. Binalia → Wanu ⟶ Mother:
    Is it yours?!   ɛlɛma

8. is it yours?! /

9. Mother → Wanu ⟶ Binalia / Mama :
    It's mine!   ɛlɛma

10. Mama → Binalia: Don't speak like that!
    ɛlɛdo sɛlasabo!

Rhetorical questions, such as those found in lines 1, 3, 5, and 7 in example (9), are frequent in family interactions involving the use of ɛlɛma. They are intended to shame the addressee so that he or she will terminate undesirable behavior. Kaluli frequently utilize teasing, shaming, and other means of verbal confrontation that focus on an addressee who cannot answer rhetorical questions without the admission of fault. These strategies of confrontation and their component rhetorical skills set the tone of many interactions, while the use of directives (such as 'put the salt away') or physical intervention is much less common. Although children may challenge adults in certain situations (and are encouraged to do so), here Mama (age 3½) tells Binalia 'don't speak like that', referring to Binalia's attempt to get Wanu to challenge his mother. When asked about that utterance, Kaluli said that Mother could get angry and take the salt away. Thus, even children evidence a sensitivity to how language is being used in interactions, sensing the consequences of particular kinds of talk. This further serves the functional importance of directly putting the burden on the addressee.

The use of ɛlɛma in these interactions is consistent with the mother's treatment of her preverbal infant, in which she puts words into his mouth. She pushes her young language-learning child into social interaction, providing the words he cannot say or may not be interested in saying. This practice provides the opportunity for the child to acquire the verbal skills that are needed later on, when mother has her next baby and the child becomes part of a peer group. It is the ability not only to repeat rhetorical questions such as 'who are you?!' 'Is it yours?!' but to use them, spontaneously in the appropriate contexts, that lead Kaluli to comment about a young child, *to halaido momada salab* 'he/she is starting to speak hard language'.

It is important to note that throughout interactions using ɛlɛma, assertion prevails. In teaching language, mothers are teaching their small children assertion itself. For Kaluli this implies strength and independence. In interactional terms this means to request with imperatives, to challenge and confront, and to say something powerful so others will bend or give. Mothers never use ɛlɛma to instruct their children in begging, whining, or appealing to others for sympathy. In learning the types of things one says with ɛlɛma, Kaluli children are learning culturally specific ways in which to be tough, independent, and assertive, which reinforces the cultural value of acting in a direct, controlled manner.

In addition to the imperatives *sama* and *ɛlɛma*, the imperative *tolɛma* is also used in conversations. In contrast to the act of speaking (*sama*), use of *tolɛma* calls attention to the importance of verbal interaction as an activity in which children are encouraged to participate.

(10) Mɛli (female, 25 months) is with her father in the house. She is not involved in any activity. Mama is not in sight.

1. Father→Mɛli——▸▸Mama:
   Mama! call out.
   holɛma

2. Mama/

3. Come and talk together with me! ɛlɛma
   nɛno to tomɛni meno!

4. come and talk together with me/

(There is no response. Seeing another child)

5. Father→Mɛli: Now you and Babi go in order
to talk.
ami Babi gain tomɛ'hamana

6. (Mɛli puts marble in her mouth) Take out the
marble! After taking it out with your hand,
you will talk!
to tolɛbi

In this episode, Father is trying to get Mɛli established in a
verbal activity, made explicit in line 3 as a directive (ɛlɛma)
to invite Mama to come and talk (to tomɛni meno). The word
ɛlɛma marks what is specific to be said, and the concatentated
form (tomɛni 'in order to talk' + meno 'come' imperative) marks
the general activity to take place. A similar concatenated form
is used in line 5, this time directing Mɛli to go in order to
talk. And finally (line 6), to tolɛbi (future imperative) is used
to indicate what Mɛli should do, but not what she will say. [7]
    In this situation, talking is being established as a way to
engage and be social. Parents assume the importance of integrating children into adult verbal activities and additionally
encourage the organization and maintenance of verbal exchanges
among children themselves. This establishes talk as a topic of
talk, instructions to talk as instructions to be social, and talk
as a modality that promotes social cohesion.
    In addition to both the desire and the necessity to develop to
halaido, children must learn to converse, to kudan 'one puts
language/words together'. The expression i kuduma 'put wood
together', is used to tell someone how to build a successful
fire, by taking a stick with an ember, putting another stick to
it to make contact and transferring the heat. Just as putting
wood and sticks together makes a successful fire, talk must
also be put together to be successful. Commenting on the
language of a 2-year-old who wasn't collaborating with or
building on the other's utterances, a Kaluli said, to mɔkudab
'he doesn't put language together'. The same expression was
used with regard to a conversation between two adults, in
which they had not agreed on what they were, in fact, talking
about.

(11) As father is leaving Mɛli (age 25 months)
my child! as for me, I'm going to converse.
niyɔ to kudumɛni
You stay here.
ge ya tɛbi.

The use of to kudan in these contexts indicates the importance
Kaluli attach to verbal interactions which are mutual, collaborative, and cohesive.

As has been seen, utterances directing a child to use language (tolɛma) and specifying what to say (ɛlɛma) and how to say it (sama) are used to promote and support young children's involvement with others in a variety of everyday interactions. The Kaluli say that without this kind of direction children would not learn what to say and how to say it. The idea is that after a child is 'shown' what to say, he or she will spontaneously use language to respond, to initiate, sustain, and control verbal interactions. However, children themselves initiate and participate in language interactions that are unlike any that their parents have shown them. Many of these exchanges are terminated by Kaluli mothers when they feel that these could impede language development or promote an undesirable effect. These situations provide an opportunity to examine what is and is not acceptable language behavior for small children, and the cultural reasons for these differences.

(12) Mɛli (30½ months) and her cousin Mama (45 months) are at home with Mɛli's mother, who is cooking and talking to several adults. Mama initiates a sequence of word play involving Mɛli which is marked by repetition, high pitch, staccato delivery, and exaggerated prosodic contours. After 10 turns this dissolves into sound play marked by overlap within turn pairs, higher pitch, vowel lengthening and shifting, and repetition. This continues for 15 more turns, at which point Mɛli's mother suddenly turns to the girls and says in a loud, authoritative voice:

Wai! Try to speak good talk! This is bird talk!
Wai! to nafa se sɛlɛiba!   ɔbɛ towɔ we!

The girls suddenly become quiet.

The mother's abrupt termination of the children's verbal/vocal interaction was not due to mild irritation caused by the noise these girls were making, since similar sound levels caused by other kinds of verbal activity would never have prompted this reaction. Her response, which was consistent with that of other Kaluli mothers in similar situations, grows out of Kaluli ideas about language development and the broader notion of taboo.

As mentioned earlier, Kaluli have very definite ideas about appropriate verbal behavior for language learning children. When asked about this word/sound play, Kaluli said it had no name and was 'to no purpose'. Purposive language is encouraged in interactions and the vocalizations between Mɛli and Mama violated these cultural expectations.

However, in addition to their ideas about how a young child's language should sound, Kaluli say that children and birds are

connected in a number of complex ways (Feld 1982: Chapter 2).
In addition to prohibiting young children from eating certain
birds lest they, too, only 'coo' and never develop hard language, children must not sound like birds, even in play.
Thus, in order to insure that 'hard language' develops, the
mother prevents a dangerous association by terminating this
vocal activity. Furthermore, she makes it explicit to the children and to the others around them, that children are to
speak 'good talk', not 'bird talk'. It is important to emphasize
that Mother does not want them to stop speaking, but to
speak properly.

Another form of verbal behavior that is not tolerated by
Kaluli mothers is the imitation and distortion of a younger
child's speech by an older child. It is important that older
children do not engage in language interactions with younger
children that are contradictory to the efforts made by adults
to ensure 'good talk' and 'hard talk'. Consider example (13).

(13) Abi (27½ months) and his sister Yogodo (5½ years) are
     alone in the house, as Mother has gone out to get wood.
     Following Abi's utterances, Yogodo repeats what he says,
     phonologically distorting his words to tease him. When
     mother returns, Yogodo continues to repeat everything
     Abi says to her, leaving him very confused and frus-
     trated. After hearing eight turns of this, mother turns
     to Yogodo and says:

     speak words/language!
     to sama

Mothers see this type of activity as not only mocking or teasing
the young child's not as yet well-formed language, but as confusing the younger child about language, its correct form and
appropriate use. Thus, an undesirable language interaction is
terminated with the explicit directive to 'speak language' (to
sama). By focusing on the form of talk rather than its specific
content, the children are not discouraged from speaking to one
another but encouraged to do it properly, on the model of 'hard
words'.

By the time a child is about 3½ years old, and ɛlɛma directives have stopped, that child's language is considered sufficiently hard so that the playing of word and sound games
with peers is acceptable. While closely timed, repetitive,
formulaic utterances involving teasing and challenging are
appropriate for older children, mothers do not want these children negatively influencing younger ones whose speech is not
yet well developed.

(14) A mother, her son (28 months), and three siblings
     (ages 5-8), are sitting around a fire cooking bits of
     food. The three siblings are playing a teasing game

about who will and will not eat, which involves speaking
rapidly and distorting words. After watching this for
16 turns, the little boy attempts to join the interaction
by interjecting nonsense syllables. The mother turns to
the older children saying:

speak hard!!
<u>halaido sama!</u>

to which one of the older children responds (teasing):
huh?, followed by the mother's repetition with emphasis:

speak hard!!
<u>halaido samɛ!!</u>

'Speak hard' implies that until this point, speech has been 'unhard'. Such a reference is always to speech in an ongoing
context. In this situation, as in many others like it, mothers
are careful that their young children do not sound less mature
than they actually are in their speaking. This is consistent
with the goals of language socialization: to enable children to
be independent and assertive by the time that they are 3-3½
years old. Independence and assertion in speech and action
are functionally valued in this egalitarian society; ability to
speak out is one important way to get what one needs.

Next, we examine situations with negative imperatives, where
sɛlɛsabo (sama) and tolɛsabo (tolɛma) are used. The use of
sɛlɛsabo 'don't say (that/it)' (parole) implies that one knows or
suspects what is about to be said, and is telling another not
to say that thing. It is also used with reference to a specific
body of knowledge or secrets. One may say 'don't say that'
or 'don't tell them' with reference to specific information. Note
example (15).

(15) A number of people are socializing and eating in the
     longhouse. A guest enters, having walked through the
     muddy jungle paths; leeches have attached themselves
     to his ankles. A child runs up to alert the guest to
     this fact, and an adult intervenes, saying: <u>sɛlɛsabo!</u>
     'don't say it!', thus directing the child not to say the
     speech specific word 'leech' while others are enjoying
     their meal. Kaluli etiquette strongly prohibits the say-
     ing of this word while people are eating.

The use of sɛlɛsabo contrasts with the use of tolɛsabo.
Tolɛsabo means 'don't talk' in the sense, 'be quiet', 'shut up',
or 'don't engage in language' (langue). The meaning is 'stop
talking' or 'do something else besides engage in language'.

(16) Isa (age 8) is teasing her brother Wanu (32 months) about who will be his wife. Father tells him to counter her teasing with:

1. Father→Wanu →→ Isa:
no! ɛlɛma

2. no! /

3. that's mother! ɛlɛma

4. that's mother! /

5. One doesn't speak/say like
that! ɛlɛma
ɛlɛdo mɔsalano!

6. One doesn't
speak/say like
that! /

7. Father→Isa: girl, Isa, you ...
that's being bad.
Shut up! Shut up!
tolɛsabowo!

In this sequence, an adult uses ɛlɛma to instruct a young child in how to provide an appropriate response to his sister's teasing. In addition, in line 5 the child is directed to say 'one doesn't say that', calling attention to the inappropriateness of what is being said. This response is yet another way to counter teasing. In such interactions the conventions of language use are made explicit to younger members who may not as yet know them or may need to be reminded of them. This sequence ends when the father, being angry at his daughter, tells her to 'stop talking'. This instructs the children as to what is and is not out of bounds and further draws attention to the social need to control the flow of talk by forcefully ending undesirable speech.

A final example completes the point that in some interactions the issue is not to say what you want to say better, but to stop talking completely.

(17) A group of children are loudly talking and playing,
and mother turns to them:

Sosas, shut up!
tolɛsabo!

Sosas is the name of a very noisy bird, one whose sounds are considered unpleasant. By comparing the children to *sosas* birds, the mother emphasizes the irritating nature of the group noise, further marking the general injunction to stop the annoying verbal activity and do something else. *Tolɛsabɔ* is used here quite in contrast to *sɛlɛsabo*; the children are being told to stop the activity of talking, not to stop saying specific things.

In these examples of learning and speaking 'hard words', children are provided both with an explicit cultural model of the importance of verbal activity, and with the importance of saying or not saying the right thing. Functionally, such a model promotes social integration into a coherent world constructed upon the importance of direct, controlled, forceful face-to-face communication. Kaluli children learn to focus upon what they want and need, even when this requires challenge or confrontation. They learn that discourse is a means to social ends, and they openly utilize sequential talk following that model. Imperatives are often heard in the language of adults to children and adults to each other, and the ability to utilize language in interaction requires an understanding of when to demand specific speech and when to demand verbal closure.

When something has been said or done, or might be said or done, the ability to refer appropriately, report, or challenge is one consequence of the way Kaluli learn 'hard words'. Such situations continually reflect the choice of formulations about what has been said in order to focus the specifics of the situation. If one reports benignly to another that 'someone said something to me ...', and the listener immediately wants to challenge the substance of the remarks, a common interruption at this point would be *ba madali siyɔ* 'it was said for no reason'. Remarks on the truth or intentions of what was said are very commonly the subject of initial interruptions in conversation, immediately letting the speaker know the listener's point of view on the reported speech. Remarks about the circumstances of what has been said must be formulated with *siyɔ* 'said', or *ɛlɛ siyɔ*, 'said like that'; these refer to a specific instance of speech or the 'said' of a report in a certain context. *Tolɔ* can never appear in these situations because one cannot have the capacity or system of language in the past; in fact, the construction is inappropriate in any utterance about the language of deceased persons.

More pointed rhetorical strategies for dealing with the reports or references of speakers are formulated with two common phrases: *ge siyɔwɔ dadaye?!* 'Did you hear what I said?!' and *ge oba siyɔwɔ?* 'What did you say?' While these can be requests for information, confirmation, or acknowledgment, they are often found breaking into or responding to the stream of discourse in order to focus reaction and challenge what is being said. Neither construction can be formulated with *to* and *tolɛma*, as both exemplify the necessity of controlling a specific instance of speaking.

Rhetorical challenge can be pushed a degree farther; escalation to threat is an important way not just to register response but to prohibit or shame someone who is doing something that is inappropriate or not approved of. In such cases the threat is registered simply with: *sameib!* 'someone will say (something)!' The implicit threat is that someone will say 'who are you?!', 'is it yours?!', or other pointed rhetorical questions that shame the addressee. Use of *sameib!* to control inter- actions that may get out of hand, rather than use of physical control, emphasizes the concern Kaluli exhibit about speaking as an instrument of social action and accomplishment. Such a threat cannot be formulated with **tolomeib!* because it is the implied 'something' that will be said that is so important to shaming as a regulatory action.

In these examples of learning, speaking, and controlling 'hard words', it is clear that Kaluli must understand when it is appropriate to talk about language, and when it is appropri- ate to talk about speaking. Kaluli discourse then is taught and utilized as an integration of linguistic and metalinguistic practice which is shaped and scaffolded by having a place in a culturally coherent world of beliefs about 'hardness', con- trol, direct action, and assertion. Kaluli discourse must be analyzed in relation to the belief system that constructs its organization and goals, as well as the social ends which it accomplishes for participants. Cultural analysis then is an ex- plicit manner of connecting form and function. We have found that constructing an analysis from the bottom up satisfies both the demands of ethnographically situated explications and the demands of explaining the ordinary and routine ways that Kaluli interactions actualize cultural expectations about language use and meaningful social behavior.

3. **Closure.** To close a story, a speech (or, in a recent adaptation among the few literate Kaluli, a letter), Kaluli utilize the phrase *ni towɔ kɔm* 'my talk/words/language are finished'. It is fitting that we close this paper by explicating why this phrase is appropriate and why the contrasting **ni siyɔwɔ kɔm* 'what I have said is finished' is inappropriate and not utterable.

For Kaluli, verbal closure implies directly that there is nothing left to talk about, at least for the moment. What is finished is the action of language, the invocation of words, the activity of talk. No such boundary is appropriately imposed upon the 'said' of speaking in a specific setting, which is always open- ended and ongoing. Verbal activities are closed by a boundary on talk, not a boundary on what has been said. The function of reaching closure, again, underscores the direct manner in which Kaluli control situations and behaviors by viewing talk as a socially organized and goal-directed actualization of the capacity for language, 'hard words'. *Ni towɔ kɔm.*

NOTES

Fieldwork in Bosavi during 1975-1977 was supported by the National Science Foundation, the Wenner-Gren Foundation for Anthropological Research, the Archives of Traditional Music, and the Institute of Papua New Guinea Studies. We gratefully acknowledge their assistance. Detailed reports of our separate work are Feld (1982) and B. B. Schieffelin (1979). The order of author's names was determined by geomancy.

1. *Kalu* specifically means 'man' (opposing *kesale* 'women') but can generally refer to 'person' or 'people'. Kaluli see the ideal form of 'hardness' modelled on maleness; women, however, are clearly supposed to be competent language users. Sex role socialization is clear in the speech of mothers to children; little boys are encouraged to use language to be demanding, while little girls are encouraged to use language to be more complacent. These issues are addressed in detail in B. B. Schieffelin (1979: Chapter 2).

2. It is worth noting that, in contrast to some aspects of metalinguistics, Kaluli do not directly verbalize about the importance of a distinction between *to* and *sama*. The clear langue/parole distinction is consistent, however, in all of our elicited or tape-recorded naturally occurring data. Further discussion of how this distinction affects Kaluli poetic concepts can be found in Feld (1982: Chapter 4).

3. There is one additional context where the term *to halaido* or *halaido to* is found. This is in the talk of debate, heated discourse, anger, dispute, or confrontation (as, for example, in a bridewealth negotiation). This sense of *to halaido* is far less prominent than the broader usage. The morphological marking *-ait* is used only to indicate anger; it is not prominent in our sample of recorded speech (83 hours of family interactions, 50 hours of song, myth, texted weeping, and more formal modes).

4. We are speaking here about interactions in an assertive frame. These characterizations do not apply equally to frames of appeal. On Kaluli assertion and appeal, see E. L. Schieffelin (1976: 117-134) and B. B. Schieffelin (1979: Chapters 3 and 4).

5. In casual adult interactions, εlεma may be used to direct a response to a speaker who is slow to respond to teasing or joking. A more marked and deliberate adult usage occurs in funerary weeping, where women improvise sung-wept texts to a deceased person lying before them. Often these texts contain lines like, 'Look up to the treetops, εlεma ...', indicating that the weeper is telling the deceased to say these words back to her. The grammaticality and pragmatics here rest on the notion that while the deceased is next to the woman in body, he or she is going elsewhere in spirit, in the form of a bird. The commanded words marked with εlεma must therefore be in the form of an appropriate utterance to a living person from one who is now a bird. 'Look up to the treetops' is such a line because it indicates that from then on the weeper will only see the deceased as a bird in the treetops. Feld (1982: Chapter 3) contains an analysis of εlεma in sung-texted-weeping.

6. Transcription conventions are described in B. B. Schieffelin (1979). Child speech is on the right and the speech of

others plus contextual notes are on the left. Single arrow indicates speaker to addressee; double arrow indicates speaker to addressee who is to address a third party. Kaluli glosses are provided only where *to*, *tolɛma*, *ɛlɛma*, and *sama*, or other forms of these verbs, are used. Full transcripts of all examples with morpheme by morpheme glosses can be obtained by writing to the authors.

7. The use of concatenated forms also appears with *sama*, particularly in interactions with *ɛlɛma*, where the child is too far from the intended addressee and is told to 'go in order to speak', *sɛmɛni hamana*.

REFERENCES

Feld, Steven. 1982. Sound and sentiment: Birds, weeping, poetics and song in Kaluli expression. Philadelphia: University of Pennsylvania Press.

Feld, Steven, and Bambi B. Schieffelin. 1980. Sociolinguistic dimensions of Kaluli relationship terms. Paper presented at the Annual Meeting, American Anthropological Association.

Schieffelin, Bambi B. 1979. How Kaluli children learn what to say, what to do, and how to feel: An ethnographic study of the development of communicative competence. Unpublished Ph.D. dissertation. Department of Anthropology, Columbia University. [To appear: Cambridge University Press.]

Schieffelin, Bambi B., and Steven Feld. 1979. Modes across codes and codes within modes: A sociolinguistic analysis of conversation, sung-texted-weeping, and stories in Bosavi, Papua New Guinea. Paper presented at the Annual Meeting, American Anthropological Association.

Schieffelin, Edward L. 1976. The sorrow of the lonely and the burning of the dancers. New York: St. Martins Press.

THE MEDICINE AND SIDESHOW PITCHES

Fred 'Doc' Bloodgood

Editor's Introduction. One of the highlights of the 1981 Georgetown University Round Table on Languages and Linguistics preconference sessions was a presentation by Fred 'Doc' Bloodgood, the last known living medicine show pitchman. A transcript of Mr. Bloodgood's presentation is included here in order to preserve an example of a once flourishing, now extinct American folk discourse genre which is not otherwise available. No medicine show or sideshow pitch of the twenties or thirties was ever tape recorded or written down. As Doc Bloodgood put it in a letter to me, until now the pitch

was not printed, stamped, stained, marked or engraved ... on anything movable or immovable, capable of receiving the least impression of a word, letter, syllable, or character, which might have become legible or intelligible, to any person or persons under the blue canopy of heaven.

A tape recording of Mr. Bloodgood's introductory remarks and demonstration pitches is also available from Georgetown University Press.

Although the transcript fails to give an adequate sense of the oral presentation, it shows dramatically that the medicine show and sideshow pitches were constructed in ways similar to those identified by Lord (1960) for oral epics: formulaic phrases woven together in a flexible but structured sequence to yield a text that sounds memorized because it is astoundingly fluent. Mr. Bloodgood produced only a few false starts and only three instances of fillers ('uh') in more than a half-hour of talk. The pitches make use of repeated rhythmic patterns, sound play, and specific details to create immediacy and vivid imagery-- features found in poetry, both oral and written.

What follows is a verbatim transcript of Doc Bloodgood's introductory remarks and sample pitches. Mr. Bloodgood did have

a chance to go over the transcript and make minor corrections.
He inserted commas and occasional underscores, corrected the
spelling of names, corrected the transcription in a few places,
and added two sentences to the pitches. No other changes were
made.

On the matter of the names of the tonic ingredients, Mr.
Bloodgood wrote the following disclaimer in a letter to me, which
I pass on:

> I will not vouch for the accuracy of the names of the roots,
> herbs, leaves, gums, bark, berries, and blossoms. But
> we have the distinct advantage that no one known to the
> medical world can dispute their veracity.
>
> In case of a challenge on this, just remember that some
> of these are probably now extinct ... like the medicine show
> people themselves ... of yesteryear. (Down the valley of a
> thousand yesterdays).
>
> ... the corrections I have listed are the nearest I could
> come. Anyway, as my dad always told me, 'Never let a
> grain of truth interfere with the story.'

I am very grateful to Mr. Bloodgood for his participation and
to Samantha Hawkins of Georgetown University and Steve Zeitlin
of the Smithsonian Institution for helping to arrange for his
appearance. Marta Dmytrenko generously volunteered to tran-
scribe the presentation.

Doc Bloodgood's oral introduction. Fifty years ago the medicine show was the only entertainment that some people ever saw.
It was their one connecting link with the outside world, and
they looked forward to its arrival with a very great deal of
anticipation. I suppose one could say it was the forerunner of
the commercial on radio or television as we see it today. The
show was usually comprised of about seven to as many as fourteen performers: singers, dancers, comedians, a piano player,
fiddler, and so forth. And after about thirty minutes of entertainment, then came the pitchman or the lecturer, followed
hopefully by the sale.

It was imperative that the moment the sale started, the music
also started loud and lively. And then to add further interest
to that magical moment, all of the performers acted as agents
for the product. In other words, they would stand poised with
a bottle of tonic in hand, waiting for a hand. The moment a
hand shot up, that particular agent would loudly shout, 'Sold
out, doctor!' And then all the other six or seven agents would
immediately echo that cry, 'Sold out, doctor!' Now on the way
back to the stage to replenish his stock, that is to get a new
bottle of medicine, that man would again scream, 'Sold out,
doctor,' and with all this repetition, you can readily understand

that the impression was created that a tremendous amount of tonic was being sold, although unfortunately such was not always the case.

At some point in the program came the inevitable candy sale. This was a box of prize candy usually put out by the Gordon Howard Candy Company of Kansas City, Missouri, which sold for as little as a dime or as much as a quarter. Now each package contained a prize of some value. However, some of the prizes were much much too large to be contained within the package, so they had coupons calling for them up on the stage. And these called for various articles, such as: safety razors, silk hose, silk lingerie, opera glasses, field glasses, pen and pencil sets, garter and hose sets, boxes of stationery, beacon blankets, tilt-top tables, many other valuable and useful articles.

Now incidentally, it was the sale of this candy that was often instrumental in allowing the show to move from one town to another. Remember, this was in the very depths of the Great Depression. And that, combined with the fact that down in Georgia they had not yet quite recovered from Sherman's march to the sea, it made selling a real challenge. Now most of us owned cars. But the show itself usually moved on a very large truck, the sides of which would let down to form a stage. One particular one that I recall was on a show I was with in Texas, that was a Packard truck--a 1912. It had solid rubber tires. What a collector's item that would be today!

Medicine shows were once as plentiful as the buffalo on the western plains, and people thought this was something that would be with us forever. And yet, a year ago this last fall, when the Smithsonian Institution decided that this was part of our American heritage which should be preserved, they had great difficulty in locating anyone who was ever even a part of it. So they placed an ad in the Billboard magazine. (That's the showman's bible.) And even after combing the entire country, they were able to locate just fourteen performers and two pitchmen. Actually they located one pitchman; the other one passed away last summer.

One of the difficulties, of course, was the fact that not one word of the material was ever written down. Any of the bits, the skits, the after pieces or the lectures. Not a bit of it. Everything was passed from word of mouth, one to the other. And what with old age taking its toll, and ancient memories growing dim, it is truly only a question of time until the medicine show of yesteryear will have vanished down the valley of a thousand yesterdays. I suppose it would be safe to assume that we are an endangered species.

Now by a stroke of very good luck, my son in California happened to see this ad in the Billboard, and he telephoned to me and he said, 'You surely should answer this'. And under extreme duress I finally did. The duress came because I felt that this would never come back. I hadn't done any of these in forty years, these pitches. Or anything like that. But I

did call the Smithsonian people, and they suggested that I submit a tape of a sample of an oldtime medicine show pitch, which
I did, and immediately I received a call from them inviting me
to be a participant in the folk life festival in October.

And my arrival on that lot was a very emotional thing, I
assure you. They had reconstructed an old-time medicine show
stage just exactly as I remember it, complete in every detail
even to the two model T trucks, one on either side of the stage,
beautifully restored. When I stood there it was as though time
had turned backward in its flight a half a century. And a
great lump came to my throat, and a thrill ran up and down my
spine, and--remember, all this, in the actual shadow of the
Washington Monument. To me it was the absolute apogee of
spine-tingling enchantment.

And when those banjos started to play and those fiddlers
started, it all came back to me just exactly as I hope it will
today. We gave a full and complete performance each day plus
many interviews and reminiscences, all of which was recorded
for the Archives of the Smithsonian Institution. They told me
that even two hundred years from now (Mr. Zeitlin told me that)
that two hundred years from now, if anyone were doing research
on medicine shows, that would be the voice they would hear.
It was very awe-inspiring to me to think that I might be able
to contribute something to our American heritage. Actually, I
suppose the only real difference between David Farragut and
Doc Bloodgood is that instead of the stirring battle of cry of
'Don't give up the ship!' etched indelibly upon the yellowing
pages of history, my contribution may be, 'Sold out, doctor,
four dollars change'.

Now just a very few words as to how I got started in this
business. As a youth I can't ever remember ever wanting to
do anything else. When I was seven my Dad took me to the
circus, and the circus was just great, but the sideshow! The
sideshow was *incredible*. And I thought to be able to stand on
that platform, in front of that long line of pictorial paintings,
and actually convince anybody of the benefits to be derived by
actually *visiting* that congress of freaks, curiosities, and mon-
strosities, that would be the greatest occupation a man could
ever have. So, the day I finished high school, I hitch-hiked
to the nearest circus, and there followed eleven of the most exciting, incredible years that a youth could ever have. With
circus and sideshows in the summer in the north, and then to
the medicine show circuit consisting of Georgia, Mississippi,
Alabama, and Texas, in the winter, and all this, I remembered
that, I think one of the things that convinced me, that to be
able to sell your goods *sight unseen*, and collect the money in
advance--that would be the ultimate in selling.

That wonderful week in Washington that we had a year ago
last October was not without its sad moments, because as I was
standing on that platform on the last and final day, it suddenly
occurred to me that it was quite conceivably possible that I was

now giving the *last* and *final* medicine show lecture that the world would ever know.

But how very wrong I was. Because last summer, they telephoned me again and said that because of the success of the Washington situation, that they were going to do a documentary film of a medicine show in Bailey, North Carolina. So, again, we flew to NC and met fourteen venerable old performers, most of which we already knew. All had been with medicine shows in the old days, one of which was Roy Acuff, and may I just say that he probably is one of the very nicest people I've ever had the privilege of meeting. So, again, we gave a performance every day and the film company from the Smithsonian took over seven miles of film which will be edited and then shown on educational TV next fall sometime.

Their attention to detail was absolutely phenomenal, even to this time the Grand Free Street Parade. They had a galaxy of model T Ford trucks with performers and musicians playing up and down the main street of Bailey, NC, while the cameras rolled. And it was my privilege to lead the parade perched on the back of a rumble seat of a Model A Ford roadster, with a bottle of tonic in one hand, and waving to an enthusiastic audience with the other. Oh, and the last two nights I really had an opportunity to sell medicine again. Now actually this was just colored water and the people were apprised of that. It was a souvenir bottle. But that which I'd waited for so long happened. When I got ready and offered that medicine for sale, a thousand people became a veritable sea of hands, each hand holding a dollar bill in it. How often I had dreamed of just this situation!

Those wonderful people of North Carolina gave us a banquet or a barbecue almost every night, consisting of whole roast pigs and other southern specialties. Then throughout the day, after the show they would come back and ask for autographs and the Girl Scouts would ply us with cookies and cold drinks. It was a memorable week in our lives, but it was also a memorable week in history. Because on Saturday, September 6, 1980, the medicine show of yesterday joined the silent ranks of the dinosaur and the dodo and the passenger pigeon. That was the end forever. And as the guitars and fiddles faded into the night air, the phenomenon of the oldtime medicine show also faded, forever. And the evening breeze seemed to sigh with sadness as it swirled the papers and the refuse of an emptying lot, as the last clarion cries of 'Sold out, doctor' vanished forever.

I've been asked to do an actual pitch one more time. It'll be just as it was in 1928, with one exception. There won't be any sale this time. I hope that you'll enjoy hearing it as much as I'll enjoy doing it for you. And if at the conclusion of our performance any time remains, I would be just more than happy to answer any or all questions, on a no charge basis, without cost or obligation.

Oh, just one more thing. It was a different era. Remember, things that were dead serious in those days, hopefully today they will prove to be entertaining or even amusing to you. But it was an entirely different age.

You will notice one thing also, that whether it be a medicine show pitch or a sideshow pitch, we used a great deal of alliteration or euphonious phrases. May I give you just a short example? For instance, in the process of describing alliteration: Now one particular show I had was a deep sea diving show consisting of a diver, a hard hat diver, and a giant deep sea devil fish or octopus. And at one point in the program I would say,

And ladies and gentlemen, I'm going to send the young man to the very bottom of that steel and glass tank for a hand to hand encounter with that death dealing demon denizen of the deep and, if fortunate, bring him to the surface for your very close inspection.

Or an example of a euphonious phrase: I once worked on a living skeleton with the Rubin and Cherry show; this was in about 1929: Walter R. Cole. Now, Walter Cole was 5'11" tall and weighed just 63 lbs. Now at a certain point in the program, I would ask Walter to raise that right arm of his, and he would put that tiny little arm over the top of the canvas, and I would say,

Ladies and gentlemen, there he sits in there, slowly wasting away, slowly becoming atrophied, slowly becoming ossified, slowly becoming petrified, and slowly turning to stone. Unable to move, carried around from one place to another by his nurse just like a mother would a babe, and yet-- apparently happy, for I have never heard him complain.

I want you to also if you will notice, that there's a great use of *comparisons* in all of these pitches too. And it's not by accident that we used the long *E* or the *AH* sound when we named freaks. The reason for that was very obvious, really. We didn't have all this sound equipment in those days and the *E* or the *AH* sound had a much better carrying quality. That's why all my 'Geek' shows or wild girl shows, were either Neva or Neola. I'm thinking of one show that I worked on where they incorporated *both* the *E* and the *AH* sound, was Leah-Lee-- half man, half woman, alive.

And when you get on the inside, ladies and gentlemen, I want you to draw an imaginary line from the very top of its head down to the very tip of its toes. And on one side you'll find this strong arm, the muscular limb, the coarse beard, the heavy features. And on the other side, the beautiful features of the feminine sex. Father, mother, brother and sister, in one body alive.

And now for the pitch of the medicine show.

THE MEDICINE SHOW PITCH

Good evening, ladies and gentlemen, and welcome to the Clifton Comedy Company. We have come to your city to stay one week, bringing you clean, moral, refined entertainment which is absolutely free. We bring with us a company of fourteen performers, each and every one an artist in his or her line. But more than that, they are all ladies and gentlemen and can conduct themselves as such. In other words, there will be nothing seen, heard, said, or done, to mar the impunity or injure the propriety, in any way, shape, form or manner of the most fastidious little lady in the community. (If you'll pardon me a second, then, you'll see how these are usually in multiples of two, four, or six. It seems to work out that way; I don't know why.)

We're sent here by the Finley Medicine Company, forty-one hundred and fifty-one Olive Street for the express purpose of introducing and advertising their product. Now we have just two products, the Hospital Tonic, and the Instant Liniment. The Hospital Tonic is a harmless preparation consisting of roots, herbs, leaves, gums, barks, berries, and blossoms. Including ginseng root, diana emma leaves, sinco, salfamettaberries, iron phosphate, cassian, mandrake, Canadian snake root, bitter apple, Chinese dragon flower, and gimico oil. And now you're going to say, 'Well, will it cure everything?'

Ladies and gentlemen, we don't have a cure-all. If I did have, it wouldn't be necessary to come out here with a show. I would set up in some small town or city and in three days' time I'd be having more business than I could handle. Friends, we don't have a cure-all, and if I were to tell you we *did* have, I would be lying to you. And I'm not *going* to lie to you.

Now throughout the week you're going to hear people calling me 'doctor', and actually I'm really not a doctor. I did attend Northwestern for two years. I'm not licensed, I'm not allowed to make calls. Soon after that, I decided I didn't want to hang out a small shingle in some little town, but I would prefer to go down the highways and into the byways in an attempt to allay the sickness and suffering that mankind is heir to. And if you could look as I do upon that vast multitude of people, people that I see going to and from me daily that I've taken off from canes, off from crutches, out of the sick bed, ah, you might say snatched off the operating table with the use of that tonic, then you wouldn't blame me for preaching.

Now, really, that's all I know. Our product is good for three things: the stomach, the liver, the kidneys. The three principal blood-making organs, or any disease arising therefrom, such as sour stomach, indigestion, constipation, female weaknesses, rheumatism, catarrh. Any disease arising from a disorderly stomach, impure liver, deranged kidneys, with the exception of Bright's disease, and friends, let me say this. If your kidney complaint has reached that stage, don't you buy a bottle. It wouldn't do you any more good than that much rain water. I would much rather you wouldn't have it.

And as I say, that's really all I know: just the stomach, the liver, the kidneys. I have a car sitting out there, a Buick. As long as it'll run, I can drive it. But if it stops, I don't get out and try to fix it. I just hail the first passing motorist. He may turn over a wire, a nut, or a bolt. I'll put my foot on the starter and it'll go along all right. Now, if Mr. Buick had made the car with stomach, liver and kidneys, then *I* could have fixed it. He didn't, I don't know anything about it, I don't *want* to know anything about it.

Now ladies and gentlemen, for me to earn my salary, it is going to be necessary for me to say just a very few words each night about the product. Tonight I would like to say a few words about the subject of rheumatism: how, as a general rule, it's treated, how, as a general rule, it's cured. On either side of that lumbar spine there are two little organs. When in a healthy condition, they weigh from two to four ounces. These are known as the kidneys, or, in other words, the sieve of the human body. And their duty in the body is the same as a sewer system is in a large city. That is, to cleanse and purify the blood.

Now let us suppose the kidneys are *not* in a good condition, and they allow too much uric or lactic acid to go out into the system. This in turn crystallizes, becomes like a lot of powdered glass. In fact, friends, if I were to take that light bulb, break it, pulverize it, powder it into the very finest of glass, and then cut an incision in my wrist, fill it full of the powdered glass, sew it up, it would heal up and, to all external appearances, seem sound and well. And perhaps I wouldn't even feel the pain--until I went to move that muscle. There would be just one difference. I couldn't take medicine in my system strong enough to dissolve the powdered glass. But if the uric acid is properly treated, it can be driven back into circulation.

And now you're going to say, 'how do we do it?' Well, I'm not going to say that a good hot liniment properly applied will not bring you temporary relief. I've had men come in my office, with rheumatism so bad they couldn't raise their arm above their shoulder, and in five minutes' time I'd have him putting his arm high above his head, free from any pain and he'd be *elated*. He'd say 'You've cured me! You've cured me, doc!' But I really hadn't. I hadn't done anything of the kind. I had driven that uric from that point to some other point.

Now, notice this, that usually it'll be settling in a point that's been overstrained previously. For example, a man who's done a lot of lifting, it'll settle in the small of the back, the lumbar region of the spine. And they say the poor man has lumbago. If it's someone like a postman that's done a lot of walking, it'll settle in the sciatic nerve of the thigh, and they say he has sciatica. In the face it's neuralgia. I don't care where it is, it's all one and the same thing--too much uric or lactic acid.

Now, friends, I *do* have a preparation that will *cure* that condition. Why? Because it goes right to work on those kidneys. Puts them in a strong, workable, healthy condition, so they can perform the work which Nature's intended them for. And it doesn't stop there. It goes to work on those other two organs, the stomach and the liver, and let me say this, that if it doesn't help you in three days, then it won't help you in three years. You bring it back to me. I'll give you another dollar for the bottle.

Now, I've had people come in my office also and say, 'I haven't taken a dose of medicine in five years or ten years'. And if you would stop and think, just think, a person wouldn't make a remark like that. Let me paint you a word picture that the smallest boy or girl in my audience can understand. Those of you that keep house, have sitting at your back door what we call a garbage can or a slop bucket. And when you get through with your breakfast dishes, you scrape those dishes into that bucket. You do the same thing with your lunch, same thing with dinner. And when the bucket gets full, you take it out and bury it or feed it to the pigs. I don't care what you do with it, but just keep that bucket in that capacity for one week's time, and then I want you to see the condition that it's in. See the filth that adheres to the sides. Smell the stench that comes from it, and stop and think, 'I've been putting that same food into my stomach not for a day, a week, but for five years--or ten years--and I have *never* cleaned it out!' (See, I told you that these would be mildly amusing, but nobody ever laughed in those days.) And, I will guarantee, ladies and gentlemen, that the very first dose of the Hospital Tonic will bring from your body, *double handfuls* of filth, slime, mucus, corruption, fecal matter, maggots, and even *worms*.

And not very long ago, we asked the Finley Medicine Company to add one more ingredient in the product--something that would pass a tapeworm--head and all. And I'm proud to say that that condition now exists. In fact, I have some specimens back there in my office. I have one in particular that I remember from a Mr. Adams, in Sanger, Texas--a brakeman on the Baltimore and Ohio Railroad. He got a bottle of the tonic on Monday night, and on Friday he came down with that in a tin can. And I washed it and measured it. It's a tapeworm that measures just over 16 ft. in length! And I have Mr. Adams' sworn statement that he used no other medicine but the Hospital Tonic in the passing of that worm!

Now there is just one more thing and then I'm all through. One more thing that I think makes that product stand head and shoulders above anything else ever offered on the market. But there is one thing about it. I can't say much before a mixed audience of ladies and gentlemen. But I will say this: If there is a man within the hearing my voice that goes to his home tonight, and he sees that poor wife, sister, mother, sitting there with her head tied up, and you say, 'What's the matter, Mary', and she says, 'Nothing. Nothing at all, John', don't you *believe* there's nothing the matter. There *is* some-thing--something she's not going to confide in you. She's not going to tell you all her troubles, why--you know the disposi-tion of a woman. The majority of them will drag themselves around as long as they can keep going, and finally they break down', and then you have an invalid to take care of the balance of your days.

Friends, I talk to you like I would my own mother, my own folks in my own home, and if I thought it'd do any good, I'd get down on this platform, on my knees, I'd *beg* you to take that woman home a bottle of that tonic. Oh, if you've got a woman like that at home, you see she's on the toboggan, on the downhill path. You want to bring the roses back to her cheeks, make her step pick up, make her feel like she should again, you'll take my advice, and take her home a bottle of that tonic. The price? The price is so low you cannot afford to miss it. It's a dollar a bottle, and with every bottle you will receive one hundred votes for the most popular lady or baby in the com-munity. I'm only going to have our agents pass among you just one time, and I'll ask you to raise your hand, turn on your lights, I'll be glad to wait on you. Thank you. There goes one right over in there. Thank you sir, very much, thank you.

And that's the way a medicine show pitch sounded in 1928. Just a couple of more things, and then I'm all through.

THE SIDESHOW PITCH

During those incredible years, I accumulated enough memories to last two lifetimes. It was for instance my very great privi-lege to tour the United States with one of the most amazing, one of the most astounding, one of the most bewildering sights: a human oddity, one of the strangest ever exhibited under the blue canopy of heaven. That was Neola, that strangest of all strange creatures. It was the very same girl that was brought here during that great evolution trial that took place in Dayton, Tennessee in 1925 between the late William Jennings Bryan and Clarence Darrow, the great criminal lawyer. She was examined at that time by some of our leading psychiatrists, Dr. Mullen, head of the Department of Psychiatry at Columbia. Dr. Mullen claimed that she had less intelligence than that of the chimpanzee or the monkey family. She was found by that great antiquarian explorer and trapper, Dr. Carter, who was exploring for animals in the lowlands or swamp regions of Abyssinia. He heard this strange tale of some fanatic natives, of a strange and curious animal that lived in the center of a deep dark cave, and investigating their story, he found it to be fact. But he found not an animal, but a human being, crouched upon a huge flat rock exactly as you're going to see her in there tonight, completely surrounded by hissing, seething monsters, some of them larger than a man's upper arm, some that could crush a human being with one coil of those enormous bodies just as you or I would crush a piece of food between our teeth.

Let me paint you a mental picture of her. She stands just 3 feet tall. Long, long arms that hang way down below the knees. Eyes that pop out and glare just like two red-hot coals of fire. But I think the most peculiar thing about her of all (and I think you'll agree when you see her) is the shape of the head. The head *tapers* at the top just like that of a coconut. She doesn't speak any language. Doesn't know any creed. Neither walks nor talks, just creeps and crawls and spends her lifetime down in that steel-bound arena, down in that steel cage, where you would not expect a dog to live for an hour.

Now all afternoon they've been asking, 'When and what time are you going to feed her?' And that moment has now arrived! Once, on this very performance, I *am* going to feed her *exactly* as you'd see her in her own native land, Abyssinia, in the north of Africa. You'll see her leap clear across that steel-bound cage, the eyes will pop out and glare like two red-hot coals of fire. Now it's way beyond feeding time. I'm going to feed her positively within the next three minutes. The price, so low you cannot afford to miss it, usually 25 for the adults, 10 for little ones. I'm going to lay away the regular adult tickets, turn back the pages of time, make children out of all of you. Now I'll say this, for a period of three minutes and three minutes only by the clock, if you can lay as much as the price of a children's ticket, that's 10¢, it's 10¢ to each, 10 to all. You may get tickets here, and I'm going to feed her within three minutes, whether one of you go, all of you go, or *none* of you go. Hold it Doctor, don't feed her just yet!

'Doc' Bloodgood's concluding remarks. Y'know, during those years, I suppose in retrospect it's natural to remember only the *nice* things, the *exciting* things that happened. One has a tendency to forget the endless rains, and the muddy lots, and the stuck trucks, and the winds that often destroyed our tents. Somewhere a half a century ago, I heard a little verse that seems to tell it all. It says,

Looping around the mountain,
Dragging across the plain,
Gay in the flowered sunlight,
And drab in the droning rain,

Man from his gypsy childhood
Is a houseless vagabond
Who pitches his tent and passes
'Til he camps in the dim beyond.

And now, ladies and gentlemen, as we used to say on the medicine show, I want to thank you one and all, for your very kind, courteous and undivided attention, wishing you a safe return to your respective homes and destinations, and a very fond good night. I thank you.